CASEBOOK
Structured Enrichment
Programs for Couples
and Families

CASEBOOK
Structured Enrichment Programs for Couples and Families

by Luciano L'Abate
and Linda Young

BRUNNER/MAZEL *Publishers* • New York

Library of Congress Cataloging-in-Publication Data

Casebook: structured enrichment programs for couples
  and families.

  "Designed to accompany Structured enrichment programs
for couples and families (L'Abate & Weinstein, 1987)"—
Introd.
  Bibliography: p. 383.
  Includes index.
  1. Family psychotherapy—Case studies. 2. Marital
psychotherapy—Case studies. 3. Family—Psychological
aspects—Case studies. I. L'Abate, Luciano, 1928–
II. Young, Linda, 1953–   . III. L'Abate, Luciano,
1928–   . Structured enrichment programs for couples
and families.
RC488.5.L346 1987   616.89'156   86–26880
ISBN 0-87630-451-X

Copyright © 1987 by Luciano L'Abate and Linda Young

Published by
BRUNNER/MAZEL, INC.
19 Union Square
New York, New York 10003

MANUFACTURED IN THE UNITED STATES OF AMERICA

CONTENTS

Section II Single-Parent Families

Section III Problematic Couples

Section IV Examples of Specific Programs

1

CONTRIBUTORS

Margaret S. Baggett, PhD
Rosemary Bleyer, PhD
William L. Buchanan, MA
Hilary P. Buzas, PhD
Cinda Caiella, MA
Joy Dance, MA
Flo P. Dawson, MA
Julie Friedman, MA
Raymond A. Gallope, PhD
Susan P. Gantt, PhD
Deborah Huntley, MA
Edgar Jessee, PhD
Jackie W. Johnson, PhD

Pat King, MA
James Kochalka, MA
John Lutz, MA
Alan Schnee, MA
Jerry Stein, MA
Margaret Taylor, MA
Victor Wagner, PhD
Kathy Weeks, MA
Steven E. Weinstein, MA
Marsha Weiss, MA
Carolyn Zweig, PhD
Bari Zwirn, MA

INTRODUCTION

This casebook has been designed to accompany *Structured Enrichment Programs for Couples and Families* (L'Abate & Weinstein, 1987), which contains the guidelines on how to conduct a structured enrichment (SE) program. These cases have been selected from the hundreds of couples and families that have been seen at the Family Study Center of Georgia State University in the past 15 years. In most of these couples and families, one member was a student who participated to earn part of the experimental credit needed for introductory psychology courses. Other couples and families volunteered to help the graduate students who needed couples or families for laboratory credit in a graduate course on enrichment. With few exceptions, these cases were the first experiences these graduate students had with a couple or a family. The first author supervised most of the cases (supervisors of the remaining cases are identified in the text); the second author selected the case reports for this casebook. (Other case studies have been published in L'Abate, 1977, and in L'Abate and Rupp, 1981.)

As you will soon find out, one of the most frequently selected programs was Negotiation (or similar programs relating to issues of negotiating, problem solving, and decision making). This frequency tends to support the first author's contention that negotiation is one of the two basic sets of skills that families need. The other set of skills is the ability to love and be intimate (L'Abate, 1986b). We hope that if we teach functional or even semifunctional families both sets of skills, we can help them prevent the future mishandling of inevitable traumas and conflicts.

These cases illustrate the application of SE to specific couples and families, a process in which the watchword must be *flexibility*. There is no need to continue a program if the couple or family (and the enrichers) are not getting much out of it. In these cases, if a program did not suit a particular couple or family, the enrichers switched to another program or used lessons or exercises from other programs. Sometimes, depending on the specific needs of the family at that particular time, a specific exercise was written for that family.

These cases also illustrate that SE is first and foremost diagnostic. If you want to know how families work (or fail to work), just try to change them! Most of these families were, by definition, nonclinical; that is, they fulfilled the two basic requirements for SE: they were not currently in professional treatment with anybody else, and they did not perceive themselves as being in need of professional help. As you will see throughout these cases, being nonclinical does not necessarily mean being functional. Even though we have tried to apply SE to as many families as were willing to be enriched, we had to drop a few families that were too dysfunctional (under too much stress, in crisis, or chaotic) to be enriched. To be enriched, families require a modicum of stability and functionality. We (Kochalka, Buzas, McHenry, L'Abate & Gibson, 1982) have found, though, that SE can be administered right after the termination of family therapy, by volunteer intermediaries or paraprofessionals who possess the personal qualifications of responsibility, warmth, and caring but who do not have paper credentials (L'Abate, 1973).

SE should be applied to families—with their written informed consent—who want it and need it and who can profit by it. All the families described in these case studies gave written consent after SE was explained to them. Names, ages, geographical locations, and other identifying information have been changed to protect the confidentiality promised them. On the consent form, the families granted permission for their records to be used for research purposes.

Most of the cases presented here were evaluated before and after SE. However, different tests were used at different times. First, the evaluation batteries for couples are different from the evaluation batteries for families because children have to be included in family evaluations. Second, we have used different test batteries during the 15 years of applying this approach, striving to improve the evaluation process by changing the composition of the batteries over time.

One shortcoming of the cases presented concerns long-term follow-up. To guarantee candid responses from the families, we asked for and received anonymous follow-ups (some at 3 months after SE). We thus cannot tell how each family has fared years after SE took place. At least a 1-year follow-up is needed after SE (see L'Abate, 1986b, for a follow-up form). After all, long-term effects are the proof of the pudding in preventive approaches (L'Abate, 1986a).

ASSESSMENTS USED IN CASE STUDIES

Dyadic Adjustment Inventory (Spanier, 1976)

Family Adaptability and Cohesion Evaluation Scales (FACES) (Olson, Sprenkle & Russell, 1979)

Family Adjustment Inventory (L'Abate & McHenry, 1983)

Family Environment Scales (FES) (Moos, 1976)

*Family Information (18-item) (L'Abate & McHenry, 1983, Appendix F; L'Abate & Rupp, 1981)

*Family Information (10-item) (Egan, 1973)

†Family Life Questionnaire (also known as Rochester Scales)

Holmes-Rahe Schedule of Events (Holmes & Rahe, 1967)

Marital Evaluation Battery (L'Abate & Wagner, 1985):

Marital Questionnaire (complete assessment will be available in L'Abate, L. [in preparation], *Research manual,* Atlanta: Georgia State University)

Likeness Grid (LG)

Priorities Inventory

Marital Happiness Scale (Azrin, Naster & Jones, 1973; also in L'Abate & Rupp, 1981)

Primary Communications Inventory (Navran, 1967)

Semantic Differential (available in L'Abate & Rupp, 1981)

Sexual Happiness Scale (Gottlieb & L'Abate, 1974; also in L'Abate & Rupp, 1981)

---

* Also known as Family Satisfaction Scales
† Reference to this instrument could not be located. The authors will appreciate information on its source.

Visual Family Evaluation Battery (L'Abate & Wagner, 1985):
  Bell-Fagan Family Symbols (B-F)
  Description of Feelings in the Family (DFF)
  Family Situations Picture Series (FSPS)
  Animal Concepts Picture Series (ACPS)

CASEBOOK
Structured Enrichment Programs for Couples and Families

SECTION I
Couples

1

A Dating Couple

John Lutz and Steven E. Weinstein

Mac, aged 18, and Edie, aged 20, are not married but have been dating each other for 6 months. Both are college students, Edie a junior and Mac a freshman. Edie said that, starting this summer, she will be taking time off from school so that she can work full-time. She is currently enployed as a secretary.

During the interview, Mac was much more vocal than Edie, who often smiled and giggled and seemed somewhat shy. Mac said that this was his first "adult" relationship and reported that his last "serious" relationship had been when he was 13 years old. Edie stated that she is more experienced in relationships because she has had three previous "long-term" relationships, two of which lasted 1 year and one of which lasted 6 months. Mac noted that because he is less experienced and younger than Edie, he sometimes uses Edie as a "surrogate" mother. Mac said, however, that he does not want to use Edie in this way.

Both reported that they currently live with their parents but that they are thinking of moving out and living together this fall. Mac identified his mother's decreasing attachment, her separation from him, and his moving out of the house as issues between him and his mother.

Mac's parents were divorced when he was 2 years old. Since then, his only contact with his father was when Mac was 13. Mac has two stepbrothers (aged 29 and 35) from his father's first marriage.

Edie, the oldest of three children, also indicated difficulty in her relationship with her mother, as well as in leaving-home issues. In talking about her 18-year-old sister, who has been married for 3 years, Edie observed that although her sister married to get out of the house, she lives across the street from her parents.

In this first meeting, we explained the concept and the format of SE. We told them that we are graduate students (not therapists) fulfilling course requirements, and we asked them to tell us the areas in which they would like to improve their relationship. Mac mentioned that one area he would like to focus on is expectations for the relationship. He noted that each of them has different expectations about commitment and what each expects from the other.

PRETEST SUMMARY

In the final part of the interview, we administered the pretest battery: Holmes-Rahe Schedule of Events, Dyadic Adjustment Inventory, and Family Adjustment Inventory.

On the Schedule of Events, Mac's score is clinically significant. Most of the endorsed items dealt with issues relating to his new job and his family. Items related to changes resulting in his new relationship with Edie were also endorsed. Although Edie's score is not clinically significant, her score is high. Many of the items she endorsed were also job-related.

Mac's and Edie's scores on the Dyadic Adjustment Inventory were compared with the norms of married persons because, unfortunately, no normative data are available for dating couples. When compared with the scores of married couples, the total scores for both are within normal limits.

On the subscales, Mac's dyadic cohesion score is above normal limits; the other scores are within normal limits. The only significant deviation on Edie's subscales is her score on the dyadic consensus subscale, which is below normal limits, indicating possible problems with agreement on important matters in their relationship. This may be related to Mac's concern about their expectations for their relationship.

On the final assessment instrument, the Family Adjustment Inventory, both have negative scores. The general areas of focus identified by Edie were family, Mac, work, and her own problem-solving ability. Her top priorities were matters concerning her family and Mac. Mac listed as his areas of focus work, home, Edie, and his insecurity. His insecurity was given top priority, followed by family issues and issues concerning his relationship with Edie.

We chose, on the basis of the interview and the pretest scores and in consultation with the supervisor, three programs that highlight expectations and roles in relationships: Assertiveness, Equality, and Negotiation. These three programs seemed appropriate because the couple had been dating for a relatively short period and were thus still getting to know each other. In addition, each indicated problems (both in their test data and verbalizations) with their differing expectations for their relationship.

SUMMARY OF SESSIONS

After the three programs were described to the couple, they were asked to select the program that they believed would be most applicable to them. The couple chose the Negotiation Program. Because the Negotiation Program was written for married couples, some of the wording had to be changed to reflect a dating relationship rather than a marriage.

Session 1

In the first exercise of the lesson called Marriage Myths, the couple defined the preconceptions (myths) they had had concerning a long-term relationship before they met each other. Edie told Mac to start. Mac stated that he had been looking for a serious relationship. Edie said that she had not been; she had recently ended a "hard" relationship (4 months earlier) and had not been dating until she met Mac at a bar.

In the second exercise, the couple was asked to compare "being in love" during the initial period of the relationship with "being in love" now. Mac said that the relationship has progressed from one of lust to one of love and added that this love entails trust and caring for each other. Edie also stated that it progressed from what was at first a sexual infatuation to love, which now entails understanding and a "comfortableness" between the two of them.

The next exercise concerns differences in attitudes and behaviors between the sexes. The couple were asked to write the characteristics they consider descriptive of men and women in general. Mac described men as mathematical, likely to keep troubles to themselves, macho (stonger), having a higher threshold for pain, and smarter. He described women as more creative, capable of dealing with stress, able to share their problems with others, weaker, better at dealing with family problems, and sensitive.

Edie described men as better equipped to handle stress, more insecure, unable to handle financial matters, better able to change the channels on the TV, and more honest with real feelings. She described women as more cunning, more sensual, more imposing, better in the home, and as persons who are supposed to be insecure.

When asked which of their descriptions fit each of them, Mac said that he is mathematical, and Edie said that she is more insecure and more honest with real feelings.

The final exercise in this lesson concerns the ways in which the partners agree or disagree, as well as how each shows respect for the other. Edie stated that they argue when they disagree. Mac noted that he was raised in a household in which "When you are angry, you are expected to scream and fight and get it out of your system." Edie reported that in her family, the opposite happens: "When you are angry, you don't fight—you keep it to yourself."

When asked how they handle disagreements, Mac said that it is hard. Edie said that Mac is better than he used to be: he now only argues with her "when something is really wrong." Mac said that Edie has also improved: unlike before, she tells him when something is wrong.

The lesson ended with a homework assignment: to be aware during the coming week of the times they meet each other halfway.

Supervision.

In supervision, the effects of the couple's different backgrounds on the relationship were discussed. The different ways their respective families handle disagreements were discussed, as were the differences in their religious backgrounds (Mac is Jewish and Edie is Baptist). It was explained that differences can be used two ways: to enhance or to destroy a relationship.

Session 2

When asked what the couple learned from the homework assignment, Edie handed us a sheet that listed examples from the past week of meeting each other halfway. We praised them for having taken the homework assignment seriously and for the effort they had put into it.

In the first exercise of Focus on the Relationship, the couple asked each other the question "Who are you?" Mac responded that he is Mac [last name], his mother's son, Edie's boyfriend, a college student, an American citizen, Mark's employee, a human being, a male, a teenager, and a Jew. Edie stated that she is Edie [last name], a secretary, the oldest child, a would-be poet, a student, Mac's girlfriend, one person, a buyer of books, a female, a namesake, and a lost soul. During the exercise, Edie asked Mac not to make faces when she was answering the questions.

Next, the couple asked each other, "What can I give you?" Mac replied that he could give Edie love, constructive criticism, security, challenge, happiness, structure, a sense of well-being, freedom, and maturity. Edie stated that she could give Mac love, understanding, acceptance, hope, herself, a partner, escape, a sense of well-being, happiness, and sincerity.

The final question they were instructed to ask each other is "What can you give me?" Mac replied with the following: love, security, sensitivity, understanding, freedom, happiness, help, laughter, structure, a different path, direction. Edie replied to this question with the following: love, understanding, acceptance, help, a different direction, security, a home, words, a resting place, and a child.

When asked what they had learned from this exercise, Edie responded that it was hard to come up with 10 items but that she felt good about hearing things that Mac wants and what he wants to give. Mac said that he enjoyed the exercise and that it put things in "a nice perspective." He found it nice to hear what Edie wants to give him. He said that it was as if he were putting in a penny and getting back $10.

The second exercise concerned rules in the relationship. Mac stated that they have a rule that neither of them dates anyone else. For homework, they were told to think about other rules they operate under.

Supervision.

Supervision focused on two main issues. First, Mac and Edie's plans to live together were discussed. The supervisor noted that according to some data, couples who have cohabitated have a higher rate of divorce.

The second part of supervision concerned a letter to the couple to identify aspects of the couple's relationship that we had observed above and beyond the SE process. It was decided that the letter, to be given to the couple after Session 4, would deal with three issues: the couple's different backgrounds, leaving home, and identity and choice of mate.

Session 3

We first asked about the homework assignment (to think about rules under which they operate in the relationship). The first rule that the couple discussed was that every night before they go to bed, they talk with each other on the telephone. They also always let each other know their whereabouts. Another rule, which Edie mentioned, is that when Mac does something with a female friend, she (Edie) is supposed to be jealous and Mac gets worried if she's not. Finally, they operate under a rule that no matter how bad the partner's parent(s) is, Edie and Mac are supposed to be nice to each other's parent(s).

The first exercise in the Communication lesson concerned the meaning of communication and the ways that a couple can communicate with each other (verbally and nonverbally).

When asked what the word *communication* meant to each of them, Mac stated that communication is the most important part of the relationship. It means that one talks about things—good and bad—no matter how one feels. He also referred to the nonverbal part of communication, stating that one can communicate "I love you" with a kiss. Edie said that communication means talking about things. She also mentioned nonverbal elements, such as touching.

The second exercise began by having both partners silently observe each other and then comment on the feelings they received. Edie said she received feelings of love and concern. Mac said that he was sending Edie a feeling of love as well as a feeling that "You're all right— everything is OK." Mac said that he received feelings of love from Edie, who stated that she was sending a feeling of love and a feeling that communicated "I understand." In this exercise, the partners were able to distinguish inconsistent verbal and nonverbal messages.

In the third exercise, the couple role-played the blaming, placating, avoiding, and preaching modes of communication. Mac found the preaching role the easiest for him and the placator role the most difficult.

The final exercise involved "it," "you," "we," and "I" statements. To practice these statements, Mac and Edie used the issue of getting married. Edie would like to get married; Mac is not ready to marry. He prefers that they live together.

In response to the "it" statements, Mac said that they are a way to make the issue more distant. Edie found it quite "normal" to use these statements. On the other hand, Edie reported that the "you" statements made the argument circular. Mac found "you" statements nice but also said that they are a way of blaming the other person. Of the "we" statements, Edie said that it was difficult to use these statements, and Mac said that "we" statements take the pressure off one person and result in "spreading" the issue. Both liked the use of "I" statements because they tend to keep the focus on the self. Both noted that "I" statements are a quicker way to express one's feelings and intentions. The homework assignment was to make three "I" statements a day to the partner.

Session 4

Mac and Edie reported that they had done the homework assignment— making three "I" statements every day. Edie, saying that she uses fewer "I" statements than Mac does, recalled that she had used these statements in talking about her illness. Mac recalled having attempted to express feelings when he used "I" statements.

The purpose of the Communication and Hurt lesson is twofold: first, to learn to listen conductively to each other, using a shared-meaning process; second, to work on sharing feelings, especially those of hurt and anger.

Two stimulus sentences, one given to each partner ("Are you planning to come over tonight?" and "Didn't we talk last week about moving in together?"), demonstrated to the couple that the messages they send each other aren't always the messages the partner receives.

In working on the shared-meaning process of emphasizing listening to understand what the partner is communicating (i.e., listening conductively) and of checking the accuracy of (but not necessarily agreeing with) what was communicated before responding, Mac chose to communicate not wanting to go to Edie's house that evening because he wanted to study; Edie chose to communicate wanting to go out with Mac alone on Friday night and not have a friend of his along with them.

In the exercise on sharing feelings of hurt and anger, Mac told Edie that he feels hurt by her allowing things to continue to bother her without "closing" them and by the way her mother treats her. Edie said that she feels hurt by Mac's flirting, the way her mother treats him, his working weekends, and his competitiveness. Asked to express to each other a wish that the partner would convey his or her hurt or anger, Edie told Mac that she wants him to tell her when he's angry and not belittle his feelings or respond by saying, "What's your problem?!" Mac told Edie that he wishes she would not hold in her anger or hurt so long before sharing it.

Listing ways in which each could encourage the partner to be more expressive of hurt and angry feelings, Mac said that he could be more patient, realizing that Edie closes her hurts more slowly, and be more encouraging of her to be open. Mac added that sometimes when he's angry, he isn't angry with her but that he wants her to listen at these times because this is his way of resolving his painful feelings. Edie said that she could encourage Mac to express his feelings of hurt and anger rather than devaluing his feelings. She added that she wants Mac to realize that many of her hurts (e.g., family ones) aren't likely to be closed for some time.

Early in this session, it became apparent that Edie and Mac have different styles of dealing with old, lingering sources of hurt. Mac reported that he tends to close them off more quickly than Edie does. During the lesson in which they were sharing how each feels hurt because of the other's actions, he had brought up her failure to seal off her old hurts. He began to berate Edie for her inability to deal with her hurts as he had dealt with his. As he continued, Edie started to cry. Mac stopped berating her and held her, telling her that he loved her. We pointed out that Edie and Mac have different styles in dealing with old hurts— neither of which is necessarily better, just different.

We gave the couple a linear (straightforward) letter at the end of this lesson, outlining areas that they need to examine more closely but that the Negotiation Program does not directly focus on—handling differences, dealing with family and separation, and struggling with identity.

Dear Edie and Mac:
    The purpose of this letter is to deal with all the aspects of your relationship that we have observed above and beyond the enrichment

process. We want to put these observations in writing because what we have seen is far too important for us to consider orally. By putting our observations in writing, we will have a better opportunity to reflect on them.

We have found these past sessions with you very enjoyable, and we like working with the two of you. We are impressed with the openness, playfulness, and care the two of you have for each other. We are also struck by your motivation to improve your relationship with each other.

Both of you have mentioned issues that relate to your own families (e.g., moving out, separating). We know that this can be a difficult process and that it can place pressure on your relationships, both with each other and your family members. We know it is tempting to try to solve the other's family conflicts because you care for each other. Do you know how to be an active listener for the other and to help each other discuss and work on possible areas of conflict? If you need to talk directly with the family members involved, stand behind each other in the process.

You have told us that you come from different backgrounds. This difference allows you to complement each other very well. Your differences can be used to enhance each other and your relationship. However, we would be remiss if we fail to acknowledge that differences can at times be an important source of conflict in relationships.

Finally, although you are currently working on your relationship, each of you is probably still actively involved in constructing your own identity. We see this process as an important dimension in the development of intimacy in any relationship.

We look forward to our remaining sessions with you. We will be happy to discuss any parts of this letter with you, but we ask that this discussion be saved for the feedback conference, when more time will be available for this purpose.

Supervision.

In supervision, we discussed Mac's Superman role in dealing with hurt and anger, as seen during the last session. He had reported dealing with some traumatic events in his life (i.e., not having a father, being kidnapped) and expects Edie to close hers off as he has done. We speculated that old hurts may regulate distance-closeness in their relationship.

Session 5

This lesson on building trust through effective communication high-lighted communication consistency across several levels (verbal and behavioral), areas of competitiveness in their relationship, and three styles, or modes, of relating (symmetrical, complementary, and parallel) in relationships.

In the first exercise, listing areas that each of them would like to be more open for discussion, Mac listed Edie's family, her upsets, and his friends. Edie brought up the price she pays for clothes, the problems she has with her family, and her liking or disliking some of Mac's friends.

In the second exercise, dealing with the inconsistencies in their behaviors that diminish trust in their relationship, Edie pointed out her saying to Mac that it's OK (when it really isn't) when he goes out with women friends and that she feels left out when he goes out with friends. Mac pointed out that he is inconsistent when he tells Edie that she is very important to him but then doesn't have time to spend with her. He added that recently his actions and words had been inconsistent when he told Edie that a classmate was just a friend when in fact his involvement with her had become more than friendship, especially on the part of the classmate.

They were unable to generate more than just a few areas in which they compete—games and styles of expressing emotion. We may have focused them too specifically toward the content level of interaction rather than toward other, metarelationship levels, such as rule setting.

Supervision.

In supervision, we discussed delineating more clearly the sequences of inconsistent behaviors and sharing hurt.

Session 6

Because Mac and Edie had not done their homework, the task—listing areas of competence and areas neglected by both—was done in the session. Edie listed the following areas of personal competence—cooking and cleaning, organizing and planning, typing, driving, dancing, and dealing with in-laws. Mac listed as his areas of competence generating ideas for things to do, persuasiveness, socializing, math, and computer games. Areas neglected by both were dishes, handling money, and handling negative feelings of upset (Mac) or jealousy (Edie).

This final lesson, Quid Pro Quo, is geared toward having each partner negotiate a desire or a need in the relationship in exchange for helping the partner achieve a need or a desire. The rules of communication ("I" statements, avoiding manipulative styles, shared meaning, congruence, no past history, and sharing feelings) were stressed in this lesson.

In the first exercise, the characteristics that Mac would like to see, ideally, in Edie included her becoming more patient, listening more carefully to what he says, taking time before responding to what he says, relaxing more around him and being less fearful of losing him, not taking on her mother's problems, working out hurts and closing them efficiently, and becoming tougher (less easily hurt). Edie told Mac that she would like, ideally, to see him be a good student, understand better what she goes through rather than not wanting to be bothered with it, be less flippant, and to flirt less with other females.

In the second exercise, each recounted to the other ways in which he or she had contributed destructively to or were failing in the relationship. Edie mentioned being too emotional, being deceptive about why she's really angry with Mac, wanting from him things that he isn't ready to give or doesn't want to give her (i.e., marriage), and giving him a hard time about her mother and her illness. Mac listed as his destructive behaviors flirting too much, not taking some of Edie's concerns seriously enough, not putting as much energy into the relationship lately, becoming defensive with Edie's mother, being generally critical of Edie, and being moody.

Edie, in expressing wishes or needs in her relationship with Mac, included a wish that their relationship be positive and that it influence her other relationships in like manner (especially with her mother), a wish or a need to get married, to feel secure, to be happy, to have the relationship work out when they get an apartment "so I don't have to go home again or you won't leave me," to be well off, and that she and Mac not be insecure. Mac's wishes and needs for the relationship included that the relationship be an avenue of growth for him, that he feel loved, that he feel secure, that he be able to teach Edie ways of making herself happy in the rest of her life even without him, to provide security for Edie, to live with her, and to feel that he has achieved something or to feel satisfied.

In the final exercise of this lesson, each chose an item from the other's wish or need list and attempted to negotiate them. Each tried to help the other feel more secure. Mac agreed that he could be more consistent (congruent) in his messages to Edie that he isn't interested in other women. Edie suggested that she could help Mac feel more secure in their relationship by not talking about other people, which upsets him, and not talking about dying.

They were only moderately successful in the negotiation, easily falling back to defending their positions without first understanding what the other was trying to communicate. In part, this may have been due to the global nature of the selected items and letting negotiation spread to many problem behaviors and sequences without reaching resolution on a way to handle one behavior before moving on to another. We made these suggestions and assigned the task of finishing the negotiation at home. At the end of this session, we administered the posttest battery.

Supervision.

Supervision dealt with the content and format of the feedback conference. It was decided that at this time no further preventive therapeutic intervention is needed, although further work in SE or individual/family work will be presented as options for the future.

POSTTEST SUMMARY

Following the final lesson, we administered the posttest battery: the Dyadic Adjustment Inventory and the Family Adjustment Inventory.

Scores for both on the Dyadic Adjustment Inventory remain about the same as on pretest. The only significant change is the drop in Mac's score on the dyadic consensus subscale, which now puts him below normal limits (at least when compared with the married couple norms). Edie's score on the dyadic consensus subscale remains below normal limits (again, when compared with married couple norms). It is not known, however, whether this score is normal for dating couples.

On the Family Adjustment Inventory, Mac's total score remains approximately the same as on pretest, improving by 8 points. Although he reported more dissatisfaction with work issues, he reported less dissatisfaction with home issues and issues with Edie. His insecurity was still given top priority, followed once again by family issues and his relationship with Edie.

In contrast to Mac's score, Edie's total score on the Family Adjustment Inventory decreased by 45 points. Although her rating of her work situation improved slightly, her rating of her relationships with Mac and her family dropped. The main reason for the increase in family problems was the increased priority given to the fact that her parents do not like Mac. Her test score also indicates an increased concern with Mac's growing up. A possible explanation for the drop in Edie's total score on this test is that she has become more committed to her relationship with Mac (perhaps a result of SE).

FEEDBACK CONFERENCE

The feedback conference was divided into four sections: (a) feedback from the couple on the program, (b) our positive feedback to the couple, (c) areas to work on further, and (d) ways in which they could carry out the suggestions for further work.

Mac's positive feedback on the program centered on its involving both of them as partners in learning about themselves and their relationship.

He said that the techniques/rules about communication and negotiation provided them with a system for working on issues in their relationship. Edie agreed with Mac, adding that the program had helped her understand Mac better and that she feared less that Mac would leave her.

Suggestions that Mac and Edie made for using the program with other couples, including dating couples like themselves, are as follows: to gear the exercises more toward dating couples, to emphasize early in the sessions a nonjudgmental, nongraded attitude toward the experience, and to delete overlapping questions and exercises.

In our positive feedback to the couple, we complimented their obvious motivation toward enriching their relationship, as shown in their completion of the program and their dedication and diligence in doing their homework assignments. We also praised them for their flexibility (and lack of polarization) in their expression of emotionality and rationality. Finally, we expressed our enjoyment of their playfulness with each other. We gave them full credit for all the benefits they had derived from the program.

We highlighted three areas that they could continue to work on: (a) communication—attempting to understand first (not necessarily agree on) what the other is saying rather than reacting or defending immediately; (b) relationship expectations—being open about expectations, needs, and desires for each other and for the relationship, and integrating the use of "I" statements (especially for Edie) into this process; (c) negotiation— taking time each week to list, discuss, and negotiate various areas of living together (e.g., cleaning, finances, socializing, sexuality, closeness-distance) in preparation for living together in the fall.

We suggested that they continue to work on these areas, using the ideas and skills they learned and worked on during the program. We also told them that they could participate in other SE programs or perhaps try covenant contracting.

CONCLUSION

Working with a dating couple demonstrated the flexibility of SE and the benefits for couples, on a continuum of dyadic commitment. Despite the fact that the wording of the Negotiation Program is geared toward married couples, we were able to adapt the material for a dating relationship and to insert into the exercises and examples meaningful material derived from earlier sessions with the couple. The Negotiation Program includes several dimensions that are useful in any intimate relationship (e.g., communication levels, styles of relating—symmetrical, complementary, and parallel—sharing of negative feelings of hurt and anger, and negotiation).

2

A Democratic Couple

Jackie W. Johnson

An enrichment couple and a control couple received pre- and posttests (Family Information and Marital Happiness Scale) at the pre- and the posttest sessions; each spouse of each couple tape-recorded approximately 10 minutes on the subject of their primary relationships and related feelings. Following the second recording, both couples were asked whether they would listen to their tapes and fill out a questionnaire about their listening experiences. Both couples agreed.

Pre- and posttest sessions were separated by 6 to 7 weeks, a period during which the enrichment couple received six enrichment sessions of approximately 1 hour each in the Negotiation Program. An interview and a feedback conference were conducted with the enrichment couple.

Because of the requirements that the enrichment couple be functional, nonclinical, stable, and cooperative, the enrichment couple was selected from my married friends.

The couple selected have been married for 6 years and have a 15-month-old healthy and adorable son named Jonathan. Paul and Angela are intelligent, highly articulate, and responsive. Many background variables are similar: culture, education, religion, and interests. According to their reports, each spouse entered marriage with similar values and similar expectations.

They live in a beautiful home in a white, upper-middle-class area. Their home is richly furnished, and magazines and books are plentiful. All sessions were conducted at their home, one session in their backyard. Their son was present on almost every occasion but never posed a problem; all other external interferences were minimal.

Paul is a well-known newspaper columnist, and his occupation has rewarded him with acclaim and financial security. Thus, this couple is financially solvent, a factor that research has shown to be highly correlated with overall marital happiness. Because of the esteem granted to Paul through his occupation, many of his ego-needs are met outside his marriage, another factor contributing to this couple's functionality and success. That is, Paul does not depend or look unrealistically to Angela to make him happy and to be all-fulfilling to him.

Angela is currently a homemaker and mother, roles she enjoys very much. Before the birth of their son, Angela had worked as a stewardess and as a teacher. Although Angela expressed happiness with her life, she also expressed throughout SE her fear of losing her personal identity. Further, she considered this a need within their family system, in that Paul could support her more in her need for personal identity.

My initial impression of this couple (borne out during SE) is that they have a highly functional marriage characterized by financial security, health, commitment to each other, involvement with their community and society, mental stability, and flexibility (i.e., neither spouse has rigid role expectations or beliefs). Paul and Angela appear to have a democratic relationship based upon mutual sharing and love for each other and for their son. Also, their marriage has not been challenged by any crises, such as financial problems. Conflicts seem minimal, with the exception of an in-law problem, which was not included in the particular program selected for them.

PRETEST AND INTERVIEW

Based upon my arbitrary selection of a 3-point plus discrepancy for any equivalent question answered by Paul and by Angela, the pretest forms show that the main areas of discrepancy were occupational satisfaction, emotional satisfaction, communication behaviors, social activities, household responsibilities, spouse independence, and sexual satisfaction. Angela mentioned several times during the pretest session that she and Paul have different frames of reference and thus their ratings would not necessarily correspond. She feared that their different ratings would be seen as a problem in their relationship. For example, Angela considers herself more emotional than Paul, whose approach to life is extremely rational and objective.

Both are aware of these differences in communication styles and personality makeup and consider this one area in their relationship in which they can improve. That is, Paul wishes Angela to be more rational, and she is trying to do this; Angela wishes Paul to be more emotionally expressive with her, and he in turn is trying to do this. Paul's extreme objectivism and rationality are perpetuated partly by the demands of his occupation but also by the way he was reared—in a family that showed little emotion. Paul stated that he wants to be more open, sensitive, and emotional in his communication with Angela and their son. The only other area he desires to change is to acquire more personal time for himself.

In the interview, Angela responded that she would like to change her tendency to become rigid as she grows older, to be better organized in order to give more time to Paul, and to improve their sexual communication. Angela does not consider that they have any sexual problems, but she wants Paul to be more attuned to her needs, such as stroking her more, and wants him not to assume that he knows what she wants. Angela has not confronted him about this but according to the Azrin scale, the happiness of spouse on "show of affection," "fondling," and "sex overall" were rated lower by 3 or more points by Paul than by Angela. His rating indicates that Paul is aware of Angela's feelings about their sexual communication. Further, Paul's ratings on empathy, warmth, self-disclosure, feelings, and emotions were 3 or more points lower than Angela's ratings, which seems to support a dichotomy in their communication styles.

Concerning the things that they are satisfied with in their marriage, Paul replied that he is satisfied with his occupation, overall family situation, and health. Angela expressed satisfaction with motherhood, support received in her relationship with Paul, and her sense of self-improvement in tennis. Paul's occupational satisfaction is an aspect that Angela feels is missing in her own life, as she is not very happy in her occupational identity and misses some of the positive aspects of having a career. However, she is not unhappy with motherhood and being Paul's wife.

Generally, Paul and Angela are very happy in their marriage. According to the pretest forms, their sexual communication in general could be more satisfying, especially Paul's need to be more emotional with Angela. Because of this couple's stability and their general lack of significant conflicts, my supervisor and I decided that the Negotiation Program would best address their needs. The exercises on communication techniques would sharpen and increase their awareness of each other's nonverbal and verbal feelings. I expected Paul to move closer to obtaining his goal of being more emotionally expressive with Angela, to state his need for more personal time, and in turn, to enrich Angela in expressing her need for more explicit sexual communication. Generally, I expected the Negotiation Program to enrich their communication within the family system and help them to become more aware of the implicit rules under which they operate.

SUMMARY OF SESSIONS

Session 1: Marriage Myths

This session reconfirmed that neither Paul nor Angela had many delusions about marriage (e.g., belief in the myth of romantic love). Both worked through a number of adjustment problems during their engagement, and, generally, adjustment to marriage was relatively easy for them.

Paul and Angela responded spontaneously to the question about how each reacts to disagreement. Neither believes that arguing is characteristic of a poor marriage, although Paul stated that they "disagree on how to disagree." That is, Paul tends to stress being rational when arguing, and Angela describes herself as having more knee-jerk reactions than Paul does. In this session, again, Paul wants Angela to be more rational in her approach to discussing issues, and Angela wants Paul to be more emotional. Paul pointed out, however, that when he expresses anger, Angela feels hurt and doesn't know how to respond.

I think that this session served as an ice-breaker for future sessions. I was tense and anxious about following the program structure and about how the couple would react. I felt solely responsible for the session's success, a feeling I discussed with my supervisor. Through supervision, I realized that I could not shoulder all the responsibility for success. The most important process in this first session is the couple's interaction concerning their differences on how to disagree, as both communicated their feelings about how they disagree.

Session 2: Focus on the Relationship

We began by discussing their reactions to the homework assignment, which were positive. Both Paul and Angela seemed to be cooperating and making an effort to be involved in SE, but I became more aware that Angela was more responsive to SE than Paul was, a fact that he also mentioned in his first tape recording.

The second session was more relaxed for all of us. In this session, Paul stated to Angela his desire for more free time. Angela was already aware of his need but replied that he had refused to accept free time when she had tried to give it to him. Further, when she has free time and Paul doesn't, she feels guilty. In a nutshell, both Paul and Angela clearly stated their impasse on the issue of free time apart from each other. Although no solutions were reached, I think that each increased awareness of the other's position. Also, they recapitulated what each wants to improve or change in their relationship. For example, Angela wants Paul to be more attuned to her emotional and sexual needs, be more interested in their child's development, and to boost her morale as a homemaker and as a person. Paul wants more understanding of his need for individual time, fewer family demands, a more rational approach to problem solving, and a cleaner house.

My general impression of Paul and Angela during this session is that both evade confrontations lest they hurt each other. In fact, Angela stated twice during the interview that she did not want to disrupt the status quo in their relationship. I found this frustrating and did not know how to respond. My readings in Crosby (1973) helped me with this frustration (i.e., conflict is a fact of life; when the negative is repressed, so is the positive). Paul and Angela seem to be verbally suppressing some of the underlying differences that each is aware of nonverbally (e.g., Angela's need for Paul to support her as a homemaker).

Session 3: Communication in Marriage

Nonverbal communication within this marriage is apparently used to convey a lot of their bad moods and leave-me-alone feelings, but both seem perceptive to each other's verbal and nonverbal communications. For example, when I arrived for this session, Paul seemed grumpy and sullen, as expressed in his silence and facial expressions. While doing the second exercise on communicating a feeling to each other, Angela said Paul communicated irritability and that he was in a bad mood. Paul replied that the feeling he received from Angela was that "I know where you are at, and it is OK because everything is going to be OK." In this exercise, the honest communication expressed between them seemed to clear the air; from this point on, Paul was over his bad mood.

The next exercise was very productive. Paul and Angela discussed a practical issue that had to be resolved that day: Angela wanted Paul to do something with her that he didn't want to do. Through the series of "it," "you," "we," and "I" statements, Paul and Angela negotiated a satisfying outcome. During negotiation, both expressed honesty and humor. I felt that today's session facilitated smooth communication between them, and I felt satisfied that SE had helped them to be together when they might have stayed apart, feeling resentful toward each other.

In the exercise on manipulative communication styles, it became clear to both of them that Paul uses placating and computing more than blaming and distracting, whereas the opposite is true for Angela. Both seem uncomfortable using the other's characteristic styles but also seem more aware of how their manipulative communication styles sabotage efforts to resolve conflicts.

Session 4: Communication and Hurt

We began this session with good feedback on the preceding session. For example, they said that Paul made an "I feel . . ." statement that he probably would not have made if it had not been for SE and that SE had helped them to clarify their practical problem of the past week, which they had resolved satisfactorily.

In this lesson, I deviated somewhat from the structure by explaining the three key concepts in this lesson before beginning the exercises. I believe that these concepts need to be stressed more than they are in the written lesson and that this explanation adds continuity to the session. I explained the crystal-ball technique, shared meaning, and what I labeled "gunnysacking" (after Crosby, 1973) in order to tag the communication process in which not facing conflict can result in the repression of negative feelings that emerge later in the form of resentment or in bringing up irrelevant past history when discussing a current conflict. Both Paul and Angela seemed to like the terms crystal ball and gunnysacking, and used them frequently in the remaining sessions.

The exercise concerning how each partner can let the other know that he or she is angry was a rehashing of earlier sessions: Paul wants Angela to state her anger rationally, and Angela wants Paul to show some "gut reactions." Not agreeing on how to disagree appears to be another impasse in their relationship. Although each affirms that an effort will be made to move toward the other's wishes, I suspect that this may be an example of accommodation within a relationship, in which the conflict over how to disagree is not resolved but tolerated as a personality difference.

Session 5: Trust

When Paul and Angela were asked to name three areas in their relationship that they would like to be more open about, both named sex (it is becoming clearer that each wants to be more expressive in this area), and Angela named conflict with her mother-in-law.

When asked about naming verbal and nonverbal communication inconsistencies, both named placating examples, such as Paul's saying, "I don't mind going to the party on Saturday night," when he really does mind. Angela is aware of Paul's true feelings. Both seem sensitive to incongruent messages, and SE seems to be helping them to align communication incongruencies (e.g., Paul is eventually telling Angela what he really feels).

Both strongly agreed that they have a parallel relationship in which they feel equal and work hard to cooperate with each other on issues. However, in the exercise on admitting a mistake, Angela seemed quicker than Paul to admit a mistake, but this may have been due to the particular incident that they related.

Session 6: Quid Pro Quo

Both were reminded of the communication rules that had been demonstrated in the past sessions. Of importance in the session is that each partner was to select a need from the other's list of needs that he or she could fulfill. This need was to be discussed until both were satisfied with the outcome. I gave all instructions according to the program structure and remained silent throughout the negotiation process, except for intervening when manipulative types of communication were used (e.g., blaming).

Paul and Angela spent at least 1 hour on the first negotiation, in which Paul chose to give Angela more time away from their son without making her feel guilty. I think Paul chose the very wish that he wanted for himself; thus, I see this choice as a projective manipulation in that Paul gunnysacked often about how much spare time Angela has in comparison with the spare time he has. The crux of the first negotiation is that Paul resented fulfilling this need of Angela's; consequently, the negotiation had negative overtones (I observed anger, hurt, and resentments in both partners).

I think that the instructions about the time limitations for negotiation are incomplete; eventually, I had to intervene and express their alternatives, as they had stated them, to help them stay on the issue. I recommend that instruction about the time limit be included in this session, as we spent 2 hours and 15 minutes in negotiation, and I felt that I intervened more than the program intended.

For the second negotiation, Angela chose Paul's wish that she be more organized. Again, I had to tell them often that they were gunnysacking, blaming, to keep them on the issue. Paul seemed to doubt Angela's sincerity about her desire to be more organized as a person and in household responsibilities.

I do not feel that I lost control in this session. Instead, I believe that the time spent on this session was worthwhile (I did think to myself, "If I were a therapist and their hour was up, I could tell them that I would see them next week"). I was uncomfortable at times because Paul selected a wish of Angela's that he was not ready to fulfill, and this is not in accord with the design of the Negotiation Program.

When I left, I knew that some wounds had been opened but that some plans had been made for dealing with those wounds. Paul and Angela did reach agreement on how to give the other what he or she wanted. I think, though, that they may have felt that SE had hurt instead of helped them. I consider this a temporary reaction, part of the old agitation process of change—feeling that things are worse than before. In reality, when people face conflict and risk growth, things typically get worse before they get better. We talked about the feelings they experienced during negotiation, and this discussion seemed to help them feel more positive about this session.

POSTTEST AND FEEDBACK CONFERENCE

The results on the posttests are mixed in comparison with the pretest results. Ratings on some items changed, some in positive and some in negative directions. Notably, Paul increased his satisfaction in relationships with close relatives, personal time, empathy, warmth, self-disclosure, and in some of the sexual dimensions; he decreased his satisfaction in feelings, emotions, confrontation, and self-exploration. From pre- to posttests, Angela remained satisfied with her communication behaviors and dissatisfied with her personal independence, household responsibilities, occupational progress, and social activities; Paul was relatively satisfied in these areas, although he could be more satisfied with personal independence both for himself and for Angela. Angela decreased her satisfaction with physical health, Paul's personal independence, and on most dimensions pertaining to her sexual satisfaction, although both rated sex in general as highly satisfying. Both slightly increased their satisfaction in communication happiness with self and spouse, perhaps a direct indicator of the effect of the Negotiation Program. Both remained very satisfied with their overall marital happiness and feelings of love for each other.

I question whether the posttests and feedback accurately reflect the impact of SE on their relationship. Many of the communication techniques and experiences shared through SE will probably be more accurately evaluated on a long-term basis. Paul and Angela may look back a year from now and conclude that SE was a very meaningful experience in their relationship.

Generally, both Angela and Paul stated that before SE, they had used many of the communication processes in the Negotiation Program but that the program had given them labels for the processes. In the feedback, both said that SE is a good idea and that its primary benefit to them was its confirming what they already knew—that they have a good relationship. This was also evidenced in their evaluation after listening to their tapes (i.e., the principal value was reaffirmation of their positive feelings about their relationship). Angela was more positive than Paul in her assessment of SE, which came as no surprise, considering that she had been more enthusiastic than Paul in the beginning. She also stated that Paul had probably received more benefit from SE than he realized. Neither wanted more SE unless they could be shown that it would be worth the time they would have to invest.

In the feedback conference, I first delineated the areas for growth in their relationship, then delineated the positive aspects in their relationship. I recommended three areas for growth: (a) less rumination about the issues between them (both have a tendency to field issues unnecessarily before taking action); (b) increased awareness of their manipulative communication styles, such as Paul's placating and Angela's distracting, in order to confront issues more directly and more effectively; and (c) working on aligning feelings and nonverbal messages with verbal messages so that their communication will be more congruent. Paul and Angela were very attentive throughout my feedback, and both agreed with my recommendations.

I delineated five positives: (a) their willingness to work on their relationship and to risk learning new things about each other; (b) their cooperation and involvement with each other's needs; (c) their sensitivity to each other's feelings; (d) their consideration and support of the roles and responsibilities that each assumes to accomplish the functional demands of their marriage; and (e) their valuing of honesty and their attempts to be honest with each other. Overall, I said that they have a highly functional marriage based upon commitment, mutual support, and love for each other.

SUMMARY

I concluded that Paul and Angela have a highly functional and democratic marriage with few, if any, significant problems. The Negotiation Program was selected because I believe that this sequenced structure would best address their needs for more open communication, for increasing their awareness of each other's needs and feelings (e.g., Paul's need for more personal time and his need that Angela be more rational when discussing issues; Angela's need for Paul to be more emotionally expressive and to support her need for personal identity), and for increasing their awareness of the implicit rules under which they operate in their marital system. I expected that SE would involve the couple and me in a fruitful give-and-take and that this interaction would produce constructive change.

Evaluation of SE depends upon three variables: the suitability of the program for the couple, their cooperation and involvement, and the humanness and the skills of the enricher. Concerning the first variable, I recommended that the Family Information form on communication behaviors specify that the behaviors being rated pertain to the immediate family only. This form posed a problem both for the control and the enrichment couple. For example, the control female stated that she rated herself as highly empathetic with the world outside her marriage but that she considered herself much less empathetic within her marriage. Both couples asked how to respond to various items on the Family Information form in light of how each behavior was defined on the communication behaviors sheet. I suggest that the definitions on the communication behaviors sheet be reworded to pertain to the category that is to be assessed (e.g., empathy, self-disclosure) so that we will have generated equivalent data that can be evaluated reliably and with construct validity. Further, I recommend that the four manipulative communication styles—placating, blaming, avoiding, and preaching—be changed to follow Satir's (1972) placating, blaming, distracting, and computing. Satir's distinction between blaming and computing seems clearer than that between blaming and preaching. Concerning the involvement of the couple, I have already reported that Angela was more receptive and positive than Paul, although in general, both were cooperative and involved in the process. Both considered SE a good idea and believed that its primary value for them had been in confirming what they already knew—that they have a good relationship.

I consider the couple's impressionistic evaluation of SE (1 week following program completion) qualifiable because I think the benefits could be more accurately assessed later, perhaps at a 1-year follow-up. I think SE was a growth-producing experience for the couple and for me. Further, I believe that the enrichment couple derived more benefits from the process than they now realize. Although no startling differences appeared between pre- and posttests for the enrichment couple (each spouse showed overall happiness with the marriage across time), changes did occur in negative and in positive directions on some dimensions. In comparison, the pre- and posttests of the control couple reveal similar results; given the multivariables in these tests and the lack of statistical analyses, assessment of the meaning of rating changes is problematical. Both couples reacted positively to listening to their tapes, but both reacted negatively to recording them (they said it was difficult to speak for 10 minutes).

Concerning humanness and skills as an enricher, Angela wrote a positive note about my work, specifically about maintaining objectivity with a couple I knew. Another evaluation will come from my supervisor. I believe that I followed the program 97% of the time; when appropriate, I contributed spontaneously to the interaction among the three of us. Also, I believe that I improved with time, becoming less anxious, more confident, and able to enjoy the process more.

3

A Functional Couple

Alan Schnee and William L. Buchanan

Carl and Julia are from middle- to upper-middle-class families. Both work part-time and attend college full-time. They have been dating each other seriously for 2 years and are thinking of getting married in the next few years. Carl is 25 years old; Julia is 21. Carl explained that he had been thinking of seeking individual therapy when Julia suggested that they come together for SE.

The couple presented a few immediate problems during the interview. Their chief concern was the amount of arguing they had been experiencing. Carl was identified as the one who needs to work on his "temper." Julia said that she needs some help because she "worries too much." The couple mentioned that they typically disagree about time spent with friends versus time spent with each other. Later, Julia said she wishes only that Carl not change his plans when they involve her because the change leaves her hanging. Toward the very end of the interview, they looked at each other, smiled, and said, with some embarrassment, that they disagree about some sexual issues.

The couple impressed us initially by their awareness of and interest in each other and the relationship. It appeared, however, that they were sometimes too involved with each other (e.g., they seemed to use a system of nonverbal signals, which appears to censor more overt behavior).

PRETEST SUMMARY

Several paper-and-pencil tests were administered to Carl and Julia, including the Dyadic Adjustment Inventory, the Family Adjustment Inventory, and the Holmes-Rahe Schedule of Events.

27

We asked them to tell us the areas they wished to work on. In addition to pretest measures, we asked them to complete daily (throughout SE) the Marital Happiness Scale.

On the Dyadic Adjustment Inventory, Carl scored 39 on dyadic consensus, 8 on affectional expression, 33 on dyadic satisfaction, 21 on dyadic cohesion, for a total score of 101. Julia scored 53 on dyadic consensus, 10 on affectional expression, 40 on dyadic satisfaction, 21 on dyadic cohesion, for a total score of 124. Both totals fall in the normal range. An item-analysis revealed no outstanding difficulties, and all items were scored in a neutral or a positive direction.

On the Family Adjustment Inventory, Carl scored 111. However, he reversed the ranking in column C (i.e., instead of using 10 for top priority, he used 1 as top priority). With the reversal, his total score is −34. Julia scored a −94 on the Family Adjustment Inventory. These scores indicate that some areas are displeasing to the couple. Carl's greatest displeasure is that he and Julia argue too much. Julia also indicated that she and Carl argue too much. Both noted areas of displeasure outside their relationship (e.g., home life, school, Julia's relationship with her mother). Carl said they "have good sex; could be better though," and Julia stated, "We don't make love enough."

On the Holmes-Rahe Schedule of Events, Carl scored 354, and Julia scored 390. Both scored relatively high, indicating that they have experienced higher than average stress during the past 18 months. Julia's greatest stressors were sexual difficulties, change in number of arguments with spouse, financial problems, change in health of a family member, and a reorganization of work. Carl's greatest stresses have been sexual difficulties, gaining new family member, change in health of a family member, and change in living conditions.

Carl and Julia agreed that communication was the area that needed the most work but that they also needed to work on arguing, Carl's temper, Julia's worrying too much, and disagreements on how much time to spend with other people (friends).

After consultation with Jim Kochalka, our supervisor, we chose three programs: Problem Solving, Assertiveness, and Communication. All involve two-way communication, so all three could help with their arguing and temper and give them new skills for dealing with each other. A program of sexual enrichment was not selected because the couple, when questioned about it, were not interested in such a program (it might have been initially uncomfortable for Julia because both of us—the enrichers—are male). However, the supervisor suggested that near the end of SE, when communication is better and a more supportive rapport has developed, an optional sexual enrichment program might be suggested for one session.

SUMMARY OF SESSIONS

Session 1

At the beginning of the first session, we asked the couple to choose one of three programs: Problem Solving, Parental Assertiveness, and Communication. They chose, with some difficulty, the Communication Program. The first lesson concerns unfair communication and the ways in which guilt, mind reading, nagging, sarcasm, and silence can be used to communicate unfairly.

Carl and Julia had some difficulty thinking of how they use guilt in communicating unfairly. However, after we gave some illustrations, they described numerous ways in which they use guilt. For example, Julia admitted that she tries to make Carl feel guilty about being around his friends when she wants to be with him alone. Carl said that he tries to make Julia feel guilty about not buying him anything when he doesn't have enough money to buy something.

In each succeeding exercise, once the couple understood the concept, they participated eagerly. By the end of the first lesson, the couple had mastered the concepts and had described a number of unfair behaviors in both partners.

Supervision.

Our supervisor suggested that we be flexible about the selection of lessons for this couple and that we concentrate on the concepts of fair fighting and feelings because the two go hand in hand. For the next lesson, we chose Communicating Feelings Versus Hostility, from the Parental Assertiveness Program. This lesson incorporates the prescribed concentration, through exercises in feelings, emotions, "I" messages, comparisons, and hostility versus "I feel" statements.

Session 2

Having been asked to enumerate as many feelings and emotions as they could, Carl and Julia had little difficulty listing approximately 30 feelings. The next exercise, however, making "I feel" statements, posed some problems. Typically, they confused "I feel" statements with blaming statements. For example, Julia said, "I feel that you always cause the arguments." Carl and Julia were encouraged to use the ways they had listed earlier to help them identify their own feelings. After some illustration, they began to get the idea; by the end of the session, Carl expressed clearly to Julia that he felt angry when she was late. Julia was able to say that she felt hurt when Carl made fun of her "less than excellent athletic abilities."

The couple seems to have a pattern in which arguments grow out of the partners' inability to own and express their feelings. Instead, they use blaming statements, so conflict and hostility result.

Supervision.

Our supervisor suggested that we stay with the Parental Assertiveness Program because the lessons seem appropriate for this couple. Because Carl and Julia spend so much time arguing, we thought that we could at least help them to argue more effectively. We believed that they were learning an important skill in the first lesson and were ready for the next step. We decided to use the lesson called Asserting Yourself, which includes making requests, saying no, righting a wrong situation, assertion, and a role-play.

Session 3

In the first exercise, the couple imparted some interesting information about the relationship of anger and hurt. They explained that they usually have a difficult time saying no to each other and that when one does say no, the partner is unpleasant to the one who said no. We explored with the couple their feelings about saying no to each other and their feelings about receiving a "no" statement. At first, both said that when one partner says no, the other becomes angry. We continued to talk about that, and they began to divulge their feelings of hurt, which were underlying their anger. For example, Julia said, "Yes, I begin to yell at Carl when he doesn't want to go out to a movie, but I guess I really feel hurt because it feels like he doesn't want to go with *me*. That hurts!" This was an important time for the couple because it allowed them a chance to be more intimate about the sharing of hurt feelings, and it helped them understand where some of their anger was coming from. The following exercises went smoothly; through a new sense of sharing, they felt more comfortable with assertion.

Session 4

The fourth lesson was not difficult to choose, for the next logical step was to help the couple fight fairly. They had now had what we thought were important prerequisite lessons (i.e., knowing what you are feeling and assertion). Our supervisor agreed.

The first exercise—where and when to fight—proved to be an important exercise for this couple. Julia said she usually just "blows up" at Carl without thinking about how or what she really wants to say to him. Carl said that he experiences the same difficulty. From these statements, we began to see the degree to which Carl and Julia are entrenched in emotional and action spheres and that it is important for each of them to begin to practice using more rationality. The exercises helped us direct the couple toward this end. We encouraged them to set a time to fight. Julia liked this idea and said that setting a time to fight will help cool her off and allow her to "think" about what she wants to say. She also said that she does not like to fight in the car, so they decided on a place where they would like to fight. Carl agreed that a "cooling-down" period would help him organize his thoughts.

The next exercises presented two concepts: how to present complaints and how to give feedback. Again, they had difficulty at first, and both had problems making "I" statements. Once the importance of "I" statements was clear, they were able to make them (they had had difficulty with "I" statements in earlier lessons as well). They demonstrated a more difficult time doing the active listening (feedback). We consistently had to redirect them. Julia would repeat what Carl said but would invariably add something (Carl had less difficulty). By the end of the lesson, the couple seemed to have a strong grasp of the material.

Supervision.

We discussed the possible functional uses of the couple's arguments. It became clearer, as the discussion progressed, that arguing is an integral part of this couple's style of getting close. Our supervisor suggested that because the fair fighting lesson was so difficult for them, we should continue on that track. (If they are going to do it, they might as well get more out of it!) We decided to do the lesson called How to Deal With Anger.

Session 5

At the beginning of the fifth session, the couple presented a very different affect from what we had seen before. They sat farther from each other than they normally did and exchanged what appeared to be hostile glances. We asked them if by any chance they were angry with each other. They told us that they had just had a fight and that indeed they were angry with each other. The task at hand for us was quite interesting. We thought, "Now we'll see if this stuff is worth the paper it's printed on." We proceeded step-by-step with the couple on the following exercises: (a) Angry Feelings; (b) Learning to Accept Angry Feelings; (c) Owning Problems; (d) Gathering the Facts. The couple cooperated with us on the exercises, although they demonstrated some behaviors seen in the preceding session (e.g., difficulty in listening—each would interrupt or would feedback incorrectly). We considered this a good opportunity for the couple to practice these skills again. By the end of the session, with the firm direction and clear structure offered by the program, the couple had heard each other and were no longer angry with each other.

Session 6

In this session, we wished to highlight a basic principle on which the preceding lessons were based, namely, intimacy. This lesson, called Intimacy (from the Working-Through Program), is different from earlier lessons because it involves the couple in insight rather than action. Also, this lesson seemed an appropriate lesson with which to close. The couple had been introduced to skills that would lessen their need to fight in order to be close, so they might be better able to step back and look at the ways they were avoiding intimacy (because they had learned better ways of being intimate). The lesson took on a quality of completeness, as the couple shared with us the fact that they did feel closer. However, they had difficulty thinking of the ways in which they avoid intimacy (much to our dismay). Because they had been learning to become more and more intimate, they had difficulty identifying areas in which intimacy is still a problem. In a sense, they seemed to believe they had "arrived" and that they weren't blocking areas of intimacy. We felt that, as this was the last session, it was more appropriate to emphasize their progress and hard work; in the feedback conference (after the posttests), we will try to help them see that more work needs to be done.

POSTTEST SUMMARY

On the Dyadic Adjustment Inventory, both Carl and Julia increased their scores, indicating greater satisfaction and adjustment in their relationship. Carl's score increased from 101 at pretest to 114 at posttest. Julia's score increased from 124 to 126. On both pre- and posttests, Julia's scores are well above the cutoff point of 100. Carl's pretest score (101) is borderline, but his posttest score (114) is well into the adjusted range.

On the Family Adjustment Inventory, Carl's adjustment scores decreased from −34 to −54. However, in his scores only in relationship to Julia, his pretest score is −24, and his posttest score is 0. Thus, although his overall score dropped, his scores in his relationship with Julia improved from a displeasing rating (−24) to a neutral rating (0). The decrease in the overall score is accounted for mostly by his ratings of finishing school, quitting his present job, and getting a new job, which at pretest he scored +45 and at posttest he scored −16.

Julia's score on the Family Adjustment Inventory improved from −94 at pretest to −77 at posttest. Both are in the displeasing range, but the posttest score is less displeasing. In scores concerning her relationship to Carl, her pretest score is 30 and her posttest score 38. Thus, she rated her relationship with Carl as pleasing on both tests, but more pleasing at posttest. The most significant change was the item "we argue too much," which changed from −12 at pretest to +12 at posttest. Julia is mainly dissatisfied with her relationship with her mother, school, and her feelings of being secure and confident in herself.

Arguing seemed to be the biggest issue of concern in Carl and Julia's relationship. The arguing persisted because of lack of communication and lack of skills in problem solving. The SE lessons were designed to increase their skills in communication and problem solving, and it was predicted that, as a result, the arguments would decrease. This is indeed what the couple reported orally and what Julia's Family Adjustment Inventory indicates.

Carl and Julia seem more relaxed and at ease with each other. They reported arguing less in the one specific situation in which they usually had arguments (i.e., in the car). At the feedback conference, they reported having argued only once in the car during the preceding 3 weeks. Overall, despite the stressors in their family life, school, and work, this couple seems to have improved their relationship.

On the Marital Happiness Scale, most scores were in the 7–9 range throughout SE. A few noticeable exceptions did occur. From Week 1 to Week 8, Carl's average weekly scores indicate that his and Julia's communication improved (self—6.7 to 8.6, partner—5.6 to 8.3). Julia also indicated improvements, in two other areas. In occupational progress, she increased her average weekly score from 5.4 in Week 1 to 7.3 in Week 8. She also indicated that their ability to work out differences increased from Week 1 to Week 8 (4.1 to 7.4); Carl's scores are consistent with that increase (7.1 to 8.3).

FEEDBACK CONFERENCE

We began with Carl and Julia's oral feedback to us. They said SE had been a very positive experience and that they had recommended it to one couple and would probably recommend it to another. What they had learned most was fair fighting and the ability to listen actively (i.e., to check out what the other has said by repeating one's understanding of it). They reported having used the techniques of fair fighting on several occasions and also that they had reminded themselves in the middle of an argument to fight fair. They said that as a result, they have argued less and feel that they are communicating better than they ever have. They reported feeling closer to each other and attributed that to the communication techniques they have learned.

In addition to feedback on the paper-and-pencil pre- and posttests, we gave feedback concerning the couple's strengths, areas to work on, and our overall impressions of their relationship. The strengths include their love and commitment to each other, which has been quite obvious and exciting for us to observe. Their ability to communicate does seem to have improved. Their use of nonverbal communication was presented as a strength: they can make decisions by checking things with each other quickly, using few words. However, the nonverbal communication is a two-edged sword in that they have a tendency to mind-read and not check out assumptions about what the other is communicating. Carl had found it difficult to tell Julia when he felt hurt and insecure; instead, he would usually get angry. He reported that now he is able to share more of his hurt feelings instead of becoming angry. Indeed, as they have learned to share their feelings of hurt, they report being "closer to each other" (i.e., more intimate).

Carl and Julia agreed with our feedback and said they believed they had gotten better about mind reading because they have become aware of it and now catch themselves doing it. They reported they are mind reading less and checking out each other's communications more.

We told Carl and Julia that we have been excited to see the growth they have experienced. We also told them that SE and covenant contracting will be offered next quarter. After we explained covenant contracting, the couple indicated that they are interested and will probably sign up for it.

CONCLUSIONS

As trainees, we find that the strength of SE is that it teaches specific skills for specific areas of attention. Further, it demonstrates graphically the theories learned in family psychology. With this couple, we were able to see the theory come to life (i.e., that intimacy occurs when hurt feelings are shared).

The format also provided logical direction for the sequence of the sessions: each session built upon the preceding session. There is an abundance of programs to choose from, and we found the lessons used with this couple very appropriate.

We recommend that the programs be better written and organized. Some lessons are repetitive, and some of the wording is so vague that we had to reword it in order to be understood. Our final recommendation is not possible, we know, but we wish that SE could last longer than 6 weeks. Both of us feel that this couple wants to continue and would benefit from continuing. We enjoyed working with them and are sad to see it end.

4

A Gifted Couple

Joy Dance

Charles (aged 22) and Laura (aged 21) have been married for 19 months. Both are attractive and have pleasant personalities. The couple met in college and began dating during their freshman year. They dated for almost a year before getting married.

Laura dropped out of school at the end of the first semester of her sophomore year, when the couple married, and now works as a secretary. She is the oldest of four children; her father is a minister and her mother a housewife.

Charles is a senior in school and also works as a youth minister in a local church. He and his twin are the oldest of five natural children and two foster children. His father is a foreman, and his mother is a housewife.

Laura is a quiet, moderately shy person, but when communicating with her husband, she seems very open and honest about her feelings. Charles's personality is more outgoing than hers. He is open and seems to have a good self-concept. Charles, much more verbal than Laura, tends to speak for the couple.

During the interview, the couple seemed relaxed and mildly curious about the program. They appeared happy and comfortable with each other. The only display of negative feelings arose when Charles asked Laura her birthdate. She retorted that he could look on her information sheet.

After an explanation of SE, they agreed to participate. The decision to participate was made between them before either answered me. I then asked the couple to complete the contract; the Family Information sheets (Laura, 9.4; Charles, 9.5); Azrin Marital Happiness Scale (Laura 9.3;

Charles, 8.8); the communication behaviors subscale (Laura, 7.8; Laura about Charles, 9.6; Charles, 8.2; Charles about Laura, 9.6). The average score for each scale is indicated in parentheses.

Because of the high scores on the rating scales, and the couple's lack of marital problems, my supervisor, Mary Allison, helped me select the Reciprocity Program. We chose this program with the intention of enriching an already good marriage.

SUMMARY OF SESSIONS

Session 1: Catharsis

The couple brought in their Marital Happiness Scales (MHS). Charles's ratings had risen 0.6, and Laura's had risen 0.1. None of Charles's rating had dropped, and social activities, money, and communication had risen. For Laura, household responsibilities, personal independence, and spouse independence had dropped, but the lowest score was still only 8. Social activities, communication, and occupational progress had come up for her. No assignments or activities had yet taken place, so the change can most likely be attributed to circumstance within the marriage rather than to the effect of the program.

In this session, both gave "love" as the strongest reason for getting married. Other reasons Laura gave were that she likes to be with Charles, has fun with him, and has things in common with him. Charles was pleased with her reasons but said that he already knew them. Additional reasons that Charles gave were that dating was getting to be a hassle and he had felt that he would have more time to study after he got married. Another reason they decided to go ahead was that Laura was ready to drop out of school anyway. She agreed with his reasons. No problems were mentioned during this first part of the session.

When asked about problems, Laura said her biggest problem is being jealous when Charles works with girls in his youth ministry. Although she does not doubt his affection, she is still jealous of his attention and time. She had been jealous even when they were dating. Already aware of her jealousy, now and before the marriage, Charles is sympathetic toward her. Another problem for Laura is accepting the amount of study time necessary for Charles while he is in school. Also, she feels that he sometimes talks down to her, like a father speaking to a child.

A problem that Charles mentioned is that Laura talks too loudly when they are in their apartment. Noise carries from apartment to apartment, and he believes that their conversations should be private.

Both were already aware of these problems. Neither became upset when they were discussed. They mentioned that they had speculated about having to discuss problems at this session. They also mentioned that they always tried to keep their communication open about any feelings in their marriage.

Another area of feelings mentioned is that Laura sometimes takes her feelings out on Charles after a bad day at work. He does not get upset and tries to be understanding. She agrees that this is the way he reacts.

Both are looking forward to Charles's being out of school. Money is tight now but will get better when he is out of school. They always check with each other before making any large purchases, so there are no disagreements about money. They do not plan to have children soon, not even when Charles first gets out of school. They want to build their relationship before they add a member to the family.

Both obviously want a good marriage and are willing to work at it. They realize the importance of communication in the relationship and seem eager for each spouse to be open with feelings. Also, they try to correct any problems, or at least be sympathetic about them.

Session 2: Old Satisfactions

A week and a half had passed between sessions because the couple had gone on vacation. Their MHS ratings had again risen. For Laura it was 9.6, having come up in household responsibilities and personal independence and having dropped 1.0 in social activities. Charles's ratings had come up to 9.7, having risen in social activities and other ratings having remained the same.

The couple had no problem listing 10 things that they do for each other. In fact, they listed 12:

Female—10 things you do for the male
  1. Do the laundry and housework.
  2. Work full-time.
  3. Keep him in mind when planning meals and cooking.
  4. Keep financial records—checkbook, pay bills.
  5. Pick up after him.
  6. Type schoolwork.
  7. Make time for him to be with family—usually Saturdays—rest of family there.
  8. Try to wait up for him when he has to study late.
  9. Go to doctor every week—to get well.
 10. Show how much I love him by being affectionate.

11. Not criticize him in public—wait until we get home.
12. Let him watch and participate in sports.

Male—10 things you do for female
 1. Keep cars up—his more than hers.
 2. Planned vacation with her in mind—except sunburn.
 3. Find a place for her to go when he is occupied in meeting at church.
 4. Arrange for adequate income by asking for raise, if needed—so she won't have to take up slack.
 5. Pull strings at church to get her a job that she will be happy doing.
 6. Make time for her to be with family—grandmother in area; sisters visit.
 7. Always try to plan so that we can eat together; only miss Tuesday night.
 8. Help her with her attitude about her job.
 9. Don't bring problems of church into the home so that she won't get a negative attitude.
10. Show how much I love her by being affectionate.
11. Not criticize her in public—wait until we get home.
12. Let her have girlfriends over—I don't mind.

The couple agreed that they do these things for each other because they love each other. Laura also mentioned that she wants to please Charles and make him happy. He stated that one reason they got married was so that they could do so much for each other.

In working on the negative aspects of the marriage, we struggled to come up with some situation that they could role-play. I finally suggested Charles's talking down to Laura, but they could not think of the last time that had happened. We finally worked on Charles's telling Laura what to do and a situation that arose on their vacation, pertaining to her getting sunburned. Although they were cooperative, they seemed a little awkward during this exercise. Charles said that he would rather people just tell him what they think and that he would probably be amused if Laura tried to rephrase his statements positively. Laura believed that positive statements would sound better and that she would feel better about replying positively.

In this session, it became more apparent that Charles speaks for the couple. He even prompted Laura on listing things that she does for him. Because they had had a little difficulty dealing with the negative aspects of marriage, I spent extra time praising their good marriage. I did not want them to start imagining negative aspects rather than seeing the good things about their marriage. Homework assignments were given and agreed on.

Session 3: New Satisfactions

There were 10 days between Sessions 2 and 3. Charles had been away at camp for a week, so they had not had a lot of time to practice the homework assignments.

On the MHS, Laura's ratings had come up 0.2, to 9.8. Ratings had risen in communication, personal independence, and spouse independence but dropped on occupational progress. Charles had the same mean score as last time, 9.7, but his score had dropped in social activities (understandable, as he had been at camp) and come up in communication.

When checking on their homework, I learned that they had been thanking each other for nice things but had found that the thanks sounded funny, so they had usually ended in laughter. They had not had much opportunity to practice stating things positively because Charles had been gone so much.

In trying to find 10 additional satisfactions, we took the following areas from the MHS as categories that could be improved: money, communication, personal independence (Laura), spouse independence (Laura), and jealousy, which had been one of the original problems. Naming these areas did not prove too helpful. Nothing can be done to improve the money situation right now, they believed that their communication had already improved, the independence category (Laura) was related to a specific incident that had been solved, and no jealousy problems had come up since they had started the program.

They had a difficult time thinking of 10 new things to do because they already do so much for each other. Laura remarked that she already does everything for Charles. They helped each other to come up with the following items:

Female for Male—additional things I could do
1. Cook chicken and dumplings once during week.
2. Go calling once a week.
3. Be ready 15 minutes early on Sunday night.
4. Get housework done by 8:00 p.m. to spend more time with him.
5. Have supper ready by 5:30 Wednesday night.
6. Empty trash in ashtray in car.
7. Not eat so many potato chips.
8. Make gravy once this week.

9. Do laundry by lunchtime on Saturday.
10. Be more understanding when he is late.

Male for Female—additional things I could do
1. Wash dishes once a week.
2. Take her to see a movie.
3. Call her once a day at work.
4. Have supper ready one night per week.
5. Stay at table until she finishes eating.
6. Wash her car.
7. Hang up suit on Sunday after church.
8. Let her drive my car.
9. Open doors for her when we go "out."
10. Empty garbage every night.

The Happiness Contract was explained to them, and both signed it. Before signing, Laura decided to change one of her items because she could not do it in the time designated.

Homework assignments were given, along with praise for their good marriage.

Session 4: Compromise

Sessions 3 and 4 were only 4 days apart. They had not had time to do many of the "new satisfactions" in their Happiness Contract but were planning to do most of them during the weekend when they would have more time together. They are continuing to thank each other for nice things, and it is not so funny now, as it is becoming more natural.

On the MHS, the scores for both had come up to 9.9, and they scored exactly the same on all scales. For Laura, that is up 0.1, as her score had risen in occupational progress. For Charles, that is up 0.2, his scores having come up in social activities and money. They had discussed their MHS forms after filling them out, so they were not surprised with their results.

For this session (on compromise), the only applicable area from the MHS (an area in which they are not completely satisfied) was social activities. They had no problem or conflict in this area, but because of time, they do not have as much social life as they desire. They did think of a problem that had occurred in the past, one that could happen again in the future in a similar situation.

Using the compromise technique, which I described in this session, we constructed the following chart:

Conflict

Charles wants to socialize with couple because he is friends with the other male. Laura does not enjoy being with the other female.

Solutions

Charles	*Laura*	*Compromise*
Stop seeing couple together, although he would really rather do things with both couples.	Would rather not associate with them but could just accept it.	1. Both go out with other couple to please Charles. 2. Laura go out alone with girlfriends.

At first, both thought that the best solution was just to give in to the other's wishes. After some discussion, they began to see that if both *gave*, each could do something to please the other without giving up something desirable. We discussed their feelings about the compromise, and they were very pleased when they realized that each of them could experience positive feelings about a situation that had been undesirable for both of them.

At this point, I felt that Charles and Laura had really achieved the intent of reciprocity as described by Azrin, Naster, and Jones (1973). "The overall feeling induced in a partner should be that the spouse is continuously striving to please him (her) and he (she) in turn will strive equally to please the spouse to maintain this attitude of 'I will try to please you since you are trying to please me'" (p. 368).

Because Charles and Laura could not define a current conflict, we talked about the compromise technique as a preventive measure to deal with problems in the future—to make their good marriage better. They agreed to try the compromise technique over the weekend, the most likely time for problems because they are together more then.

At the close of the session, they shared some feelings about the program. They said that they had discussed the program frequently and consequently were talking more about their marriage. They also believed that hearing from an outsider that they have a good marriage has had a positive effect on their marriage.

Homework assignments were given.

Session 5: Sexual Feedback

We skipped the fifth lesson in the program because the couple did not want to fill out the Wildman Sex Survey (they were not having any problems and were pleased with their sex life). They felt that the survey could be of value if they were experiencing any difficulty, but because they are not, they prefer to keep this aspect of their marriage private. They offered to write a statement that they chose not to complete the survey.

I believe that Charles and Laura were being honest about their sexual satisfactions and were not trying to hide anything. Additional reasons for not filling out the survey could be their conservative religious views and also their acquaintance with me.

In checking with my supervisor, we decided that only the exercise on compromise (Sexual Feedback Lesson) could be done, so this could be included in Session 6.

Session 6: Summing Up

Their MHS scores continued to be high. Charles's stayed the same (9.9), but Laura's dropped in occupational progress (9.8). This decrease was due to a difficult week at work. Laura said that she has no desire to continue her education but plans to continue clerical work.

Charles and Laura have continued to acknowledge the nice things that they do for each other and now feel comfortable doing this and really enjoy it. They have also been trying to state disagreements positively, which has made them more aware of the tone of their statements and of thinking before speaking.

Charles and Laura had brought in their statements from their contract to show me how they had negotiated some of the things that they could not get done. When they realized that they could not fulfill part of their contract, they decided that each would eliminate the same number of items so that the contract would be equal (they agreed to do the other things later when they had more time). From this negotiation, I felt that they were getting a good understanding of the program. The couple had also used the compromise technique successfully.

I suggested that they try the compromise technique to work on the jealousy problem. They could not come up with a situation or an example. Laura finally said that most of her jealous feelings had occurred when they were with the couple discussed in Session 4. The other girl continually touched men when she talked with them and it made Laura jealous. That couple had moved, so they were no longer a problem. Other times that she had been jealous were at church when the teenaged girls touched Charles when they were talking with him. She said that this was bothering her less as she grew to understand that this is typical behavior for teenaged girls; also, she knows that her husband does nothing to encourage their attention. When jealousy does occur, they always talk about the situation, and Charles tries to be particularly reassuring. This is not the approach that Knox (1975) recommends for dealing with jealousy, but I did not discuss his suggestions with them.

Another accomplishment they have achieved through the program is better communication. Completing the homework assignments has forced them to talk more about what they are doing in their marriage, and consequently they have become more aware of each other's feelings. They considered the length of time required for the program beneficial because it has given them time to practice the new techniques. Also, knowing that they would have to report on their progress has been a stimulus to their achievement. Both again mentioned the positive effect of hearing from someone else that they have a good marriage. Charles also believes that the experience of being helped could be of value to him in the future as a minister.

We also discussed the value of the techniques in dealing with future problems and how the use of the techniques can help prevent problems.

POSTTEST SUMMARY

Both MHS scores were again 9.9. The score was up 0.1 for Laura, but the same for Charles. Each had all 10s except for 9s on money. The MHS scores have increased from the pretest: for Charles, 8.8 to 9.9 (+1.1); for Laura, 9.3 to 9.9 (+0.6).

On the posttest Family Information, Laura's score rose from 9.4 to 9.9. Charles's rose from 9.5 to 9.9. On the communication behaviors of the Family Information, the "female about self" rose from 7.8 to 9.8; "male about self" rose from 8.2 to 9.9; the "male about the female" from 9.6 to 9.9; the "female about male" from 9.6 to 10.0.

Although none of the posttests show a marked increase, I consider the increases significant because the scores were already so close to the top. Although it is difficult not to be skeptical about the high scores, I believe the evaluations were honest. Charles and Laura seem very happy, and they feel that they have a good marriage, especially after the positive reinforcement they have received. The rise in the few original low areas was, I think, due to both spouses' efforts to build self-esteem.

Although Charles and Laura are not as romantic as described in Crosby (1973), they do seem to be very much in love with each other. The relationship almost sounds as though it were still in the honeymoon stage, but they have had to face several stressful situations in their marriage (school, work, finances) and have dealt with them maturely.

Although many young marriages do not work out, this one, because the partners have similar backgrounds, maturity levels, and values, should have a better chance than a marriage in which the partners are from different backgrounds and have different value systems (Knox, 1975; Schulz & Rodgers, 1975).

Even though this couple is very close, theirs is not a symbiotic relationship because they do not depend entirely on each other for need satisfactions and self-identity. They seem to have fairly high self-esteem, Charles's a little higher than Laura's. Their roles in the marriage fluctuate: sometimes both are on the adult level; at other times, she is the child and Charles the parent and vice versa. The couple can be described as moderately differentiated, as they are learning to negotiate in many areas of their relationship. In some aspects of their marriage, though, Charles expects conformity.

In L'Abate's (1986b) aspects of a good marriage—seeing the good, caring, sharing the hurt, forgiveness, responsibility, protectiveness, and enjoyment, Charles and Laura's marriage rates high because these qualities are apparent in their relationship.

Their marriage has the potential to continue to be a good marriage if they continue to be open and honest with each other without being hurtful. They also show concern for each other's physical, emotional, and pleasure needs. I do not think that they will ever be highly differentiated because Charles expects too much conformity, but I think they will be sufficiently differentiated to be able to negotiate within their marriage.

FEEDBACK CONFERENCE

The feedback conference was held 16 days after the final session of the program. Charles and Laura turned in their final Marital Happiness Scales, and each had scored 9.9, the same as their scores on the preceding forms.

We discussed the results of Family Information and their Marital Happiness Scales. Although they had not been aware of their actual scores, they had been aware that, overall, the scores had improved.

The couple had experienced no new problems since the last session. They were using the techniques they had learned during the program and were still observing the Happiness Contract, although they had been very busy, school having started for Charles.

Laura will be taking a night course this fall and is considering trying to finish the requirements for a two-year secretarial certificate. She seems to be more interested in developing more of her own interests, outside her job and her role as wife.

We discussed some of the strengths in their marriage, open communication being the strongest. Although Charles is much more verbal than Laura, at this time both are allowed to express their feelings. We discussed the importance of continuing this expression of feeling to maintain their good marriage.

5

A Rational Couple

Pat King

When Lynn and Elias were asked why they had chosen SE over other programs (e.g., projective testing), Lynn replied that SE seemed more interesting and more applicable to her immediate situation. Elias did not respond to Lynn's statement or reveal any of his own opinions.

Lynn and Elias have been married for 4 years and have a 21-month-old son, Zaki. Lynn, aged 24, was born of middle-aged parents (her mother is now 60; her father is 80). She attended public school except for 1 year at a church-affiliated academy in the northern part of the state. She has two older brothers, aged 32 and 35. Lynn's upbringing, therefore, has been very traditional, particularly as the youngest child and only daughter of Southern Baptist parents. Lynn now attends college, working toward a degree in nursing.

Elias, aged 31, was born in the Middle East and is the third of eight children. His parents and four siblings still live in the Middle East; Elias and three brothers live in the United States. The entire family is Muslim (Lynn has recently converted). Elias has a degree in mathematics and is working on a master's degree. He is employed as a night manager at a large hotel.

Lynn and Elias have recently moved into a large house in an upper-middle-class neighborhood. At this time, living in the house are Lynn's parents, Elias's three brothers, one brother's wife, and Lynn, Elias, and Zaki. This situation appears to be permanent, as three additional bedrooms were being finished at the time of the interview.

INTERVIEW

During the interview, I was struck by the degree to which Lynn, especially, put forth an effort to give an impression of a healthy, stable

47

marriage. Throughout this interview, Lynn spoke of her happiness in being a wife and mother and her ability as an individual in independent activities. At intervals, however, she attempted to persuade Elias to "help" her do SE so that she could obtain the experimental credits she needs. Elias repeatedly asked me whether the sessions would involve anything personal. He said frequently that he didn't care to get involved in SE if the sessions pertained to personal matters in the marriage. I told him that he and his wife would be instrumental in choosing the program, so getting involved in personal matters would be of their own choosing. This appeared to satisfy him, as he agreed to participate provided an undue amount of time would not be required. I then explained the time requirements (number of sessions and length of each session), which were satisfactory to both partners.

Lynn and Elias then completed their pretests, with a great deal of deliberation on certain statements. (Neither Lynn nor Elias answered most of the questions concerning their sexual activities.) When they finished the pretests, we agreed on the time and place for the next meeting.

Enricher's notes.

Elias and Lynn apparently perceive a healthy, stable marriage as extremely important. However, they seem to place as much emphasis upon impressing others with the health and stability of their marriage as upon their own feelings of happiness and stability. Second, to achieve this happy marriage, Lynn and Elias have invested a great deal of energy in maintaining a traditional power structure. Elias appears to be a very powerful, dominating figure in the marriage, controlling the big decisions and, apparently, the marriage in general. Lynn, on the other hand, appears fully entrenched in her role as Hattie Homemaker. I even got the impression that she attends college primarily to please her husband and to impress others rather than for her own self-fulfillment and satisfaction (she entered college shortly after they were married). Lynn's and Elias's expressions throughout the interview were very controlled; apparently this is habitual for them.

In general, even though Lynn and Elias are young, this marriage appears traditional; both partners have very specified roles. They seemed to be trying to impress me with their marital healthiness and stability, partly by their emphasis on controlled feelings and "computing."

PRETEST SUMMARY

The pretest results seem to agree with my admittedly biased impressions. On the pretest, Lynn, in particular, rated most aspects of their marriage as highly favorable (scores of 9 or 10). The activities that she rated somewhat lower were more external events, such as household responsibilities (5), money (8), or social activities (self—8, spouse—6), even religious participation (3). She rated her husband as very strong, fast, helpful, and powerful. In contrast, she saw herself as more noisy, harmless, soft, helpful, but unimportant. Results of the Marital Questionnaire indicate that, for Lynn, the main dysfunctions in her marriage were in the areas of computing and taking responsibility. There were also some concerns about placating and distracting (avoiding marital issues).

Elias's test results are equally interesting in that they basically complement Lynn's. Elias saw himself as more helpful, aggressive, useful, and independent; he visualized his wife as noisy, harmless, helpful, and soft. Lynn saw herself as somewhat unimportant; Elias, however, considered her quite important and strong. Elias's answers, in general, were not as extreme as Lynn's. For instance, in rating his satisfactions with his marriage on several dimensions, Elias's answers were more diversified (rather than mostly 9s and 10s), which may indicate a more realistic view of marriage in general and his marriage in particular. Elias appeared to be most dissatisfied with social activities (self—2, spouse—4), money (2), and occupational progress (2). Again, however, the lowest ratings were the dimensions that appear to be most external to the marital relationship per se. In agreement with his wife's, Elias test results rated computing and taking responsibility as the main areas of dysfunction in the marriage. However, there are also lower scores in the areas of likeness (degree of self-differentiation), priorities, and seeing good. These results are somewhat surprising because they indicate that Elias may not really be as satisfied with the pattern in his marriage as the impression he gives.

Supervision.

I met with my supervisor, Victor Wagner, to discuss my impressions and the interview. He expressed some hesitancy about my seeing this couple, because of their emphasis on control and privacy. However, we finally agreed that the program could go ahead as planned.

In planning for this couple, I soon realized that it would be important to maintain control of the sessions at all times. For this reason, I decided to meet this couple in an office at the university, making it somewhat easier to keep the emphasis upon working on the marriage rather than socializing.

SUMMARY OF SESSIONS

Session 1

The first session consisted of choosing a program and doing the first lesson.

I had carefully considered the programs available and had selected four programs that I considered appropriate for Lynn's and Elias's needs: Assertiveness, Equality, Reciprocity, and Negotiation. Considering the obvious dominance-submission dimension in their marriage, I believed that Assertiveness would be the most appropriate. This judgment seemed reinforced by their apparent lack of focus on feelings (of self and of partner) in the marriage. In addition, the Assertiveness Program contains elements of the Reciprocity Program and, indirectly, elements of Equality and Negotiation. After a discussion with Lynn and Elias, Assertiveness was selected.

The first lesson was intended to help Lynn and Elias understand assertiveness thoroughly. This was accomplished by discussing definitions of assertiveness, submissiveness, dominance, and reciprocity. In addition, the goal of assertive behavior—attaining give-and-take in the relationship—was discussed.

In discussing these definitions and issues, Lynn and Elias openly, although unemotionally, admitted that they had not achieved a consistent balance of give-and-take in their marital relationship. Lynn believed that she gave more to the relationship but emphasized that she enjoyed doing so. To Elias, give-and-take meant compromise. Most of his answers in this session were very concise. I learned later that Elias feels that he has trouble with English and is thus quite conscious of what he says, contrary to my initial impression that he was attempting to remain uninvolved and thereby retain control of the situation.

Both partners believed that assertiveness means standing up for one's rights. Neither could recall a situation in which either had been assertive.

Lynn and Elias were clearer about their conceptions of dominance and submission. Lynn said that at times she is submissive because she is afraid of hurting Elias's feelings. This was discussed at length, particularly with reference to the meaning of assertiveness. I stressed that maintaining clear communication and checking out the partner's feelings (rather than assuming that he or she feels a certain way) minimizes the possibility of hurting one's partner. I also mentioned situations from my own experience, particularly those in which I have undermined a relationship by being "submissive" (but actually getting what I had desired in the first place). Lynn agreed that she had acted similarly at times and that it might be better if she maintained clear and open communication with her husband. The discussion on dominance brought forth the response from both that dominance means getting your own way, even, at times, regardless of the partner's desires and feelings. Elias admitted at this point that he is the dominant partner and at times doesn't like it.

The discussion on reciprocity was rather brief because related aspects had already been covered. Lynn and Elias did agree that although their marriage has not always been characterized by reciprocity, reciprocity is desirable. After the homework assignment was given, we agreed on arrangements for the next session.

Enricher's notes.

During this session, Lynn and Elias appeared more relaxed and more open than during the interview. Despite earlier doubts about the efficacy of attempting SE with this couple (because of their overwhelming concern for privacy), I was finding them very verbal and interesting. My initial impression of the power structure in the marriage was reinforced by Lynn's and Elias's statements about dominance and submission.

Supervision.

My supervisor agreed that there seemed to be a change in this couple's behavior, particularly with respect to openness and friendliness. Again, he stressed that I must maintain control of the situation throughout the program.

Session 2

In Session 2, we discussed the responsibility for assertive behavior in marriage. Lynn and Elias discussed this topic at length. Both felt rather strongly that each has the sole responsibility for his or her own behavior, although at times they, especially Lynn, find it difficult not to take the responsibility for the partner's behavior. They arrived rapidly at these conclusions, independently of my comments. Their awareness was somewhat surprising, yet it does indicate a potential for change in their dealings with each other.

In the second part of this session, each partner was asked to role-play assertiveness in front of a mirror while the partner observed and noted certain aspects of assertiveness (such as the clarity of communication). This exercise did not work particularly well for Lynn and Elias because they had difficulty being serious while looking in a mirror and rehearsing an unfamiliar kind of statement before two other people (the partner and me). Lynn's statement, which concerned losing weight, was particularly lengthy. Elias noted that she appeared to be pleading with herself rather than being assertive. We discussed briefly the difference between pleading and assertiveness (in being assertive, one maintains control of a situation with respect to one's own behavior). By pleading with herself, Lynn was, to some degree, undermining herself. Elias's statements, very different from his wife's, were much more direct and (as Lynn noted), to some extent, threatening.

Enricher's notes and supervision.

Although both appeared actively involved in the first part of this session, they were only minimally involved in the second part. I encouraged them to give each other feedback about their assertive statements, but they found it increasingly difficult to remain serious. I believe that they become involved only in things that are directly applicable and meaningful to them. The supervisor agreed but carried my idea further by saying that this couple seems to become involved only in concrete matters. Although this idea may be accurate, the couple's willingness to take responsibility for their behavior and their willingness to attempt the role playing (even when it was not applicable) does seem to indicate a potential for change and growth within their marital relationship.

Session 3

In Session 3, Lynn and Elias were asked to role-play assertive statements to each other (although neither was allowed to respond to the partner's assertive statement). This session went extremely well, and both seemed involved in the exercises. The first exercise in this session (the negligent newspaper boy) particularly interested them because the situation has happened to them (again, the applicability). Lynn's statement was quite pleading: she very meekly asked the boy if he wouldn't mind putting the paper on the porch. Elias's statement was quite aggressive and directly confrontive. He demanded compliance or the subscription would be cancelled.

When giving feedback to each other, Lynn's pleading and Elias's threatening were rapidly brought to the foreground. When we discussed the advantages and disadvantages of both kinds of statements, I emphasized a combination of the two. That is, Lynn's consideration of the newspaper boy's feelings and Elias's control of the situation as the consumer were viewed positively; their placating and aggressive attitudes were viewed as undesirable.

After some modeling, both Lynn and Elias modified their statements to include only the positive elements. The final statements approached assertiveness to a much greater extent. The second and third exercises went more smoothly, primarily because both partners were concentrating on modifying their instinctive statements. Aspects of all three exercises were discussed (e.g., the police officer as an authority figure and the consequences of being too aggressive or submissive with him).

During this session, Lynn and Elias willingly gave each other feedback. Lynn at times appeared to really enjoy telling Elias his faults in assertive behavior.

Enricher's notes and supervision.

This session appeared particularly appropriate for this couple because the situations were nonthreatening (i.e., outside the marital situation). My supervisor and I wondered about Lynn's enjoyment in giving feedback to Elias. We speculated that this may be one situation in which she can compete with Elias and have sanction for doing so. In addition, in this situation, Elias may not realize the competition aspect—thereby giving his wife a nonverbal go-ahead. Considering the rigid role structure in their marriage, this may be the one situation in which Lynn can compete and win.

Session 4

In Session 4, we dealt with assertive behavior in the marriage. Lynn and Elias were asked to role-play different situations; however, they were not allowed to respond directly to each other's statements. The three exercises in this lesson were appropriate, and Lynn and Elias participated actively—both in verbalizing their own assertive statements and in giving the partner feedback. The accent was on achieving a balance between *placation* and aggressiveness, or as we talked about it throughout the program, "coming more to the middle." Lynn and Elias worked on changing their behavior and at intervals asked me for feedback.

At the beginning of each session, Lynn and Elias were asked to describe ways in which they had been assertive during the preceding week. They always responded with an appropriate situation and appeared to be proud of themselves for doing so. At the beginning of this session, when they were asked the usual question, Elias casually mentioned that Lynn was becoming a great deal more assertive and outspoken in their daily life and that he was feeling somewhat uncomfortable about it. Although he acknowledged his feelings, they did not discuss this situation to any extent.

I had chosen to write a paradoxical letter to this couple. The main aspects of the relationship that I mentioned in the letter are (a) the traditional and rigid role structure in their marriage, (b) the subtle competitiveness, and (c) the stress on their marriage at the expense of individuality. Although I preferred to write a paradoxical message, I also believed that Lynn and Elias would be able to discern and appreciate the subtleties underlying the paradox and would perhaps be somewhat less threatened than they might be by a linear message.

At the end of Session 4, I gave each partner the following letter. Elias called me later that night and angrily questioned the validity of the letter. I asked him to delay his comments until the feedback conference.

Dear Lynn and Elias,

I really have enjoyed working with you for the past 6 weeks. Throughout our sessions, I have seen you work really hard on becoming assertive. I believe that with time and continued efforts the two of you can reach the goal of asserting yourselves and developing a more balanced marital relationship. It is obvious that you care about changing and about keeping your marriage as a growing, vital process, particularly in providing a basis for a lot of support for each other.

Sometimes, however, although both of you have a capacity for insight, you may have some difficulty being aware of your own and your partner's feelings. There may be too much emphasis upon maintaining emotional control in your marriage at all costs. With time, however, I believe that you will become more comfortable and will place a great deal of importance upon maintaining clear, open communication.

Finally, I really appreciate the way in which you make your marriage and your togetherness the primary target in your relationships rather than placing all your emphasis upon Zaki. You really seem to have your priorities straight!

Thanks again for working. I know that you have seen the benefits in your relationship.

Enricher's notes and supervision.

Lynn and Elias appear to have become steadily more open with each other and more cognizant of each other's feelings. Although they still have some difficulties overcoming their initial responses to situations, they are more aware of their need to do so. Beginning in this session, the submissive partner, Lynn, was requested to make the assertive statement and the dominant partner was asked to give feedback. At times, though (with the approval of my supervisor), I asked Elias to make the assertive statement because the situation seemed much more applicable to him and because I felt that he, too, could profit from some degree of change. Sometimes Lynn and Elias found it difficult to acknowledge their feelings outwardly or to describe the partner's feelings in a given situation, but a simple reminder was enough to help them make more appropriate, assertive statements.

With respect to Elias's discomfort about Lynn's growing assertiveness, my supervisor suggested that this area should have been followed up more. In reviewing the situation, I agree.

Session 5

Lynn and Elias entered the session on time, and it soon became quite apparent that Lynn was quite angry about the letter. After commenting favorably on my literary style, she proceeded to deny the statements in the letter. Following a suggestion given by Dr. L'Abate, I calmly agreed that I am not perfect and that it really was a relief to know that I could be wrong. The deflation of Lynn's anger was almost visible. I then asked Lynn if she would delay comments about the letter until the feedback conference. She agreed, and we began Session 5.

Again, they worked on assertive statements within the marriage, but this time they were allowed to respond to each other. Surprisingly, this session proved to be one of the better sessions in the entire program, not only because of its applicability (losing the car keys, disciplining the child) but also because Lynn and Elias participated intensely in responding to each other and in working through the situations assertively.

They spent approximately 15 to 20 minutes on the exercise about child discipline and used appropriate, clear statements throughout this exercise. I listened carefully and gave them positive feedback only when they had finished the entire sequence. For the first time, Lynn and Elias worked together to find alternative solutions to the problem rather than accepting one partner's statement as fact. Although their solution may be seen as a form of compromise, it basically involved a very appropriate level of give-and-take, or reciprocity, in that each partner clearly stated an opinion and the solution reflected the opinions of both partners. For example, in the exercise on child discipline, Lynn stressed the continuity of discipline from one parent to the other; Elias stressed that she should tell him how she disciplined Zaki so that he could be consistent. They agreed that in the future they would discuss the situations and agree on the disciplinary measures.

In the example in which Lynn role-played having lost her keys in her pocketbook, Elias arrived at a very interesting and original solution. Rather than berate his wife for losing her keys (which she has done on occasion), he offered to help her find them by lighting a match so that she could see into her pocketbook. Although this was first done in jest, I pointed out that the lighting of the match could easily be an appropriate response, provided it was accompanied by an appropriately assertive statement. Both partners were intrigued by this solution and stated that many times an impulsive action, such as the lighting of a match, could be changed into an appropriate action by making an appropriate assertive statement.

Enricher's notes and supervision.

Obviously, Lynn and Elias have come a long way since the interview. They have become intensely involved in being assertive, and although Elias is still somewhat uncomfortable, he has admitted that it is a pleasant change to hear Lynn standing up for her rights and acknowledging his feelings as well. During this session, I gave a great deal of positive feedback because I felt that they were working, not to please me, but to obtain benefits for their own marriage. Indeed, I did very little other than read the exercises. I wonder whether Lynn and Elias were subconsciously (or consciously!) trying to prove to me that my letter was wrong. My supervisor approved my handling of Elias's unique solution to the lost keys as well as my allowing Lynn and Elias to continue their discussion about child disciplinary practices.

Lynn and Elias in this session did bring up the question of when assertiveness is appropriate and when it is inappropriate. We discussed this to some extent, but I delayed extensive discussion until the final session (lifemanship and diplomacy). Lynn raised the point that assertiveness may not be appropriate when one's partner is very angry or upset and has given indications that he or she cannot listen. I considered this an appropriate statement rather than an indication of Lynn's placating behavior.

Session 6

In Session 6, the final session, we reviewed the concepts and behaviors they had learned throughout the program. We also discussed the appropriateness of being assertive in certain situations. They decided that in certain situations nothing can be gained from assertiveness and it might thus be better to wait until the partner has cooled down before stating one's opinions. I stressed during this session that Lynn and Elias will have to keep working on assertiveness until it becomes more natural for them.

Enricher's notes.

Lynn and Elias were quite relaxed in this session and engaged in an intelligent, open discussion. They acknowledged that, although they have become more open with each other about their feelings, they do not yet feel natural in being assertive. They insisted that they will definitely continue to work because they have already felt the benefits in their marriage.

FEEDBACK CONFERENCE

During the feedback conference and posttest session, I stressed their continued work on assertiveness. After they completed the posttests, I thanked them for their hard work throughout the program. They declined to participate in another SE program immediately but indicated that they may be interested later.

PRE- AND POSTTEST EVALUATION

Several interesting patterns emerged in the pre- and posttest analysis. The pretest scores indicate a great deal of marital happiness and satisfaction. However, as I noted earlier, these scores may have been inflated because Lynn and Elias were intent on impressing others and upon maintaining emotional control. I got these impressions primarily from Lynn's test results, although it was evident that Elias glorified the aspects of his marriage that he considered most private and "personal." Their combined pretest total (Marital Questionnaire, Family Information, Marital Happiness Scale) of 1,052 is quite high and is based upon the number of items rated 8 or 9 with general respect to either happiness or satisfaction. Their pretest scores on the Marital Questionnaire, however, approximate the mean for married couples (97.4, provided in L'Abate's norm tables), although Elias scored significantly lower than Lynn on this questionnaire. When their pretest scores on the Marital Questionnaire are added together, the combined score (183) is 1 standard deviation below the mean for married couples. The questions on this test were apparently subtle enough that Lynn and Elias were not able to project a glorified image of their marriage. As noted earlier, both Lynn and Elias revealed the same dysfunctions in their marriage—computing and taking responsibilities. In addition, although Elias scored significantly lower than Lynn, his pretest results indicate some difficulties with self-differentiation (likeness) and with establishing priorities. The main dissatisfactions noted were the external events, such as money and occupational progress.

Both partners' scores dropped in general from pretest to posttest. For Lynn, a decline in overall happiness was accompanied by a corresponding increase in her overall satisfaction with aspects of her marriage (Marital Happiness Scale vs. Family Information). When these tests are considered in this kind of pattern, the increase in satisfaction is even slightly greater than the decline in happiness. In interpreting this pattern, I speculate that as Lynn has become more assertive and outspoken, she has felt a loss of role specificity and rigidity. If true, this perceived change in her marriage has left her with a less rigid part to play. Consequently, she has been forced to perceive her marriage more realistically. When the rose-colored glasses were removed, some of her elation about her marriage departed also. However, by seeing her marriage more realistically, she is becoming more satisfied in it—particularly with the prospect of growing and changing.

Elias's posttest results are somewhat different (and difficult!) to analyze. His posttest scores indicate a decline in both happiness and satisfaction, although his scores on the Marital Questionnaire increased slightly. After the posttest, I learned that Elias is experiencing a great deal of job dissatisfaction and has begun to look for other employment. This occupational dissatisfaction can be noted particularly on the Marital Happiness Scale and on the Family Information and perhaps is reflected in a generalized dissatisfaction and unhappiness at this time. Considering Elias's emphasis upon control, I would expect him to have some difficulty separating job-feelings from marriage-feelings.

The change in this couple was particularly noticeable in their scores on the Marital Questionnaire, although Lynn's score declined (perhaps, again, reflecting a more realistic view of her marriage). On this questionnaire, Lynn showed increases in areas that indicate a degree of freedom from placating, computing, and distracting. In addition, there was an increase in the area of taking responsibility. There were decreases in the areas of forgiveness, protectiveness, and seeing the good. This pattern seems quite appropriate, however, considering Lynn's general submissiveness, the role structure in their family, and the program used with this couple. Lynn seems more willing to assert herself in her marriage and consequently is less willing to give herself up to taking care of all the emotional needs of her husband. In other words, Lynn apparently no longer fears that she will certainly hurt her husband's feelings by making an assertive statement. These scores may also be interpreted as evidence of Lynn's willingness to take more responsibility for the well-being of her marriage, partly by recognizing her own liabilities. Lynn has, I think, engaged in some self-confrontation as well as the confrontation of her marriage.

Elias's results on the posttest Marital Questionnaire are highly significant, almost amazing. On the likeness subscale, his increase from a score of 6 to one of 9 indicates an increasing level of self-differentiation. This aspect would seem to be particularly important, considering his position of power within the family structure and considering the fact that the level of differentiation within the marriage is mostly determined by the husband's level of self-differentiation (L'Abate, 1976). In addition, there were increases in establishing priorities, in his enjoyment of his marriage (7 to 10) and in seeing the good. The decreases in placating, distracting, caring, and sharing hurt are minor and do not appear particularly relevant. Finally, Elias showed an increase in his freedom from computing. This increase was possibly due to the emphasis on awareness of feelings throughout the program and Elias's growing awareness of his needs in this area. This increase could indicate his willingness to share some of his power with his wife.

In general, the posttest results, although they show an overall numerical decline, reflect some very positive changes in both partners. Analysis of the Semantic Differential indicates that both partners now see themselves as more equal to each other, Lynn in particular becoming more aware of her own inner strengths. Lynn and Elias may also be more aware of the importance of individuality of each of them and may be seeing each other as persons rather than as glorified representations of husband and wife. If this is true, SE with this couple may be assumed to have been successful to some degree.

SUMMARY

Lynn and Elias proved to be a very interesting couple with whom to work. In L'Abate's theory (1976), this couple could thus be placed in the "sameness" section of the differentiation continuum. They appeared to use a great deal of digital thinking, particularly concerning the very rigid and specific roles in their marriage. Although Lynn and Elias voluntarily participated in SE, I wonder about Lynn's underlying reasons for signing up.

Learning to settle conflicts in a somewhat different manner than they were accustomed to seems to have taxed the level of self-differentiation for the marriage and for Elias. Although it cannot be said that Elias's increase in the likeness subscale of the Marital Questionnaire indicates a permanent increasing level of self-differentiation, it does appear that this very positive change in him has produced a positive change in the marriage.

With respect to the four basic aspects of marriage (self-survival, self-confrontation, reconciliation of differences, and sharing of hurt feelings), Lynn and Elias may now be involved primarily in self-confrontation, especially as they become more equally involved in reconciling their differences. At this time, the emphasis upon the sharing of hurt feelings within the marriage seems minimal. However, theorists such as Fromm, Sullivan, and L'Abate have shown us that until self-confrontation occurs, there can be no genuine sharing of hurt feelings, and consequently no genuine intimacy. I believe that Lynn and Elias now have the potential for a truly intimate marital relationship, provided they maintain their interest and involvement in growing and changing. Although Lynn and Elias will probably continue to maintain a somewhat traditional family structure, it has now become quite important for them to be seen as individuals, both by each other and by outsiders. Thus, there does appear to be a greater balance of give-and-take in their marriage—primarily because of a growing sense of self within the marriage.

6

A Couple Under Stress

Steven E. Weinstein and Julie Friedman

Nancy, aged 23, and Gerald, aged 24, are a black couple who have been married for 3 years. They have a 2½-year-old son, whose name is Terrell.

Nancy and Gerald lived in another city for 2 years while Nancy attended college. During Nancy's leave of absence for childbirth, they returned to their hometown to be closer to their families. Nancy has since enrolled in a local university and is currently a junior, maintaining an A average. Nancy has a twin sister and one younger sibling.

Gerald, the second of five children, works in a factory. He reported that he works an average of 60 to 80 hours per week. He has a high school education and graduated with a C average; however, he stated that he has a reading disability.

In our first meeting, we introduced ourselves and explained the concept and format of SE. We told the couple that we are graduate students (not therapists), fulfilling course requirements. We then asked the couple to name areas in which they would like to improve their marriage. Nancy suggested communication as a topic, and Gerald agreed. Terrell was also present but slept throughout the session.

PRETEST SUMMARY

We administered the pretest battery, which consisted of the Holmes-Rahe Schedule of Events, the Dyadic Adjustment Inventory, and the Family Adjustment Inventory. Initially, Gerald handed his Schedule of Events form to Nancy while he held the sleeping Terrell. When told that the tests were to be completed individually, Gerald reported that he could not read very well. At this point, we suggested that one of us read the items to him and record his answers. Gerald agreed, and this procedure was used for the entire pretest battery.

Our initial clinical impression was that poor communication in the marriage was entirely probable in light of the present state of the marriage and the number of significant changes in their lives in the past few years. Not only does Nancy go to school full-time and Gerald work the equivalent of two jobs while the couple must care for a young child, but as evidenced by the Schedule of Events form, major changes in the past 18 months have included moving and starting a new job and returning to school. The couple has had little time to themselves since marrying 3 years ago. Their son was born less than 6 months after they were married. A high level of stress was particularly noticeable in Gerald, as can be seen by his significantly high score on the Schedule of Events.

On the Dyadic Adjustment Inventory, the total scores for both Nancy and Gerald are within the normal limits for married persons. The only subscale that falls below normal limits is Nancy's dyadic consensus score, indicating a problem with their agreement on matters of importance in their marriage.

The final assessment instrument that we administered was the Family Adjustment Inventory. The areas of concern that Nancy listed were income, in-laws, parenting, and communication. Communication was given the top priority. Gerald listed income, lack of time with family, and dissatisfaction with work and with his reading ability. His top priority was his reading ability, followed by dissatisfaction with the amount of time spent with his family.

In view of the initial impression and the pretest scores, and in consultation with the supervisor, we chose three programs that highlight communication, an aspect of the marriage to which both partners had given a high priority. The three programs were Equality, Communication, and Negotiation.

Our supervisor suggested that we reframe the stress that both spouses had been experiencing in terms of the stressors that are normal life cycle events and those that are idiosyncratic to their marriage. This was done at the beginning of the second session.

SUMMARY OF SESSIONS

Session 1: Marriage Myths

After a description of the three programs already mentioned, the couple were given the choice of selecting the program that they believed most applicable to them. Gerald suggested the Negotiation Program, and Nancy concurred.

In the first exercise in the lesson, we asked the couple to define the preconceptions (myths) they had had before marriage. Nancy began by saying that it was rather difficult to be married. She reported that it requires a giving from both people. She said that before marriage she had thought that she could make her partner more like her. Gerald's response was similar. He also talked about giving up more of himself than he had expected, saying that he had thought he would be "the man, the boss."

In the second exercise, we asked the couple to compare their conceptions of being in love before and after marriage. Gerald commented that that was a difficult task. After giving it some thought, he stated that the playing, hugging, and kissing before marriage grows into a oneness after marriage. He added that what he meant by this statement is that after marriage the partners join and become one. Nancy thought that love was exciting at first but said that she now considers this a childish attitude. After marriage, she stated, the excitement of romantic love declines, and this childish infatuation is replaced by a more mature, though still romantic, love. Gerald agreed with her statement.

The next exercise concerned gender differences in attitudes and behaviors. We asked for written statements, but because of Gerald's poor reading ability, this exercise (and all subsequent exercises that required writing) was done orally; we wrote their responses on the blackboard and then reviewed them. In this exercise, Gerald described men as rough and smart. He described women as serious, gentle, sexy, and dangerous. Nancy described men as egotistical, selfish, ambitious, dreamers, and generous. Women were described as romantic, sensitive, compassionate, and smart.

The characteristics that Gerald considered applicable to him are *generous* and *dreamer*. Nancy said that he should have added *egotistical*. She described herself as serious, gentle, sensitive, smart, compassionate, and romantic. Gerald said, "You think," and laughed. As for untraditional jobs that they perform in the marriage, Nancy said that she takes out the garbage, and Gerald reported that he mops the floor.

The final exercise in this lesson concerns the ways in which the couple agree or disagree, as well as how the spouses show respect for each other. The part on disagreement illustrated a sequence of interaction that was discussed later in supervision. Their responses to this exercise followed this pattern: (a) they have a disagreement; (b) Gerald withdraws and keeps quiet; (c) Nancy gets even angrier and yells more; and (d) Gerald gives in to Nancy's demands. Nancy said she knows that to show respect for Gerald's viewpoint, she should remain calm and listen to his side. Gerald stated that he should simply say, "We don't agree, and it's just my opinion." Our supervisor suggested that we pay close attention to see whether this sequence recurs during subsequent sessions.

We ended the lesson with a homework assignment. They were instructed to be aware during the coming week of the times that they meet each other halfway.

Session 2: Focus on the Relationship

When asked what they had learned from last week's lesson, Nancy responded that she had not realized that her attitude toward men was so negative. In response to the homework assignment, Nancy said that she had agreed to have a family portrait taken. In addition, she said that Gerald had bought some furniture and she had agreed to keep it. Gerald had agreed to speed up doing things (Nancy had complained about his slowness), although he said that he had not yet had a chance to accomplish this goal.

In the first exercise, we asked, "Who are you?" Nancy stated that she is a woman, nice, a mother, a Christian, a student, a wife, a lover, sensitive, a clock-watcher, and a giver. Gerald said that he is Gerald, a husband, a father, a man, a brother, a giver, a man of love and a Christian, wise, a minister of reconciliation, and an uncle.

During this exercise, Terrell was quite disruptive—crying and whining. Gerald was able to quiet Terrell most effectively by hugging him. Nancy's attempts to quiet him by giving him a toy to play with were unsuccessful.

The next question was "What can I give you?" Gerald replied that he could give Nancy more time, more love, a daughter, understanding, some clothes, help her to finish school, guidance, joy and laughter, peace, and a new stereo. Nancy said that she could give Gerald quality time, a vacation, a home, some clothes, more help around the house, a baby, more self-confidence, strength, discipline (they laughed), and money to fix his teeth.

In reply to the question "What can you give me?" Gerald said that he could give Nancy a vacation, quality time together, material things, more love and affection, peace, a baby, a new home, guidance concerning the word of God, new toaster, and new clothes. Nancy said that she could give Gerald love, a new baby, some support, knowledge, more time together, security, compassion, more understanding, and happiness.

When asked what they had learned from this exercise, Gerald replied that it had helped him to realize the love that Nancy has for him and the things they need to do for each other.

When asked about the rules they have in the marriage, Nancy stated that they have the following rules: (a) Both say "I love you" when they talk on the telephone. (b) They always shop together. (c) They always kiss each other before leaving each other in the mornings. (d) She is responsible for mailing the bill payments. Gerald reported the following rules: (a) He notifies her of business transactions. (b) If they fight, they make up before bed. (c) If Terrell is bad, they discipline him with the "rod." (d) On a day when they have to get up early, they put Terrell to bed earlier than usual. (e) If they have guests, he helps her in taking care of them. Their homework assignment was to think about additional rules in the marriage.

In supervision we discussed the fact that Gerald is slow in doing things. Our supervisor noted that Gerald's slowness may be his defense against Nancy's pursuance in an argument.

Session 3: Communication

When we asked about the homework assignment, both said that they could not think of any more rules in their marriage. Both said, however, that the past week's lesson had helped them to "think about things more."

The first exercise concerns the meaning of communication and the ways that a couple can communicate with each other (both verbally and nonverbally). Nancy stated that she believes communication means being able to talk with each other and understand each other's ideas. Gerald agreed with Nancy's definition. When asked about nonverbal means of communicating, Gerald said that making love is a form of nonverbal communication. Nancy said that the way they look at each other is another form of nonverbal interchange.

Terrell again acted-out. This time, Gerald threatened him with the "rod" (a paint stick).

In the second exercise, both partners were asked to observe each other silently and then comment on the feelings they received. Gerald reported that he received feelings of love, joy, and peace. Nancy said she received the feeling that Gerald loves her. In this exercise, the couple was also able to distinguish inconsistent verbal and nonverbal messages.

The third exercise involved the playing of the blaming, placating, avoiding, and preaching modes of communication. Nancy said that the preaching role was easiest for her and the placating role the most difficult. Gerald stated that, for him, the avoiding role was the easiest, the blaming role the hardest.

In the final exercise, Nancy and Gerald were asked to make "it," "you," "we," and "I" statements. Both felt that "I" and "we" involved more positive feelings than did the others. "You," Nancy said, makes one feel like a blamer. The homework assignment was to make three "I" statements a day to the spouse.

In supervision we talked about the appropriateness of the program for this couple. Our supervisor felt that this program was not producing sufficient results. At his request, we searched for a more appropriate program. As we were unable to find one, we continued with the Negotiation Program.

Session 4: Communication and Hurt

Gerald stated that they had forgotten to do their homework. Nancy reported that it had gone quite well. Suspecting that the couple had not completed their assignment, we stressed the importance of completing the homework.

In the first exercise, we explained metamessages. Both were able to understand the concept by practicing the statements from the exercise.

In the second exercise, using the shared-meaning process, the couple discussed Nancy's decision to attend summer school instead of staying home to sew clothes. Nancy had difficulty letting Gerald know that she understood him. Nancy observed that they need to work on this exercise more often.

The third exercise deals with hurt and angry feelings. Nancy said that she feels hurt when she is ignored, when she is asked to do things she does not like to do, when Gerald yells, and when things bother Gerald and he does not tell her. Gerald stated that he feels hurt when Nancy changes the subject when he is talking and when she yells.

In response to "How do you wish your partner to let you know that he or she is angry?" Nancy said that she would like Gerald to tell her what is wrong and talk to her in a peaceful way. Gerald stated that this is what he was going to say and then laughed. Gerald then said that he realized that he displaces his anger from his job onto Nancy and knows that this is wrong. He noted that instead of remaining angry, he should tell her that he has had a rough day at work. Nancy said that it would be ideal if they could interact with each other this way but that many times they lose their self-control. The homework assignment was to practice the process of shared meaning.

In supervision we discussed the couple's lack of affect, which had permeated the sessions. Our supervisor suggested that we outdo their blunted affect by speaking more slowly than we had been. We also reviewed the unusual discussion concerning Nancy's decision to attend summer school rather than sew clothes. The supervisor suggested that when Nancy or Gerald makes an odd statement, we should look puzzled and comment on the statement or ask a question about it.

Session 5: Trust

In response to the homework assignment on shared meaning, Nancy said that "it was different." Gerald said that this process helps one to know what the other person is talking about.

In response to the first exercise, both reported that they are totally honest with each other and could not think of areas in which they have been dishonest with each other. Following our supervisor's suggestion, we commented on how unusual this was.

In the second exercise, Nancy noticed inconsistencies between words and actions when she sometimes says to Gerald, "I don't care." Gerald could not think of any inconsistencies.

In the third exercise, both admitted that "yesterday" was the last time they had admitted being wrong. Nancy had made a mistake on the preceding day when Terrell had needed discipline and she had not given it to him. Nancy stated that although she was at first angry when Gerald pointed out her mistake, she later agreed with him that she had been wrong. Gerald stated that on the preceding day he had gotten upset because he had had trouble fixing a light. Nancy had told him that he should not become so distressed. He later agreed with her that he should not have gotten so upset and that he should learn to relax.

In the next exercise, Gerald could not think of any areas in which he competes with Nancy. Nancy stated that she feels jealous when Gerald has a "revelation from God" and that she feels she has to compete with him by citing a passage from the Bible.

In naming the areas that each is responsible for in the marriage, Gerald said that he is responsible for basic needs, house repairs, income, and transportation. Nancy said that she is responsible for cooking, buying food, cleaning the house, paying the bills, and balancing the checkbook.

At this point, Terrell (disruptive during most of the session) began to act-out uncontrollably, crying and demanding a piece of chewing gum. We remained silent and observed the interchange between Nancy and Gerald as they tried to parent their child. Nancy told Gerald to go downstairs and buy a pack of chewing gum for Terrell. Gerald refused. The sequence in which Gerald gives in to Nancy's demands was not evident here. If we had not been present, however, Nancy might have become angrier and Gerald might have ended up giving in to her demands. Nancy did not get angrier, however. Instead, Gerald took Terrell out of the room for what he called a time-out. After he succeeded in calming the child, they reentered the room and all was calm. We ended Session 1 by giving the couple their homework assignment—to think of areas in which each of them demonstrates competence.

We suggested that, if at all feasible, they get someone to baby-sit with Terrell. Nancy and Gerald commented that it is rare for them to have a chance to be by themselves, without their son. We suggested that they try to do things together, without Terrell. The possibility of getting a baby-sitter and the suggestion that the couple try to find time for themselves had been discussed in supervision. In response to our lowering our affect level during the session, Gerald, after the session, inquired whether the male enricher was tired!

Supervision focused on the necessity of stressing the importance of the homework. We talked about asking the couple whether they could find a time and a place to complete the assignments. We also talked about heavenly revelations and the cultural differences in religious practices.

Session 6: Quid Pro Quo

The couple entered without Terrell, saying that their son had been with a baby-sitter for the entire weekend (sessions were held on Sunday evenings). In addition, Gerald had had Saturday off from work (a rarity). They said that they had been able to do things as a couple for the first time in quite a while. They had forgotten to do the homework.

Before beginning the exercise, we reviewed the rules of communication, which had been illustrated and demonstrated in the preceding lessons. Both said they remembered the rules.

In the first exercise, Nancy stated that, ideally, she would like Gerald to be wiser, have a better job, make more money, and have more time to spend with Terrell and her. Gerald was able to summarize what Nancy had said except that he forgot the statement about getting a better job. Nancy reminded him. Gerald wanted Nancy to see herself more highly than she does. Nancy interpreted this to mean that she needs a higher level of self-esteem and that she criticizes herself too much.

In the second exercise, Gerald stated that he could improve their marriage by spending the time he has with his family more wisely. After summarizing Gerald's statement, Nancy said that she could also do better things with her time, have more patience, and worry much less. Gerald correctly summarized Nancy's statement.

Nancy's wishes and desires in the marriage were as follows: to have another baby, more leisure time together, a nice house, a job she likes, more wisdom, to be more beautiful, to be able not to worry, and to give to the "children" a good education at a good school. Gerald's wishes and desires were as follows: to have another baby, a new home, more time with his family, a new (good) job, a better relationship with in-laws, more wisdom, to come up with an invention, and for his whole family to have a better relationship with Nancy and Terrell.

In the third exercise, each was asked to choose a topic that he or she would like to negotiate. As usual, Nancy suggested a topic and Gerald agreed, saying that it was the topic he was going to pick. The topic was having another baby. We were silent while Nancy and Gerald discussed when to have their second child (who, they stated, would be a daughter and whose name had already been chosen). The issue involved either moving to a new home and then having the child or having the child first and then waiting until they had enough money to move later. They successfully applied the methods of communication they had learned throughout the program (e.g., summarizing the partner's statement and using "I" statements). Nancy, however, did become impatient at times, instructing Gerald to make up his mind. Nancy agreed to live in the present house and to have a baby now if Gerald would agree to fix up their home. This agreement represented concessions from both of them, so we congratulated them for having just negotiated successfully for something each of them wanted. They both smiled and said that they were pleased with the positive feedback.

They had not been completing their homework assignments, so we asked whether they could set aside an hour in a place where they would not be distracted. Although they could not give a specific time, they did agree that they could get together after Terrell goes to sleep. They were told that with this in mind, we would give the final homework assignment—to negotiate an important issue between them.

POSTTEST SUMMARY

At the end of Session 7, we administered the posttest battery: the Dyadic Adjustment Inventory and the Family Adjustment Inventory.

On the Dyadic Adjustment Inventory, Nancy's total score improved significantly (more than 1 standard deviation). Her dyadic consensus score, which is significantly below the mean on the pretest, is within normal limits on her posttest. Her other scores also improved on the posttest (although not more than 1 standard deviation).

Gerald's total Dyadic Adjustment score dropped on posttest but remained within normal limits. The most noticeable drop on the subscale scores is in dyadic satisfaction, but this, too, is within normal limits.

On the Family Adjustment Inventory, Nancy's total score increased dramatically. Specifically, her top priority (dissatisfaction with communication in the marriage) changed from −50 on the pretest to +30 on the posttest. She ranked priorities similarly on pre- and posttest, but she gave less weight to communication problems with in-laws on the posttest. Proving herself as a person through raising her son was given more priority on the posttest.

Gerald's total score remained approximately the same. His priorities on the pretest and the posttest were ranked similarly. Dissatisfaction with his reading ability remained of primary importance.

Note that as was done at pretest, the male enricher read Gerald the items on the posttests and recorded his answers. The posttests, however, were administered to Gerald in a separate room. Two confounding variables may have affected Gerald's scores. First, the items were read to him and recorded by the enricher. The results might have been different if Gerald had been able to complete the tests by himself. Second, his wife's presence during the pretest administration may have affected his responses.

The fact that Nancy's posttests show some improvement is in keeping with our clinical impression that SE has been helpful for this couple. We believe that Gerald also improved, although his objective test scores do not substantiate our opinion. His improvement was evident in his ability to incorporate into later exercises the skills he had learned earlier. The inherent limitations of self-report measures must also be considered in interpreting the objective measures.

FEEDBACK CONFERENCE

The couple's progress was discussed with our supervisor before the feedback conference. The following comments and suggestions, which had been discussed in supervision, were given to the couple. First, we highlighted the couple's strength in handling a significant number of life stressors, such as poor income, Nancy's full-time study, Gerald's working the equivalent of two jobs, and the raising of a 2½-year-old child. Second, we suggested that they discuss with each other the impact of having another child (financial, emotional, and time factors) so that they would be better prepared for the addition of a new family member. When we made this suggestion, the couple stated that they had continued to negotiate the issue of having another child since the preceding session and that both had agreed to delay for a while, waiting until they are better prepared (financially and emotionally) to have another child.

Finally, we made a suggestion that tied in some of the needs of both partners (as assessed through the pretest data). We emphasized the facts that Gerald wants to improve his reading ability and that both want to spend more time with each other. To help them work toward improving these areas, we suggested a "less structured educational intervention" in which Nancy would help Gerald learn how to read. The couple were told that this format could "kill two or three birds with one stone." Not only could Gerald improve his reading ability but both could continue to work on their communication skills. At the same time, they would be able to spend an allotted time together. Both expressed interest in this suggestion. At the end of the session, we realized that Gerald should also teach Nancy a skill, perhaps how to do basic home repairs.

We asked Gerald and Nancy to critique the program. Both were quite positive about the experience, stating that they had gotten much more than they had expected. Gerald said that the sessions had brought out many things of which he had been unaware. For example, the lesson about blaming, placating, avoiding, and preaching had brought out facts about each partner of which he had been unaware.

Gerald said that SE is like "looking in a mirror" because it forces a person to focus on himself or herself and to think about what he or she does. In conclusion, he stated that he would recommend SE not only to married couples but also to couples contemplating marriage.

Nancy reported that SE has aided her in being able to think before she speaks. She said that before SE she expressed herself without first thinking about what she was going to say and the consequences. Now, however, she reported that she has learned to monitor herself. Also, she said that she now views Gerald in "a different light." Before SE she had taken many things about him for granted. Overall, Nancy said that the program has helped her to restate feelings more constructively, thus improving her ability to negotiate and communicate. Note that, although we have reversed the order for purposes of discussion, in the session, we asked the couple for feedback on SE before we made our suggestions to them.

THEORETICAL INTERPRETATION

In this section, we try to discuss Nancy and Gerald in terms of personality development within the marriage and the family. With regard to the A-R-C (Apathy-Reactivity-Conductivity) model, we believe that Gerald most exemplifies the apathetic style and that Nancy is most like the reactive style (L'Abate, 1986b). Gerald's apathetic style can be seen in his use of avoidance. In arguments, he tends to withdraw. In the exercise in which they played the avoiding, placating, blaming, and preaching roles, Gerald said that the avoiding style was the easiest for him to role-play. In contrast, Nancy typifies the reactive style, becoming quite angry when she is upset and exhibiting a somewhat rigid stance in which she strongly resists giving in. (The Negotiation Program seemed most helpful in helping both spouses to use the conductive response style.)

In terms of power, Nancy apparently has the most power in the relationship, at least overtly. She is the achiever, and she appears to make the most decisions, although she might disagree on this point, stating that she always consults Gerald. Before they practiced negotiating skills, however, Nancy always seemed to come out ahead in terms of getting what she wanted. Gerald has the greater power on a covert level. His slowness in doing things, along with his withdrawal in arguments, is his way of counteracting Nancy's overt power.

With regard to priorities, the couple does appear to place their marriage ahead of work. Terrell, however, takes priority over the marriage. Much of the couple's interaction takes place in the context of Terrell. They spend very little time together without him. Evidence that work is lowest in priority is Gerald's Family Adjustment Inventory, in which he gave least priority to work-related matters.

The marriage may also be assessed in the being, doing, and having dimensions. Although, as already stated, work does not take precedence over the marriage, doing is very important to this couple. This is reflected in Nancy's full-time studies and what seemed to us a high need for achievement (having talked about her A average) and in Gerald's working the equivalent of two jobs. The need to be a better parent (as expressed on the Family Adjustment Inventory) is a concern of Nancy's. The fact that Gerald is not able to do more things for his family was one of his areas of concern on this test. Having also plays a large role in their marriage in terms of their lack of money and goods. Gerald expressed his concern about the lack of income, which also prevents his doing more for his family. The couple mentioned in several sessions that they own very few material goods. Gerald mentioned, for example, his desire for a toaster and a stereo.

The Negotiation Program helped the couple work on the being aspect of their relationship. Initially, Nancy and Gerald had some difficulty with exercises in which they used "I" statements or reflected on the partner's statements. At the conclusion of SE, however, they seemed to have improved their ability to use these skills. This improvement was exemplified in negotiating the issue of when to have another child.

The program may also have helped the couple to increase their level of intimacy. The lessons that assisted them with communication helped them to be more open with each other. A more open relationship would, one hopes, increase the sharing of hurt feelings and fears (an essential ingredient in achieving intimacy).

SECTION II
Single–Parent Families

7

A Mother-Daughter Dyad

Cinda Caiella

SUMMARY AND EVALUATION

This report details SE with a nonclinical family consisting of a mother, Rachel, and a 9-year-old daughter, Jennifer. In the interview, the only need that Rachel expressed was their need to spend more time together and to find things to do together. Although there was no specific program in exactly that area, we sought lessons that would be fun for the family to do together and that touched upon the way the family spends their time together and apart, on each member's fantasies had about what it would be like to have lots of money and time, on their skills and interests in artistic endeavors, and on active, experiential and role-playing lessons that would involve both of them and that would appeal to the 9-year-old child.

It was apparent from the beginning that the divorce and the where-abouts of the father were volatile issues. Rachel clearly indicated that these topics were hands-off, even though Jennifer did tease us by reading a story about parents who divorced. We followed the mother's lead and stayed away from that area. The mother and the daughter were stuck in rigid mother and daughter roles, so we attempted to check that area as well as do preventive work by introducing lessons on leaders and followers, hoping that each could see how Jennifer could help her mother and gain self-esteem by getting approval for her actions. This lesson flopped. Next, we decided to try metaphoric, right-brain activities, such as sculpting and drawing.

The drawing exercises were enjoyable, although Jennifer became some-what frustrated at her inability to produce what she wanted, particularly in comparison with her mother's artistic talent. However, we (the mother and the enrichers) congratulated Jennifer on her imagination in drawing her time-map, and this seemed to please and surprise Jennifer. Both often responded literally to the "wordy" programs and seemed leery, fearful, and somehow threatened by exercises that called for affectional exchanges and labeling positives in self and the other family member. Control is important to Rachel, but during SE she began counseling at school and began to take steps to decrease the family's isolation and the stress they were experiencing from recent changes.

We did find limitations in reaching this family with the educational format of SE but do not consider them significant because the mother and the daughter are nonclinical and are not seeking further service from us. Our gentle feedback about the nonobservance of emotional expression in the family was misunderstood: Rachel interpreted our remarks to mean that we considered the family very expressive and flexible. This appears to be her myth of how the family operates, although Jennifer gave us clues to the contrary in Session 1 (the divorce story), Session 2 (wanting hugs and kisses for doing a good job), and most of the remaining sessions. Jennifer would use baby talk or become distracting when the program became somewhat intense (as well as when she seemed to tire of "wordy" lessons). Rachel and Jennifer relaxed as we went along and seemed reluctant to part in the final session. Sculpting was the pivotal lesson: although few comments were made about the revealing sculptures, the remaining sessions were more relaxed. In the sixth session, the experiential joyful exercises were still beyond the family's capabilities. Rachel disciplined Jennifer off and on but disciplined less in the later sessions.

SE with this family was a powerful diagnostic tool to test their reactivity, their ability to express emotion, the extent to which they are undifferentiated, and their ability to learn from the lessons. The lessons that used the family's strengths were more successful than the ones that attempted to address their (perceived) deficits.

SUMMARY OF SESSIONS

Interview

All sessions were held at the family's apartment. Rachel stated that she had not lived there long and that Jennifer had come to live with her only recently. The apartment, decorated in neutral tones, was pleasant. Jennifer brought in her cat to inspect us. We explained the purposes of SE, and the contract was signed.

Rachel attends college and works part-time; Jennifer is in fourth grade and goes to an after-school program. Rachel mentioned that Jennifer has attended five schools and is used to moving. We administered pretests to Rachel; Jennifer tried reading some of the questions but could not understand the words, so we asked her to draw her family and her school.

The only area Rachel could think of that the family needed help with was deciding what to spend time on and what they could do together.

Enrichers' notes.

We wondered whether Rachel was recently divorced, as there was no mention of Jennifer's father. The family seemed reserved. We began with the Clarification of Values Program, with family members sharing with each other likes and dislikes regarding fairly neutral items.

Supervision.

Our supervisor warned us to stick to role playing and active lessons in order to keep the child interested. He suggested that we use lessons from several programs, rewriting them if necessary, or that we write lessons appropriate for this family. The idea is to use nonverbal activities, play, and have fun.

Session 1

For Session 1, we used exercises from the lesson called Using Your Imagination (Knowing Your Family Program).

Pretending some more.

Everyone was given clay with which to fashion something. Rachel made a bust of George Washington, Jennifer made a dinosaur and a child riding on its back, and the enrichers made a mouse and a tree with leaves. We commented on the artistic talent evident in the bust and the imagination in the dinosaur model. Rachel said that there is much talent in her family. She (and a brother) are avid photographers, and she has modeled with clay many times.

Robot.

Everyone was instructed to be tight and tense and to act like robots, making the noises of machinery rather than words. All of us participated, but Jennifer kept trying to talk a lot, bumping into furniture.

Clown.

Everyone was instructed to act free and loose, to be a clown and make faces.

Again, all of us participated, but we (the enrichers) were more relaxed than Rachel and Jennifer. Rachel reported that she liked the robot more than the clown, finding the robot more "normal" than the clown. She also commented that she has wanted to do mime.

Imagining.

In this exercise, we pretended to be in a dark movie theater, watching an animal on the screen. (Note that the coenricher, an undergraduate, is referred to as assistant enricher to distinguish our responses when we participated in the exercises.)

What animal do you see?

Daughter: Weasel.
Assistant enricher: Horse.
Mother: Hyena.

What is it about to do?

Daughter: Bite me.
Mother: Bite me.
Enricher: Chase me.

What noise does the animal make?

Daughter: My animal changes into a koala; it makes no noise.
Mother: The hyena cackles [she describes but does not make sound].
Enricher: Whinnies.

In a cage, how does the animal feel?

Mother: Pacing.
Daughter: Pacing, unhappy.

Uncaged, what does the animal do?

Daughter: The hyena chases me.
Mother: The hyena goes to the Serengeti National Park.
Enricher: The horse runs free on the beach.

Machine.

Rachel and Jennifer were asked to work together to make a machine, without talking, touching only. They took some time to make a machine—

a foot-stomping machine, Rachel called it. She tried to get Jennifer to follow her gestured directions and touched parts of Jennifer's body when she wanted her to do certain things. Neither made much noise. Jennifer danced and laughed and tried to talk. They did the exercise quickly and seemed glad to get it over with.

We finished the lesson in approximately 45 minutes and spent the rest of the time talking with Rachel and Jennifer. We learned that Jennifer reads many books, loves Monopoly, and talks to and about her cat a lot.

Enrichers' notes.

We divided up during this session, the assistant enricher participating with the family to help them relax and to make the exercises go less quickly. Even so, we finished early. Rachel and Jennifer did all the exercises quickly, but especially the ones in which they were asked to produce something nonverbally.

Supervision.

How conductive are Rachel and Jennifer? They sound very reactive, as in their choice of animals. Is Rachel more like a robot in real life? It takes a really free person to be a good mime. She is defined by her daughter. Use the A-R-C model (L'Abate, 1986b) to look at the parent-child relationship. Note that reactive parents confuse roles.

Session 2

The lesson was taken from the Clarification of Values Program. In an addition to the lesson, we asked Rachel and Jennifer to tell us their favorite stories.

Jennifer was ready with her favorite story: she read from Judy Blume's *It's Not the End of the World,* a story about parents who divorce (first mention of divorce in this family). The section she read is about the woman's serving cake with mocha icing, which the man hates. He says *"damn,"* and the cake ends up on the floor. Jennifer used baby talk in reading some sections and was not always understandable.

Rachel said that *Alice in Wonderland* and *Peter Pan* were her favorite stories when she was a child.

Basic definitions.

What is the meaning of the word *value?*
Jennifer didn't know, Rachel smiled, and the assistant enricher answered.

Important issues.

What are three things you like to do?

Mother: So many—dance, read, be with people I like, go to the beach.
Daughter: Disney World and Six Flags, play kickball, read, play dodge ball and tennis, modeling clay, Stephanie. (Rachel explained that Stephanie was Jennifer's friend when Jennifer stayed with her maternal grandmother.)

Values.

Do the activities you listed require people, money, or planning?
Jennifer said she didn't know what *value* means and asked, "Does it mean money?" Rachel responded that it means worth. She went on to say that most of the things they like don't require money, although they do like to go to movies together and that does cost. She stated that the other activities are partly with people and partly alone.

Important beliefs.

What is your favorite vacation place?

Mother: Tropical beach.
Daughter: Bahamas or Hawaii [hasn't been to either].

What is your greatest personal achievement?

Daughter: Being born, poster of balloon for art project.
Mother: It's hard to think . . . maintaining household.

What is your most prized possession?

Daughter: Kikki [the cat] and teddy bear [showed us and said that she's had the bear since she was 2 years old].
Mother: A material thing? Maybe the glass bowl on the table (from my grandmother, who got it when she was 13 and got married) or maybe my silverware.

Finish this sentence: I am striving to become——

Daughter [quickly]: . . . rich, rich, rich.
Mother: . . . the best person I can be, making fuller use of my abilities.

Feelings.

I get angry when people——

Daughter: . . . when people—when Mommy yells at me, when Kikki bites.
Mother: . . . when people won't listen to what you're telling them or trying to tell them.   [Enricher: Do you mean Jennifer?] No, people behind a desk, red tape, pencil-pushers.

I feel best when people——

Daughter: . . . don't know . . . when I do a good job? And get a hug and a kiss.
Mother: . . . when people respond positively—that covers a lot of things—when you can talk about self and feel rapport with people who appreciate what you're doing.
[At this point Jennifer begins to say to her mother, "You go first."]

I am proud of—

Daughter: . . . . yourself. [Enricher: What do you like? What are you good at?] Monopoly.
Mother: . . . Jennifer. For myself? Flexibility, adaptability.
Daughter: Why of me?
Mother: You're a very special person, with good qualities, even if you weren't my kid.
Daughter: . . . Mom's taking me to Six Flags.

I admire people who——

Daughter: Ask Mother first.
Mother: . . . are stable and in control of their lives.

Who are some of the people you admire? What do you admire about them?

Mother: From real life? My mother especially; my older brother, a conscientious, dedicated person—to his job and family, not money.
Daughter: A movie star, John (from "Dukes of Hazzard," a television show), because he's cute; Stephanie, because she's nice and my best friend.

Again, this session took only about 45 minutes. During the final minutes, Rachel told us a story she remembered from childhood, about a king with three sons. Each, in turn, is to take a pear to the neighboring king; each son meets a witch who asks what the son has in his bag. The first two try to trick the witch and end up with a rock and dust; the third son tells what is in the bag and is rewarded with gold. The witch's tag line for each is "We shall see when the journey is ended," which Rachel remembers and likes to think of still.

Enrichers' notes.

We used this lesson against our supervisor's advice because we had mentioned it as a possibility to the family and Jennifer was eager to read us the story she had selected. We jumped around within exercises because of what seemed to fit the family—they are very good at introspection but fearful of sharing emotions. The lesson did prove, as our supervisor had predicted, to be too "wordy" and "heady" for Jennifer's attention span. The assistant enricher observed that Jennifer seemed to be showing off and monopolizing our attention with baby talk. Try lesson on leaders and followers.

Supervision.

Jennifer is parentified to a certain extent. Check again the Single-Parent Program, or ask about loss of father, what fantasy father would be like. Is it OK for Jennifer to speak of her father? Mother and daughter do appear reactive, and Rachel is more on the child's level than she should be. To the lesson about leaders and followers we might want to add the roles of Kantor and Lehr (1975), including the bystander role. We also might want to try sculpting the family—as they are now, as they were in the past, and as they will be (or would like to be) in the future.

Jennifer's regression and activity are controlling, manipulative, reactive behaviors, which protect Rachel (Jennifer does these things instead of disagreeing with her mother). Jennifer is competing with Rachel. We should use humor to counter this behavior, implying that we know the kind of game Jennifer is playing, thereby taking her power away by giving it to her.

Session 3

Leaders and followers.

Because the family has only two persons, this exercise was modified so that each person could act as leader. We also made the exercise more experiential so that it would be more appropriate for Jennifer. Each person takes a turn being leader while everyone else is a follower. The followers decide while the leader is out of the room how they will behave toward the leader (follower, distracter, or bystander).

Jennifer wanted to go first, having a game in mind. Rachel and I decided to act as followers; the assistant enricher would refuse to participate and become a bystander. Jennifer walked around the house, upstairs to her room, to the bathroom, to the linen closet, back downstairs to the kitchen, opened the refrigerator door, and returned to the living room. Rachel and I followed, doing all that Jennifer did (we did not walk across her bed, step into the bathtub, or fit into the closet). Upon returning, we talked about what it was like to lead. Jennifer said that we didn't do everything that she did; we answered that we didn't want to and discussed how much leaders can do if followers don't follow.

Allocating responsibilities.

What does the leader do?

Mother: Is in charge of things.
   What does the follower do?
Daughter: It's OK sometimes.
   Who decides? What kind of leader does this family want?
Daughter: A mother.

Considering the opposite.

What if leaders and followers were opposite?

Mother [incredulous]: If I did everything she wanted to do?
   What do you need a leader for?
Daughter: Nothing. Could stay up and eat junk food.
Mother: I am totally free already.

Assuming leadership.

This exercise was modified so that each person could take a turn being the leader.
   Rachel became leader and led us in a game. She very quickly said that she had a game while Jennifer was suggesting several (telephone, Monopoly). Rachel asked everyone to talk quietly, if at all. Jennifer

wouldn't be quiet and had to be quieted by her mother. We talked quietly about school matters, including Jennifer in the conversation, but she got increasingly loud.

What happens when followers don't follow?

Rachel said, "It depends on the situation. With kids, you have to adapt to them; with adults, you can make them obey to a certain extent or forget about them, but with kids, you have to be in charge and responsible."

I became leader next (after allowing Jennifer to play one potato, two potato, to determine who would be leader). Then I asked each person to tell the others one good thing that had happened that week or something that he or she felt proud of.

Assistant enricher: Grade on test.
Mother: Score on Regents' test.
Enricher: Language test for master's.
Daughter: [She had wanted to go first.] Making a puppet for the show at after-school.

Enrichers' notes.

This session was short, only 40 minutes. I rushed questions somewhat when neither family member could answer the questions. The concept seemed difficult for them, and both seemed captured by the idea that a mother is a mother and the only leader in the family. We had hoped that switching the roles of leader and follower would counter the reactivity and locked-in roles of this family. We felt that the session flopped, although the family's discomfort and their inability to answer the questions and perform the role plays were instructive. For example, when asked what would happen if leaders and followers changed places, Rachel answered that she was totally free already and Jennifer assumed she would be able to stay up and eat junk food.

The family considers that only the mother does any leading, and her response differentiating the way she handles adults and the way she handles children (having to be in charge) highlights the set roles and reactivity in this family. For example, at the end of the session, I asked Jennifer what she was good at, suggesting that a leader is someone who is good at things. Jennifer answered, "baking cookies," and went to the kitchen to get us some of her first batch ever. This question and Jennifer's response surprised Rachel, who asked, "Jennifer, a leader?"

We agreed that the session was too wordy and that activity is a must for Jennifer. We worked at ignoring her interruptions, but she became more babyish. She spent a lot of time talking about or to the cat but still did not mention her father. (We had also hoped that this lesson might bring up that subject.) Jennifer did show us her picture album.

Supervision.

Our supervisor agreed with our decision to stick to active lessons from now on. Next in our plan was sculpting, as discussed in the preceding supervisory meeting. The supervisor suggested that we use the word-association test for the A-R-C model (L'Abate, 1986b), as this family is so reactive. We are to congratulate them on being hooked by opposites.

Session 4

The first exercise was written by Dr. L'Abate, to teach couples and families about reactivity and conductivity.

Word associations.

A list of words is read three times by one family member. The first time through, the other member is to respond with the antonym of each word; the second time, with a synonym; finally, with a word different from the stimulus word. Jennifer wanted to read first. (See charts)

Words (read by Daughter)	Mother's Answers		
	Opposite	Same	Different
no	yes	negative	apple
false	true	untrue	head
night	day	evening	knife
wrong	right	error	radio
white	black	blanc	light
hard	soft	solid	rock
down	up	below	beneath
bad	good	evil	cat
fast	slow	quick	runner
cruel	kind	mean	cigarette
big	little	gigantic	orange
soft	hard	mellow	drink
weak	strong	puny	tea
noisy	quiet	raucous	TV
stupid	smart	dumb	chair

Words (read by Mother)	Daughter's Answers		
	Opposite	Same	Different
yes	no	uh-huh	meatloaf
true	false	not a lie	apple
day	night	morning	orange
bright	dark	colorful	grape
black	white	dark	indigo smoke
simple	hard	easy	bobcat
up	down	high	parakeet
good	bad	perfect	United States of America
slow	fast	walking fast	poke
kind	mean	nice	blanket
small	big	little	Peter
tough	weak	mean	pizza
strong	weak	tough	tushie
quiet	loud	no noise	me
smart	stupid	knows a lot	Superfudge

We asked the family to talk about the exercise. Rachel said that the easiest was giving opposites, because that's naturally the way language is made. Jennifer said giving the different responses was fun. Rachel thought the words were bland and that more emotionally charged words might be better. She pointed out the difference between a different word and an unrelated word in the third round of answers.

Sculpting.

Without talking, the sculptor is to arrange the family according to the enricher's general instructions. The sculptor is to choose someone else to represent himself or herself in the sculpture.

Rachel began. Directions were to place family members as they would typically be in the apartment. Jennifer began to talk, and Rachel reminded her of the directions.

Rachel placed Jennifer on sofa, watching the TV screen. She placed me (as Mother) in the director's chair (she called it the most comfortable chair), also facing the screen. When questioned, she said that neither was looking at the other, although they might laugh at something on the TV screen. She did the sculpture very quickly.

Jennifer was to sculpt the family as it typically is. She, too, placed me (as Mother) in the director's chair. Rachel (as Jennifer) was made to recline on chaise lounge, on a blanket Jennifer spread out. Jennifer then lay on top of her mother, her back upon her mother. She wiggled a little. When questioned, she said that she was Kikki (the cat). Rachel laughed and agreed that this scene was very typical. I asked Jennifer how her mother typically acts in this scene. Jennifer replied that her mother does not watch TV but studies and looks down at a book, not paying attention to Jennifer and the cat.

Rachel was asked to sculpt her family of origin. She has three brothers and a sister, as well as many other relatives. She asked everyone to imagine that all the family was sitting around the square coffee table in the living room. She explained that the occasion was a birthday party for her brother. I (as Rachel's father) sat on one corner; Rachel (as her mother) sat next to me. Jennifer (her mother as a girl) sat across from the parents. Rachel explained that her father was drinking wine; she (played by Jennifer) wanted no cake or wine, only yogurt. (Jennifer acted-out a lot during this sculpture, saying that she wanted cake and refusing to be quiet.) Rachel explained that there were so many of them at home that it seemed like they were having a birthday party all the time and it is that kind of occasion that she remembers when she thinks back.

Jennifer was asked to sculpt the family as she remembers it, from when she was 4 or 5, just before she began school. (This should be far enough back for her to have to include her father.)

Jennifer immediately remembered an amusement park in Missouri where they went frequently. I (as Jennifer's father) sat in the car and drove, with Jennifer (as herself) in the middle and Rachel (as herself) on the passenger side. Next, Jennifer put her mother (as Jennifer) in the director's chair facing sideways, as if she were in a boat that Jennifer went in by herself while her parents waved goodbye to her.

Jennifer then brought out picture albums showing herself as a younger child, her father, and the park. Rachel mentioned that some of the pictures were taken by Jennifer's father and that some are of the parents before Jennifer was born. This was the first mention of Jennifer's father, although nothing was said of his whereabouts or contacts with the family.

We chatted for the remainder of the session, approximately 10 minutes. While Jennifer was showing pictures to the assistant enricher, Rachel mentioned to me that she had begun going to the Counseling Center for vocational testing and counseling and that she would like to be in some groups there. She would like to transfer into a major in which she could use her creative potential.

Enrichers' notes.

Rachel and Jennifer enjoyed the word-association exercise. The reactivity was apparent in the ease of listing opposites as opposed to the longer time necessary to name different words. Jennifer repeated her mother's responses or answered for her. Certain responses were by sounds, such as "bad cat" (which they use frequently for the cat) or "white light," or by familiarity, such as "soft drink." Jennifer immediately recognized that the second list contained antonyms of the first list. She also spoke the word *loud* in a loud voice and acted out a few of the other responses.

The sculpting was easily done and was very revealing of family patterns. Both sculpted typical family patterns involving no interaction between mother and daughter. Each was absorbed in separate activities and seemingly unaware of the other. When Rachel sculpted her family of origin, Jennifer became confused about who she was playing (her mother) and was unable to respond as herself (wanting cake). In Jennifer's sculpture of the family when she was 5 years old, she played herself at one point. At the end of the session, Rachel and Jennifer were relaxed and shared the family picture album with us, and Rachel talked about her counseling at the Counseling Center and her desire to be in a group with other people like herself. This session was most productive.

Supervision.

We discussed our plan to concentrate on drawings next. Only two sessions remained, and the assistant enricher, who had been helping plan sessions, agreed to prepare and lead the sixth session.

Our supervisor was pleased with results of the word-association exercise. He remarked on the lack of interaction in the sculptures and suggested having the family draw where they spend their time in the apartment in order to highlight their separation from each other. He remarked that these are two distant, parallel people.

Session 5

Family maps.

We asked Rachel and Jennifer to draw maps of the places they go during the week. Jennifer brought the drawing materials, and Rachel and Jennifer sat on opposite sides of the coffee table and began working in earnest, oblivious of us. They talked some but not enough to disturb their concentration. Jennifer showed her map first. The places were drawn along a line that curved from one side of the paper to the other. She explained her typical day: going to school and to the playground (she drew the table and her bed outside the house along the line). Jennifer was surprised at the praise, especially from her mother. She decided to keep her picture.

Rachel's map showed little buildings at road intersections to mark where she and Jennifer usually go—grocery store, university, school, Jennifer's grandmother's, gas station.

Scribble drawing.

Each was told to begin scribbling on a piece of paper to "loosen up." They found this fun, and Jennifer concentrated on her scribble. Then we asked them to make drawings of their scribbles—whatever came to mind. Rachel's is two people seated on a couch, one behind the other, very close, with sphinxlike faces looking in the same direction. Jennifer scribbled across most of her page in heavy diagonal lines. She used black chalk to follow the same lines, which she labeled "ocean" and "waterfall." She then made fingerprints all over the page, dirtying her hands. Rachel liked the texture of the picture, and the assistant enricher thought it looked like foam on the water. Jennifer was not happy with her picture but wanted to keep it.

Family portrait.

Rachel used chalk to make heads of her and her daughter, the heads flowing into each other. The heads are bent, and the eyes seem closed, surrounded by a mist of hair and chalk lines. The impression is soft, somnolent, with unclear boundaries between the two heads and a sharper one separating them from the background.

Jennifer started drawing, then became unhappy with her picture, so she began on the reverse side of the paper. (I think she had drawn herself, her mother, and her grandmother, but she did not want to discuss that picture.) Her final picture shows her mother, herself, and the cat enclosed by a line (similar to the jump-rope line in her map drawing); another girl and the girl's mother are outside the line. Jennifer said they are her friend and her friend's mother (Rachel explained that the woman is her sister-in-law). Also in the picture are a partially completed figure of a tall girl and a spiderweb. The girl was drawn as Jennifer first began (on the drawing she abandoned); she drew the spiderweb while she was talking about her portrait.

Enrichers' notes.

This session was the most successful in many ways. The family seemed to enjoy it and put a lot of effort into their drawings. Jennifer became restless and more critical as time went on. However, the praise she got for her map, especially from her mother, seemed to please her a great deal and to be an unusual experience for her. The session lasted only

50 minutes, but Jennifer seemed tired, so we dropped the idea of having them collaborate on a drawing. The discussion during the drawing was relaxed, and the atmosphere in the apartment was warmer than before. Rachel talked about going out that week and that Jennifer would have to finish her school project. Rachel was firmer with Jennifer during this session than we had seen before. We noted that the drawings show confusion of boundaries.

Supervision.

Our supervisor remarked that Rachel must have high art standards, because of the quality of her drawings, and that Jennifer must feel that her drawings do not measure up. Perhaps that is why Jennifer did not let us have her pictures. The area we need to discuss with this family is separation. He suggested that we look at the programs on adolescence and simplify some exercises for use with this family. We could have them place themselves along a single line representing a dimension such as how close-separate they feel from each other. Also, we could ask them to role-play telephone conversations, having them sit back to back.

Session 6

Relaxing and hearing.

We asked Rachel and Jennifer to close their eyes and relax. Then each was to tell the sounds she had heard while relaxing. Rachel had heard the rain, the heating system, a car's tires, and Jennifer's scraping her legs together. Jennifer had heard the heater and the rain.

Fantasyland.

With eyes closed, think of the most peaceful, lovely place you could go to.

Daughter: Yummy, a candy place, where I can eat as much as I want to and nobody tells you when to go to bed.
Mother: A beach—a big, big, big, white beach, with lots of water, not many people around, walking down beach, blue water, really green.

Colors.

We asked Jennifer and Rachel to look around the room and take turns naming colors until all the colors in the room had been named.

Spending.

Suppose this family had $10,000 and 1 month off school and work. Taking turns, tell us how would you spend this money.

Mother	Daughter
Buy stereo	Buy TV
Buy clothes	Candy and junk food—Doritos and dip
Take a trip	Go to the beach
Someplace warm	Egypt, Hawaii, and take Mom with me
Buy a rug for room	Six Flags over Georgia
Buy a piano	A house?
Can't	A swimming pool?
Buy furniture	Save—for braces and college

Conflict.

A rich relative dies and leaves you $1 million, but you must take care of his 20 cats.

Rachel and Jennifer agreed there would be no conflict. Jennifer would love 20 cats, and Rachel said they would buy a big house with a yard.

Survival.

The family is alone on a deserted island. How would you survive?

Daughter: No food. I'd starve to death—have to go fishing.
Mother: Look for clams to eat.
Daughter: Look for coconuts.
Mother: Try to find place to get out of sun.
Daughter: Build a home. Eat bananas.
Mother: Yeah, build a house.
Daughter: Make placemats and plates.
Mother: Need that for surviving.
Daughter: Need clothes if they wear out.
Mother: Leaves.

Danger.

Suppose you get a raft and are floating out to sea with three days' food and water. You have lost sight of the island.

Daughter: Sharks. Swim.
Mother: Ration food so it would last 2 weeks.
Daughter: Easy for you to say. We could make a fishing pole to catch fish. Build a fire and make smoke signals.
Mother: Build a fire in a boat?

Telephone role-play.

Sit back to back on kitchen chairs and pretend to be 1,000 miles apart, talking on telephone. Don't look at each other.

Daughter [turning around]: What's your number?
Mother: Just call any. Hello.
Daughter: Hello.
Mother: Jennifer, is that you?
Jennifer: Yes.
Mother: What are you doing?
Daughter: Eating dinner.
Mother: So, how are things going?
Daughter: Fine [swinging feet].
Mother: What else are you doing?
Daughter: Swimming.
Mother: That's nice. What else?
Daughter: Not much. What are you doing?
Mother: Busy as usual. In school. What else is new?
Daughter: Kikki had 25 babies, and we're keeping them.
Mother: Bye.

In talking about this exercise, Rachel said that the conversation would be the same if Jennifer really were 1,000 miles away, that one has to pry things out of her, just like Rachel's brother. In fact, she said that when Jennifer stayed with her grandmother, the conversations were just like that. Jennifer said, "You had to pay for the calls."

Saying something nice.

Say something nice about yourself.

Mother: I feel like I've lost a pound.
Daughter: I like myself, and I am pretty (baby talk). (We support Jennifer's statement about herself.)

Say something nice about each other.

Mother: You're getting to be more helpful.
Daughter: You're not waking me up so early.

Doing something nice.

Each was instructed to do something nice for the other without speaking. Rachel got up and left the room, came back with jelly bean for Jennifer. After thinking a long time, Jennifer took her mother's teacup into the kitchen but came back with a cup of tea for herself. Rachel looked puzzled and amused.

Joyful experiences.

Think of a joyful experience you would like right now.

Mother: A special delivery comes—a gigantic check, certified, for me.
Daughter: A delivery man comes and gives me a piano.
Mother: A piano?

Joyful messages.

Taking turns, write each other a joyful message.
Jennifer got paper for herself and her mother and began to write. Rachel said she would speak instead of writing.

Mother: Jennifer, we've just inherited a million dollars and we're moving to Florida.
Daughter: I thought it had to be between . . . [hands her mother a note, which says $90 million].
Mother: We seem to have money on our minds.

During the discussion in the last 10 minutes, Rachel commented on how many of the exercises concerned money and said that money is her major concern. Jennifer had been sitting next to the assistant enricher, who was leading the session, and trying to read over her shoulder. Then Jennifer took the manual and began to ask all of us questions and to write the answers. During the session, she had begun talking baby talk and seemed restless.

Enrichers' notes.

The family totally misunderstood "joyful experience" and were concerned with money and with fantasies. They showed strained feelings about doing something nice—no emotional connections. This was true in telephone conversation, in which Rachel drilled Jennifer with questions. Rachel seemed to miss the point of the exercises more than Jennifer did. In fact, Rachel seemed to be competing with Jennifer, for example, thinking of more color names. As was true in earlier drawings and in sculpting, the confusion of self with other and the enmeshment and reactivity were shown. The only difficulties with the session were that parts were a little too "wordy" and that the family misunderstood the directions for the joyful experience exercise.

Supervision.

For the feedback conference, in addition to asking whether the family wants further services and explaining what services are available, we are to tell Rachel and Jennifer the strengths we've observed—they are articulate and imaginative, they have clear roles, and they are protective of each other. Also, we will tell them what we have not seen—affection and the expression of affection (we should comment that we wonder whether they would like to do something about that).

FEEDBACK CONFERENCE

We collected the completed assessments that had been given out at the end of the preceding session. Jennifer had prepared a map for us (in different colors) similar to her original map for the session on drawing. Rachel made many comments about the assessments and remarked that many of the questions did not apply to a two-person family in which one person was a small child. Also, she considered the anchors of the scale, *all the time* and *none of the time,* too strong.
  What did you get out of SE?

Mother: Some of the exercises were not appropriate.

  Which sessions were the best, and which were less enjoyable?

Daughter: The modeling clay and last week's.
Mother: You liked being leader and that thing with the words [word associations]. I liked drawing, modeling clay, telling your favorite story. About SE, it has been interesting to see what we're doing. For a lot of people, activities would be better—rather than just asking questions. That's especially true with a small child, although asking the opinions of children is good. Oh, also good was seeing a movie and seeing yourself as an animal. It's hard with just the two of us. A group might be more fun.

We discussed options for further service. Rachel said that she would be continuing in counseling and was cutting back on her work hours to make room for that and that she would probably be going there for a long time. She said that she and Jennifer needed more time together. In fact, during spring break for the elementary schools, she plans to take Jennifer to school and to work with her to show her what goes on there. Jennifer seemed excited about this.

In our feedback, we told them we had enjoyed our time together and appreciated their experimenting with us in using new programs. We had also appreciated their letting an observer (the assistant enricher) into their home. We saw them as having imagination and creativity, and we had found the sessions fun. We saw them as having clear roles and being caring and protective of each other. We had not observed (until this session, when Jennifer got into Rachel's lap and was hugged) much open expression of affection. Rachel answered quickly that, yes, they are an affectionate family and that they hug a lot.

In the family's feedback to us, Rachel said it had been nice having someone observe. Jennifer wanted to know when we would be coming back and when she'd see us again.

Enrichers' notes.

We were astounded that Rachel had either misheard or misunderstood our feedback about their not expressing affection well. We discussed how Rachel, preoccupied with the divorce (which she has still not discussed), must not have prepared Jennifer for the divorce, for living with her grandmother, or for living with her mother in a new apartment on limited money. We had been concerned about the family's isolation, so we feel that Rachel's continuing in counseling is good, in that she needs support during this transition. We enjoyed the sessions and believe that the active lessons were best for this family.

PRE- AND POSTTEST EVALUATION

We discussed in supervision, before the interview, which assessments to administer to a single parent and a 9-year-old child. We administered the Family Information, the Holmes-Rahe Schedule of Events, and the Family Adaptability and Cohesion Evaluation Scales (FACES). The tests were given during the interview, before the first SE lesson, and as a posttest that was completed between the sixth session and the feedback conference.

Jennifer looked at a FACES and was interested, but the vocabulary was beyond her, so her test was to draw a picture of her family. When she had done this, she was asked to draw a picture of her school. For posttest, she drew a copy of her map of how she spent her time during the week, one of the exercises for Session 4.

We considered the Family Environment Scale, but Rachel said that the questions were very similar to those in the FACES and that both contained questions that were not appropriate to her situation.

Pretests

Rachel is a 34-year-old white female, "unmarried," a senior in college. She is the second child of five children and the oldest girl. She rated her parents as "completely loving" toward her, 75% authoritarian in raising her, moderately permissive in attitudes toward her dating. She sees her mother and father as 90% satisfied with their marriage.

Holmes-Rahe Schedule of Events.

Rachel circled many events as having occurred within the past 18 months: being separated, being divorced, beginning school, a new school, and changes in living conditions, working hours, residence, finances, number of family get-togethers, church attendance, recreation, and habits. The summed mean value of these changes is 364. Most concern changes in marital and residential status, and in school attendance.

FACES.

Rachel left four items blank, saying that they did not apply: parents agree on how to handle the children; family members share the same friends; it seems as if males and females never do the same chores in our family; and there is strict punishment for breaking rules in our family. The computations resulted in an adaptability score of 160 and a cohesion score of 222. The adaptability score puts her in the rigid category, and the cohesion score puts her in the disengaged category. (Her social desirability score is 35, very close to the mean of the rating scale.)

Rachel's ratings are near the high cutoff for each category. Two of the items she left blank were counted in the adaptability score, and two were counted in the cohesion score (which does not substantially alter the scores). In a rigidly disengaged family, according to the clinical rating scales of the FACES, the emotional bonding of family members is low, generational lines are rigid, coalitions are weak (with perhaps a family scapegoat), time apart from the family (physically and emotionally) is maximized, decisions are primarily individual, and friends and recreation are primarily individual. Assertiveness styles are passive or aggressive, leadership is authoritarian, roles are rigid, and rules are rigid and strictly enforced. Most of these descriptions seem to fit this family. Rachel sees herself as sole leader, decision-maker, and does not see Jennifer as a source of help or support. At times Rachel sees Jennifer as a helpless child and at others seems to expect her to think and act like an adult.

The sessions brought out the distance and separation of the two during their time together in the apartment, and we saw very little interaction, especially affectional interaction, between them during the sessions. The generational boundaries are tight. Jennifer's family drawings show a question of external boundaries, of who really is in the family: Rachel's drawing shows the tightness of the internal boundary.

The FACES brought to light issues that had not been clear from our initial interactions with the family.

Posttests

The changes from preassessment to postassessment are few.

Holmes-Rahe Schedule of Events.

Rachel's summed mean value score is 343. It has now been 18 months since the marital separation but less than 18 months since the divorce. Food habits have changed, as have social activities (she did mention going out). It has been 18 months since the move to this apartment, but Rachel has more recently changed her jobs. The changes are somewhat less than they were at preassessment.

FACES.

There is little change—the biggest difference is that at posttest Rachel left more answers blank, which primarily affected the cohesion score, lowering it 20 points.

In addition to the items she left blank at preassessment, Rachel left the following blank on postassessment: The parents in our family stick together; family members seldom take sides against one another; and we know very little about the friends of other family members. Rachel said that with just a young girl and herself these questions did not apply. She sees herself as flexible, which explains why she left blank the items about rules. The other questions refer to parents (plural) or to differences in the males and females in the family.

SUMMARY

It was apparent from the first page of Family Information, on which she classed herself as "unmarried," that the divorce (never mentioned, only checked on the Holmes-Rahe) was an extremely volatile issue. This issue became clear during sessions; the father was mentioned only after we engineered Jennifer's sculpting to include her father. Then Jennifer brought out family pictures in which her father was present, and Rachel mentioned that the father had taken some of them and even commented on a picture of him without any hair (in the army). Despite the lack of discussion about the divorce, it was apparent that the family's financial problems and isolation must have stemmed from a sudden change. Jennifer's baby talk and attention-getting behavior are understandable: she seems to sense the volatility of this issue but has many questions. The first story she read us was about a child whose parents divorced. However, none of Jennifer's behavior seems to be getting the responses from her mother. Rachel misunderstood our feedback at the final session that we had not seen much affection expressed in the family, saying, "Yes, we're very affectionate." Rachel has begun going to counseling and expressed the wish to be in a group with others who have problems similar to hers. The isolation of the family is apparent, although Rachel did mention going out (even then, Rachel's brother acted as baby-sitter).

The Holmes-Rahe scores reflect the stress of many changes. The FACES point out the stress and the family's rigid boundaries, especially generational ones that prevent the members from supporting each other very much. In the sessions, when Jennifer led an exercise or was seen as competent, this surprised her mother. The family's trouble with emotional bonding was apparent in every exercise calling for spontaneity, for expressing joy, for working together. The sculpting pointed out the distance between them.

8

Emotional Inhibition

Margaret S. Baggett

This single-parent family consists of the mother, Anna Jean Thompson, who is 35 years old, and her two daughters, Jeanine, who is 10 years old, and Rebecca, who is 8. Although it was hoped that the family would be "normal" (no identified patient, no family member receiving psychiatric care or services or having received these services within the past year), the Thompson family is not. Jeanine emerged as an identified patient, exhibiting highly explosive behavior through the fourth session. Because the family was cooperative, we continued the program. The family had applied for SE after the YWCA in a neighboring town informed its members about the SE program.

BACKGROUND

The mother, Anna Jean Thompson, is a research biochemist. The older daughter, Jeanine, is very bright. She evidenced surprising perceptiveness throughout the sessions, though her impulse control was very poor. During the summer she attended a public school program for gifted youth. Rebecca, the younger daughter, is also bright, according to her mother, and attended a day camp during the summer. She loves horses and art, and we admired some of her artwork. Though loving, she is quite withdrawn and regressive.

Anna Jean is divorced. She married in 1963 and was separated in 1972 after having sought help, unsuccessfully, from a marriage counselor. The divorce was finalized in 1973. Both families are Catholic; this is the only divorce in at least three generations. However, Anna Jean gets along very well with her parents and her sister. She also tries to arrange visits for the children with their paternal relatives.

The family resides in a well-kept middle-class neighborhood. The Thompsons' brick house is small but neat. Though well manicured, the front lawn is not large. It does sport a large pine tree, which invites one to climb to the top of its thick, spreading limbs (this is not allowed, however). The backyard is spacious and level, with a yard and a house for Licorice, a friendly black dog with a suspiciously poodle look to her furry shape. Surrounded by hedges, the yard also contains a swing set, a picnic bench, and a truck tire enclosing a sandpile.

Inside are a small living room, a dining room, a kitchen, a hall, two baths, and three bedrooms. There is a chance for privacy, even in these small quarters. Until recently, the girls shared a room (Jeanine's room used to be the den). There are no plants, and though the living room furniture (including a piano) is ample and tasteful, the dining room has no table. The family eats in the kitchen at a small table cramped against one wall.

This family is very attractive. Although Anna Jean is a little plump (she loves to cook, and cookbooks fill the shelf above the refrigerator in the kitchen), she is large-boned and carries this little bit of extra weight well. Her short blonde hair frames an intelligent, sometimes impish-looking face. Neatly dressed, she appears neither younger nor older than her age, though her speech is mature, quite serious, positive, and well-informed. From time to time, her blue eyes twinkle as she flashes a lovely, large grin. I find her warm, though a bit formal.

Neither girl looks exactly like their mother. Jeanine has blonde hair and blue eyes, but her features and her frame are more petite than Anna Jean's. She is very pretty, with soft, healthy skin. At first she wore her hair long, but during the summer she had it cut to nearly shoulder length. Quick to overreact, Jeanine finds sitting still difficult, unless she is engrossed in a book. She also bites her nails. She wears reading glasses and also began wearing orthodontic braces before the sessions ended, but she seemed not to mind them.

Rebecca has long, light-brown, naturally curly hair and blue eyes. Because her vision is poor, she wears glasses or contacts all the time. She is cute rather than pretty, and her face appears to be a little swollen at times. Though loving, she is withdrawn, dependent, and regressive, sucking her thumb, lisping, speaking in a low baby-voice, and disappearing into her mother's arms or against her side whenever possible. Most of the time she appears to be in a dreamworld.

All family members look clean and well cared for; their clothes, their hands and nails, their hair, skin, and teeth are always fresh and clean. The overall atmosphere is a caring one, but there is a sense of underlying tension and watchfulness.

Twice a week during this summer, Anna Jean, who has a bachelor's degree, attended evening classes in mathematics. She listed her interests and hobbies as the Solo Parents Club (YWCA), her children, music, and reading. This family is an active, involved family.

Edward, Jr., Anna Jean's ex-husband, comes from a Catholic family, as does Anna Jean. Three generations live in this city, though Edward is now living in another state. A printer, like his father, Edward was an only child. He got along poorly with his mother, who separated from but never divorced his father when Edward was 7 years old. His mother, who died last year, was, according to Anna Jean, an alcoholic. Because of his poor relationship with his mother, Edward treated his wife and his girls in less than optimal ways, according to Anna Jean, and she became concerned for their daughters. She describes Edward as immature and self-centered.

Edward's father was the second of five children, only two of whom had children. Anna Jean describes this generation as living in the past, with their parents and siblings. One brother, who had two children, died a year ago. The youngest never married. Edward's paternal grandparents are dead. His grandfather, also named Edward, was a furniture builder, and Edward's father got along very well with him. It is not known how he got along with his wife, Anna. She is described as very loved, very active in the church, "a saint." She named her first daughter after herself. Both her daughters married, but neither had children. It is interesting to note their names—Anne and Jean.

On Edward's maternal side, his mother, Evelyn, was the second of four children. In effect, however, she was the oldest child because her older brother died when he was 7 years old. She, too, lost her father, whom she idolized, when she was quite young. Her mother, a housewife, did not get along well with her, even though she was the only daughter. Perhaps Evelyn had hoped to marry a father, and Edward, her husband, had hoped to marry a saintly mother. Whatever happened, the marriage failed. On the paternal side, there is a pattern of sameness in the men and evidence that they got along well with one another. On the maternal side, there is a pattern of conflict between mother and children, whereas the father was much loved.

Anna Jean's paternal ancestors came from Germany in the late 1800s. Her paternal grandmother spoke German, and her paternal grandfather, Albert, was a steelworker. None of the grandparents on either side are living. There were twelve children; after some died of typhoid or were killed in World War I, Albert and his wife had other children. Out of this group, there was only one girl. One son had a boy to carry on the name; the rest did not have sons, and one was a bachelor. In Edward's family, his paternal grandparents also had one son who remained a bachelor. The second youngest son, George, became Anna Jean's father.

Retired, he lives in a neighboring state. Anna Jean describes him affectionately as the strong, silent German type, like his own father. He had
difficulty expressing his feelings and ruled quietly but very strictly (as
did both grandparents, whose children were too frightened of them to
share much affection with them).

George gets along well with his wife, Marguerite, who is closer to
Anna Jean. She reflects some French ancestry in her volatile nature. Now
66, Marguerite wanted to become a nurse. However, although she completed high school, she had missed a grade in school and could not go
into nurse's training. She was young when she began working in an
office but was almost 26 when she married. She is the fourth of nine
children, seven of whom are living. Both Anna Jean's parents came from
large families and are near the middle in birth order.

Marguerite's parents were from Michigan. Her father did odd jobs
when he was not working in a plant. Her mother was a "liberated"
woman. Besides singing in a choral group and giving Marguerite piano
lessons, she went to play Bingo alone, as her husband would not take
her. The oldest son, who was petted and pampered, is now an executive
in Texas but is married to his job. Marguerite was depended upon to
look after the other children. One sister, a widow, works full-time and
has four children. Anna Jean disapproves of the fact that the sister has
often left her children with Marguerite.

Anna Jean's sister, who is 2 years younger than she is, is a professor
at a midwestern university and has two boys.

In Anna Jean's family, which is much larger than Edward's family,
there seems to be more differentiation, as demonstrated in the variety
of names, locations, and professions. Movement has taken place from
lower-middle class to upper-middle class, and the women have engaged
in occupations other than housewifery. Anna Jean's less than adequate
relationship with her father probably influenced her unsuccessful marriage. She was truly strong to set a divorce precedent in this large Catholic
family!

PRETESTS

Bell-Fagan Family Symbols (B-F)

On the Bell-Fagan Family Symbols, the general pattern looks similar
for Anna Jean and Rebecca, with Jeanine defined in opposition to them.
The sibling rivalry shows up as opposition in at least three of the six
measures. Jeanine is lowest on the anxious-afraid scale and highest on
anger and on sadness. Rebecca is lowest on quiet and highest on loving
and happy (which corresponds with her self-presentation level) and on

anxious. Anna Jean is lowest on four of the six areas (angry, sad, loving, and happy), and highest on quiet. The closest Anna Jean and Rebecca get is on anxious-afraid; they are furthest apart on happy. Rebecca and Jeanine are closest on happy, and their patterns, although they appear oppositional, are really not very far apart on any of the areas.

When individual scores are subtracted from total family scores, Anna Jean sees her girls as angrier, sadder, more loving, and happier than the girls see their mother and sister. Jeanine sees Anna Jean and Rebecca as highest on anxiety; she also sees them as lower on anger, sadness, loving, and quiet. Rebecca sees Jeanine and Anna Jean as lowest on anxious-afraid and on happy (Rebecca does seem to have the happiest, least volatile disposition in the family). She sees her sister and her mother as highest on quiet (which I am inclined to disagree with). In the general pattern, Anna Jean's scores seem depressed compared with those of the girls. Here again, she sees the girls' relationship as having greater magnitude than her relationship with each of the girls.

According to individual scores, Jeanine and Rebecca see themselves as similar, except on anxious-afraid, on which Jeanine is again low. Anna Jean's pattern is similar to those of the girls, but, again, closer to Rebecca's and of lower magnitude. Rebecca is, again, highest on happy, Jeanine on anger and sadness. They have flip-flopped on loving, Jeanine seeing herself as more loving than Rebecca (perhaps this reflects how she would like to be). Anna Jean is again very low on happy, which seems realistic.

Description of Feelings in the Family (DFF)

Anna Jean and Jeanine appear to be mad and distracting; Rebecca is characterized as smug and sad, balancing them. On the B-F, Rebecca seems the most undifferentiated, since she can be seen as like Jeanine or like Anna Jean. Here, it seems, she is reacting to them, keeping the peace, or the balance. Rebecca, or the younger daughter, is characterized as mad and smug, the mother and the teenaged daughter oppose her, as they are characterized as sad and distracting. All the males are characterized as mad and distracting. Does this family have a digital view of male-female roles? Is Rebecca, not Jeanine, the identified patient? Is Jeanine more like her mother than her father, and is Anna Jean reacting to those traits in Jeanine that are like herself rather than like her ex-husband?

This composite family score is characterized as mad and distracting, which agrees with the self-presentational level. So does Rebecca's sadness, if it is considered in terms of insecurity and placation. On how the members see the other pairs (with their own scores subtracted out), essentially the way they see the whole family, Anna Jean sees the girls as distracting, and this is surely accurate. When the individual's scores for self are multiplied by 3 to present a more comparative magnitude, Anna Jean sees herself as mad and smug; Jeanine sees herself as mad and distracting. Both pictures seem to agree with reality, although Anna Jean is also distracting. Rebecca sees herself as smug and sad (perhaps when she withdraws, she is in deep contemplation).

From the Bell-Fagan, it might be hypothesized that Rebecca is aligned with her mother, or even her sister. To see her balancing them is a surprise, unless it can be explained on the grounds of lack of differentiation—she is reacting, not responding.

Family Situations Picture Series (FSPS)

Anna Jean and Jeanine balance each other. Rebecca, again, is different, with much greater magnitude. Both she and her sister selected more than 50 cards. The teenaged daughter and the younger daughter are characterized as blaming and distracting; the rest of the family is characterized as blaming and computing. No scores fall in the placating range (a few placating cards were chosen for Anna Jean). The individuals see the others similarly to the way they see the whole family (scores obtained by subtracting out the individual's score). When the score of each individual is multiplied by 3, Jeanine is characterized as blaming and distracting; her mother and her sister are together, being characterized as blaming and computing. This is how Jeanine and her mother saw themselves on the DFF, also.

Animal Concepts Picture Series (ACPS)

In general, there does not seem to be much differentiation among the members of this family on the ACPS. If anything, they seem to desire even less differentiation. Anna Jean is stronger, more powerful, bigger, "badder," and more dangerous. Rebecca is the most good, the most harmless, and the most pleasant. Jeanine, however, comes out as the most powerless, the smallest, the most helpless, the slowest, the quietest, and the most passive. This pattern does not match the self-presentational level, but, in light of a probable collusion between Rebecca and Anna Jean, it might fit. Ideally, the family wants the girls to be closer together, but the general pattern remains the same.

There is a general lack of differentiation. In comparison between how the individual sees herself, multiplied by 2 to make the magnitude comparable, and how the others in the family see her, the general pattern repeats itself: Anna Jean sees herself most nearly as the other family members see her. Ideally, there would be more differentiation, and the discrepancy of how each would like to be and how others would like her to be would be widening. I hope to see more differentiation exhibited on all the posttests. Though still within the normal range, Rebecca's difference score of 48 is the highest (below 50 is normal).

Holmes-Rahe Schedule of Events

Anna Jean scored 229 for the stresses she encountered during the past year. Above 150 indicates that illness may be a result of too much stress. According to this barometer, Anna Jean might be expected to have a problem with her health (I believe she commented once that her cholesterol level was high). On the stress scale for the past 10 years, she scored 416. That, also, is probably very high, but I have no standard by which to measure it.

Kinetic Family Drawings

The tests were completed at the kitchen table, but the drawings were done on the coffee table in the living room. Both Anna Jean and Rebecca drew stick figures. Rebecca drew the family reading, everyone smiling. She put Jeanine next to Anna Jean. Both her mother and her sister have hands, but Rebecca does not. Does she see them as more aggressive? Also, Rebecca's book is not in front of her as her mother's and her sister's are. Does she reveal herself and her thoughts more often than the others do?

Anna Jean's immature stick figures are another sign of lack of differentiation and perhaps a denial of sexuality. She places herself between the children, which can be seen as togetherness or as herself preventing their togetherness. Likewise, in Rebecca's picture, does Rebecca see Jeanine as a threat to her closeness to her mother?

Jeanine's picture looks much more differentiated, and the sibling rivalry is clear: she is observing Rebecca and Anna Jean, solemnly, from a distance, as they cook. Rebecca looks happy, but Anna Jean seems to be yelling. Something is burning on the stove. Could that represent their smoldering, unresolved feelings regarding the divorce? Could the picture's detail reflect Jeanine's rigidity and compulsiveness? Rebecca is drawn very small, perhaps reflecting her immature behaviors. Jeanine seems to see herself as outside the family circle, and Rebecca is between Jeanine and their mother.

House-Plan Drawings

Anna Jean's favorite room is the living room, but she spends most of the time in the kitchen. Rebecca likes "Mommy's room and Jeanine's room" (dependency? placating? or maybe hers is too messy!) but spends the most time in the bathroom, "hiding, reading, putting on my contacts." Jeanine's room is her favorite, and she spends the most time there. Jeanine seems to have definite boundaries, rigid ones, between what is her and what is not her. Although she seems to yearn for more closeness, she likes her distance. Rebecca seems to melt into the other two persons in her family. Jeanine drew her floor plan compulsively, using a ruler. Rebecca completed hers quickly, in any old fashion.

SUMMARY OF SESSIONS

We used lessons from Single-Parent Families because the divorce was clearly an unresolved issue in the family. Because we felt the family needed work on expressing feelings, we chose lessons from the Helpfulness Program. In retrospect, I wonder if it might have been better to make the last lesson (sharing the hurt) the next to the last, deleting the lesson on caring, which was similar to the lesson on seeing the good. I think some other lesson that would follow the sharing of hurt feelings might have reinforced any progress made with this lesson, as the sharing of hurt feelings is a significant unresolved issue in the family.

Session 1

In this session, we discovered that Anna Jean had talked only superficially with the girls about the divorce and the feelings involved. The first lesson brought out these feelings, and Jeanine, saying her mother loved Rebecca more, ran from the room in tears. Rebecca admitted in a small voice that at first she had blamed herself for the divorce but she later blamed her mother and her father. We tried to end the lesson on a more pleasant note by completing the drawing tasks. Although our effort seemed to work, Anna Jean tried to draw one of us aside and make a plea for individual help for herself and for Jeanine. She admitted that Rebecca was "her baby."

Session 2

This session began solemnly, the family perhaps apprehensive after the first session, and distracting behavior began to emerge. We asked

Anna Jean to sit between the girls on the couch in hopes of placing her equally with them. We suspect a coalition between Anna Jean and Rebecca, who is withdrawn, immature, and placating. Rebecca was quite unresponsive in this session, perhaps because Anna Jean was interacting more with Jeanine this time. Some resistance to the lesson was offered in Jeanine's saying "I don't understand" and in Anna Jean's attempts to glean more meaning from the terms than we intended. We discussed six ways of relating that do not get people what they want in a family. Jeanine ran from the room a couple of times in tears.

Session 3

Having exposed some of the more hurtful aspects of their family life to the Thompsons, we enjoyed this lesson on positive feelings (as did the family). Alliances seemed to be changing; Anna Jean and Jeanine seemed much closer tonight. Rebecca was quite withdrawn and at one point even moved away from the others to a chair. Anna Jean seems to have difficulty relating positively to both girls at the same time. Anna Jean and Jeanine criticized Rebecca about her thumb sucking and about her messy room. Rebecca let her fangs show by verbally attacking Jeanine, albeit weakly. Passive-aggressive is more her style. She has subtle methods for upsetting Jeanine so that their mother will admonish Rebecca and attend positively to Jeanine. She instigates the situation, then comes out of it "smelling like a rose."

Anna Jean tends to mention how much she sacrifices for the girls (she thinks she is presenting herself as a good mother). I wonder whether she resents being in full charge of the girls and having to bear the responsibility of the situation alone, when her own emotional needs are so sorely unmet. The family seemed to enjoy talking about their more positive aspects, though they focused on material rather than emotional ones, and Jeanine had no emotional outburst. Sibling rivalry was quite apparent, however.

Session 4

In this session, we again dealt with positive aspects of the family, seeing the good. At the end of this session, we gave each member of the family a paradoxical letter bringing up some of the behavior we had detected that had not been specifically addressed in the sessions. The letter concerned alliances and the protective aspects of distracting behavior.

Jeanine and Anna Jean were in conflict again, and Rebecca now appeared contented. She participated more than ever this time. Jeanine left the room in tears two or three times, provoked subtly by her mother and sister. Is Jeanine the safety valve for the family? She was verbally critical to Rebecca throughout the session. We made several attempts to deal with Jeanine's outbursts. At first we complimented her on her ability to express her feelings. Then we asked her mother to go to her and to put her arms around her. Sometimes she responded to that. I think the compliments made her cry more, but perhaps she needed to express some of those feelings in an accepting atmosphere. When the outbursts continued, we reminded her that one of the sessions had dealt with telling someone about hurtful feelings in a nonhurtful way. She tried this, and it seemed to work for a time, but she lost control (or rather, gained it) again. This time we congratulated her for her ability to gain control and disrupt the meeting. There were no more outbursts after that, but that statement was made just before we gave the family the paradoxical letter. Something worked—there were no more outbursts during the last two sessions.

Session 5

Before this session, Anna Jean, upset, called one of the enrichers and asked for an explanation of the letter. The enricher professed inability to act alone in responding, and Anna Jean vented some of her feelings before hanging up. Session 5 began with our asking Anna Jean to express to everyone the feelings she had expressed in the phone call. She did, briefly, and we asked her to deal with both of us next time.

The lesson dealt with caring, and Anna Jean commented that it was very much like the preceding week's lesson. The distractions were minimal, and no one (except Rebecca) said anything about Rebecca's thumb sucking, which continued. Jeanine did not run out of the room. The family seemed like a threesome for the first time, though Rebecca stayed physically closer to their mother. There was some joking and laughter today. This family seems to enjoy focusing on positive aspects, some of which they have been unaware of, in my opinion.

Session 6

This session concerned dealing with hurt feelings. The family members were not able to talk about hurt within the family, except for one minor incident, and instead focused on how they share hurt incurred outside the family. There were long silences between responses, and Rebecca was very quiet again. She had just been swimming, and Anna Jean said the chlorine made her sleepy. Jeanine became upset but was able to control herself rather than the situation, and stayed in the room. They discussed some of the ways they might better express hurt feelings. Anna Jean and the girls touched each other frequently.

POSTTESTS

The posttests were completed at the Thompsons' kitchen table, as the pretests had been. Rebecca remained at the table this time rather than scattering her cards on the floor as she had done during the pretest. Before the test began, Rebecca and Jeanine argued and pushed each other in an attempt to vie for the same position at the table. (If sibling rivalry has been reduced by SE, I saw no evidence of it.)

The posttest data were not evaluated from as many positions as the pretest data because the changes from pre- to posttest are not extensive enough to warrant this further data manipulation.

Anna Jean spent the most time on the tests, especially the last one (ACPS), which is paradoxical, as she expressed an aversion to the testing and appeared quite disgusted with it. The very fact that the test was distasteful to her, on the other hand, may have explained her laboring over it. She did believe that the ACPS was the only valid test.

Rebecca made fawning remarks to her mother about her selections. Besides being placating, her comments were rather undifferentiated ("nice," "good," "I like——").

Jeanine again expressed admiration for her mother's strength and appears to want to be strong, also. She finished the tasks the quickest, even though she picked up more cards than the other two on both the DFF and the FSPS, and read magazines while she waited. Rebecca appeared to be in a world of her own, responding least verbally.

Bell-Fagan Family Symbols (B-F)

A general comparison of the pretest and the posttest scores on the B-F suggests more differentiation among the family members on the posttest, except on the happiness scale, on which they are closer together. The overall pattern of Anna Jean's scores being more depressed than those of the girls holds true as in the pretest data, except that she is much higher on anxious-afraid. Anna Jean seems to be in opposition to the girls (anxious-afraid, angry, and sad), but Rebecca seems to be in opposition to her mother and sister on loving, quiet, and happy. Perhaps this reflects Anna Jean's heightened post-SE awareness of her collusion with Rebecca to the exclusion of Jeanine, as well as the girls' possible beginnings at acceptance of each other.

Anna Jean is highest on anxious-afraid, on angry, and on happy; although she was fairly high on anxious-afraid on the pretest, she was lowest on angry and on happy. Perhaps by enabling her to release some of her anger, SE has also allowed Anna Jean to be happier. Maybe the release of her anger has, however, made her more anxious and afraid. She is still lowest on sad.

Jeanine remains highest on sad but not as high on angry or loving as she was on the pretest. She is also highest on anxious-afraid; Rebecca has the least position on that scale. Jeanine is very close to her mother on loving and happy but close to Rebecca only on happy. Interestingly, as Anna Jean became happier, both girls became less happy; as Anna Jean became angrier, the girls became less angry. Is this another signal denoting lack of differentiation, not only generally, but with specific reference to the girls' relationships with their mother? How attached to Anna Jean are her girls? (Or, by virtue of the number of cards available that express happiness, when one person gets the cards, another does not!)

Rebecca became quieter as Anna Jean became much less quiet. This agrees with Rebecca's phenotypical behavior. She is also much less happy and anxious-afraid. The relative position of family members remained the same on sad. Rebecca seems much more in opposition to her mother on the posttest scores in contrast to the pretest scores, on which she seemed much more like her mother. Is this her lack of differentiation, her reacting rather than responding? Perhaps the coalition between Rebecca and Anna Jean is indeed weakening, the resultant change in scores reflecting the reorganization occurring among the three of them.

Description of Feelings in the Family (DFF)

As was apparent in the general overview of the B-F posttest results, Anna Jean appears also to be defined in opposition to the girls on the DFF. Again, she is characterized as mad and distracting, and Rebecca and Jeanine are characterized as sad and smug. Rebecca was sad and smug on the pretest as well, but Jeanine was characterized as mad and distracting and flip-flopped on the posttest. Both magnitudes in each direction are greater for Anna Jean and Rebecca; Jeanine seems much more smug than sad. This is consistent with Jeanine's phenotypical behavior but not entirely consistent with the B-F results, on which she is less angry but sadder. The pretest is congruent with her catapulting move from being mad and distracting, but from the B-F prediction, one might expect her to have rated higher on the sad scale.

Rebecca's results on the B-F are lower on happy on the posttest, which might agree with the posttest feeling rating, which was sadder than on the pretest. Her phenotypical behavior also seemed quieter and sadder.

Anna Jean remained essentially the same, characterized as being mad and distracting, except her magnitude increased from pre- to posttest. This agrees with her posttest B-F increases on the anxious-afraid and angry subscales. The total family scores changed from mad-distracting on pretest to sad-smug on posttest.

Perhaps, again, as Anna Jean was able to express some of her anger, she experienced more anxiety. Her girls then reacted to her by becoming less close to her and closer to each other. There seems to be more differentiation among the three on the posttest scores than on the pretest scores.

However, the family seems less differentiated than on the pretest. Everyone except the teenaged daughter seems to be characterized as sad and smug; the teenaged daughter is characterized as mad and smug. The family members are smug rather than distracting and sad, except the teenaged daughter, who is mad. Less differentiation is shown between males and females, meaning, perchance paradoxically, that this family's view of male-female roles is not so digital as it appeared on the pretest. From the preceding two tests, some changes appear to have taken place in the Thompson family. They do not seem great enough, however, to warrant an additional breakdown of the data.

Family Situations Picture Series (FSPS)

The posttest results showed less variability than the pretest results. Anna Jean selected 3 fewer cards (33) than she did on the pretest. On the pretest, Rebecca and Jeanine selected 52 and 54 cards, respectively, but Rebecca selected only 23 cards on the posttest. Jeanine again selected approximately the same number, 59 cards.

In a comparison of total responses, Anna Jean had 59 on the pretest and 58 on the posttest (normal range). Jeanine, however, had 97 on the pretest and 106 on the posttest, which is in the range of overresponsivity and receptivity to conflict and undercontrol. This certainly agrees with her behavior, though I would have preferred to have seen her score decrease. Perhaps she has to express some of her anger and frustration before she can learn to rechannel and control the rest more appropriately. The B-F indicates that Jeanine is less angry but more anxious-afraid and sad, the feelings scores backing this up. This area of evaluation underlines the premise that she is the identified patient. Rebecca's scores were 92 on the pretest (in the same range of undercontrol as her sister) but decreased to 37 on the posttest. This places her in the range of denial, repression, and overcontrol. (I am not certain that Rebecca always understood her task on the test, though we explained to her as clearly as possible. She seemed to be in her own world a good deal of the time.) Perhaps this range is reflected in the greater magnitude on smug on the feelings scores and her great increase on the B-F quiet score. It could be that she observes that the alliances in the family are changing and does not know how to react, as she appears to define herself with reference to her mother and sister. As a result, she is withdrawing until things settle and she can emerge to reassume a self-definition. Rebecca is as much or more in need of help as Jeanine, in my opinion, though Jeanine remains the safety valve for the family, the obvious identified patient.

Anna Jean's scores did not change much from pre- to posttest. Computing and distracting are still her salient areas, although computing fell 3 points (perhaps, in spite of her rigidity, she is emoting more). Jeanine was highest on blaming and distracting on the pretest and on distracting and computing on the posttest. Perhaps she is beginning to gain some control, even as her mother is beginning to relinquish some. Rebecca was much higher on blaming and computing than on distracting and placating on both tests. I would have expected from her behavior that she would be much higher on the latter two. As a family, they have changed from blaming and computing to distracting and computing. The overall average response score for the family ranged from being extremely open on the pretest (83) to average openness (69) on the posttest. This change was due to Rebecca's scores. Despite the score change, however, functioning seems to have improved. In reality, I see the family as average to closed.

All three scored in different ranges, Jeanine remaining characterized as blaming and distracting, as on the pretest. Anna Jean changed from placating-computing on the pretest to placating-distracting on the posttest. Rebecca also remained characterized as blaming and computing, but the magnitude of her responses dropped considerably. The total family changed from blaming-computing to just computing. Rebecca seems to have made the greatest change by this measure.

The father and the older son are omitted from the scores altogether, the younger son having received only one score, in blaming. All the scores are quite small in magnitude in comparison to the pretest scores. I have no explanation, only questions. Have they repressed feelings about significant males? Did they understand test instructions differently on the pre- and the posttests? Have they expressed some of their hurt and anger about their father and, as a result, felt less inclined to demonstrate it on the test?

Animal Concepts Picture Series (ACPS)

Anna Jean again chose for her actual self a kangaroo, seeing that as protective. In her second sorting, she chose a St. Bernard rather than a dinosaur (pretest), which she thought reflected her anger (and perhaps some guilt—a dinosaur was not a very pretty animal, it was not smart, and it did not survive). Her ideal selves were birds (though not the same picture) and a stag on the pretest and on the posttest, though not in the same order. Does she want to be powerful and carefree? Again she chose a butterfly for Jeanine for the first sorting on actual self; for second sorting, she chose a clam on the pretest and a snapping turtle on the posttest. She seems to see Jeanine as "flitting about" but with a shell about her. She would rather have seen her as a gull and a St. Bernard (more caring) on the pretest and as a puppy and a bird (more carefree) on the posttest. She saw Rebecca as a horse and a kitten on the pretest and as a horse and a seal on the posttest. Rebecca loves horses, and she is soft and vulnerable. Ideally, Anna Jean would have liked Rebecca to be a bird and a squirrel (carefree, thinking ahead) on the pretest and a chipmunk and a bird on the posttest. Anna Jean's responses remained quite consistent from pre- to posttest, which coincides with her rigid nature. The most change indicated from this comparison seems to be a slightly better acceptance of her own anger (dinosaur to St. Bernard). She sees Jeanine as rigid and impenetrable and wants her to be more lovable, looser, more carefree. (She could profit by those changes herself. Again, I wonder if some of her conflict with Jeanine may be, in addition to Jeanine's reminding Anna Jean of her divorced husband, she also reminds Anna Jean of herself, projected for protection, of course.) She sees Rebecca as soft and vulnerable but wants her to be more industrious and responsible, as well as to remain carefree. (Anna Jean does seem to have many self-defeating behaviors!) She sees herself as protective but longs to lessen the responsibility she labors under, the responsibility that mothering apparently entails for her. This responsibility is evident in her speaking of sacrificing what she wants or needs so that the children can have what they need. This analysis reflects the general atmosphere of the household—obvious caring, but unresolved, underlying tension. According to these scores, Anna Jean wants to eliminate that tension.

Jeanine's answers seem to reflect that she sees her mother as strong and wants her to remain that way. Actual animals on the pretest were a leopard and a bear for her mother; posttest animals were a lion and a stag (her mother selected the latter as her self-ideal twice). Her ideals for her mother were a lion and an eagle on the pretest and a zebra and a leopard on the posttest. For herself, Jeanine selected the same actuals, the panda and the llama, on both tests. She apparently sees herself as warmer and cuddlier than Anna Jean and Rebecca do. Ideally, she wanted to be a butterfly and a stag (strong and mature) on the pretest and a stag (majestic, proud) on the posttest. Note that Jeanine's ideal (stag) on both tests is what Anna Jean described as her own ideal both times. It is also what Jeanine chose as actual for her mother on the posttest. Even the words she used to describe the stag were similar to those she used to describe her mother. Though Jeanine often finds herself in opposition to her mother, she respects her and wants to be like her. Jeanine sees Rebecca as innocuous—a sheep and a puppy on the pretest and a horse and a sheep on the posttest. She would like to see her be a chipmunk and a mouse (pretest) and a hummingbird and a bee (posttest). Like her mother, Jeanine remained fairly consistent in her animal responses.

Rebecca likewise chose a stag and a deer for her mother on the actual division of the pre- and the posttests. She said of the animals, "pretty," "cute," "I like it," "nice," all of which point to her immaturity. On the actual-self part of the pretest, Anna Jean was a dinosaur and a deer; on the posttest, she was a whale and a stag. Rebecca's ideal for her mother seemed to indicate that Rebecca wanted her to be less powerful: her pretest ideals were a chipmunk and a bear, and her posttest ideals were a puppy and a mouse. Perhaps the mouse indicated her wish for even less power for her mother, reflecting Rebecca's confusion at the changing alliances. Rebecca saw Jeanine as a skunk and a seal (one tried to bite her once) on the pretest. These choices seem indicative of sibling rivalry: Rebecca sees Jeanine as threatening. She seems to be denying some of this on the posttest (or beginning to deal with it), seeing Jeanine as a bird and a poodle. Ideally, she would like to see her sister as a panda and a raccoon (pretest) and as a bird and a frog (posttest), which seem less threatening. For herself, Rebecca chose two kinds of horses for the actual (pretest) and a horse and a puppy for the ideal. She loves horses— does this mean she likes herself? On the posttest, she selected a dinosaur (Anna Jean selected this for her actual self on the pretest) and a mouse for the actual. (Has her self-esteem declined?) She is perhaps both identifying with her mother and feeling helpless. She chose a deer and a dinosaur for her ideal (posttest), which is like her mother yet more powerful. On posttest, Rebecca did not choose a horse for anyone, though it is her favorite animal. Is this part of her denial? A horse is an animal she likes and identifies with. By refusing to select horses, was she attempting to negate part of herself?

An overall view of the scores discloses what looks like more differentiation on the first four measurements but the same or less on the last six. Ideally, this family wants to be even less differentiated, perhaps because they are frightened by the changes, possibly those in alliances, that are occurring. Their relative positions remained essentially the same on the actual-self score. Anna Jean was the strongest, most powerful, biggest, most helpful, most dangerous, and most aggressive. Rebecca had scored highest on good and pleasant, but the family saw Jeanine in those positions on posttest (which does not coincide with behavioral observations). Contrary to behavioral observations and to the pretest results, Rebecca was the noisiest on both the pre- and the posttest results.

On the ideal-self, the family wants the girls to be stronger, more powerful, and bigger; they want the mother to be weaker, less powerful, and smaller. This corresponds with Rebecca's apparent desires, shown in the analysis of her selection of animals. Basically, those seem to be the most salient changes; the remaining categories are very close, even somewhat closer and less differentiated than the pretest ideal. The ACPS, as I see it, does not reflect much progress in change; the other tests, particularly the first two, seem to indicate some change, albeit minimal.

FEEDBACK CONFERENCE

Anna Jean, Jeanine, and Rebecca sat on the couch, in contrast to the seating arrangement that had excluded Jeanine at our first meeting. Although all looked happy and touched one another frequently, they appeared somewhat anxious. Anna Jean was smiling, but her arms were crossed as we spoke, Jeanine was biting her nails, and Rebecca was sucking her thumb.

When I asked what they had learned, Jeanine answered first, as usual, saying that she understands her feelings better and is now more understanding and accepting of Rebecca. Rebecca said she had had fun, a somewhat immature remark. Anna Jean said that she has examined her feelings, motives, and behaviors more carefully but feels the need for more concrete ways to improve their relationships so that they can really change. Surprisingly, as the first session seemed so traumatic, Anna Jean said she would have liked to have pursued those issues in depth. She said she needs more structure and she had hoped to develop more loyalty between the children. Rebecca and Jeanine said that some of the questions had been hard to understand and difficult to answer. Anna Jean suggested that the ages of the children should have been more carefully considered.

Anna Jean mentioned the letter again, reiterating that it had really upset her and she felt the family deserved an explanation. She said that the letter was really very difficult for the children to understand and that she had had to explain it to them as she had understood it. She wanted more specific suggestions about how to improve and stated that she had disliked the tests and thought that another type, such as inkblots, would have been more effective.

I listed the positive aspects of the family and asked whether they wanted to pursue some of the areas that had been brought up. Anna Jean seemed to equate asking for help with admitting great weakness or dreadful problems, but she wanted the names of agencies in her area, so I gave them to her.

CONCLUSIONS

In my opinion, SE just scratched the surface with this family. I think some of the areas of concern were uncovered and dealt with, but their greatest problem—sharing hurt feelings, mainly about the girls' father—still festers.

The Thompsons love, admire, and care about one another; they are strong, a family of leaders. They are physically attractive, bright, articulate, and sensitive. They have the capacity to look to the future and plan accordingly.

Anna Jean has not dealt with her own feelings about her ex-husband and the divorce. She was strong enough to divorce him, even though she comes from a long line of Catholics who have avoided divorce, but she has not accepted it on a deeper level. As a result, Anna Jean projects her own and her husband's less likable personality traits onto Jeanine. More of the good and loving qualities are attributed to Rebecca, with the result that she is regressive and immature. Anna Jean suffers from the guilt of being a "bad" mother because she made the children suffer through a divorce and is unable to cope with their sibling rivalry. She therefore derives some pleasure from the pain she inflicts upon herself by sacrificing something she needs or wants so that her children can have more. She tends to distract from the real issues by focusing on external areas, such as the girls' loyalties or Jeanine's emotional outbursts or Rebecca's thumb sucking. The focus she places on herself is the issue of becoming inappropriately angry with the girls; she does not seem to see the real problem. Anna Jean seemed to want more than she got out of SE. I hope she will pursue therapy, which is really what she had in mind. Until she understands herself better, she will not be able to deal effectively with her children's problems. Perhaps she would respond to behavior therapy, at least initially, as it represents a more structured approach than the more traditional methods.

Although the main problem remains to be dealt with, we did see some positive changes, and they are reflected in the tests. Anna Jean is sharing more physical contact with her girls, is more aware of her alliance with Rebecca, and seems to be actively including Jeanine more often. Jeanine, in turn, seems to be accepting Rebecca a little more. Also, Jeanine seems to be beginning to try to improve her poor impulse control. Both girls identify strongly with their mother, though the areas of identification are different. Jeanine selected the strong, compulsive, computing side; Rebecca chose the softer, more loving, dependent, and placating side. I think the whole family is more aware of the need to express feelings and has practiced doing this in nonhurtful ways. If only they could express their hurt, starting with Anna Jean . . .

9

Adolescent Acting-Out

Hilary P. Buzas

The Powells, a clinical family, were selected by the juvenile court outreach team to participate in SE in addition to their weekly therapy sessions. The family had been referred to therapy by the court after the daughter, Patty, had run away from home after fighting with her mother and threatening her with a butcher knife. The family had been in therapy for 1 month when SE began. The eight sessions took place at the juvenile court outreach center. The lessons were selected from several programs.

BACKGROUND

The Powell family consists of the mother, Helen, aged 36; the daughter, Patty, aged 17; and the son, Pete, aged 8. Mrs. Powell, who has been divorced three times, had married her first husband, Patty's father, when she was 3 months pregnant with Patty. Pete's father, Mrs. Powell's third husband, resides in the same town as the other three family members. Mrs. Powell works in an office. The family resides in a middle-class, suburban neighborhood, and the children attend public school. They live in a comfortable house with a swimming pool. Each family member has a separate bedroom.

Helen's mother and father live nearby, and Patty frequently stays with her grandmother after a fight with her mother. Initially, all three appeared amiable, gregarious, and, except for Pete, eager to participate.

Helen is the oldest of seven children, five girls and two boys. Her father, the second of five children, is retired. Her mother, aged 56, is a housewife and often takes care of Patty and Pete. Both parents are in good health. Helen describes her father as one who "gives in a lot,"

117

particularly to the mother. She describes her mother as dominant, the disciplinarian in the family. Helen's paternal grandmother is alive and lives in another part of the state; her grandfather is dead. Helen's maternal grandfather and grandmother, who had lived in a rural area near a large city, are dead.

Helen is occasionally in contact with her third ex-husband, Bob, as Pete often visits his father. Helen stated that she and Bob "get along now" (they used to fight) because "he doesn't have to come to me" and "I don't have to answer to him." Helen has no contact with her first or her second husband.

PRETESTS

The Family Environment Scales (FES) and the Family Adaptability and Cohesion Evaluation Scales (FACES) were administered to all three members of the family; Pete, however, did not successfully complete the test, nor did he wish to do so.

The scores on the FACES are expressed in terms of the degree of family cohesion and adaptability. Patty, the daughter, scored low both on cohesion and on adaptability, demonstrating that she perceives the family as having little emotional bonding and high individual autonomy (disengaged) and of being highly organized (structured). Helen scored high on adaptability and mid to high on cohesion, which suggests that she perceives the family as having somewhat close emotional bonds (connected) and minimal organization (chaotic) or shifting rules, roles, and power structure. According to these scores, the mother and the daughter seem to have very different views of the family; however, this discrepancy can be seen as the views of an adolescent attempting to leave home and of a parent at this life-cycle stage. The FACES subscales of Cohesion and Adaptability are similar to L'Abate's A-R-C model and model of priorities, respectively (L'Abate, 1986b). When the scores are interpreted according to L'Abate's models, the daughter is seen as perceiving the family as apathetic yet having definite roles; the mother sees the family as reactive and as having undefined roles or priorities.

The scores on the Family Environment Scale (FES) are expressed in terms of 10 subscales: Cohesion, Expressiveness, Conflict, Independence, Achievement Orientation, Intellectual/Cultural Orientation, Active Recreational Orientation, Moral/Religious Emphasis, Organization, and Control. Patty sees the family as controlled (rigid rules) and somewhat low in cohesiveness and expressiveness. This is consistent with her perception of the family as expressed on the FACES. Helen sees the family as controlled, somewhat low in cohesiveness and low in participation in recreational activities.

An average of the family members' scores on the FES indicates that on the whole the family is seen as slightly low in cohesiveness and somewhat high in control (rigid rules).

The results of the FACES and the FES depict a family that exhibits few extreme characteristics (that is, their scores fall primarily within the standard range), except for their differing scores on control and cohesiveness within the family.

After discussing the family and test results, the supervisor commented that, although the son did not complete the pretests, he should be included in SE. He also suggested that we choose a lesson from the program Separating Teenagers From Their Parents to address the issue of leaving home and/or running away.

SUMMARY OF SESSIONS

Session 1

Exercise 1.

Do you think that wanting to leave home or get away tells something about how this family works or fails to work?

Patty: I've always wanted to leave home. I'd cut my arm off to be free. This family doesn't work for me.
Helen: A child shouldn't leave home until they're of age and have a job. It's dumb to leave home if parents pay for food and housing.
Pete: I don't want Patty to leave home, makes me feel bad—sometimes it makes me feel good [laughs].

Exercise 2.

How do you allow each of you to be an individual in his or her own right?

Helen: I take time for myself, and I let others have time for themselves.
Pete: I get to ride my bike.

Exercise 3.

How does leaving home relate to how this family allows its members to be individual adults in their own right?

Helen: I don't know. I don't know why Patty wants to leave home.

Patty: This family doesn't let me be myself. I have to always watch myself and what I do.
Pete: That goes for me, too.

Exercise 4.

Sometimes it is difficult for members of this family to see themselves as interdependent. What do you think about your interdependence?

Helen: I'd like a little cooperation, but I don't get it.
Patty: This family has failed—I don't want to depend on them.
Pete: I don't want you to depend on me.

Exercise 5.

I wonder whether leaving home represents a way of changing things and whether you can think of better ways of becoming individual adults.

Helen: I don't want my life to change.
Patty: Getting older—like 18—would help me be an adult.
Pete: When I get older, I'll be an adult, too.

Session 2

Exercise 1.

How do you use guilt in the family?

Pete: I don't do that.
Helen: I do. I use those same words—I say, "I do everything for this family without getting anything in return."
Patty: I go insane to get my way. I can't make Mother feel guilty; I can't get Mother to do anything.

Do you think making your family feel guilty is worth it to you?

Pete: I don't do things in order to make them feel guilty.
Helen: It depends on what my original gripe was about. Sometimes I don't care if they feel guilty. I want them to say "poor Mother."
Patty: No, I think there are other ways, but I can't think of them right now.

How do you use crying to make your family feel guilty?

Pete: That's my question—I do it all the time to get my way.
Patty: I cry because I'm sensitive, not to make anyone feel guilty.
Helen: I don't cry to make people guilty. I cry if I'm very sad or extremely
    mad.

Exercise 2.

Can you think of a time when you tried to do something nice and
your actions were misinterpreted? Did it cause hurt feelings?

Patty: I've done plenty of things to be nice and Mother thinks I do it
    for other reasons—that really hurts me.
Helen: I don't do that. It hasn't happened to me.
Pete: They never think about me—only when I'm eating [laughs].

Exercise 3.

Have you used the number game or bragged, and do you think this
gets your family anything?

Helen: I can't think of a time when someone did that.
Patty: I don't do it.
Pete: I don't brag.

Exercise 4.

How do you feel when someone is sarcastic with you? Do you think
sarcasm helps this family?

Helen: Sarcasm doesn't bother me.
Patty: Mother is sarcastic with Pete and me. It sometimes hurts my
    feelings.
Pete: I don't pay any attention to them.
Helen: Sarcasm doesn't help any family, but we're not really sarcastic in
    this family.

Exercise 5.

How do you feel when someone gives you the silent treatment?

Helen: I feel terrible.
Patty: I'd love it if they'd ignore me.
Pete: It would feel fine to me.
Patty: Mother doesn't give anyone the silent treatment.

Homework.

Think of what you could do to change things for the better in this family.

Enrichers' notes.

The first lesson ended too soon, so we, along with the family, decided to do another lesson—one focused on improving family communications. The family had expressed their interest in that area, and we felt such a lesson would be helpful to them.

During this session, Pete had difficulty sitting still. He often walked around the room and engaged in distracting behavior (e.g., picking up things from the desk, opening and closing the door). Some anger and resentment appeared to exist between Patty and her mother; however, both were very cooperative and spoke freely. Also, Patty seemed mildly depressed.

Supervision.

Our supervisor suggested that we ask Pete to draw pictures during the sessions to inhibit his walking around the room. He also commented that a lesson that would generate conversation between family members (talking directly to one another) might be of value.

Session 3

First, we discussed the homework from the preceding session. The homework assignment was to think about what each could do to improve the family. Helen said that when she was angry she would try not to get upset. Pete said he could feed the dogs and cat. Patty said she could make dinner for her mother and Pete.

Introduction.

How are feelings expressed and heard in this family?

Helen: Pete slammed the phone down on me.
Patty: Slamming doors and pots, screaming.
Pete: Breaking windows, busting doors.

Exercise 1.

Complete this sentence: The thing I like most about you is——, and the thing I like least about you is——

Helen: Pete, you are a loving child, but you don't mind. Patty, you are my pride and joy; you are egotistic, bigoted, and self-centered.

Pete: Mother, you work and get the money; Mother, you scream at me. Patty, you help me with homework; you tell me to shut up.

Patty: Pete, you go away every other weekend. You are uncontrollable and don't get spanked enough. Mother, you never neglect your responsibilities and never avoid them; you need to enjoy life more and go out more.

Exercise 2.

All repeated their likes and dislikes (expressed in Exercise 1) and then repeated what they had heard about themselves.

Exercise 3.

Complete the following: I have a complaint about you. It is——, or you did——

Helen: I have a complaint, Pete, that you don't always mind or listen. Patty, I have a complaint when you are on the phone and whisper. This brings feelings in me to light and brings back bad memories.

Pete: Mother, you scream at me. I have a complaint, Patty, when you tell me to shut up.

Patty: I have a complaint about you, Pete, that you should do your schoolwork right and not have to do it over because of errors; and I don't like you [her mother] watching TV in Pete's room.

Exercise 4.

Complete this sentence: It hurts me to see you——

Helen: Pete, it hurts me to see you not mind; Patty, I see you as a young adult who is all mixed up about what you want to do. I know what I'd like for you to do, but I'm afraid you'll not do this and make the wrong decision.

Patty: What hurts me about you, Pete, is that you don't realize what you're going to have to go through. You now have a worse emotional problem than I ever did, and you throw temper tantrums and cry. Mother, it hurt me when you went on strike and you wanted us to have food and things and you were under stress.

Pete: It hurt me, Patty, when you hit me. It hurts me, Mother, when you scream at me.

Exercise 5.

Complete this sentence: What I want from you is———

Patty to Pete: . . . not to misbehave and to be good. I want you, Mother, to be happy with me when I grow up and to like whatever decisions I make and not be mad at me or hold them against me, whether they're right or wrong.
Helen to Pete: . . . to respect my wishes.
     to Patty: . . . to feel you can come and talk to me if you need to.
Pete to Helen: . . . to quit screaming at me.
     to Patty: . . . to quit telling me to shut up.

Exercise 6.

Complete this sentence: I want to compliment you about———

Helen to Patty: . . . your behavior lately—you've been so good. I'm proud of your schoolwork and your overall actions over the past 3 weeks.
Helen to Pete: . . . the good papers you brought home from school today.
Patty to Helen: . . . your behavior over the past 3 weeks. You've been like a mother; you've respected me and have been nice to Jimmy [Patty's boyfriend].
Patty to Pete: . . . putting the dishes in the dishwasher.
Pete to Helen: . . . getting us money and buying us food.
Pete to Patty: . . . I don't know one for you [pause]—that you helped me with my schoolwork.

Finish this sentence: It makes me feel good to see you———

Patty to Helen: . . . enjoying yourself.
Helen to Pete: . . . bring home good papers and pay attention to what I say.
Helen to Patty: . . . I felt fantastic when you discussed with me a problem Jimmy had.
Patty to Pete: . . . help Mother.
Pete to Helen: . . . let me ride my bike and don't scream at me.
Pete to Patty: . . . help set the table.

Finish this sentence: I am glad you are my [mother, daughter, son, etc.] because———

Helen to Pete: You are so loving and precious, although you're restless. You are like your dad. I love you so much.

Helen to Patty: Just think of what you would have become [cries]— because I'm your mother, I hung in there with you and knew you could become one of the finest women in the world.

Patty to Pete: [teasingly] I couldn't write an essay on that subject. One day I might appreciate having you for a brother.

Patty to Helen: You have shown me many things and have taught me a lot and have given me the qualities to cope with and understand things.

Pete to Helen: You buy me food.

Pete to Patty: You help me with my homework.

Enrichers' notes.

Pete rarely moved about the room this session (as suggested, we had given Pete paper and crayons). Although he was drawing, he paid attention and answered all the questions asked of him.

Everyone appeared to enjoy this session; Helen commented afterward that she had liked it. The family appeared to be getting along better and to be less angry with one another, although Patty still appeared somewhat depressed.

Pete rushed out the door at the end of the session; twice during the session he had asked how soon they could leave.

Supervision.

Our supervisor commented that Pete should continue to draw during the lesson, thereby inhibiting his distracting others. He also suggested we select another lesson on the expression of feelings, as the last one had gone well.

Session 4

Has this family been able to express and accept feelings more?

Helen: I've talked less about feelings or about anything else.

Pete: I've talked more.

Patty: I don't know.

Exercise 1.

What do you like and dislike about yourself?

Pete: This is the hardest question. I can't think of anything unless when I'm fussing at my mom.

Helen: I can't think of anything I don't like about me. I'm a good old down-to-earth person; I'm economical, efficient, highly diplomatic (I can cuss someone out and they don't know it). I'm good to the children. I like to think I'm a good mother, although the children will disagree. I'm close to my sister and brother, and I'm a good housekeeper and worker.

Patty: I don't like anything about me. I dislike myself because I think of where I could be and I could be richer, like people who live in mansions. I like to draw. I like that I like horses, I like that I can do math easily; I can sometimes pick up things quickly. I'd like to be someone else.

Exercise 2.

What are you going to do to change into a better person?

Helen: I could communicate with and understand Pete's and Patty's wants and wishes more. If I could understand, I'd be a better family member.

Patty: I'm ready for a change, although I don't think I could change anything. Maybe I could eat better. Also not imitate anyone in my family. Even my grandmother makes me nervous.

Pete: I could quit fighting at the dinner table.

Exercise 3.

Tell us what it is that you wish or want to become.

Helen: I want to be a millionaire and not have to work. (Pete then said, "But then you'd have to put up with me.")

Pete: I want to be a bike racer or a football player.

Patty: I'd like to be a Hawaiian native on an island or the owner of a million-dollar racehorse.

Exercise 4.

Tell us your goals and what steps you can take to reach those goals.

Helen: I would be worth an awful amount of money dead. My children would be rich.

Patty: I reach my goal when I become 18. I can do what I want. I could reach this goal by going to sleep for a year. [She is now 17.]

Pete: I would reach my goal by growing up and entering bike races.

Exercise 5.

How realistic are your plans in relationship to your wishes?

Helen: Mine don't fit. No way for me to become a millionaire.
Patty: I'll never be a Hawaiian native or a racehorse owner, but I will become 18 and be able to do what I want.
Pete: Mine fit because when I'm older, I can enter races.

Exercise 6.

What is it that is hard for each of you to say?

Helen: It is hard for this family to say "I love you." I can usually talk about anything, except I am fearful of correcting Patty—although I have done it.
Patty: I can't talk to Pete about mechanical things, and I can't tell Mother that I broke something or that I got a bad grade.
Pete: I don't know anything hard for me to say.

Exercise 7.

What feelings does this family not allow?

Patty: Kind ones—anger, sometimes.
Helen: I don't get to express my aggravation when Patty ties up the phone. I also can't say I feel neglected.
Pete: I don't know, but I can't sock someone in the nose.

Enrichers' notes.

During the session, the family was very attentive and cooperative. Helen and Pete seem to communicate freely; however, Patty seems fearful of expressing negative feelings to her mother. She carefully avoids any direct confrontation with her mother and expresses her anger by saying she wants to be on her own.

Supervision.

Our supervisor recommended selecting a lesson to address Patty's fear of speaking openly and expressing her feelings.

Session 5

For Session 5, we used the lesson Sharing of Hurt Feelings (Program 39A, Styles in Responding: The A-R-C Model).

Exercise 1.

What does it mean to share your hurt feelings with someone?

Helen: It makes you feel better to share hurt feelings.
Patty: It makes you feel like someone cares.

Do you agree that sharing of hurt feelings means telling people you are close to not only about your victories and happiness but also about your pain and defeats?

Helen: I agree. I can do that.
Patty: I agree, but I don't always do that, especially if it's a family problem. I usually don't share that.

Exercise 2.

How do you share your hurt feelings with each other?

Helen: I'm a Cancer, so I take so much and then I go into a depressed shell. I know Patty caught me in a bad mood this week. I couldn't fix the deficiency in the checkbook, and the car broke down, so I went into a bad mood. Even my tone of voice changed.
Patty: I don't always talk about my feelings because I don't think they can help. I just usually get depressed or mad.

Does it make you feel better to share your hurt feelings with the other members of the family?

Helen: If I talk about problems, I can get out of my bad mood and get better.
Patty: Like I just said—I don't usually talk about what hurts me because I don't think they can solve the problem.

Exercise 3.

Taking turns, please share with us something that is hurting you at this moment.

Helen: Having to ask people to do a favor for me, like for a ride to work since my car is being repaired.
Patty: Jimmy [boyfriend] having to work at night.

How did it feel to tell your family about your pains and defeat?

Patty: It's nice to know they care enough to listen, but it won't solve the problem. They can't do anything about it.
Helen: It helps to tell things. It makes me feel better.

How did it feel to hear about the hurt of the members of your family?

Patty: Oh, well, what can I do? Sometimes I feel bad.
Helen: Sometimes I feel really sad. It hurts me to know Patty is sad.

Exercise 4.

We want each of you to go to each member of your family, touch that person, and complete the following: I am glad that you are willing to share your hurt with me. I know——

Helen: I did that last Tuesday night [touches Patty's hand]. I'm here, I want you to understand and do something for me—share with me what your problems are, talk to me more.
Patty: [parroted the first sentence of the statement as she held her mother's hand]

Exercise 5.

How could each of you do a better job of sharing your hurt with the members of your family?

Helen: I can't do it any better than I am. I ask Patty to share her hurt feelings with me.
Patty: I could tell my mother more.

How could this family better use the sharing of hurt to make each member happier and stronger?

Helen: To get closer to one another.
Patty: If I talked more, my mother would be happy.

Enrichers' notes.

Pete was unable to attend this session. He stays with his grandmother until his mother gets home from work; bad weather prevented her driving him to the session.

Patty and her mother always select the same chairs, separated by a table, which provides some physical distance. Although a couch is in the room, only Pete sits there.

This session exemplified Patty's resistance to discussing problems with her mother (typical of adolescents) and her mother's persistence in attempting to communicate with Patty.

Helen said at the beginning of this session that she was in a bad mood because her car had broken down. Her negative mood and frustration were reflected in her responses during this session.

Supervision.

Our supervisor suggested that the last session should generate positive feelings so that SE would end on a happy note. He suggested a lesson on having fun as a family.

Session 6

Exercise 1.

What has been the most fun you have had as a family?

Patty: Going to the beach.
Helen: Our trips up North and out West.
Pete: Swimming in our pool—doing flips and diving off floats.

Exercise 2.

What fun are you planning to have as a family in the future?

Pete: Going to Illinois on an airplane.
Helen: Enjoying the pool and being with my children during my summer vacation. I'll be home for a month.
Patty: Enjoying our pool this summer.

Exercise 3.

How can this family have more fun together? What will you do to have more fun?

Helen: First we need to spend more time together. We could go to a movie.
Pete: Help Patty and Mom from telling me to shut up. I'll tell them to shut up.
Patty: Not be together—go to the beach.

Exercise 4.

What plans can this family make to get more fun out of life?

Helen: Plan a vacation, plan a shopping spree, plan a picnic to the lake.

Pete: Plan a vacation to Myrtle Beach or Maine—I've never been there.
Patty: Plan a vacation to Florida to the beach, maybe St. Augustine.

Exercise 5.

Outline the steps and stages of preparing to have fun together for a week. Where would you go? What would you need to do to get there? What would you do when you get there?

Patty: We would go to the beach. We'd drive to Florida and lie in the sun and go swimming. We'd stay in a motel or hotel.
Pete: We'd go to Miami—we'd mail ourselves to Miami. We'd catch dolphins and drive the dolphins back home in a car filled with water.
Helen: We could fly to Alaska and take sightseeing tours of all Alaska. We'd stay in a motel in most cities, but we'd stay with a friend in Fairbanks.

FEEDBACK

Because of scheduling problems, the feedback was done immediately after Session 6.

We asked the family to express their reaction to and impression of the sessions, specifically noting what they have learned and what they would have liked to have learned.

Patty mentioned that she had learned that other people have family problems and that her family and others care about her problems, even if they can't help with them.

Pete said he had not learned anything and that the sessions had been boring.

Helen said that she had definitely learned that there is a right and a wrong way to do things. She also said that no matter how hard she tried, Patty still had not changed. She also commented that Pete is too young to benefit from SE. Helen believes that she has learned to be more diplomatic in dealing with people, particularly at work, and that she has tried much harder to talk with Patty and Pete. She expressed a desire to learn more about communicating with her children and then added, "although I've learned a lot."

We gave the family the following feedback (strengths listed first, 1–5, followed by weaknesses, 6–8).

1. The family members seem to care a great deal about one another.
2. The members are bright, lively, enjoyable individuals who are willing to improve themselves and learn new ways of interacting and communicating with one another.

3. They are responsible and hardworking, as is exemplified by Patty's good grades at school, Helen's competence at her job, and all the family members' acceptance of household tasks.
4. They are sensitive to and concerned about one another, willing to help one another (e.g., Patty helps Pete with his homework).
5. Pete exhibits much enthusiasm and assertiveness.
6. They exhibit some difficulty in adapting to changing roles (e.g., Patty's becoming a young adult; Helen's losing her role of parenting her first child and instead becoming more of a loving companion and consultant for Patty).
7. All show some difficulty in helping Patty to leave home successfully and become an adult. Patty may be pushing too hard, and her mother may be holding her back.
8. They tend to hurt one another as a means of gaining distance from one another. For instance, Patty becomes depressed and moody so that she will be left alone.

PRE- AND POSTTEST EVALUATION

The Family Adaptability and Cohesion Evaluation Scales (FACES) and the Family Environment Scale (FES) were again administered to the three family members. As on the pretests, Pete did not complete the tests, so we cannot report his scores.

The posttest results of the FACES indicate that Patty perceives the family as having low emotional bonding and high individual autonomy, and as being rigidly organized (family has little ability to alter its power structure, role relationship, and relationship rules in response to stress). These perceptions are consistent with those indicated by the pretest results. Helen's posttest results indicate that she now perceives the family as flexible (able to alter its structure, role relationships, and relationship rules in response to stress) and connected (balanced between individual autonomy and bonding). Thus, before SE, Helen perceived the family as chaotic, capriciously shifting rules, roles, and power structure; following SE, she sees the family as flexible, able to shift roles, structure, and role relationships as needed to adapt to stress and circumstances.

In a comparison of Patty's pre- and posttest FES scores, she now perceives the family as slightly less controlling (rules are less rigid), more cohesive and supportive, allowing more assertiveness and self-decision making, less involved in outside activities, slightly less competitive, and more organized.

Helen sees her family as controlled, slightly low in cohesiveness, and low in participation in outside activities (similar to her pretest scores on the FES). In contrast to her pretest scores, Helen's posttest scores indicate that she perceives the family as somewhat less expressive, more independent, and slightly more achievement-oriented.

An average of family members' FES scores indicate that after SE the family is perceived as more cohesive (members are concerned and committed to the family), more independent (assertive, self-sufficient, making own decisions), having more organized family activities, and more explicit and clear in stating rules and responsibilities.

SUMMARY

Our initial impressions of the family, supported by the FACES and the FES, were that this family is struggling with adjusting to an adolescent's emerging independence (leaving-home issues). As typical of a situation in which the first child is preparing to leave the nest, the mother is attempting to tighten her control while the daughter is rebelling against this control and closeness.

The family as a whole was amiable, courteous, and cooperative. The mother responded quickly, but thoughtfully, to all questions and appeared extremely interested in the sessions. Patty actively participated in all the exercises. Sometimes her answers seemed guarded or cautious, as if she was trying to avoid conflict.

Pete frequently appeared distracted; however, he readily answered questions, proving he was attentive despite his rambunctious behavior.

SE seems to have been beneficial in that it blatantly demonstrated the effect that all members have on a family problem. No one person is seen as responsible. Also, these sessions provided an opportunity not only for positive interactions between Helen and her daughter but also for the expression of feelings in a near-neutral atmosphere. Much can be said for SE as a ritual in which family members not only learn to, but are also given permission to, state their feelings honestly.

10

Parentification
(Psychosomatic)

Carolyn Zweig and Flo P. Dawson

This single-parent black family consists of the mother, Vanessa, aged 31; her 8-year-old daughter, Tanya; 6-year-old son, Grant; and 4-year-old son, Kalyn. Vanessa said that she was looking for something she and her children could do together and that she had some concerns about her relationship with her daughter. Only the mother and the daughter participated in SE (the sons were too young).

Vanessa is a slightly built woman who first appeared rather depressed and overwhelmed, but after we had established rapport, she became much more animated and verbally expressive. She is articulate but tends to use inappropriate verb endings. The daughter, Tanya, is the child of a 2-year marriage that ended in divorce the year Tanya was born. An attractive 8-year-old, Tanya was very friendly; she did not say much, but eye contact and smiles were easily elicited. The two sons are from a second marriage, which lasted 5 years and ended in divorce 3 years ago.

The first husband, who was described as totally inadequate, has no contact with the family. The second husband, a bus driver, lives nearby and visits irregularly. He sends money for child support and occasionally takes the children out with him. Vanessa said that she and her ex-husband are complete opposites: he is high-strung and loses his temper easily; she does not let little things bother her. While married, they frequently argued over "nothing important," and threats of physical abuse were common (he did beat her up a few times). She also described herself as "very spirited." She said that her husband was never home and became involved in extramarital affairs, so they "just drifted apart."

134

After the divorce, the threats of abuse continued, this time in order to get her to take him back. To stop the threats, Vanessa had him put in jail for 9 months, after which he stopped harassing her. She now views him as very supportive and believes that they get along much better now that they are divorced.

Vanessa worked for a while after the divorce but quit because she could not handle work and her family. She is enrolled in the medical technology program at a local university and said that school is much easier than working. She stated that she has attended college off and on for years but never seems to complete what she starts. At one point she went for vocational counseling and was referred to a psychologist who saw her for a while (for what Vanessa described as nervous spells, during which her hands would begin to shake uncontrollably). Since she has been going to school and has "more structure" in her life, she feels much better.

Vanessa is the third of seven children. Two other children, one her age and one 5 years younger, were born from her father's extramarital affair, which lasted for years. Vanessa considers these children part of her family because her mother was aware of the affair and helped to raise them after their natural mother died. Another child was born from another extramarital affair, but he was raised by his mother. She also had twin siblings, one of whom died at birth and the other as a young adult. Vanessa mentioned that she is happy that she does not have twins, for one twin is always strong and one is always weak. One brother is an alcoholic and has recently spent a year in jail for wounding a man during an argument. One sister, who lives nearby, was described as "holier than thou"—she doesn't smoke or drink and is deeply religious. Because of this sister's attitudes, Vanessa does not get along with her. One other brother is also an alcoholic. She described her youngest brother, whom she considers a mama's boy, as quiet, steadfast, and dedicated— like her father. Only he is living in an intact family. The youngest sister, who is living with Vanessa until she decides to divorce her husband, was described as lazy and extremely depressed: "She will lay in bed all day." The other siblings are either divorced, separated, or have children who were born outside marriage.

Vanessa described her mother as highly erratic, uncontrollable, and an alcoholic. She had a gun and would periodically point it toward her husband's head. Vanessa's father did not seem too threatened by this but would take the gun from her and proceed to calm her down. A gentle man, he always made sure they had enough to eat and had shoes to wear. He was rarely home, however, because of his long-standing common-law marriages. Because he saw that the children were cared for and he could be counted on, he is considered the most stable influence in her life. Vanessa grew up frightened of her mother's temper, yet she now visits her regularly. Her mother (now 63 years old) and her father (78 years old) live in a rural area in another part of the state and are "still going strong." This pattern of fragmentation—divorces, separations, children outside marriage—as well as "nervous conditions" and alcoholism, is prominent throughout the extended family.

Vanessa is the only one in her family who has been interested in going to college, for that matter, the only one who has any interest in education. She believes that her family views her as "weird" or "crazy" for going to school. They cannot understand why she wants to "waste her time" and feel that she is just lazy or she would go to work.

Vanessa and her three children live in a somewhat rundown apartment complex. There is no furniture in the living room, not even a light. The small kitchen has a table and chairs where Vanessa entertains her friends, and religious plaques are hung on the walls. When we arrived for the interview, several women friends were visiting. Upstairs are two bedrooms: Vanessa and her sister share one; the children share the other. Vanessa baby-sits for neighbors' children to make some extra money. It was brought out that Tanya is often the one who ends up watching the children and is also the one who has to clean up the mess. Vanessa seemed somewhat embarrassed by the lack of furniture in the living room, saying that the children would destroy it anyway and that they have room to run around.

One of the issues in this family is what Vanessa described as her irritability with Tanya. She is often irritated with her and behaves differently with her than with the boys. She believes that Tanya's lack of cooperation and responsibility in doing the chores assigned to her and taking care of herself have contributed to the difficulty. For example, Tanya often has to be reminded to make her bed and clean up her room, and she balks at having to do the dishes and take out the garbage. Vanessa said with exasperation that she has to get up and make breakfast because Tanya will not do it for herself.

Another issue, according to Vanessa, is that she herself has a great deal of trouble managing and structuring her time. She cannot keep a schedule and has great difficulty even getting up and getting out in the morning. (When I called her one morning to arrange an appointment, Vanessa was awakened by the phone and realized that the children were not yet ready for school.) Vanessa mentioned that Tanya feigns headaches when she doesn't want to do something (Vanessa believes that Tanya got that idea from Vanessa herself, who has migraines).

PRETESTS

Vanessa and Tanya were both very cooperative and attentive, and seemed to enjoy the testing. Vanessa was particularly helpful in clarifying some of the tasks for Tanya and making sure she understood what was expected of her. We noted that Tanya tends to be rather concrete in her thinking and needs concrete and structured explanations. In this respect, her mother was very much attuned to her needs and provided structure so that Tanya readily understood what to do. Tanya seemed to enjoy being able to score her tests and was surprisingly quick and efficient in copying numbers from the cards to the scoring sheets. Her mother did not rush her or in any way give more than the very minimum structure and guidance when needed. She seemed to trust Tanya's ability to follow through on her own.

Two interaction tests were given first. Each family member was asked to divide a total of $2.95 between them. Vanessa gave herself $1.20 and gave Tanya $1.75. Tanya also gave herself more ($1.60) than she gave her mother ($1.35). Vanessa said that when she has extra money she likes to give Tanya some so that she can have a good time; she added that she wishes she could do this more often. Tanya looked as if she was trying to divide the number of coins evenly, as if she did not know the value of each coin.

Vanessa and Tanya were then asked to agree on a restaurant they would like to go to. Without negotiation, interaction, or conflict resolution, they quickly agreed on Red Lobster. So that we could understand better their methods of problem solving, we asked them to decide on a vacation they could take together. Tanya immediately thought of Disney World but couldn't remember its name. Her mother helped her identify it. When Tanya said her father had promised to take her, Vanessa laughed and responded, "Well, you go with him; I'll stay home." This trip was apparently an unrealistic expectation on Tanya's part, yet Vanessa allowed Tanya to keep her dream. From these interaction tasks, it appeared to us that Vanessa wants to give to Tanya and that Tanya's wants come first when the family plans an activity. Both Tanya and Vanessa seemed pleased with the decisions.

The Bell-Fagan Family Symbols Test (B-F) helped capture the underlying feelings and emotions in the family. The areas in which the feelings of one family member showed extreme deviation from the feelings of the other are the afraid-anxious and the angry categories. Vanessa was seen as much more afraid-anxious and angry than Tanya. On the other feeling states—sad, loving, quiet, and happy—mother's and daughter's scores are very similar and tend to fall near the norm. The results of the test led to the tentative hypothesis that Vanessa and Tanya have a highly reactive relationship, in which sameness (I am like you) or oppositeness (I am the opposite of you) is the interpersonal style.

On the Description of Feelings in the Family (DFF), Vanessa and Tanya saw each other differently. This test represents the intensity of four feeling states: mad, sad, smug, and distracting. Vanessa saw the family as fairly close to the norm yet within the mad-distracting quadrant; she perceived very little sadness in the family. Tanya, on the other hand, perceived a significant amount of sadness in the family as well as a relative amount of distracting behavior. Again, this test points out the oppositeness of family members. The family sees the members as falling within the distracting-sad quadrant. The younger daughter column (YD) is particularly represented as being more distracting than anyone else, which corroborates our observations of Tanya. Feelings of smugness were not readily alluded to. Tanya's behavior suggests that her inappropriate giggling may be a cover-up for underlying feelings of sadness.

The Family Situations Picture Series (FSPS) has four categories related to Satir's typology of family dysfunctions: blaming, placating, distracting, and computing. This test often points to the identified patient. On this test, the daughter was seen as significantly different from the mother. Tanya saw the family in the blaming-computing quadrant. This may be how she perceives her mother's relationship with her; and in this respect, she may consider herself the victim of blaming and computing tactics. If she could release some of her suppressed anger, perhaps her apparent sadness or depression would be lifted. Her mother fell within the norms on this test, indicating that she perceives all four behaviors existing equally within the family. The family as seen by the members fell in either the distracting-placating or the blaming-computing quadrant. No significant deviations are noted except that, again, the picture representing mother and the one representing youngest daughter were placed in opposing positions, mother in the blaming-computing quadrant and daughter in the distracting-placating quadrant. This supports other test data that mother and daughter seem to be reactive to one another.

In the Animal Concepts Picture Series (ACPS), which might be considered a more projective test, mother and daughter are closely aligned. Their sameness is remarkable, demonstrating a lack of differentiation. Their ideal perceptions of themselves and each other are very close to their actual perceptions, possibly indicating their feelings of being fixed, unable to anticipate or create change in their lives. Symbolic interpretations can be made from the particular animals picked by each member for self and other. Vanessa's ambivalence is suggested by her choices of horse and leopard for her actual sortings and squirrel and alligator for her ideal. Perhaps she wants to be gentle but at the same time needs to be aggressive in order to survive. Vanessa's choices for her daughter— rabbit and sheep for actual and bird and squirrel for ideal—point to her perception of Tanya as rather passive, harmless, and vulnerable. Note that none of these animals are domesticated or accessible to human contact. Possibly, then, Vanessa has difficulty showing warmth and love to Tanya. The daughter perceives herself similarly, picking the chipmunk and the rabbit. Tanya's choices of a kangaroo and a bird for her mother may indicate that she perceives her mother as motherly yet somewhat unavailable and fleeting.

Vanessa and Tanya were asked to draw pictures of the family doing something together. Vanessa drew a picture of her three children playing in their bedroom—each involved in a separate activity. She left herself out of the picture, saying "I'm in the next room." Tanya, too, drew a picture in which both her mother and her siblings were excluded. She drew herself in the kitchen getting ready to eat breakfast and said that her mother and her brothers were still upstairs. Tanya's drawing indicates some need for structure and support in her life (her drawing was close to the edge of the paper). Projectively, she seems to be looking for some nurturing from her mother. The most striking observation is that each omitted the other from the drawing, which seems to indicate a sense of loss or frustration in not being able to meet each other's needs.

Vanessa had mentioned several issues that had to do with her vague description of her "irritability" and "abruptness" when interacting with Tanya. We did not observe their supposedly conflictual relationship during the interview and pretests. In fact, we were rather impressed with Vanessa's ability to relate to Tanya positively and directly. It was also apparent that Vanessa may have some concerns about Tanya's ability (Vanessa had also signed up to have Tanya tested). Unsure of her real concerns and expectations, we decided that we needed to further clarify the issues. We discussed this objective with her, and she readily agreed. We decided to start with Solving Problems Together, a lesson from the Eclectic Program. This lesson should help us look at Vanessa and Tanya's interactions and their relationship.

SUMMARY OF SESSIONS

Session 1

We found Vanessa and Tanya waiting (they had arrived early by bus), and they seemed excited and eager to begin. Vanessa left an empty chair between her and Tanya, allowing one of us to sit between them. Vanessa obviously enjoyed answering the few remaining questions about her family (for a genogram). We expressed our pleasure at working with families who are as interested in SE as they were, for it shows that they care about each other. Vanessa had signed up for many extra hours of experiments at school, and she was returning to Georgia State for each session after meeting Tanya at home.

Vanessa and Tanya were given 5 minutes to think of the main problems in their family. Throughout the exercise, words such as *major* and *negotiate*, were changed to more familiar terms, such as *worst* and *come to an agreement*, respectively.

Then we asked which three problems are most troublesome to the family. Although Vanessa said that Tanya's coming in by sundown was their main point of disagreement, she quickly relinquished her problem in favor of Tanya's, which was the fighting, noise, and mess made by the boys that Vanessa keeps during the day. Tanya complained that she has to clean up their mess. (Other problems mentioned were Vanessa's inability to get up in the morning, to follow a schedule, and to get Tanya to do the dishes.)

When we asked them to write down all possible solutions to one of the problems listed, they chose the agreed-upon problem of the boys who stay at their apartment during the day. Of all the solutions suggested, they decided that separating the boys when they become too noisy and Vanessa's helping Tanya to clean up were the most appropriate.

Vanessa and Tanya chose washing dishes as the second problem to solve through negotiating, but when the time came to swap roles, Tanya was embarrassed and reluctant. After some coercion, she did role-play her mother's part (although she covered her face with her hands). Vanessa did such a good job in Tanya's role of making excuses that Tanya realized that her mother does have difficulty when she asks Tanya to wash the dishes. Tanya responded that her stomachaches and headaches (possibly learned from her mother, who also has headaches) are frequently the reasons she is not always available for household duties. Vanessa remarked that Tanya is outside almost constantly from the time she arrives home from school and that she often asks Tanya to do the dishes just to keep her inside for a while. Tanya agreed to be more cooperative about washing dishes, and her mother agreed to stay nearby while she washes them.

Their homework assignment was to consider which other problems they would like to work on in the remaining sessions.

Enrichers' notes.

As Vanessa revealed her expectations for Tanya (cleaning her room, preparing her breakfast, cleaning up after the boys, dishwashing, and taking out the trash), we questioned whether an 8-year-old could shoulder this much responsibility. We had one view of Tanya as a parentified child but one who is struggling with psychosomatic stomachaches and headaches and remaining outside to shift some of the responsibility back to her mother. We could also see the vicious cycle in which Vanessa seeks closeness, physical or emotional, through involving Tanya inside the apartment while Tanya seeks escape from work by remaining outside. Tanya's desire to play outside seems appropriate to her age.

Vanessa does seem to be sending a double message. On one hand, she wants to be closer to Tanya, to have her help in the house (where Vanessa functions inadequately); on the other hand, she pushes Tanya away by overloading her with responsibilities. Another problem is that, although Vanessa seeks closeness, she tends to intellectualize when she deals with Tanya. These conflicting messages may contribute to Tanya's incongruent behavior—distracting facial expressions, giggling, and hiding her face when interacting with her mother and other adults. This same conflict may be responsible for Vanessa's complaint that she feels irritable when she deals with Tanya; that is, she knows what she wants but goes about it in the wrong way, which results in an "irritating," incongruent response from Tanya. Vanessa remarked that she feels confused when Tanya responds incongruently: "I don't know if I have said something funny."

One other factor may be relevant in their relationship. Tanya is the child of Vanessa's first husband, who left abruptly for another woman and did not offer to help them financially. All these first impressions considered, we decided to offer them three options for the lesson to be covered in the second session: Seeing the Good, Caring, and Sharing of Hurt Feelings. Vanessa quickly responded that she would like to do the one on sharing hurt feelings.

Supervision.

In supervision we talked about the special needs of this family and the fact that some modification of the programs might be necessary.

Session 2

The Sharing of Hurt Feelings deals with hurt feelings in the family and what it means to be able to share such feelings. Asked to share a hurt feeling, Vanessa said that she was feeling good and that she really didn't have any hurt feelings, adding that we had caught her on a good day. This reaction was perhaps typical of a more action-oriented, impulsive person—what one feels at the moment is all that is taken into account. We asked her to attempt the exercise anyway and think of a time when she had felt hurt and to tell Tanya about it. Again, Vanessa was unable to express her feelings directly. She related an incident in which she was not paid on time for baby-sitting a neighbor's child. She asked Tanya what she should do about it—that is, should she stop taking care of the children or just trust that eventually she will get paid? The expression of anger or hurt that was underlying her frustration was not dealt with or even acknowledged. Tanya simply shrugged her shoulders in response to her mother's question—taking on her distracting posture. In an attempt to involve Tanya more directly and also to encourage Vanessa's awareness of her underlying feelings, we asked Tanya to imagine how she would feel if she were her mother. Again, Tanya was unable to respond at this level.

It was then Tanya's turn to express hurt feelings or something that was bothering her. She couldn't think of anything, so Vanessa suggested that she talk about the time she had come into the house crying because another child had picked on her. Vanessa did not address the apparent underlying feelings of hurt and sadness; instead, she addressed her belief that Tanya shouldn't allow others to take advantage of her and should fight back and defend herself. That way, the other children won't pick on her anymore. We tried in the remaining exercises to elicit underlying feelings, but at no time were feelings expressed directly. Instead, Vanessa and Tanya described behavior or incidents.

Enrichers' notes.

Feeling states seem particularly difficult for this family to talk about. This is an action-oriented family, with very little reflective ability for understanding the feelings beneath the action. For example, crying is the way of dealing with hurt, and fighting is the way of dealing with anger and hurt. Tanya was easily distracted and fidgety. She seemed uncomfortable in this session, often hiding behind inappropriate giggling. We continued to be impressed, however, with Vanessa's method of explaining more difficult directions so that Tanya could understand. There was practically no eye contact between mother and child, although Tanya was attentive when her mother spoke to her.

Supervision.

It was felt that this family lacks a model for talking about feeling states. Therefore, rather than trying to facilitate this ability, which might continue to frustrate the family (and us), we decided to switch to a more behavioral and less abstract program, Single-Parent Families.

Session 3

First we asked Vanessa and Tanya what they thought of last week's lesson. Vanessa said that she realized that she never actually thinks of "feelings" and instead is aware only of what she is doing. In this respect, the preceding lesson seemed to have some meaning for her in that her awareness of herself was somewhat expanded. She said that "a lot of people tell me, 'You look like you've lost your best friend.' I'm probably just meditating when they say this." Tanya said that last week was OK. She was not particularly responsive one way or the other. Because of her constant, unexpressive smile, it is difficult to know what she is feeling or thinking.

Asked what it means to this family to be a single-parent family, Vanessa responded that being a single parent is really no different from when she was married. By this she meant that her job with the children is no different because her husband was never home anyway. However, she did say that her responsibility is different in that she knew that in case of an emergency she had someone else to turn to; now she can count only on herself.

In the second exercise, we asked about some of the special problems this family has had. Vanessa initially had trouble thinking of any special problems; in fact, she said there are fewer problems now than when she was married. She did elaborate on how difficult it had been to find an apartment—a place where there is some grass and space for the children to play and a place that she can afford.

In Exercise 3, we asked about the disadvantages of being a one-parent family. She mentioned that she had started to work but found the situation almost impossible because she had no time to spend with the children. She subsequently quit her job and found that she became much more relaxed and patient with the children. She would like to spend more time doing things with her children, but she is often just too tired. Getting the dishes washed uses up just about all the energy she has.

The last exercise dealt with feelings about the divorce. We asked Vanessa and Tanya whether they have ever blamed themselves or each other. Vanessa answered that she didn't blame "him" or herself for what happened. She said that when they were married, everyone was just going their separate ways—they were not together anyway. "Nothing was free-flowing or relaxed." She described her ex-husband as very anxious and quick-tempered. She described herself as just the opposite: "I don't get upset over little things like he did. We just drifted apart. It would bug him that I could just tune things out and he couldn't." Vanessa looked tearful at this time but did not touch on that; instead, she laughed lightly and said, "I told him, 'don't bug me.' "

We, as well as Vanessa, tried throughout the lesson to get Tanya to respond and participate. Vanessa pointed out that Tanya probably doesn't remember too much because she was so young at the time of this marriage. However, Tanya did recall an incident when her parents had a big fight in the kitchen. "Remember," she said, "when you threw that pot of peas at him." Vanessa then talked about how her husband would threaten her and how she would pull his bluff until someone exploded. While relating these incidents, Vanessa and Tanya laughed and made joking remarks. To stop her ex-husband's harassment and threats to get her to come back to him, Vanessa arranged to have him put in jail. She was pleased with this solution because after he was released, he didn't bother her anymore. Vanessa concluded by saying that after two divorces she won't get herself into those situations anymore—"Yet it's hard to find a good man."

Enrichers' notes.

This family seems to have many more advantages than disadvantages in being a single-parent family. The most significant change seems to be that there is no longer the threat of physical abuse between the spouses. The mother is more relaxed and is perhaps able to relate to her children more adequately. The sameness-oppositeness personality characteristics, or extreme reactivity in the family (as described by L'Abate, 1986b), were highlighted in this lesson. Without real awareness, Vanessa described repetitive reactionary sequences that occurred. Action-oriented behavior and impulsivity are strongly evident in the way family members have dealt with one another. This is consistent with our impression that the short-circuiting of emotions and the lack of reflective ability lead to impulsive behavior in this family. Tanya seemed generally uninterested and unimpressed with the content of this lesson. Vanessa impressed us with her apparent ability to accept as almost normal what seems to be a high level of conflict and instability. Although the content of what she said suggests that she is objective and removed from the past, her tearfulness points to underlying feelings of sadness and pain.

Supervision.

The supervisor pointed out how this family fits the A-R-C model of interpersonal styles, specifically the reactive modality (L'Abate, 1986b). Vanessa expressed the spouses' extreme reactivity in describing their behavior and their oppositeness. The question was raised about the appropriateness of SE for economically and culturally deprived and depressed Black families. Because we have modified the lessons to meet the family's level of understanding, we believe that SE may very well be helpful. Our general impression at this time was that the program was going well, so we decided to continue it. To get Tanya more involved in the lessons, our supervisor suggested that we could interact with her more effectively by allowing her to tell us what to write on the blackboard or have her do so herself.

Session 4

Vanessa said that she felt good about the preceding lesson because it had reminded her of what to avoid the next time around. She appeared rather tired and somewhat depressed, saying that she had had a hectic weekend and had got no sleep. Tanya, too, seemed very tired, hardly able to hold her head up. We thanked them for making a special effort to come to the session.

We combined two lessons, which gave us somewhat more freedom in choosing appropriate exercises. The first exercise focused on some ways of relating that do or do not work. We gave several examples of ways that usually do not work: forcing, coaxing, withholding, criticizing, provoking. Vanessa responded that she often uses force to get Tanya to do what she wants her to do and that force works for her. She said, "I scream to get her to do something. She might get defiant, but I just ignore it and then she'll go ahead and do it."

The second exercise is based on the assumption that force and similar methods do not work, and the family is asked to demonstrate how they do not work. Because this family did not respond as expected, we omitted the second exercise.

In the third exercise, we asked them to take each other's place and to demonstrate each other's way of relating. In this family, Vanessa (as Tanya) should act defiant in response to Tanya's (as Vanessa) screaming. They tried, without much success. Vanessa was willing to role-play, but Tanya acted embarrassed and self-conscious. We told Tanya that we would close our eyes so that we could not watch her. She then proceeded to role-play her mother but giggled throughout.

We then switched to a lesson on relationships outside the family. This lesson ran more smoothly, and Vanessa and Tanya were much more interested in the exercises. In the first exercise, we asked them to talk about how they work with their relatives and how they can get more from their relatives. Vanessa first talked about her ex-husband and the financial support that he gives her. In this respect, he is very reliable. He also takes the children with him occasionally, giving her a welcomed free day. Next she talked about her sister, who is temporarily living with her. She said that she cannot count on her sister for anything—not even to change a light bulb. Her sister is just there; she doesn't do anything unless asked. She doesn't cook or clean. On the other hand, she doesn't bother anyone either, so she doesn't make Vanessa "real angry." Vanessa's description of her sister suggests that she is a depressed, withdrawn, and apathetic person. Vanessa said that "she is not in tune with her surroundings." Another sister who lives nearby comes to visit once in a while now that her phone has been disconnected. On these occasions, her sister talks about her own problems, wanting Vanessa to hear her out. Clearly, Vanessa's family cannot offer her much support. Her sisters, too, are single parents and overwhelmed with their own problems. As Vanessa described them and her relationship with her extended family, they do not seem to have the capacity or the resources to be of any help. Vanessa appears to be the most competent one in her family and the central switchboard when any crisis arises. Vanessa did recall some old friends that she could contact again and possibly reestablish their friendship. She seemed hopeful about this idea.

In the next exercise, we dealt with the family's relationship with neighbors and how it could be better. Tanya's friendships were brought up. Many children in the neighborhood return home from school to an empty house; the children then call Tanya and ask her to come over and play. Vanessa does not allow this because there would be no supervision. Vanessa mentioned she has not met many neighbors because they work. She knows the children but not the parents. She also mentioned that one child often asks Tanya to go to special places (an ice-skating rink or the movies) but never follows through, leaving Tanya upset and disappointed. Tanya admitted that she always believes this friend and hasn't learned that she often makes up "stories." This problem was left unresolved, as there seemed to be no adequate solution.

Next, we asked about the family's relationship with the school and whether this could be improved. Vanessa considers the school OK. She does not have much contact with the school, but she believes that a lot of time is wasted and that little learning takes place. Tanya talked a little about some of the things she does in school and said she likes to read. We saw no apparent problems with their relationship to the school. Before they moved to their current neighborhood, Vanessa felt that the school had not prepared Tanya in the basics—reading, writing, and arithmetic. Tanya talked about her best friend and some of the things they do together. For homework, they were asked to think of new ways of behaving, within or outside the family, that would be helpful to them.

Enrichers' notes.

This session, particularly the lesson on outside relationships, went well; the family was quite responsive to the exercises. We believe that Vanessa has come to a better understanding of her role in her extended family, that she is always giving of herself and never receiving anything in return. She also was able to vent some of her frustrations with her sister, who doesn't take any responsibility for household chores. We believe that this session hit upon some important issues in this family and allowed some thoughtful observation and possible reframing. Vanessa was able to come up with some ideas about how she could extend her friendship network and call upon some people from her past who could be helpful to her.

Supervision.

We noted that this family has few available resources and that depression, lack of energy, and lack of consistency and stability contribute significantly to their difficulties. Their strengths are considerable, however, and we believe that SE is helping them use and focus those strengths more effectively. Vanessa and Tanya seem to be doing well with this program, so our supervisor agreed that we should continue it.

Session 5

We began by asking Vanessa and Tanya about the homework assignment. Had they been able to think of new ways of behaving within or outside the family that would be helpful to them? Vanessa replied that she already allows her sisters to stay with her whenever they are having trouble but that she has to let them alone when they are too inconsiderate. She said it does not work to be assertive with her sister about helping around the house, so she just asks her to leave when she (Vanessa) has had enough. Vanessa also stays on good terms with her second ex-husband, who helps support them.

What about *new* ways? Vanessa and Tanya had decided to refuse to keep the boys when Vanessa does not receive payment from their mother. We agreed and congratulated Vanessa for being able to set limits when she feels she is being taken advantage of. Although Vanessa said that she had no other problems to work on at this time, we told her that we had chosen today's lesson because of issues she had mentioned at the beginning of SE.

In the first exercise, we asked them to choose a situation "in which you did not agree with some other family member but for some reason said nothing about it; then tell the family member about it." Vanessa chose an instance in which Tanya was still at a friend's house after dark. She told Tanya, "You remember what I told you about that—you are not allowed out after six o'clock."

In the second exercise, we asked them to describe their feelings about the situation, without blaming or criticizing each other. Vanessa responded that she was mad and worried because Tanya is too young to be out alone after dark. She also stated that it felt OK to express her feelings to Tanya but that she was "flustrated" because it "didn't do any good."

We then asked Vanessa to express her frustrated feeling by beginning with a positive statement. Vanessa practiced a positive statement by telling Tanya that she is old enough to be trusted and that she knows Tanya can accept the responsibility for getting in on time. She then summarized by differentiating between blaming and saying something positive to Tanya. Making a positive statement was a new idea to her, and she seemed to like it.

In the next exercise, we instructed Vanessa and Tanya to ask themselves, "What am I frustrated or angry about?" and to express it directly.

Tanya practiced expressing a frustrating situation to Vanessa, using a positive statement first. When she had difficulty, her mother demonstrated it again, and Tanya then responded, "I like you, Mother, but you need to help me clean up the boys' mess." That was pretty good for Tanya.

We concluded by making a list of what each of them does for the other. We asked whether they realized how much each does for the other and whether they let the other person know how much those things are appreciated. As we talked, Tanya drew a valentine on the chalkboard; inside were the words, "I have the best mother in the world." Vanessa again began to intellectualize, saying, "Well, look at that—I didn't know you felt *that* way." After some coercion, Vanessa finally gave Tanya a big hug and a kiss on the head. Tanya had no trouble responding to this and smiled from ear to ear.

Enrichers' notes.

We have observed that Vanessa lacks warmth and has difficulty expressing positive feelings to Tanya. Vanessa illustrated again in this session that she deals more successfully with relatives and outsiders than she does with Tanya. She is more interested in improving that situation through parental and verbal skills than through expressing her feelings, which fits her need to intellectualize. We had hoped that this lesson would offer a balance in feedback to Tanya and thus contribute to improving her self-image. We were not disappointed. Who could have asked for a better ending?

Supervision.

Because of our concern that Vanessa's expectations for Tanya are too high for her young age and that they contribute to her incongruent behavior, we suggested an improvised parentified-child program for the last session. It would include correlating the distribution of responsibility and authority with the parent. This suggestion fit right into the context of our most recent session, in which we listed the things that Vanessa and Tanya do for each other, the list illustrating more or less how responsibility is divided within the family.

Session 6

We began our improvised parentified-child program by looking again at the list from the preceding session. Vanessa and Tanya agreed that Vanessa has more responsibility and is the boss in the family. We congratulated them for being aware that these two jobs go hand in hand

and told them that many families are not aware of this. At this point, it became clear that Tanya's list of jobs around the house is longer because her jobs are rotated and that she rarely performs all of them on any one day. We discussed a regular weekly schedule that they could negotiate each week. Vanessa agreed that this would cut down on her nagging and provide more structure for her.

When they agreed that Tanya gets to play more than Vanessa, we asked Vanessa whether she ever gets to "play." She talked about her prospects for dates, who usually are only interested in "bedding down," and decided she might contact a nice man who had asked her out recently. She also enjoys the women friends who visit her. We asked about the church, but she said she had rejected getting involved in church "busy work" but occasionally visits different churches.

We closed the session by asking the following: "As there are only two people to share the responsibility and only one person can be the boss, how can you be more supportive of each other in your responsibilities?" Tanya answered that she would like working together rather than alone; Vanessa said that she would like to spend more time with Tanya. We ended by telling them that, although the boss does and should have more responsibility, we liked the way they are able to share the responsibility in the family because it indicates that they care about each other.

Enrichers' notes.

Although we still see Tanya as a parentified child, we are encouraged that all the jobs she listed are not totally her responsibility. This point had not been made before, although we had talked about the jobs at length. No matter how the responsibility is distributed, we are glad that *they* see Vanessa as carrying more responsibility as well as being the boss in the family. By giving them a chance to look at the list together, this lesson clarified Vanessa's need to perform a parent's share of responsibility in the family. It also allowed them to differentiate the household responsibilities on the list from the other things they do, letting them know that each cares about the other.

POSTTESTS AND EVALUATION

The posttest session went smoothly because Vanessa and Tanya were familiar with the cards and the procedure. Tanya's distracting behavior was considerably less than in the pretest session. Her behavior was more appropriate, and she worked swiftly for her age, occasionally talking to herself: "Oh, I know what I'm looking for" and "I remember this."

Vanessa, however, maintained her constant slight smile and her slow speech and movement.

The mother's concern had been her irritability with the daughter. On the Bell-Fagan Family Symbols (B-F), she had predictably scored high on afraid-anxious and on anger on the pretest. Her other scores are aligned with the center of the graph, parallel but lower than the daughter's scores. The daughter had scored very low on afraid-anxious and angry, which coincides with her early clinical picture of feeling loving toward her mother. The pretest scores indicate the same-opposite aspects of their relationship (as described in the preevaluation), as each took the "re-actor's" position toward the other.

On the posttest, these widely divergent scores on afraid-anxious and angry are dramatically closer together, toward the center of the graph; the other scores (sad, loving, quiet, and hostile) are further apart. More specifically, the mother's loving score dropped on the graph, and she became significantly quieter; the daughter's sadness and hostility decreased somewhat. Among the most dramatic changes on posttest is the closing of the mother's and daughter's widely divergent afraid-anxious and angry scores. These results are supported by our clinical observations: as Vanessa practiced positive feedback and negotiation with Tanya, she felt more successful, and her anger and anxiety decreased. We hope that she can continue to move from being a "reactor" toward the position of a "conductor" in their relationship, taking charge of family problems and pushing them to resolution.

Other dramatic changes are Vanessa's drop on the loving scale and rise on the quiet scale, changes that do not coincide with her behavior in the clinical setting. She maintained her caring and concern for Tanya throughout the sessions and was able to move from "showing caring through doing" to some physical demonstration of affection. She was consistently verbal and less quiet than Tanya. Although there is no clinical evidence for this, we wonder whether some outside event influenced her choice of symbols, causing her to make unique associations in her choice of cards. Only an extended clinical relationship could follow up the significance of this dramatic shift on the loving and the quiet scales.

Tanya's sadness and hostility decreased somewhat, which is supported by our observation of her. Her sadness, apparent on the DFF, seemed to be hidden by and somewhat related to her distracting behavior. Her behavior became more appropriate as the sessions proceeded, possibly indicating that she had less reason to be sad and inappropriate as she was able to negotiate herself out of the parentified-child "trap" and to feel more hopeful. Her interpersonal style had been consistently action-oriented (accompanied by a decrease in emotional and rational components). This style was evident in her distracting and in her passive-aggressive style of not cooperating with Vanessa. Her decrease in these behaviors probably coincided with her decrease in hostility on the posttest.

Vanessa had seen the family slightly in the mad-distracting quadrant on the Description of Feelings in the Family (DFF) pretest but saw them more clearly in the sad-distracting quadrant on the posttest. These results are supported by the B-F and by our clinical impressions: Tanya's distracting behavior decreased (as she was encouraged throughout the session to negotiate her responsibilities and her needs with Vanessa); Vanessa's anger decreased (as she became more successful in dealing with Tanya), and her sadness increased. The changes from mad to sad (mother) and from distracting to smug (daughter) illustrate the reactivity and oppositeness still active in their relationship. Vanessa's increase on the distracting continuum might be seen as a denial tactic and logically would accompany her simultaneous shift toward sadness. Vanessa's lack of affect (sad, depressed) and her slight smile and intellectualizing (denial, distracting) were characteristic of her throughout the sessions. In summary, apparent positive changes on the DFF posttest are the mother's decreased anger and the daughter's decreased distracting behavior, which make negotiation more feasible.

Vanessa and Tanya saw most of the family member figures in the sad-distracting quadrant on the pre- and the posttest, which coincides with the daughter's continued sadness and the mother's increased distracting on the member-sees-family section and seems to be an accurate representation of this family.

On the Family Situations Picture Series (FSPS), the mother's view of the family has changed from a computing but almost neutral position on the pretest by moving slightly into the distracting-placating quadrant; the daughter's view of the family remains in the blaming-computing quadrant, similar to the pretest but somewhat closer to the blaming end of the continuum.

As mentioned earlier, we were impressed with Vanessa's verbal skills and her ability to intellectualize about her background and her family members. These characteristics of her interpersonal style are supported somewhat by her position on the computing axis on the pretest; the clinical changes that we saw supported even more her new position on the posttest (she became less angry and more placating as she and Tanya worked together on specific problems). Her increase in distracting on the posttest coincides with the increase in distractibility on the DFF posttest, both of which might be explained by the simultaneous increase in sadness (which she denies by distracting). Tanya continued to view the family in the blaming-computing quadrant, which possibly indicates that she agrees with us about her mother's characteristic computing behavior. Her continued view of the family as blaming may indicate that the changes we observed in Vanessa in the sessions did not carry over in practice.

A second contributor to the continued blaming status may have been Tanya's occasional insistence on choosing cards because she remembered them from her pretest choices (in spite of our continued reminders that the choices were to be chosen based on the present). The sameness-oppositeness in this family's reactive stance may also have contributed to producing an opposite (increased blaming) reaction in the daughter's view of the family as the mother switched from the computing view to a more opposite (distracting-placating) view of the family.

Most of the family member figures were seen collectively in the blaming-computing quadrant on the posttest, which coincides with the daughter's view of the family and shows little change from pretest. The young daughter figure, still seen slightly in the distracting-placating quadrant by the family, again is supported by the mother's view of the family and shows no change from pretest. These positions are consistent with our clinical observations of the family's positions on the E-R-A model of differentiation (L'Abate, 1986b): the mother is higher on rational (computing) and lower on emotional and action aspects; the daughter is higher on action (distracting) and lower on emotional and rational aspects.

The results of the Animal Concepts Picture Series (ACPS) show almost no change on the 10 scales from pretest to posttest. Vanessa and Tanya are closely aligned, both in their actual and in their ideal graphs before and after SE. Very slight differences between them were observed on the actual small-big scale and the ideal slow-fast scale on the pretest. On the posttest, the daughter, being more flexible, moved closer to the mother by becoming bigger and slower. This alignment represents the lack of differentiation between mother and daughter, which coincides with our clinical impression of Vanessa. (She talked about her high expectations for and irritability with Tanya, indicating that she would like Tanya to be more like herself.) According to the A-R-C model, Vanessa and Tanya are reactive in their interpersonal styles, reacting with sameness and oppositeness to each other. This relationship is apparent in the B-F and also in the DFF.

Vanessa chose for herself a bird and an octopus (actual) and an ox and an elephant (ideal) on the posttest, indicating that she sees herself as fragile but sometimes able to escape (fly) from her problems and that she would like to feel much stronger, possibly to get what she wants by overcoming opposition. Tanya chose for herself a kangaroo and a rabbit (actual) and a cat and a horse (ideal), indicating that she feels— as she wrote on the blackboard—that Vanessa is a good mother and takes care of her (kangaroo) but that she is difficult to catch, touch, or hold; Tanya would like to "cuddle" and would like her mother to sit around and be accessible for "petting" and for "riding" more often. On the posttest, Tanya chose a cat and a bird (actual) and a rabbit and a bird (ideal), possibly indicating that she, too, feels fragile but needs cuddling and would like to need it less (rabbit) but does not mind being fragile (bird) because she can escape, as she frequently does by soaring about the neighborhood with her friends until after dark. The mother chose for her a lamb and a kitten (actual) and a lepoard and a horse (ideal), possibly indicating that she correctly perceives Tanya's nature—harmless, dependent and emotionally available—but would like her to be stronger (horse) and more cunning (leopard) as she begins to go out into the world. This impression is supported clinically by Vanessa's concern that Tanya may be in danger when she is out alone and by Vanessa's lecturing and coercion as she attempts to prepare and strengthen the developing Tanya. Although very small changes are apparent on the ACPS posttest, the graphs reveal the lack of differentiation in this family, and the animals selected coincide with characteristics shown on the other tests as well as with our own clinical impressions.

FEEDBACK CONFERENCE

When asked how she felt about SE and whether she had learned anything, Vanessa replied that SE is different from what she had expected (she had been seen previously by a psychologist) but that it has been helpful to her and Tanya. Tanya said that she liked SE but that it lasted too long. She liked writing on the blackboard. Vanessa was especially glad that it had given them something that they could do together, which was her main reason for coming. We told her that many parents are reluctant to ask for help or information and that her coming and staying throughout the program proves that she is a good parent and that she cares about her family, especially that she and Tanya care about each other. We also told them that we were impressed with the amount of responsibility they have and how well they manage it.

We noted that their support system is lacking and that, if for no other reason, they may want to consider continuing in SE, although other options are (a) to stop at this point but continue to work on the skills they have practiced in the sessions, (b) to stop at this point and forget the entire experience (do nothing), or (c) to enter family therapy. Vanessa thanked us and said that she would like them to work on their own until she feels the need to call again.

11

A Family Under Stress

Marsha Weiss

The Baker family consists of three members: Kathy, aged 33, and her two children, Christy, aged 16, and Clark, aged 4.

BACKGROUND

Kathy, Christy, and Clark live in a two-bedroom apartment in a close-in suburb. Kathy and her husband divorced 3 years ago after 13 years of marriage. Two years ago, Kathy and the children left a medium-sized city in a neighboring state, where her ex-husband and her extended family reside. Her husband has since remarried (his girlfriend of 11 years) and has a 6-month-old son.

Kathy works full-time and is a full-time undergraduate student. Having "grown up with nothing," she considers it crucial for her to get a college degree in order to feel secure financially. She is petite, attractive, energetic, verbal, and hardworking.

Christy is a high school junior and until she was recently fired for refusing to work overtime at a fast-food restaurant, she worked 12 hours a week after school. She is attractive, athletic-looking, very quiet, and expresses only negative feelings about herself, her family, and life in general. She has no friends and does not date; her primary pleasure is derived from playing tennis. She asserts that she would like to get out of school as soon as possible and work as a model or a tennis pro or in any other job at which she could make a lot of money. She does not want to go to college, which is extremely upsetting to her mother.

Kathy's ex-husband, Carl, is 6 years older than Kathy. She met him when she was 14 years old. Her parents were extremely religious and strict, and Carl represented fun and excitement. He took her to the movies, dancing, and offered all kinds of other forbidden fruits. Her parents refused to allow her to marry. Finally, they allowed her to marry at age 16 because she was pregnant. She quit school and went to work. She attended night school after Christy's birth and got her high school diploma, then attended business school, where she learned skills that allowed her to get a better job. Kathy's mother cared for Christy when Kathy was at school or working.

Carl was rarely home. He spent a great deal of time gambling and dating another woman. (Kathy became aware of this relationship years later.) Kathy's main social relationship was with Christy. She says, "We kinda grew up together."

A year after Kathy and Carl were married, Kathy's sister-in-law shot Kathy's brother and killed him. Claiming self-defense, she was not arrested. Kathy's mother, unable to cope with the death of her son, attempted suicide by shooting herself in the head. She survived but was crippled. During her mother's hospitalization, Kathy found out that Carl was having an affair and made him leave their home.

Soon after, she began an affair with one of her teachers from high school, who was then working in social services and who helped her with some of the financial arrangements for her mother's hospitalization. She found the relationship very satisfying but broke it off because it upset Christy.

Carl kept begging her for a reconciliation, and after 6 months they began living together again and had a large home built in the country. Kathy soon became pregnant with Clark. Things were good for a while, but then Carl returned to his former habits. Kathy decided to just accept their lifestyle and found her satisfaction in her relationship with Christy.

Two years later, a woman called Carl; Christy told Kathy to pick up the extension. After hearing Carl tell the woman how much he loved her, Kathy decided to get a divorce.

The family eats breakfast and dinner together except for the evenings when Kathy has classes. Kathy helps Clark get ready in the morning while Christy prepares breakfast. Christy and Kathy share the housework and child care. Christy often baby-sits, although recently Kathy has begun employing a neighbor to baby-sit.

Kathy has been dating Brian, a man she met at work, and spends some of her evenings with him. Other evenings are spent studying.

The Bakers rarely go out as a family.

Christy, Kathy, and Clark visit their hometown monthly. Kathy spends the time with her family while the children visit their father.

The family has few friends and no relatives nearby. Brian is really their only outside contact. They don't attend church or participate in any social groups.

The family is highly stressed. Kathy's schedule puts extraordinary demands on Christy as well as Kathy. In addition, this family has had to adapt to a large reduction in their financial status, forcing Christy into a part-time job in addition to her schoolwork and family responsibilities.

Brian's entry into the family has also been quite stressful. Christy resents his involvement with Kathy: he has replaced her as Kathy's primary companion and confidante, in addition to further reducing the time that she and Kathy spend together.

Kathy is unsure of her feelings for Brian and whether or not she wants to marry him. He himself is not sure that he wants to get married because he wants children (Kathy cannot have another child).

Finally, Christy will be having cosmetic surgery on her knee in a few months, which will make it impossible for her to play tennis, her primary satisfaction. The family appears to be having a great deal of trouble coping with these stresses.

PRETEST RESULTS

The family completed the pretests in businesslike fashion. Although Christy worked very quickly, she did not appear to be rushing through it.

On the Bell-Fagan Family Symbols (B-F), most of Kathy's and Christy's scores hover near the midrange. Christy, however, ranks very high on the afraid-anxious scale; Kathy is lowest on this dimension. Their scores come together at loving, slightly above the midline. On the dimension of sadness, Christy is considerably higher than Kathy. Christy's happiness score is her lowest, but it is within the midrange. Her rating and Kathy's rating are close on this dimension.

On the Description of Feelings in the Family (DFF), Christy and her mother placed the family on opposite ends of the distracting-smug continuum. Christy rated the family as slightly sad and highly smug; Kathy rated the family as somewhat sad and extremely distracting.

Their joint scores (how the family sees the members) suggest that Christy is slightly sad and that Kathy is both sad and distracting.

On the Family Situations Picture Series (FSPS), both rated the family as slightly blaming, but then their ratings diverged. Christy rated the family as somewhat distracting; Kathy rated the family as highly distracting.

In how the family sees each member, both mother and daughter were rated as blaming, but the mother is also seen as somewhat distracting. The young son was rated as extremely distracting and somewhat placating.

Overall, there is little difference between the family's actual and ideal choices on the Animal Concepts Picture Series (ACPS). There are differences, however, on a few specific dimensions. Kathy and Christy would like Christy to be stronger and less bad, Kathy to be more pleasant.

For the actual choices, Christy chose a clam and a pig to represent herself; Kathy rated her as a bull and a snail (actual). Their choices reflect great polarizations. Kathy chose a panda and a growling tiger to represent herself; Christy chose a cow and a puppy to represent Kathy.

For the ideal choices, Christy chose a doe and a butterfly to represent herself, and Kathy chose for her a butterfly and a puppy. Both wish for the same kind of Christy. Kathy chose a deer and the seal to represent her ideal self; Christy chose a doe and a puppy for the ideal Kathy.

The generational boundaries in this family are very poor (Minuchin, 1974). Christy, coparent and "spouse" for many years, is now being replaced by Brian as "spouse" but still is required to perform many parenting functions. She appears quite depressed and angry. She has socialized very little with peers and has not yet been able to make any real friends here.

Christy blames everything on the lack of money. She believes that if she had more money everything would be wonderful. Kathy said that she used to be very materialistic but has found that even though she had many material goods during her marriage, she was unhappy. She wishes Christy could understand that "money can't make you happy."

Kathy appears to want to return to a more traditional parent-child relationship with Christy, yet she needs Christy to earn money and help with the housework and child care. Christy would like the privileges and freedom of childhood (being taken care of) yet does not want to relinquish her peer relationship with her mother.

The test results suggest that Kathy and Christy have opposite perceptions of the family. For example, the DFF results indicate that Kathy sees the family as highly distracting; Christy sees it as extremely smug. These perceptions are supported by clinical observation. Kathy sees her responsibilities to her children as difficult and confusing; Christy sees her mother as not really caring about her.

The generational boundaries of this family must be strengthened. Christy must be encouraged to develop more peer relationships; Kathy must take over more of the parental responsibilities. In addition, both must be able to increase their awareness of each other's wants, desires, and problems. The Single-Parent Families Program was chosen because it deals with these particular issues.

SUMMARY OF SESSIONS

The family agreed to try the Single-Parent Families Program, even though they believed that they had resolved all the problems related to the divorce. Because my clinical impressions and the pretest results indicate that poor intergenerational boundaries are a serious problem in this family, I am using the program despite the family's comments.

Session 1

Exercise 1 in the lesson called The Meaning of Single Parenthood asks the family to discuss the ways in which the divorce has changed the family. Both Kathy and Christy asserted that the divorce has had two main effects on the family: they have less money, and they moved to a new city. Both feel that the family relationships are largely unchanged because Carl was never around much before the divorce anyway.

Exercise 2 asks the family to describe the special problems that they have had as a family. Kathy stressed being overwhelmed because she doesn't have enough time to support the family financially, go to school, and take care of Christy and Clark. Christy argued that the only real problem is not having enough money.

Exercise 3 asks for the disadvantages of being a one-parent family. Both reiterated their responses to Exercise 2.

Exercise 4 asks the family to talk about times when the family members blamed themselves or each other for the divorce. Both denied any blame. Asked how they have dealt with feelings of anger, guilt, hurt, Christy denied these feelings, saying that only the lack of money upsets her and that she doesn't like her mother's boyfriend, Brian. Kathy said that she feels guilty about not having enough time for her children. She also expressed her confusion about her relationship with Brian and whether she wants to get married. She is not sure whether she really loves Brian or whether she just wants the security of a permanent relationship.

I asked the family to think about all the feelings they experience during the coming week.

Enricher's notes.

Christy is a very unhappy girl who is in the role of parentified child. Kathy wants her to get out more on her own, yet she needs Christy to help her take care of Clark. Kathy expresses some guilt at putting Christy in this position and at not having enough time to be a proper mother. Christy thinks of money as the answer to all of her problems, making money the "villain." We hope that SE will help clarify some of the family relationships and problems.

Supervision.

My supervisor noted how much can be learned about a family through SE. He agreed with my conception of the mother-daughter enmeshment.

Session 2

The second lesson deals with how the family members relate to each other. In Exercise 1, we discussed ineffective ways of relating; then I asked the family whether or not they use each of the following ways of relating: (a) coaxing; (b) forcing; (c) judging, criticizing, or putting down; (d) denying responsibility for actions; (e) masking feelings; (f) provoking; and (g) defiance. I also asked how well each works for them. Kathy said that none of these methods work but that she occasionally lapses into criticizing the children. She said that this works with Clark but that she has found that doing things for Christy is the best way to get Christy to do things for her. Christy denied using any of these methods, but Kathy argued that Christy constantly masks her feelings and is often defiant.

In Exercise 2, the family was asked to demonstrate how they get into any of these patterns. Christy refused, saying that none of the patterns fit. Exercise 3 asks the family members to exchange places, using the other's style. Christy (as Kathy) criticized Kathy (as Christy); Kathy (as Christy) refused to comment and went to her room. Christy said that was all and that she couldn't go any further with the role-play. Exercise 4 asks the family to decide what may work for them as a family and to remember that compromise may be necessary. Christy said that nothing can be done, that nothing will ever change, and that everything is hopeless.

Enricher's notes.

Christy appears to be getting very upset during these sessions. She withdraws, consistently expresses hopelessness, and looks as if she is about to cry. SE is, we believe, bringing to the surface a lot of hidden feelings and problems that Christy is unable to cope with. I believe she also fears change. Kathy has said that when she attempts to deal with problems, Christy withdraws (she does the same thing during our sessions).

Supervision.

My supervisor said that it is impossible to continue with this program as long as Christy refuses to participate fully. He recommended the Confronting Change Program, which will be used next week. I am to reassure Christy, telling her I'm sorry it's upsetting, but that it's OK to talk about upsetting things. I will also point out that things usually get worse before they get better.

Session 3

We had to skip a week because Christy was visiting her father. She and Kathy had argued the week after our last session, so Christy went to spend the weekend with her father. In Lesson 1, Why Change?, I asked about the meaning of change. Kathy said that change could either improve or hurt their relationship. Christy said she didn't think things could change anyway and that she didn't really want to talk about it.

Exercise 2 asks how each person thinks change will take place. Christy said that she didn't think any changes would take place. Kathy asked Christy why she thought that, but Christy shrugged and wouldn't answer. Kathy said that she thought they both needed to change. "I don't think that just one of us can do it." Christy agreed, then said to Kathy sarcastically, "You go first."

Kathy reported that during the past week Christy had told her that she wanted them to spend more time together. Brian was out of town and Kathy had extra time. Christy found this unsatisfactory; she said she wanted things to be like they were before Kathy became involved with Brian.

Exercise 3 asks the family member who appears to be resisting change whether she or he enjoys having the power to defeat the family. Christy repeatedly stated that she has no power to change anything.

Exercise 4 tells the family that each person has the choice to stay the same, thus defeating themselves and others, or to change. Finally, I asked, "If you really want to change, how does each of you want to change?" Christy could think of no productive changes; she just said, "I'm just tired of living like this. Then she added, "Just to be a better person, to be easier to get along with. There's no use in me trying to change if nobody else is going to change. They say they're going to change but they don't." She and Kathy then discussed an incident in which Christy had talked about moving back to their hometown and Brian had promised her a car if she would stay here. She stayed but so far has not gotten the car (Kathy says that she has not as yet saved enough money). Christy brought up this incident as proof that things will never change. Kathy expressed her concern and her desire to find a way to spend more time with Christy.

Exercise 5 asks why anyone should want to change. Kathy said that pride is a major factor: she has always strived to be better and to live up to her expectations; she wants to improve herself. Christy said she wants to change "because something's got to be better than this."

Exercise 6 reads, "If change is to take place, it is to satisfy ourselves. How can we satisfy ourselves and others in the family?" Kathy, answering first, said, "I think when we get along, I feel at peace. I don't like to be in a turmoil." Christy said she didn't know and expressed annoyance because "all the questions seem to be asking the same thing."

Enricher's notes.

Christy is very angry and depressed and refuses to participate fully. She denies blocking change; rather, she asserts that change is impossible. Kathy wants to improve her relationship with Christy, yet Christy is put into a number of binds. For instance, if she makes more friends and Kathy becomes less concerned about her well-being, it is likely that they will spend even less time together. Christy would like to be happier, but she doesn't want to do anything that might further change their special relationship or reduce the amount of time they spend together.

Supervision.

The supervisor suggested not continuing SE if Christy is unwilling to participate. He suggested that I recommend family therapy and that I give them three sources for therapy.

Session 4

Kathy and Christy, after having been given a week to consider whether or not to continue SE, decided not to continue. Kathy asked whether this had ever happened before and was reassured when told that SE was developed for families without too many problems and that many families with more difficult problems switch to therapy. The family then completed the posttests.

POSTTEST RESULTS

Once again the family worked quickly.

On the Bell-Fagan Family Symbols (B-F), Kathy scored very high on sad and loving; Christy's most extreme score is her low happiness score. Christy ranked very high on the afraid-anxious scale.

On the Description of Feelings in the Family (DFF), Christy and her mother rated the family as being far apart in how they handle feelings in the family: Kathy sees the family as distracting; Christy views the family as smug and sad. In terms of how the family sees each member, the categories mother, young son, and teenaged daughter (the actual configuration of the family) were rated as distracting; the younger daughter picture was rated as smug.

On the Family Situations Picture Series (FSPS), both Christy and Kathy saw the family as distracting, though Christy considered them also placating and Kathy rated them somewhat on the blaming side of the continuum. In terms of how the family sees each member, the mother is blaming and computing, the older daughter is distracting and blaming, and the young son is both distracting and placating.

Overall, there are few differences between the real and ideal pictures chosen on the Animal Concepts Picture Series (ACPS), although Kathy and Christy are somewhat more differentiated in the ideal. For the actual choices, Christy chose a clam and a pig to represent herself; Kathy chose a seal and a moose for Christy. For ideal choices, Christy chose a deer and a butterfly for herself; Kathy chose a puppy and a butterfly for Christy. For the actual Kathy, Christy chose a leopard and a kitten; Kathy chose a bull and a lion. For the ideal Kathy, Christy chose a lamb and a kangaroo; Kathy chose a kitten and a deer.

Although no real changes are shown in the posttest, some small changes are evident. Christy is more anxious and afraid. She is less smug and sees the family as less distracting.

TERMINATION

After they completed the posttests, I told Kathy and Christy that I believed they, along with Brian and Clark, should strongly consider family therapy. I said that Christy seems extremely depressed and that Kathy seems unhappy with how things are going in the family. Kathy said that no one else wants to go to therapy and asked what should she do. I suggested that if she is the only one in her family who wants to be happier, she should go to therapy on her own. I then said that obviously Christy has a good reason for keeping things the way they are.

Supervision.

The supervisor supported my comments to the family and approved the termination of SE.

12

A Psychosomatic Family

Margaret Taylor

Milton Rawls, aged 49, came to the Family Study Center on referral from a local mental health center, having requested help with individual and family problems. He was having difficulty controlling his own children and the children in the ninth grade class he teaches. Mr. Rawls reported that he had had a heart attack recently and that he had stopped teaching in the final 3 weeks of the school year on his physician's recommendation. As a result, though he had tenure at the school, he had been put on probation and was trying to decide whether or not to return to teaching in the fall.

Mr. Rawls has a master's degree in education. His language skills are excellent. Gray-haired and considerably overweight, Mr. Rawls breathes heavily, with a wheeze (he smokes unfiltered cigarettes). He is divorced and has five children, four of whom still live at home.

Three of the children came in with Mr. Rawls. Mandy, aged 17, has completed high school and is living at home and working full-time. An attractive young woman, she has long brown hair, dresses neatly and attractively, and has a rather mature air about her.

Dan, aged 16, has dropped out of high school, having completed the tenth grade. He lives at home and does odd jobs for friends and relatives. Dan dresses casually in jeans and T-shirts, has moderately long hair, and a youthful appearance.

Randy, aged 13, a student in junior high, is quite physically active. He has shoulder-length blond hair and wears sport clothes and a baseball cap. He is quite talkative and at times is distracting (playing with the footstools and drumming his hands on the table).

An older son, Jimmy, aged 22, is married and is in the navy, currently stationed in Virginia. A daughter, Dorrie, aged 14, usually lives with Mr. Rawls but is spending the summer with Jimmy and his wife.

INTERVIEW

The family reports that the children's mother is living with a man to whom she is not married; her lack of room for the children is the reason for Mr. Rawls's temporary custody of the children (by voluntary arrangement).

Mr. Rawls reported that he and his wife were divorced after 14 years of marriage, for reasons he says he is still trying to understand. That marriage was his first, and he has never remarried. After the divorce, the parents twice took the issue of custody of the children to court. The children have generally lived with their mother, who has moved them back and forth between Dallas, Texas, and Atlanta every 6 months for approximately 2 years. While in Texas, the children were frequently cared for by their mother's relatives, particularly an aunt, and they report having experienced a confusing sequence of parental figures with differing ideas of right and wrong. As a result, the children report that they have always had a close relationship among themselves, serving one another as best friend and confidante in the absence of other stable relationships. The family agreed with my observation that the children seem in some ways to function as an independent family unit, apart from their parents.

This is the second time the children have lived with their father. The first time followed their having been evicted from an apartment, with their mother, leaving her with no place to take the children.

Mr. Rawls stated that long ago he and his ex-wife agreed not to discuss their marital problems with the children and that he has held to that agreement.

The Rawls family seemed warm and affectionate with each other. Mandy seemed to play a wife-mother role in the family, particularly in relation to Randy (giving and withholding chewing gum and instructing Randy to sit down and be quiet). Throughout the interview, the family laughed easily and spoke affectionately about and to each other. Some gentle teasing occurred, particularly between Dan and Randy. Whenever a member of the family used a word Randy did not understand, he asked its meaning and was cheerfully given a definition, without overtones of put-down. The three children expressed concern about their father's school problems and several times indicated that they consider the students' behavior "ridiculous." Although they said they were unclear about the reasons for their participation in treatment, they expressed a willingness to participate in whatever way is indicated.

Mr. Rawls expressed concern about Dan's dropping out of school. When Dan said he plans to return to school, Mr. Rawls responded skeptically and repeated his assertion that school is important and that Dan should not have dropped out.

We described SE, and the family enthusiastically agreed to participate. We explained the possibility of further and perhaps different forms of treatment following SE and they seemed pleased. Both Dan and Mandy expressed an interest in individual treatment, and we explained the value of working with the family as a whole. An appointment was set for the next session, and contracts were signed.

Enrichers' notes.

This family's evidence of caring for each other seems a significant family strength. The openness with which members spoke of their history and problems suggests a capacity to profit from intervention. The father seems to receive the least support in the family in that he is somewhat isolated from the unity of the children's system. His school problems and heart condition, coupled with the way he describes his inability to cope at home and at school as well as his obesity and heavy smoking, suggest some cause for concern over the possibility of covert suicidal behaviors or at least some submission to ill health. A program designed to provide opportunity for mutual family support and to help them define and more comfortably fulfill their roles in the family seems indicated. We suspect that Mandy functions generally as a mother in the family and that some clarification of roles and work with related feelings would be helpful.

Supervision.

We agree that the Rawlses are a clinical family and that intervention more extensive than one SE program may be indicated. We are concerned about Mr. Rawls's health and the possible self-destructive overtones in his behavior and affect. We feel comfortable working with the family and believe that they can profit from SE.

SUMMARY OF SESSIONS

Session 1

Mr. Rawls, Mandy, and Randy arrived on time but said that Dan had gone to the airport to see a friend off and would be late. Mr. Rawls said he doubted that Dan would come at all. We began pretests (described in the Pre- and Posttest Evaluation section). Dan arrived about 20 minutes late and was also tested.

The family members were cooperative during the testing and generally worked steadily and quietly. Randy asked what some of the cards were supposed to represent and was told he could decide what they mean to him. Mr. Rawls said several times that he had no idea why he had chosen certain cards or assigned them in certain ways (he did not specify which cards he was referring to). Mandy asked why all the people in the cards looked so unhappy. Dan thumbed through the "feelings" deck (Description of Feelings in the Family, DDF) and handed it back to me saying, "All of them."

The family laughed easily and seemed to enjoy the testing. Randy took an interest in the cards that were chosen for him on the Animal Concepts Picture Series (ACPS) and moved around the room trying to see which cards had been chosen. Mandy hid her choices from him, and a friendly tussle resulted.

Enrichers' notes.

At this point, we were concerned primarily with test scoring and plans. Our impressions of the family remained unchanged.

Supervision.

Our supervisor suggested that the father's health condition may be worthy of consideration in a program on death and dying. He suggested that we mention this possibility to the family and further suggested that we find out more about any medication the father may be taking. We discussed other programs, and our supervisor suggested the Helpfulness Program as an alternative.

Session 2

We described three programs (Transactional, Death and Dying, and Single-Parent Families) and asked the family to choose one. All expressed surprise at the suggestion of a death and dying program, but then Dan said, "Well, Dad's had a heart attack." Mr. Rawls expressed a preference for the Transactional Program, saying he did not want to go back over the issues surrounding his divorce or deal with issues of separation and death. Mandy said she thought dealing with difficult issues might be the most important for them. Randy said he thought we should use Death and Dying because "that would make us say how much we care about each other." After we and the family assured Randy that the family's caring for each other could be expressed in other programs, all agreed on the Transactional Program.

We began immediately with the first exercise in the first lesson: What does it mean to be a man or woman in this family? Mr. Rawls focused first on being a father and was encouraged to speak of other aspects of being a man. He complained that the two were hard to separate but said that being a man has to do with taking care of the family financially, wanting peace and quiet at home, and being responsible. He said he had never expected to be the man in a family without a wife and that this is hard for him. Randy said being a man means earning the money for the family and taking care of the family by buying what they need. Mandy echoed similar ideas but emphasized the need for a man and woman to share household responsibilities as a partnership, especially if the wife works. She also made the only mention of emotional roles, saying that a man should love and appreciate his family, especially his wife. Dan returned to the notion of financial support and need for peace and quiet at home.

In general discussion, the family achieved some consensus that the man's role is that of provider and the woman's that of homemaker, that each must support the other, and that some role flexibility is necessary if, for example, the wife works.

This discussion was extremely lengthy; all family members had difficulty deciding what to say and how to say it. Randy stopped the discussion frequently to ask what a word meant. Mr. Rawls frequently strayed from the point to complain about the "chaos" of the family's lifestyle. He also frequently directed the discussion, particularly with questions. When Dan said that one part of a man's role is to discipline the children, Mr. Rawls pursued the point (asking Dan how a man should do so) until we returned the focus to the lesson.

Because the first exercise had taken so long, we did not do every exercise in the lesson. In response to the question "What does it mean to be old or young in your family?" Dan described being young in terms of freedom to pursue interests and adventure. Mandy said she feels both old and young, at which Mr. Rawls expressed surprise. Mandy distinguished old and young primarily in terms of responsibility, saying that with age comes more responsibility for self. Randy said that being young is more fun. Mr. Rawls claimed ignorance of what it is to be young because times have changed since he was young. Encouraged to describe himself as a youth, he described himself as independent and hardworking but said he dated a number of girls and enjoyed himself. He contrasted his behavior and values as a youth with those of his own children, particularly in his dedication as a student. Frequently he spoke disparagingly of "kids today."

Asked "What happens in this family if something happens to one of you?" the family described various behaviors: blaming each other, supporting each other, and drawing closer as a family. They cited the occasion when the oldest son left home to join the military: they had pretended he wasn't leaving, then drew closer to each other when he left.

As the session ended, the family members decided they should talk with each other more often, and Mandy suggested they make an effort to have meals together.

Enrichers' notes.

The family seems to have difficulty staying on the point. More explicit directions requiring far more limited verbal exchange would probably help.

Mr. Rawls is very controlling of the discussion and requires restraint, particularly from launching into tirades about his children's disorderly lifestyle. Randy seems to be the most open about expressing warm feelings in the family.

The family might benefit from less intellectual and more nonverbal interactions. We agree that a change of program is in order and decide on the Helpfulness Program. We agree that Mr. Rawls will need strong control. We are concerned about his physical condition as a possible manifestation of suicidal feelings and about the fact that he is not in individual therapy (as we had been told) but in assertiveness training (according to his report). We have noted his emphasis on his own pride and his complaint that his marriage and his family are failures on his part.

Supervision.

We reported to our supervisor our concerns about Mr. Rawls's physical condition and our plans to change to another program. He emphasized the importance of dealing with Mr. Rawls's health, with all the family present, not Mr. Rawls alone. He concurred with our choice of the Helpfulness Program.

Session 3

Beginning with the first lesson, Seeing the Good, we followed the plan for the lesson closely. The family arrived at a definition of seeing the good in each other that is close to the definition in the manual. Asked the ways that family members show that they see the good in each other, Mr. Rawls said he doesn't show it much at all but concentrates more on the bad. Mandy and Dan agreed that they show that they see the good in each other by complimenting each other. The family generally agreed, however, that they don't see the good in each other and show it, often enough.

Asked to say something good about each member of the family, Dan focused on skills or abilities, telling his father that he is a good teacher,

Randy that he plays drums well, and Mandy that she does a good job keeping the house. Mandy, too, told her father that he is a good teacher, Randy that she likes his enthusiasm and energy, and Dan that she admires his musical ability. Mr. Rawls expressed amazement that Dan had liked his teaching and that Mandy had ever seen him teach at all. Mandy reminded him she had once been his student aide.

Mr. Rawls complimented Mandy on her taking responsibility around the house, Dan on his intelligence, and Randy on his energy. Randy, when it was his turn, became very fidgety and made several attempts to begin, stopping each time to ask again what he was to do and to think. The family urged him to go ahead, saying, "C'mon, Randy, you can think of something." After much hesitation and laughter, Randy told Mandy he likes her bracelet, his father that he likes his watch, and Dan that he likes the way he plays guitar.

When we asked how they felt about the exercise, Randy said, "Didn't bother me," and began moving around the room, making noise and complaining about the cigarette smoke. The others agreed that they had felt good while doing the exercise. Mandy said she found it somewhat embarrassing. Mandy and Mr. Rawls tried unsuccessfully to get Randy to rejoin the group. I then asked Randy to join in or to refrain from making comments, as he had been doing across the room. Randy then quieted down.

The family was asked to think of a situation with both good and bad aspects. Dan offered an example—his giving Randy a hard time by teasing him and fighting with him, saying that it's hard on Randy but that it's good for him to learn toughness.

For homework we encouraged the family to practice seeing the good in each other.

Enrichers' notes.

This program seems more appropriate and affords more control, especially of Mr. Rawls's tendency to focus on his complaints about the others' behavior.

We were both surprised that Randy, who had expressed a desire for the family to let each other know that they care about each other, had had such difficulty and had seemed so anxious in this session. We also noted Mr. Rawls's ineffectiveness in controlling Randy. Perhaps Randy is adept at getting strokes from the rest of the family but, at the same time, is very threatened by the prospect of showing warmth and caring verbally. In a sense, Randy exemplifies the family's dialectic of closeness and distance—they show warmth in the sessions but do not eat meals together at home.

Session 4

For this session, we used the lesson called Caring. The family discussed what it means to care for someone and agreed on synonyms, such as *protection, concern, looking out for, taking care of.* They also agreed that they show caring for each other by physical affection, helping each other, and doing things together.

In the next exercise, each family member stood up and said, "I am a person, and I am important," then said to each other member in turn, "You are a person, and you are important, and I care about you." Afterward, everyone but Mr. Rawls said it felt good to say and hear that they care for each other; Randy, who had done this exercise with no trouble, agreed. Mr. Rawls said he had felt silly and that they already know he cares for them. We then discussed the value of hearing directly that someone cares, even though we may already know it.

Asked to show their caring for each family member nonverbally, Mandy and Randy jumped up, Mandy hugged Dan (who remained seated), and Randy hugged his father (who also remained seated). Then Mandy and Randy hugged each other, and Dan extended his hand to his father. Mr. Rawls laughed and said, "Oh good, that's OK," and shook Dan's hand. Then Mandy hugged Mr. Rawls, and Randy shook Dan's hand. Mr. Rawls said he was glad that Dan had just shook his hand—that it was okay for Randy to hug him because "Randy's just a little fella" but that Dan is a man and "I'm not attracted to men." He laughed and seemed quite nervous. Dan did not respond to his father's comments. The others said that it had felt good to show affection.

Asked how they might better show their caring for each other, all agreed they could help each other more. Dan said he could play drums with Randy more often. Mandy suggested that all of them could help with keeping the house. A family discussion of the housekeeping problem followed. Mr. Rawls accused the children and their friends of keeping the house a mess. Mandy said they have begun controlling their friends' behavior more. Randy said that their friends would be neater if they themselves were neater. Mr. Rawls disagreed, saying their friends just have bad manners. After more discussion, the family began to focus on how they might improve.

All agreed to work together to clean out a junk room. Mr. Rawls suggested reinstating a schedule of shared assignments, which had failed in the past when Jimmy (the oldest son) had refused to do his job. The family agreed to try the system again, and Mr. Rawls said, "I feel like I can get this family organized!" Dan became somewhat withdrawn during the talk of assigning jobs; when questioned, he acknowledged his belief that he would be assigned only the jobs he hates. More negotiation followed, with all members participating energetically. We stopped the session, assigning the continuation of their discussion and plans for homework.

Enrichers' notes.

Mr. Rawls showed more self-confidence than he had in other sessions. The family worked well together toward a solution of a family problem, and Randy seemed less anxious than last week. Mr. Rawls seems to have great difficulty with physical affection with other men. Mandy seems to give and receive affection most freely.

We are pleased to see the family working so energetically to solve a problem as a way of showing caring, but we are apprehensive that Mr. Rawls may be set up for another sense of failure. This program seems very appropriate for this family.

Session 5

First, we asked how the housecleaning project had been going. The family reported, all talking at once, that they had been getting rid of junk, had borrowed a truck to haul old furniture away, and that they expected to get the regular clean-up schedule going once the junk is out of the way.

We congratulated them on their good work and went on to the next lesson, Sharing of Hurt. The family equated sharing hurt with sharing problems; we suggested that the two are different. Mr. Rawls, who saw no difference, said he doesn't share his problems with the children because he doesn't want to "burden" them and because they couldn't solve his problems anyway. He also said that Dan and Jimmy don't bring their problems to him any more now that they're older. All agreed that Randy and Mandy freely share their hurt feelings.

When asked to share a hurt with the family, Dan said he is angry and frustrated that he has several broken guitar strings. Randy said he is frustrated because his drumsticks are cracked. Mr. Rawls said he is upset that Dan won't stop banging on the piano, and Mandy said she is upset about the school district they live in and wants to move out for Randy's and Dan's sakes. Asked how they felt about sharing their hurts, Dan and Mr. Rawls said it had given them some important information that explained each other's irritating behavior (concerning Dan's piano playing).

More discussion on the family's not sharing of hurt followed. Mr. Rawls said that he can't share his hurt with his mother because she always offers pat solutions to his problems. We pointed out the contradiction between that feeling about his mother and his using the children's inability to offer solutions as a reason for not sharing his problems with them. Mr. Rawls remained adamant about not sharing his hurt with the kids. He refused to participate in the next exercise (sharing a hurt with the family) until he had heard the others do it and was satisfied that he did not have to agree to share his hurt with them. The others, with much physical affection, invited each other to share their hurt as directed in the exercise.

For homework, the family was asked to listen to and discuss the song "He Ain't Heavy, He's My Brother" (Randy had sat on Mandy's lap during the last exercise; when Mr. Rawls told Randy to get down, Mandy said, "He isn't heavy").

Enrichers' notes.

Mr. Rawls seems to hold onto his parental role at the expense of interpersonal closeness with his children, none of whom are too young to offer him support. He continues to evidence a tendency to separate himself from them and to focus on the differences between himself and them.

The family clean-up project seems very successful, and their energy level for the project remains high.

Session 6

We continued the program with the lesson called Forgiveness. Asked what forgiveness means, the family agreed on the synonym *overlook*. They had difficulty distinguishing between forgiving each other's imperfections and abandoning their expectations that the other do better. Mr. Rawls focused on his responsibility for teaching his children and seemed to consider forgiveness the antithesis of teaching.

The family agreed that they tend to take forgiveness for granted rather than ask for it or offer it explicitly.

Because of the length of the discussion and because the family seemed to be having such difficulty understanding the concept of forgiveness, we moved on to the fourth exercise, having the family practice verbalizing their appreciation of each other's humanness and inability to be perfect. Each family member performed the task, but Randy had the most difficulty remembering what he was to say and understanding the task.

We then led a general discussion of the difference between forgiveness and retaining some expectations about specific behaviors. The family agreed that the "big things" requiring forgiveness are "big" because they involve moral or social values, and they arrived at an understanding that they can forgive each other for not living up to each other's values yet continue to uphold those values. Mr. Rawls frequently lapsed into lengthy discussion of Dan's inconsiderate behavior and had to be controlled repeatedly. Mandy said there isn't much she needs to forgive others for, but that there are many things for which she hopes she is forgiven. We discussed the importance of asking for forgiveness as well as letting others know when they hurt us.

Enrichers' notes.

This session did not go as well as the others. The family seems polarized into two ways of dealing with faults: The children accept and forgive without holding grudges; Mr. Rawls blames and equates forgiveness with total permissiveness. Because the family does not seem ready for this lesson, we will stay with the concept and try to help the family understand how forgiveness has a part in a family.

We will continue with the Helpfulness Program and note the family's difficulty with forgiveness as a focus of possible future work with them.

Session 7

For today's lesson, the last in this series, we skipped to the lesson called Enjoyment. We hoped that this might lead the family to interact with each other in enjoyment as well as problems.

Asked what enjoyment means to the family, Dan and Mandy emphasized the importance of everyone's doing the same thing, having fun together. All agreed that enjoyment is having a good time.

When asked how they enjoy themselves individually, each reported an activity. Mr. Rawls watches TV, Mandy dates, Randy plays sports and drums, and Dan plays guitar. Asked how they enjoy themselves together, they agreed that they enjoy going out to eat together, which they often do after our sessions. Mr. Rawls commented that they really cannot afford to eat out but said he tries not to bring that up. He also said that they used to enjoy doing things as a family when the kids were younger but that now they are never home, all going separate ways.

The family was then instructed to go out of the room and spend 10 minutes doing something they enjoy together. They readily agreed and went out. When they returned, we asked what they had done, and they reported they had gone out on the plaza and walked around. Mr. Rawls said that Randy had run ahead of them, and Randy laughingly told of walking on the rim of the fountain. Mr. Rawls said he felt that they had not really been together: Mandy and Dan had walked together, he had been somewhat apart, and Randy had been far away. Dan and

Mandy disagreed and said that all of them had been together. Randy said he had not felt apart from the others.

The family was then asked how they might enjoy themselves more. Dan suggested that they listen to music together, but Mr. Rawls stated that they enjoy different things and that, for example, he can't tolerate the music Dan likes, that it is "repugnant" to him. Mandy suggested that they go out to dinner together. Dan suggested travel and camping.

For their homework, we encouraged them to plan some enjoyable activity together and do it.

Enrichers' notes.

Mr. Rawls's negativism continues, as does his focus on the past. The family seemed to have different perceptions of the enjoyment exercise. Mr. Rawls seemed to feel excluded; Dan, Mandy, and Randy seemed satisfied with the attained degree of togetherness. Mr. Rawls, ironically, expressed the most vehement complaints about distance in the family but seems to separate himself from the others the most.

Session 8

This session was devoted to the posttests. The family cooperated well and worked quietly. Mr. Rawls balked at the Animal Concepts Picture Series (ACPS) and complained that none of his children seem like animals to him. However, he did complete the test.

Supervision.

We reported that we have scheduled the feedback conference and that we plan to point out as family strengths the family's openness to receive help and their willingness to work on their problems. Our supervisor suggested that we congratulate them on their loyalty to each other in defining themselves in terms of their similarities and differences and that we mention the concomitant risk that they may not be uniquely themselves.

CLINICAL ASSESSMENT

Mr. Rawls is clearly the identified patient in this family. It is he who sought help and who presents problems at work and at home. In addition, he tends to separate himself from the children in a number of ways: he points out differences between his own values and interests and those of his children; he declines to share his problems or hurt feelings in an attempt not to "burden" them; he complains frequently and vehemently about the children's friends, their irresponsibility, and their activities. Mr. Rawls's posture is generally a blaming one, and in discussions he frequently engages in lengthy tirades about his dissatisfaction with the children. He says that it seems to him that the family lifestyle is "chaos" and that the children are "going straight to hell." He speaks frequently about "the way things used to be when the children were younger," saying that in the past the children did what he said, were respectful, and that the family had fun together.

In spite of his strong negativism about the family, Mr. Rawls devotes his time and attention almost completely to his children. He has no outside activities other than his work and stays at home to be available to the children and to take care of Randy. He seems to have little life of his own.

Mr. Rawls describes himself as a failure in his marriage, his child rearing, and his work. He describes a past in which he was a successful teacher and had what he believed was a good marriage and wonderful children. He says he cannot understand what has happened, how he failed. In this, as in other areas, Mr. Rawls is quite digital in his thinking. Issues for him are clearly right or wrong, acceptable or unacceptable, successes or failures. He frequently says "always," "never," "should," "should not," and describes things and events as "repugnant," "intolerable," and "horrible." Rarely does he moderate his position or permit differences not to be opposites.

Dan is the focus of many of Mr. Rawls's complaints. Although the children were carefully named so that their names would sound similar (Jimmy, Mandy, Danny, Dorrie, and Randy), Dan insists, over his father's objections, on being called Dan, and his doing so seems to represent a level of differentiation that is unacceptable to Mr. Rawls. Dan's having dropped out of school seems to be a primary focus of Mr. Rawls's blaming (the similarity of Mr. Rawls's own school situation and Dan's seems significant). Dan states that he plans to return to school in the fall because he now feels a need to do so. Mr. Rawls repeatedly expresses doubt that Dan will do so, and this doubt seems consistent with his own approach to life, which is based on right and wrong absolutes rather than personal feelings and needs. Dan's response to his father's criticism is generally to argue minimally and then to withdraw from the conflict and make his own decisions.

Mandy, though she is the oldest child at home (and in fact not a child at all in age or responsibilities), has completed high school, works full-time, and bears most of the responsibility for meals and housekeeping, is grouped by Mr. Rawls with the others as a failure in child rearing. Mandy rarely argues with her father on this point but seems to go about her work and other activities with self-confidence and an easy-going manner. On the issue of housekeeping, she supports her father, complaining that she rarely has help with those responsibilities. Frequently, she brings up facts that her father seems to have overlooked, for example, pointing out positive aspects to arguments. Mandy seems to give and receive physical affection most freely, and her affection toward Randy has a maternal air. With her father, however, Mandy vacillates between little girl, sitting on his lap, and adult, inviting him to share his problems with her and taking initiative to help him run the household.

Frequently, Mandy is the spokesperson for the children in the family, defending them, stating their concerns, and expressing their wishes. Dan is both respectful and protective toward her and frequently gives evidence that he is proud of her. She, in turn, supports and defends him.

Randy seems in many ways the closest of all the children to Mr. Rawls. He is warm and affectionate with his father and becomes quite anxious at the prospect of his father's developing some outside interest of his own. Much is made in the family of Mr. Rawls's attending Randy's baseball games. Randy is concerned that the family let each other know that they care about each other but sometimes has great difficulty verbalizing his own caring for other family members. He represents the family's dialectic of closeness and distance—wanting to be close yet fearing a total lack of differentiation.

PROGRESS DURING SE

Although initially Mr. Rawls tended to control the sessions by repeating directions and by beginning tangential discussions of what is wrong with members of the family, by the end of the program this behavior had lessened considerably. He seemed much less critical in later sessions than he had at the beginning.

SE brought clearly into focus the dichotomy between Mr. Rawls and the children as a group. Frequently, Mr. Rawls's reactions to exercises were negative, whereas the others' reactions were positive. Often, he hesitated to participate or declared that what they were asked to do was "silly" or "useless." In the feedback conference, however, he acknowledged that his children were not, in fact, "going straight to hell," as he had first thought, and that he had been impressed with their insight, their participation, and their maturity in the sessions. He also acknowledged that his older children are now adults in their own right, largely beyond his influence, and that he has not done such a bad job raising them as he had thought.

Also brought out was Mr. Rawls's self-destructive inattention to his own physical and emotional needs. He was confronted in various ways by the family (as well as by us) about his insistence on holding in problems and allowing himself no outlets for enjoyment, possibly at the expense of his health.

Perhaps the most significant change was Mr. Rawls's developing sense of competence and power, not only in seeing more good in his children but in developing through the family's housecleaning project some confidence that he could "get his family organized." During SE, Mr. Rawls made the decision to retire from teaching, collect his pension, and seek other work. He made this announcement with an evident sense of relief and of control over his own fate, not despair. Mr. Rawls seemed to have come to see his teaching as something he no longer wants to do rather than as another failure.

All family members seemed to be taking advantage of an opportunity to talk to each other about family issues and problems, to share feelings, and to plan for changes. The family resolved (and began an attempt) to work together to clean the house, share in housekeeping responsibilities, and plan activities together. Most basic among these resolutions was a decision to try to have meals together, something they reported as a rare occurrence.

Randy emerged as a family member with good insight into problems and the ability to act constructively rather than depending on the family totally to manage problems for him. It was Randy who pointed out to his father that smoking cigarettes in his current state of health is no less a problem than Dan's occasionally smoking marijuana. The family often talked over Randy's head, even about Randy himself, but the family seemed to gain insight into Randy's importance as an individual in the family.

At a minimum, the family had an opportunity to practice sharing feelings, particularly warm and supportive feelings, with each other. In almost every session, they reported that they had rarely done the things they have been asked to do in SE—seeing the good, letting each other know of their caring for each other, forgiving each other, or enjoying themselves as a family. By doing these things with each other, the family has seemed to develop more awareness of each other as individuals and of their dyadic relationships within the family.

PRE- AND POSTTEST EVALUATION

On the pretest of the Bell-Fagan Family Symbols (B-F), it is difficult, as in all the tests, to clearly discriminate the identified patient. Dan seems more afraid-anxious and angry than the rest of the family. Mr. Rawls seems least angry; otherwise, his scores are in the midrange among family scores. Mandy ranks as happiest and Randy, surprisingly, quietest. Dan ranks as most loving, Randy as least loving. If a guess were made about the identified patient solely on the basis of the test scores, Dan would probably be selected. However, his scores may simply reflect his higher level of differentiation in the family and the concomitant frustration in the family setting.

On the pretest Description of Feelings in the Family (DFF), the family members see the family clearly in the mad-smug quadrant, again with the exception of Dan, who selected all cards and therefore scored in the center of the graph. Consistently, the family sees the members in the mad-smug quadrant as well. The family's initial difficulty in expressing feelings (other than frustration and anger) and their tendency to intellectualize (particularly Mr. Rawls) seem clearly reflected in the scores on this test.

The pretest of the Family Situations Picture Series (FSPS) reveals results very similar to those on the DFF. In general, the family members see the family and the family sees the members in the blaming-computing quadrant. An exception is Mandy, who sees the family as slightly distracting. Mr. Rawls's constant blaming of family members is certainly reflected in this test; however, his estimation of the family's blaming-computing features is considerably lower than Dan's or Randy's.

On the pretest of the Animal Concepts Picture Series (ACPS), Mandy's scores (not Dan's) seem to follow least the family pattern of similarity set by the others' scores; all difference scores between actual and ideal profiles are comparatively low (Dan's, predictably, were highest, Mr. Rawls's lowest). According to these scores, the family seems generally satisfied with their level of functioning and not particularly eager for Mr. Rawls to change.

On the DFF and the FSPS, the number of cards chosen by family members indicates neither withholding of information nor excessive reporting of symptoms.

The posttests reveal some changes in the family's perception of itself. On the B-F posttest, Mr. Rawls's scores distinguish him more clearly as the identified patient (his scores are highest or lowest on most variables). Dan is seen as least loving rather than most loving, as on the pretest. Mandy continues to rank as happiest. Dan is seen as much less quiet than on the pretest. Mr. Rawls has moved to the position of most angry yet most loving.

On the DFF, scores are generally much less smug, though still mad, on the graph of how the family sees the members. In looking at how the members see the family, Dan sees the family as more mad than before, though the rest of the family sees itself as less so. Mandy's perceptions of the family have moved from very mad-smug to the center; perhaps she has come to see more sadness and more distracting in her family or perhaps she has felt keenly Mr. Rawls's vote of confidence in her and Dan at the end of SE.

On the FSPS, Mandy sees the family as very distracting and blaming, no longer mildly so. The contrast between her posttest scores on the DFF and the FSPS may be related to the fact that the DFF shows individuals alone and the FSPS shows family members relating. Perhaps her perception of individuals in the family have changed but her view of the family as a whole is more blaming and distracting. Randy's scores on the FSPS have moved from very computing–very blaming to very computing–slightly placating. Some of this movement toward distracting and placating also is evident in how the family sees the members on the posttest.

On the ACPS, Dan now has the lowest difference score between actual and ideal rather than the highest. Randy has replaced Dan in having the highest difference score; Mr. Rawls's is next highest. On this test the identified patient is still quite difficult to distinguish.

On the whole, the tests confirm the family's mad and blaming stance and reflect their computing and distracting components as well. To some extent, the contrast between pretests and posttests suggests that the family may have become somewhat less satisfied with their family functioning and more aware of Mr. Rawls's separateness from the rest of the family. The changes in their perceptions of each other and of the family as a whole are consistent with their expressed desire for further treatment.

RECOMMENDATIONS

The Rawls family requested further help. Offered a choice of another SE series or family therapy, they seemed generally to prefer therapy but wanted time to make a decision. They plan to involve Dorrie in future treatment if she is willing.

Mr. Rawls's desire for a less structured intervention may be related to his apparent desire to talk freely about his complaints about the family, a desire that was firmly limited in SE. However, a less structured format will permit more exploration of the family interactions that have been identified as problems, the etiology of them, and the means by which they are maintained. With sufficient control of Mr. Rawls's tendency to take control of sessions, family therapy may be highly productive.

Therapy may also help the older children move out on their own, differentiating themselves from the family system. In many ways, it is as important for the family to begin to separate as it is for them to be closer emotionally. They will need some assistance to deal with separation without blaming and to leave without rebellion or self-definition through oppositeness.

The family seems highly motivated to change and grow; this characteristic is perhaps their greatest strength.

13

Depression

Raymond A. Gallope

The Carter family was referred by a local mental health center where the mother is being seen for chronic depression. When we asked her about the problem, she said she knows she has a problem but that she also finds it difficult to understand her children now that they are becoming adolescents. The children said that they fight a great deal.

The family consists of the mother, her son and daughter, and Mrs. Carter's mother. According to the mother and the children, the grandmother would not participate. Mrs. Carter is 38, has a high school education, is divorced, and works full-time. She is overweight, has pleasant features and short black hair, and wears glasses. She appears to be a chain smoker. Sharon, aged 14 and a ninth-grader, has long brown hair, blue eyes, and braces on her teeth; she is pleasant-looking but not pretty. Sam, aged 12 and a seventh-grader, is of normal stature and has light-brown hair, brown eyes, and handsome features.

Mrs. Carter was married in 1963 and divorced in 1968 or 1969 (she couldn't remember which). She and her husband separated a year before the divorce (he traveled and drank a lot). He remarried a short time after the divorce but sees the children now and then. Four years ago, Mrs. Carter had a nervous breakdown, which followed, as she calls it, "a constant high." She is currently depressed, worries a great deal, and is seeing a counselor. Her mother lives in the house and often takes care of the children while Mrs. Carter is at work. Mrs. Carter attributes "part" of her depression to the fact that her mother has control of the children and takes away some of Mrs. Carter's "motherly" duties.

The grandmother has had a series of nervous breakdowns and professes an antipathy for psychiatrists. Mrs. Carter's father was an elevator mechanic who died 5 years ago; her parents were divorced when she was

6 years old and she saw little of her father after the divorce. She commented that the reason for divorce was that her father drank too much. An aunt and an uncle kept her during much of her childhood. Before the divorce, her family lived with her grandparents until they died. Mrs. Carter's only brother died at 37; she has one older sister who lives in the Midwest. Her family is not very religious but professes to be Methodist.

There appears to be a pattern of intergenerational sameness, which, if maintained, would confer on Sharon the status of identified patient. Both Mrs. Carter and her mother had husbands who drank, were divorced early, had nervous breakdowns, and lived with their parents.

SUMMARY OF SESSIONS

Session 1

Sharon and Sam sat at opposite ends of the sofa; Mrs. Carter sat in an armchair next to Sharon. Sam and Sharon immediately requested soft drinks, so the session was delayed until they returned. I then explained SE, and the family members signed a contract. The family was then asked what they expected to get out of these sessions. Mrs. Carter said she knows that she has a problem but that she can communicate with the kids. However, she commented, understanding is not good because they are becoming adolescents. Sharon then said she fights with Sam who, in turn, said that he feels picked on. As Sharon put it, Sam "bites like an evil snake." The grandmother usually intervenes and punishes them (Mrs. Carter is usually not at home). Sam then said he would like to see more of his mother, who responded that she has to work to support the family. Sam left the room and Sharon went after him (Mrs. Carter appeared unaware of his absence and made no effort to go after either child). She also did not remember what grades the children were in.

Next, I administered the Bell-Fagan Family Symbols (B-F) and the Description of Feelings in Family (DFF). They were quiet during the tests except for some laughter from Mrs. Carter and Sam. Sharon had a difficult time with both tests. On the B-F she took a long time, finally picking no cards for herself. She then picked only two cards on the DFF. Mrs. Carter and Sam had to choose for her while she complained about how difficult the tests were and how she couldn't do it. We ended the session by discussing program choices. I suggested Single-Parent Families and Reciprocity as possibilities.

Enricher's notes.

Mrs. Carter seemed apprehensive and often laughed nervously. Sam was the most verbal and distracting. Sharon appeared quiet and resentful, at times hostile and resistant. She seems immature for 14, and the family seems to reinforce her immaturity by saying how quiet and tongue-tied she often is. Mrs. Carter seemed out of control: the children did what they liked and spoke as if they were her peers (e.g., "Keep quiet!"). The grandmother seems to be replacing the mother in the family as the one in control and is perhaps the transmitter of an intergenerational pattern. Sharon's anger may be her attempt to resist this pattern. The children appear to be relating to each other as the grandmother relates to them—by punishment. The first lessons of Single-Parent Families seem appropriate to help uncover any latent feelings about the divorce and bring more into focus the family's relationship patterns.

Session 2

Sharon and Sam went to get candy while I waited with Mrs. Carter (I had earlier observed the children badgering her for money just before they entered the lab). The final two tests—Family Situations Picture Series (FSPS) and Animal Concepts Picture Series (ACPS)—were administered after the children returned. These tests were done more quickly than the first two, as Sharon showed less resistance to them.

Before beginning the program, I asked the family to change seats, asking Mrs. Carter to sit between Sharon and Sam on the sofa. They hesitated but complied. We then began the first lesson, which concerns feelings about the divorce. They said they hadn't given much thought to what it means to be without a mate or a parent. Sam then said he can't do as many things. Mrs. Carter mentioned financial and recreational problems (the family cannot travel as much as before). She believes, however, that the divorce has made the family better. Sam agreed. Mrs. Carter then said that a man could discipline the children more. At this point Sharon spoke up and agreed the family cannot do as many things as they did before the divorce. Mrs. Carter said she has never blamed herself for the divorce; she added that originally she was hurt but she really doesn't think about it much any more.

I commented on Sharon's quietness, and the family said that she is shy. Sharon said that sometimes she is afraid in a crowd but doesn't know why. I attempted to explore her feelings about the shyness but got nowhere, as she refused to talk. Mrs. Carter then said that Sharon "is just like that."

We ended the session with family sculptures. Sharon posed Sam hitting Mrs. Carter with a pillow. Mrs. Carter had Sam sitting at her feet and

Sharon beside her, but no one was touching anyone else. Sam had Mrs. Carter slapping Sharon, with Sharon crying and Mrs. Carter looking angry. I asked the family for more sculptures. Sharon had Sam chasing her and Sharon hiding behind the mother. In another, Sam made a fist at Sharon, who was kicking him as the mother ran into the room. Mrs. Carter had Sam and Sharon standing next to each other, holding hands and looking up at her, standing with her hand slightly raised as if lecturing. No one wanted to change his or her sculptures except Sam, who wanted his mother to sit with her arm around Sharon.

When I asked for comments, Mrs. Carter said she was surprised that the fighting was so prevalent in the sculptures. The children had no comments, but Sharon did mention that they usually fight when their grandmother is not at home.

The homework for each session was to think about the topic of the lesson and to explore their feelings about the lesson.

Enricher's notes.

I am impressed by the anger in this family and by the hurt feelings, which are not easily expressed. Mrs. Carter again appeared out of control and may have been denying the anger, perhaps to maintain the status quo. She seems to be trying to assert control by lecturing. In the sculptures, there were indications of Mrs. Carter's protection of Sharon as well as indications of their coalition within the family's intergenerational framework. Positive feelings were lacking, as was closeness. The family appeared uncomfortable sitting next to each other and seemed to prefer distance. Sam showed the power and leadership he has in the family, and Sharon may be using her withdrawal as a rebellion against her mother. In conclusion, the family appears to relate by fighting and forcing; positive and hurt feelings are repressed. There was more laughter in this session, but it was nervous laughter, especially from Mrs. Carter.

Supervision.

It was decided to emphasize positives and try to get the family to express their feelings.

Session 3

Mrs. Carter called to cancel one session because she could not get away from work, so we did two lessons in Session 3.

The family entered the room and assumed the same seats as in the first session. I commented on this and asked them to sit with their mother in the middle on the sofa. Mrs. Carter said she was uncomfortable in this position because the family never sits together on the sofa at home.

I asked again about the sculptures they did last time. All responded that they were silly.

We then talked about ways of relating in the family, and they indicated that coaxing, forcing, criticizing, and judging are used often, withholding and denying responsibility less frequently. In acting out these situations, Sam used force on Sharon, who reciprocated; Mrs. Carter used force with both Sam and Sharon. I asked them to switch roles, but they seemed to get very little out of this reversal. When asked to think of better ways of relating, they had some difficulty. Sharon said they could ask each other nicely instead of yelling and forcing. When I asked them to try this, the mother, especially, found it difficult. She said that it was easier to talk about asking nicely than to do it.

We then went on to the next lesson. Mrs. Carter had, by this time, moved to a side chair to get a cigarette and had stayed there. Sharon and Sam moved to opposite ends of the sofa. The family members were asked to write two situations that made them angry or frustrated and then relate the situations to the person concerned. Mrs. Carter had the most difficulty relating her feelings without criticizing or judging.

They were then asked to talk about a situation at home and express their feelings about it. This exercise did not go too well: Sam refused to express any feelings about the issue. I then asked them to write 10 things each of them does that are good for the family. Sharon wrote 2 specific things, Sam listed several specific deeds, and Mrs. Carter listed 10 general stereotypic issues (e.g., care for the family).

The last was a fantasy exercise in which the family sat in a circle, holding hands, and imagined walking down a country road. Mrs. Carter and Sam told their fantasy about what they saw and smelled, but Sharon could think of nothing. She said she was seeing black and felt frustrated. I pointed out that during this exercise Sam had difficulty maintaining his grasp of his mother's and Sharon's hands. Sharon started crying and then the mother cried because, as she put it, Sharon was crying. When I commented on their strength in crying, Sam said it was difficult for him to cry. When I asked Mrs. Carter to hug Sharon, she wiped a tear away but did not hold her. Mrs. Carter then said she didn't know whether the children should come to the sessions if the sessions weren't helping them. She then said that all of them must try together at home if the sessions were to help.

Enricher's notes.

There appears to be much hurt (disguised as anger) that is not being expressed. Mrs. Carter, in playing coenricher (e.g., asking the child 10 questions), maintains distance, and her stereotypic comments seem to preclude change. In this session, when threatened with a change in Sharon that she didn't understand, she suggested excluding her from the sessions. The mother and perhaps the grandmother seek sameness in Sharon but not closeness.

Sharon and Sam were very distracting during this session (e.g., Sharon played with a cigarette pack, and Sam looked at the clock—he wanted to see a movie on TV). This session brought out further evidence of their intergenerational pattern: Sam is excluded from the things his mother and Sharon do (e.g., it's difficult for him to cry, to hold hands, to express his feelings about a family situation). The family seems to maintain distance because closeness would be a threat to one's power in the relationship.

Supervision.

The supervisor suggested that I use Expressing Feelings, the second lesson of the Introductory-Experiential Program.

Session 4

Sharon and Sam entered the room with candy and drinks, as usual. I had congratulated both on their distraction, and the effect of this tactic was to be seen in this session.

The family had difficulty addressing comments to each other (each speaker would look at me) and maintaining eye contact with the person addressed. Both Sharon and Sam on a few occasions said "mad" instead of "sad" in expressing a hurt. They also had a difficult time saying what they liked least about their mother. Mrs. Carter wanted Sharon not to look sad, to participate more, and to express more of her feelings. Sharon was quiet and withdrawn, appearing sullen much of the time. Sam was very distracting (e.g., looking at the clock, tearing cups and bags). Both children said they wanted their mother to stop smoking. Several times, Sharon mentioned her grandmother as involved in her feelings toward another person (intergenerational process). Sam acted-out (pulled off his mother's glasses) when I turned to change the tape. I commented on how the children turn each other on and make each other happy (e.g., they laugh when looking at each other).

Many of the sentence completions, such as "I feel good when . . ." and "I'm hurt by . . ." were nonspecific (e.g., "nice," "mad"). When pressed for more elaboration, they resisted.

We ended with a nonverbal exercise—holding hands and concentrating on feelings. They were told to touch each other's faces, arms, if they wanted to. Mrs. Carter did the least touching; everyone mostly just held hands. We then ended the session. No one expressed any feelings about the exercise.

Enricher's notes.

I believe that Mrs. Carter has the greatest investment in no change. Perhaps she brings the children to focus on them so that she can maintain distance. When confronted with exercises, she usually does not fare too well. I felt defeated by Sharon's withdrawal and Sam's distraction during this session. There was incongruent laughter from all members, especially when expressing hurt feelings. Mrs. Carter seems protective of Sharon, who was sometimes defiant towards me (e.g., "I answered already. Why are you asking me again?"). As a male, I may be eliciting behavior precipitated by intergenerational transmission.

Supervision.

It was decided to disallow candy and drinks in the sessions as a possible way of decreasing distraction. Also, the supervisor suggested four possible strategies for dealing with Sharon's withdrawal: (a) prescribing the symptoms—telling her to withdraw, (b) congratulating her and pointing out what she gets from it, (c) having Sharon role-play the enricher, and (d) telling the family about my feelings of defeat about the withdrawal.

Session 5

When Sharon and Sam came in with food and drink, I said that I found it distracting to work while they were eating, so we would wait until they finished. It was hoped that, as they were apparently eager to finish each session, they would not prolong it by bringing food in the future. They were told the session would not be conducted if eating or drinking persisted.

After a few minutes, I asked them how they felt about last week's session. Sam said he found it hard to do and he would rather not. Mrs. Carter said they do express feelings but not all the time. Sharon said that it is hard to express some feelings, such as negative ones. I then began a lesson Talking about Yourself (Intermediate-Experiential Program) in an effort to elicit the feelings that concern each person, especially hurt and positive feelings.

In response to the first exercise (saying what you like and dislike about yourself), Sharon could not answer. I offered her encouragement, but she still did not answer. I then told her how good she is at getting attention in the family by remaining quiet. At this, she began to cry and said she was mad at me. When I asked why, she said to her mother, "He doesn't know when to stop." I commented that she expressed her feelings well, for everyone could guess how she was feeling at this time.

We went on to the next exercise (saying how you could improve yourself). Sharon ran from the room with a nosebleed. Sam went after her, and when she returned, I commented on the "red badge of courage" she was now wearing on her sleeve. Everyone laughed and Sharon appeared to be more relaxed and outgoing.

The session ended with a baseball game in which I was the umpire. Everyone participated and seemed to enjoy the exercise.

Enricher's notes.

The family was quiet and reserved. Perhaps thinking about oneself at this point was too threatening for a system based on blaming and externalizing. Sharon was evidently affected by my statement and seemed more outgoing toward the end of the session. Both children appeared nervous and fidgety without the distracting food. Mrs. Carter said at one point the children do not want to come; perhaps this was a statement about her also not wanting to come. The resistance from the family as a unit was greatest in this session.

Supervision.

Because of the family's resistance to change, the supervisor suggested I select appropriate exercises from the Introductory-Experiential Program.

Session 6

In this, the final session, Sharon and Sam sat on opposite sides of the sofa; Mrs. Carter sat next to Sam in a chair (the prevalent pattern for all sessions). Sharon and Sam said they had had fun playing baseball and would like to do something like that again.

I asked whether the family wanted to be there. At first the children said no. When I said that we could stop if they liked, they retracted and said they had only been kidding. Mrs. Carter said she had seen change in the children, but they did not admit to change.

I then started the lesson called Settling Discord (Introductory-Experiential Program). The children said that their mother makes the final decisions in an argument, but in the exercises Sam seemed to speak for the family very often. In their family play, a mother finds two orphans at the door; the orphans can't decide on a movie to see, so the mother tells them to watch TV. They then quarrel about a TV program, and Mom spanks both and sends them to bed. The roles were rotated among the family members. Sam and Sharon seemed to enjoy spanking their mother. The children thought the exercise was fun; Mrs. Carter thought parts of it were silly.

Enricher's notes.

There was really not much discord between the mother and the kids; she acquiesced in most instances. The children were unruly and disruptive toward the end of the session, especially Sharon, who once more challenged me (e.g., "Do you want to be here?"). Mrs. Carter was plainly out of control, and though she made attempts, they were futile. I threatened at one point to stop the session unless Sharon stopped playing with a table. Fighting and forcing were again prevalent, as was a lack of positive emotions. Sharon's behavior was different, perhaps rebellious. The issue of change is important: the family apparently wants change only if "forced" to say so (e.g., when I said, "We can stop the session if you like").

Supervision.

The supervisor suggested that I concentrate feedback on two central issues. One is the use of power (family members use power to defeat each other by force, essentially playing a win-lose game). The other issue is intergenerational sameness, especially as it is revealed in Mrs. Carter's relationship with Sharon. By forcing, protecting, and denying, she is attempting to pass on the specter of identified patient to the next female— Sharon. Sharon seems to be rebelling at times by being opposite, her only alternative under the pressure of sameness. Difference is not tolerated. When Mrs. Carter is quiet, Sharon talks and vice versa. Sam is perhaps the outsider here but is still being viewed as men in preceding generations (e.g., defiant, harmful, powerful, a leader). Being a part of the system, he maintains sameness by forcing Sharon as their grandmother forces him.

FEEDBACK CONFERENCE

The family completed the posttests much more quickly than they had completed the pretests. Sharon turned her back to me while she did the

Bell-Fagan Family Symbols; I later discovered that she merely dealt the cards into three piles. She challenged me by asking to see the notes on the family in my notebook (e.g., "Do you not want us to see it?"). After completing the tests, Sharon and Sam sat in the beanbag chairs; Mrs. Carter and I joined them. With the lights dimmed and everyone relaxed, I began the feedback.

First I asked what the family had gotten from SE. Mrs. Carter said she could see change in that they are more considerate of each other's feelings. She thought some lessons had been better than others (e.g., the expression of feelings). Sharon and Sam said they don't fight as much anymore. Sam liked the last two sessions, in which they had played baseball and acted out the family play (which Sam made up). I then mentioned that how much the family cares for each other is evident in how much they fight. If they didn't care, they would be indifferent. I also commented on their sense of humor and ability to be involved in family activity. Next I mentioned family power and how it is used to defeat another family member. Sharon said she didn't understand, so I explained how the win-lose game is played between her and Sam. Mrs. Carter asked how to combat this, and I replied that further work will be necessary to switch to a win-win pattern. Finally, the intergenerational pattern was mentioned. Mrs. Carter and the children agreed that the pattern does exist.

After hearing the options available to them, Sharon asked why they had to come back. I explained that the decision was theirs but that if they wanted to come back the participation of the grandmother would be mandatory (this had been stipulated in supervision). Mrs. Carter agreed that her mother should participate but was pessimistic about her agreeing to do so. The children agreed with their mother. I pointed out that perhaps when the grandmother sees the changes in the family she may change her mind about participating. The family said she would probably not notice any changes because she is often "deaf" to their interactions. I suggested they talk it over with the grandmother.

Enricher's notes.

Sharon continued to be more outgoing but less disruptive than in the preceding session. Mrs. Carter and Sam were quiet. Again, I had the impression of a resistance to change as revealed by the total rejection of the grandmother's participation. When I suggested coming to their home for further sessions, Mrs. Carter rejected the idea, saying it was important to be away from the house. My impression of the family's potential for change is not great unless a shake-up of the intergenerational pattern occurs.

RESULTS OF PRE- AND POSTTESTS

Bell-Fagan Family Symbols (B-F)

The results show similar profiles for Sharon and Mrs. Carter; Sam's deviates significantly from the other two. Mrs. Carter and Sharon take turns, so to speak, being higher on any one dimension except sad, on which they are exactly the same. Sam is higher than either Mrs. Carter or Sharon on all dimensions but highest on afraid-anxious. He has approximately the same level in all other dimensions because his profile flattens out after the first dimension.

The closeness of Mrs. Carter and Sharon is evidence for the hypothesis that they are locked in a pattern of intergenerational sameness. However, the fact that Sharon picked no cards for herself leaves some uncertainty. Sam's outsider status is apparent in his deviant profile.

On the posttest, Sam's scores dropped significantly so his deviance from the family is less evident than on the pretest. Mrs. Carter has taken Sam's place as highest on afraid-anxious; the rest of her profile remains essentially unchanged. Because Sharon had dealt out her cards on this test, her postenrichment profile must be considered invalid. The change in Mrs. Carter's score on afraid-anxious may reflect a concern about the end of the program. Sam's lowered scores may indicate positive change. However, any changes on these tests may be due to poor reliability of the instrument, so hypotheses must be tentative.

The pretest clearly shows the pattern of sameness that Mrs. Carter and Sharon evidenced in the sessions. The pretest can be considered the family's defensive posture—Mrs. Carter and Sharon linked together behind Sam as the leader. Sam's leadership quality was often evident in his willingness to answer first, to volunteer for exercises, to make a decision.

Family Situations Picture Series (FSPS)

The pretest clearly shows the family's externalizing characteristics. In their patterns of concern and force, they blame one another. The distraction so much in evidence in the sessions is also reflected in this test.

In the posttest, the two close members—Mrs. Carter and Sharon—flip-flop from blaming to placating; Sam, as the outsider and leader, stays the same but less extreme (the closeness referred to is psychological, not physical; distance is constantly maintained in this family as a tactic for maintaining power). The family saw the female pictures in the same pattern, a flip-flop to placating. This pattern may be seen as evidence for the dialectic of opposites typical of a system locked into sameness.

They vacillate in extremes, with no in-between. The flip-flop is not as extreme, however, in the placating quadrant, on which Mrs. Carter and Sharon are closer to center. This may be taken as some evidence of disruption in the system as a result of SE; if the system were the same, one would expect extreme placating, just as there is extreme blaming.

Description of Feelings in the Family (DFF)

The pattern seen in the FSPS is again revealed in the DFF. On the pretest, all are in the mad-distracting quadrant, with the exception of Sam, who is in the mad-smug quadrant. This result reflects the fighting and hostility in the sessions, especially in the sculptures. Sam's smug position may be a result of his outsider status. Also, all the pictures are seen in the same quadrant (mad-distracting), with the exception of the male pictures, which are in the mad-smug quadrant, and the mother pictures, which are in the sad-distracting quadrant.

In the posttest, the flip-flop of the mother and Sharon is seen in their move to sad-distracting, although, again, as in the FSPS, they are closer to center. In fact, Mrs. Carter is zero on sad. Sam stays in the same quadrant but increases on smug. The female pictures flip-flopped and the male did not: all were seen as distracting instead of smug.

One can again see the dialectic in action, but it is not as strong as it would be if no change had taken place in the system. Some disruption in the coalition between Mrs. Carter and Sharon may be inferred to have resulted from SE, although the certainty is low. Sam seems to have maintained his status.

Animal Concepts Picture Series (ACPS)

On the pretest, the pattern of the female coalition and the male outsider again emerges. Mrs. Carter and Sharon are very close in both actual and ideal, somewhat closer in ideal. Sam is the most deviant and considered the strongest, most powerful, and most harmful. In the ideal, Sam is closer to the family pattern. Interestingly, Mrs. Carter comes closer to Sharon in the ideal (Sharon changes very little). I am reminded of Mrs. Carter's crying because Sharon cried, answering for her, protecting her, and rationalizing her behavior (e.g., "That's the way she is"). Sharon's lack of movement in this case has somewhat better prognostic value for an eventual split in the intergenerational pattern than if she had moved closer to her mother.

On the posttest, Sharon is seen as weaker, smaller, and less powerful than before. This may reflect her vulnerability as exposed in the sessions (e.g., crying). Sam and Mrs. Carter are essentially the same. In the ideal, Mrs. Carter and Sharon change places exactly: Mrs. Carter is seen as the weakest, smallest, most helpless; Sharon is between her mother and Sam in these characteristics. For Sharon to be different, she must be opposite to her mother, who must be seen as defeated and one down. This pattern was reflected in their behavior (e.g., the mother verbal, Sharon quiet). One good sign is the increase in difference scores for Mrs. Carter and especially for Sharon. Sam's difference score remains essentially unchanged.

In conclusion, there is some converging evidence from test results to support my impressions from the sessions. All tests show in some way the sameness pattern in Mrs. Carter and Sharon; the FSPS and the DFF show the blaming, angry, and internalizing characteristics of this family as they force and fight to win and defeat one another. Sam's outsider position (perhaps the mover, in Kantor and Lehr's [1975] terminology) and his status as leader, powerful yet harmful, are especially evident in the ACPS test but are revealed in all tests. Perhaps he is a substitute father and, as such, has the attributed qualities of the males in preceding generations. Positively, the absence of extreme dialectical reversal may indicate some increase in differentiation through heightened awareness. Also, the difference score (indicating some desire for change) is more prominent on the posttests. Finally, Sam's lowered B-F profile may indicate decreased anxiety as a result of SE.

CONCLUSIONS

This family, without the participation of the grandmother, who is perhaps the architect of the sameness pattern and the control agent in the home, shows poor prognosis for either SE or therapy. She is likely to sabotage any significant changes. The extreme distance that is used to maintain the power to defeat and the intergenerational sameness must be altered to increase differentiation and precipitate growth in the family. The family shows potential in its humor, ability to work together, and the caring they show for one another.

SECTION III
Problematic Couples

14

An Uproar Couple

Anonymous*

INTERVIEW

At the interview, pretests were administered, and 10-minute tapes were recorded by each partner on the subject "What I think is important to myself and my mate."

Tom, aged 28, and Debbie, aged 22, are unmarried but have lived together for 2 years. Her home was in the West, where she met Tom. After knowing him for 2 weeks, Debbie moved with him to a large city in the South.

During the interview, the couple said that they believe their relationship is best when both are meditating often. They expressed a desire to be more open in their relationship and said they have been trying to accomplish this by more meditation. Tom considers Debbie more open than he. Debbie wishes to be more productive and independent. They explained that they can see that their problems are repetitive and that through meditation they are making progress in looking "beyond the superficial manifestations to the source."

In the taped segments on what is important to them, both stressed meditation. Tom spoke of raising consciousness, becoming aware of his totality, and being more open. These would come about, he said, by increasing the time and effort invested in meditation. He added that this is the most important thing for Debbie to do, also. Debbie was concerned with "the practice of our spiritual development" in order to become "two whole individuals" rather than "two halves," as is necessary to form a whole relationship. Like Tom, she stressed individual rather than

---

* This student wishes to remain anonymous.

195

interpersonal growth. She spoke of the importance of allowing and assisting the other person to become fulfilled independently through career or other interests. Unlike Tom, she spoke of commitment to the relationship—that she had sacrificed a lot to come here with Tom; that when times are hard she believes she "made a mistake" but that awareness of her commitment holds them together. She also talked about the importance of "ignoring" her own feelings of being a martyr.

Enrichers' notes.

Two impressions stand out from the interview. The first is the emphasis placed on the individual path of spiritual development. The result of this in the relationship is that problems are viewed abstractly, with little emphasis on concrete interaction. The second impression is a shade of uncertainty about their commitment to each other, a theme that was expanded throughout the program.

Supervision.

E. E. Dunne, our supervisor, suggested the Negotiation Program as a means of increasing openness in communication, particularly the communication of emotion. We discussed other programs that might have merit for this couple.

PRETEST RESULTS

The pretest results reveal some potential weak points in their relationship. On the 10-item Family Information, Tom revealed that he was dissatisfied with his self-disclosure and with feelings and emotions. Debbie was dissatisfied with her empathy and self-exploration. This pattern of communication difficulties proved to be a dominant theme in the sessions that followed. Also evident from the tests is Debbie's dissatisfaction with her role (self-exploration and personal time were marked low). Sources of disagreement were social activities, as rated on the Family Adjustment Inventory. Sex was an area of great discrepancy (each sexual area on the Azrin Marital Happiness Scale was marked to indicate that one person was more satisfied than the other). This issue came up in discussion later; Debbie said she would like them to be more open in discussing sex.

SUMMARY OF SESSIONS

Session 1

First, we reviewed programs with the couple so that we could decide on one together. In talking about the Cohabitation Program, Tom and Debbie said they plan to get married—they've "been through all that." When we asked if they were agreed on this decision, Tom said that they were. We also discussed Equality, Assertiveness, Reciprocity, and Negotiation, but we concentrated on Reciprocity and Negotiation. The Reciprocity Program was presented as dealing with concrete behavior, the Negotiation Program as dealing with feelings. The Negotiation Program was finally chosen to increase the couple's openness.

We began with the first lesson (Marriage Myths) in the Negotiation Program. The couple discussed their earlier expectations about living together. Each had thought the other was an entirely different person at the time. Debbie's impression of Tom was that he was very social and self-reliant (e.g., could cook for himself). These assumptions are not correct. Tom thought Debbie would make a good cook and added, "I expected a nurse." However, Debbie doesn't enjoy homemaking. They kidded each other about trying to pull the wool over each other's eyes during those first 2 weeks.

Debbie explained that her view of a relationship was "like the movies." She said that before she became involved with the guru Maharaji movement she thought that marriage was the ultimate fulfillment. Tom said that his early experiences of romantic relationships were "carnal and empty." He now sees love as something you work at and grow into. Debbie said that the men in her early relationships had just wanted her body but she had kept hoping that each one would "be the *one*" with whom to establish intimacy.

Debbie and Tom each made a list of both male and female sex-role expectations, then described the items in terms of each other's behavior. The lists were fairly stereotypical, and their descriptions of each other's behavior largely fit the stereotypes as well. Then Debbie said that sex-role definitions are a main problem for them and added that that problem may be a factor in her overemotionality. She also described the following role conflict. When she works, Tom does not assume his share of the housework. When she doesn't work (as is true currently), Tom is resentful and has overly high expectations of Debbie as a homemaker.

The couple next described their differences in communication. They said that in the past, Tom has shown a tendency to "get cold"; Debbie "gets emotional" and tries to "keep it going," or as she explained it, tries to change the situation. They said that they have realized lately that you "can't solve anything" by arguing, so they have been "dropping the whole thing." Tom explained that Debbie gets irrational and that he thinks it's "better to wait until she calms down." He said, "People don't act rational when they're caught up in their emotions. If you're ever going to get anything straight you've got to be rational." Debbie complained, however, of being left with a feeling of unresolution and claimed that the problem usually doesn't get discussed.

Enrichers' notes.

Evidenced in this session were the very tenuous position in which their relationship started and their naive views of love at that time. It was apparent that the religious movement rather than interpersonal experience had provided them an avenue for changing their attitudes about love and relationships. The communication problems they discussed showed that Tom has a tendency to deny the emotions that result from problem issues (calling them irrationally based) and that Debbie tends to become emotional about Tom's response to the situation. Their "new" attitude toward problem situations was essentially the recognition that problems are negative and must be avoided or "dropped." They also showed confusion about the allocation of responsibility.

Supervision.

Our supervisor suggested that we keep the discussion grounded in specific behaviors and that we balance disagreements so that no one wins and no one loses. It was also suggested that we offer the formula "I feel —— when you ——" as an appropriate way to state feelings.

Session 2

Tom and Debbie were very relaxed, not at all serious. The first exercise in this lesson (Focus on the Relationship) begins, "Who are you?" Debbie's responses were fairly stereotypical: an independent role, student, was given first; the second word given, *primi*, relates to her religious pursuit. Tom's responses were more heavily philosophical: light, primi, infinite, and everything.

For both partners, the marriage role was near the middle of the list, indicative of their individualistic attitudes. They differed in the way they described this role: Tom was described as Debbie's "friend"; Debbie called herself "a mate."

To the next question, "What can I give you?" Tom's responses were stereotypical, as were Debbie's. In discussing the responses, Debbie said she was surprised by Tom's statement that she could give him "someone to talk to." She said, "Somebody to listen to—that's what you give me."

Enrichers' notes.

This session did not reveal much except that Tom sees himself as more a friend than a mate and that Debbie is accustomed to Tom's not talking much; instead, he listens to her.

Session 3

First, we reviewed the homework. The couple had arrived at the "rules" of their relationship. Tom cited several examples of things he does not *talk about* with Debbie, such as jokes about her family or other people; also, he does not tease her or scare her. Debbie cited things she does not *do*, such as disturb Tom when he is practicing or touch him when he is meditating. Tom appears irritated at the thought of the limitations on his communication. This tension was apparent before the session began. Tom's irritation upset Debbie, as evidenced later when she cried.

Tom explained they have different senses of humor and are two very different people. He considers her sense of humor childish; she claimed that his is cruel and sarcastic. With these issues unresolved and anger and hurt still apparent, the session was begun.

When we asked, "What is communication?" the couple concluded that there is much nonverbal communication and even communication by the act of silence. Their tension was still apparent in this discussion.

In the next exercise, we asked Tom to communicate a nonverbal message to Debbie. He communicated that he felt "bugged." Debbie thought this was because she had been interrupting us. Earlier she had caught herself doing this and had tried to stop. At that point, she had reached out to touch Tom for reassurance (a very standard nonverbal gesture for them). She did not receive any reassurance at the time, so she knew he was "bugged."

Then Tom explained that Debbie often fails to meet his expectations, which makes him angry. He said it seems that, in spite of her promises, she'll "never change." Debbie explained that she does a lot of things that bother Tom. She considers most of them trivial but is trying to change.

Next, Debbie was asked to communicate nonverbally to Tom. Before she began, Tom said, "She's hurt—she's going to cry." She did, saying she felt "real embarrassed." We reassured her that she need not feel embarrassed by her tears.

In further discussion, it was pointed out that Tom had not even noticed that Debbie had interrupted us. A discussion ensued about exactly why Debbie cried, and she finally attributed it to the fact that Tom had said she would "never change." Tom explained again that they are two very different people. For example, he "thinks before he acts" but she "acts without thinking." We confronted Tom with his wanting her to be like him and pointed out that Tom probably loves her spontaneity and that her qualities that are opposite to his may attract him.

We had each person ask a question of the partner nonverbally; the partner was to give the answer the other person wanted. This deviated from the program but allowed them to make up nonverbally.

Next, Debbie was to ask a question of Tom and he was to ignore her. She asked, "Are we going to visit my parents this summer?" When Tom was to ask Debbie a question and be ignored by her, he said sarcastically, in a high-pitched voice, "When are we going to get married?" He then added, "That's what she's always asking me." We pressed Tom to ask something he seriously wanted to know, but he persisted in asking, "When do you want to get married?" Finally, he asked, "When are we going to eat dinner?" Debbie ignored this, as instructed, but said later, "I can really get to him by being silent."

Each partner was asked to communicate verbally but conceal the message nonverbally. Each described the nonverbal component (e.g., facial expressions) clearly and specifically, and cited other instances of incongruence they had observed in the past.

We asked Debbie to role-play the blamer and Tom to play the preaching role; Debbie was to avoid his communication. We asked them which role each was better at. Tom said he was best at preaching and disagreed when Debbie said she was good at it. Debbie considered Tom a better placater, and he disagreed with that. Debbie said she was good at blaming. Tom said that although placating was easier, the preaching role was more natural: "I understand that because it just flows."

Tom and Debbie got into a discussion about separating while Tom goes on tour with a band. They spoke of how it had become clear to them that they do need to separate.

Following this, we explained "I" statements, telling them that one can speak only for oneself, which is communication of a fact and that all talk of "you" and external events is based on assumption. Debbie and Tom got very excited and mentioned times when they had discussed this truth.

Next, we offered the general formula "I feel —— when you ——" and related this statement to a disagreement they had mentioned earlier. Tom could have said, "I feel embarrassed when you are noisy in public," rather than making blaming statements.

For homework, the couple was asked to make three "I" statements every day. Tom said, "We'll make a million of them."

Enrichers' notes.

In this session, the couple's avowed communication block appeared early. Tom was feeling increasing irritation, and Debbie was overemotional and self-critical for inappropriate reasons (interrupting the enrichers). Tom's attitude following this incident centered first on how different their personalities are and then switched to sarcasm, as shown in his asking, "When are we going to get married?"

The exercise on manipulative techniques was a learning experience for both of them. Tom could see which technique is "most natural" for him. Debbie thinks of herself as a preacher, not a placater, but Tom has the opposite impression of her. (I am inclined to agree with Tom, that Debbie is a placater rather than a preacher.) Debbie did recognize her blaming tendencies, however. It may be that the ongoing frustration between the couple clouded Debbie's perception at that point.

The frustration Tom showed in his sarcastic remarks continued until the final discussion, in which both agreed that a separation would be good for them. Only after that did they discover the importance of making statements such as "I feel —— when you ——."

Session 4

At the beginning of the session, Debbie said that she had arrived at some great insights about herself and her role: "I have been looking at Tom as a father and just kind of playing house." She explained that she had not been assuming responsibility for her share of their life. After a discussion with Tom, she had begun to realize how much responsibility is necessary. "I was feeling mad, but I started to think about why I was mad. I realized I've been living in a fairy tale." Then she stated that she realized that Tom never intends to get married and that she had just taken it for granted that they would someday get married. Tom said, "I felt relieved that she realized these things. It was just going to end soon if she hadn't."

We asked whether they had used the statement "I feel —— when you ——." Debbie had said, "I feel bad when you snap at me," but Tom could not "remember" how he felt or reacted to the situation.

Beginning the lesson called Communication and Hurt, we gave written ambiguous messages to each partner to deliver to the mate. The exercise was designed to point out that one message can be construed differently under different circumstances. Tom and Debbie did not respond well to the exercise, so we explained the point of it.

In the next exercise, we asked the couple to engage in a conversation in which they were to use restatement techniques (feedback). They discussed what kind of car to buy. Tom said that they should buy one with an automatic transmission because "it would last longer if we both were driving it." Debbie interpreted his remarks to mean that she can't drive well. Tom explained that after anyone else drives his car, "it just doesn't feel the same." Debbie asked Tom to show her how to drive it right. During the discussion, we intervened often to elicit restatements from each partner. Tom said, "What I hear you saying is that you're getting into how you're inadequate and can't change." Debbie finally restated this message as "I want you to be more specific about how I should drive the car."

Because of the restatement techniques, the couple had to lay their cards on the table. Tom reflected to Debbie his perception of her inadequacy and defensiveness, which are stumbling blocks to him. Likewise, Debbie reflected to Tom her perception of the vagueness of his statements. The exercise seemed to leave them frustrated, perhaps somewhat hurt.

The partners were instructed to take turns saying, "I feel hurt when ———." The first three or four responses of each partner had to do with communication: "You don't understand me, don't listen to me, aren't interested in what I say." During this exercise, tears came to Tom's eyes; at the end, they hugged each other.

In the next part of the exercise, we asked how each partner would like the other to show hurt or angry feelings. Debbie told Tom, "I wish you would just say it instead of making me guess around and feel bad about it."

In response to the same question, Tom said that Debbie freely shows her feelings in the way she walks and acts. "It's very clear," he said. He added, "Maybe she could bring it up faster and not make it last so long."

Enrichers' notes and supervision.

Debbie's realization that she had not assumed her share of the responsibilities and her immature sense of Tom as a father are steps toward maturity. The couple's earlier claim (Session 1) that they intended to marry was overturned, and each person's real expectations were revealed and accepted. For Debbie this is a step from fantasy into reality.

The discussion about the car pointed out inadequacies in their communication system. As the next exercise was begun, Tom and Debbie still appeared frustrated and hurt by the feelings that had been expressed. Apparently, this frustration and hurt contributed to the extent to which Tom was able to express his hurt feelings.

This lesson again resembled the couple's avowed theme of Tom's irritation and Debbie's self-depreciating emotions. Providing the couple with the structured restatement techniques (shared meaning) was particularly appropriate at this time because it allowed them to reflect each other's communication style, painful though it was.

As we talked about this couple after the session, we realized that each of us has a very different view of Tom and Debbie. I have tended to identify with the partner who is weaker, at least on the surface. That is, I consider Debbie somewhat the victim of Tom's denial of emotions and logical manipulation. On the other hand, the female enricher feels more supportive of Tom and has wished to confront Debbie about her passive aggression, her tendency to manipulate from an inferior position of placating and the abrogation of responsibility. These realizations have helped us become more aware of our biases and, we hope, more effective as enrichers.

Session 5

A review of the homework revealed that Tom and Debbie had not done many of the "I feel" statements or the shared meaning homework.

For the first exercise in the lesson called Trust, we asked Tom and Debbie to name the areas in which they do not feel open to communication. Both felt they hold back communication in some areas.

Tom: I would like to be more open about my innermost thoughts and feelings.

Debbie: I would like us to be more open about sex.

Tom: It's not really hard for you to talk about it; it's just hard for you to get me to listen. I'm just not into that facet of my consciousness. I don't think about that unless I'm really doing it.

Debbie: If I waited for you to bring it up, we'd never talk about it.

Tom: You don't know that. If you'd get to know me a little better, you'd know when it's the proper time to talk about such things. I don't think you're really concerned about the problem but only thinking about yourself.

At this point, we played back the tape of the preceding conversation, then asked them to repeat the conversation, speaking in terms of "I feel —— when you ——."

Debbie: I feel we should discuss this.

Tom: I do too, but at the appropriate time—when we're both feeling objective about it. The best time for me to talk about it is when I'm not involved in it.

Debbie: What I hear you saying is that when we're not involved in it, you don't want to talk about it, but you don't want to when we are involved either.

Tom: Since I'm not perfect and since I suffer a lot from my emotions, I feel you could get more from me if you would just evaluate the situation and see where I'm at.

Debbie: I've brought it up, but you've made me feel I didn't have any right to bring it up.

Tom: You're bringing up things when I'm into something else.

At this point, I asked Tom what he does when it's a "bad scene."

Tom: When that happens, I'm not looking to someone else to understand it; I'm looking to myself to understand it. That's not just in that situation, that's in a lot of situations—a procedure I have.

The female enricher remarked that Tom seems to try to solve all problems by himself, even those concerning his interactions with others. "What would happen if you just blurted it out to Debbie? Can you trust her to accept it?"

Tom replied: "No, I just don't think she understands a lot—understands me. There have been times when she's missed the point entirely. . . ." Asked how he felt then, Tom explained that he felt hurt and empty when that happened.

The female enricher asked them to name other areas that are not open to communication. Debbie was obviously irritated at this point, so the female enricher turned to her and asked, "Are you irritated at me?"

Debbie replied angrily, "Both of you. You didn't give me a chance to explain it. I do understand Tom [when he expresses himself], but I don't say what he wants to hear. So I think that should change your entire interpretation."

The enricher then explained that she was "only interpreting that Tom *felt* you didn't understand. That's all." Debbie accepted this but with her nose in the air.

Tom further explained that he wants someone to listen to him without interpreting what he says or saying it back. "I just want to get it out and be vulnerable."

Debbie said, "I just don't know what he wants me to say."

After we urged them to use "I feel" statements, Tom said, "I feel frustrated when I put you in the position of having to think about your reaction."

Debbie responded, "But if I don't, you say I missed the point of what you said." We then suggested that if the communicator does not feel the message is being heard, he or she should ask for a restatement.

In responding to the exercise on congruence, both partners recalled tendencies to promise one thing but not do what they promise. On the subject of facing imperfections, both gave examples of admitting fault.

Of their styles in relating, the couple said they compete for attention and that they also compete in conversation. Tom commented that after a movie, Debbie dominates the conversation.

When we asked about areas of responsibility, Tom said he feels responsible for telling Debbie what she is responsible for. Debbie said, "Sometimes I feel responsible for keeping things light so they don't get too heavy."

Enrichers' notes and supervision.

Tom's reluctance to deal openly with emotion-laden issues was evident in this session. He prefers figuring out emotions "objectively" by himself and wants Debbie to approach him on such subjects only when he is in just the right mood. In this dialogue, Debbie was trying to point out the illogic of what Tom was saying (a form of preaching) instead of seeking an expression of his feelings when those uncomfortable subjects arise.

Regarding Tom's "important" communications, it was apparent that it is hard for Debbie to know when he is "being vulnerable." Tom admitted "frustration" at putting Debbie in a position of having to think about her responses at such times. Tom's "vulnerability" seems armored with defenses of when and where and how Debbie should respond to him. But in a sense, Debbie manipulated by placating when she said, "I don't know what you want me to say."

Session 6

When we arrived for the session, the couple were reluctant to have the session because they were in the middle of an argument. Because of rescheduling problems, it was decided to go ahead with the session.

We attempted the first exercise in the Quid Pro Quo lesson, asking Debbie to begin because she was passive and avoiding the interaction. She began to cry and recounted the reasons that she was upset. Tom had been sick, and neither had had a chance to meditate. They had been shopping that day, and Tom had acted irritable. Debbie, trying to be understanding, had bottled up her own hurt and frustration. Later, in the car, Tom had asked her what was wrong. When she tried to explain, Tom told her she was frustrated for the wrong reasons, paranoid, etc. His response had made her feel "boxed in." At this, we reminded them to use restatements and "I" statements.

Debbie: I felt responsible when you were snapping for no reason, and I felt victimized.

Tom: I hear you saying that you know you weren't the cause of it but you were the one to catch it. Well, I feel really frustrated when you assume such things—when you don't believe me.

Debbie: Do you deny that you were irritable?

Tom: Right, but it wasn't like you dramatized it.

Debbie tried to drag in earlier similar incidents, but we reminded her of the rule about no past history. She responded, "I tried to communicate sincerely later [in the car]. He told me to shut up." Tom admitted he had ignored her because "What you were saying had a totally invalid foundation. I explained that you were fighting for a cause that was wrong." We pointed out that Tom's statement was a form of manipulation by logical argument (preaching).

Next, the partners were asked to role-play the scene at the store, using restatement and "I feel" statements. Debbie voiced her frustration, and Tom admitted his irritation. They again launched into an argument to defend or justify their frustration and had to be continually reminded to make appropriate statements.

Tom and Debbie complained of two other communication problems. One was that Debbie wanted to know what to do when Tom denies he is irritated. We told her she has the right to keep expressing her own feelings of frustration that arise from such a situation. Second, it was revealed that Tom does not accept Debbie's feedback, or restatement. But Tom, too, stated that when he understands Debbie's communication she doesn't believe him and "keeps on doing it." We kept reminding them to use restatements and to ask for restatements to ensure accurate communication and reception.

In talking about their argument during their shopping trip, we explained that it is Debbie's responsibility to bring up her feelings at the moment she feels them and that it is Tom's responsibility to actively accept them without rationalizing their inappropriateness or threatening her. Throughout the session, the couple remained angry and kept slipping into generalities about each other. We kept structuring the conversation and became more directive as the session went on, including preaching about why it is important to express feelings immediately.

Toward the end of the session Tom acknowledged his "impatience" as a basic "flaw in my personality." He also added, "We have a bad habit of being committed when things are going well but not when things are rough."

Debbie responded, "Yeah, we want to leave every day."

When we reminded them, "You're still together," both said, "Yeah."

Enrichers' notes and supervision.

This session was totally dominated by the unsettled issue of the communication breakdown that day at the store. They were so emotionally wrapped up in it that it was impossible to keep them on the program.

The initial reasons they gave for their problem were that they had not had a chance to meditate and that Tom had been sick. We believe that the day's events pointed out each partner's intolerance for negative emotions. Tom denied any real irritation or anger several times in the session and tried to convince Debbie that the basis for her negative feelings was invalid. Debbie tried "to bear" the hurt and anger she felt (rather than expressing it immediately) until it seemed grossly disproportionate and inappropriate to Tom when she did express it. Debbie defended her negative emotions, insisting that Tom had caused them by his irritation. This strong need to justify negative emotions may be due to the couple's spiritual attitudes.

We intervened often to get Tom and Debbie to restate each other's communications and to avoid blaming. As the session progressed, we became more and more directive in stressing the need for the immediate communication of feelings and open reception by the listener. Eventually, we advised them to be more accepting of emotions in their immediate context and not to rationalize them away in either spiritual or blaming terms. The advice did not appear to be taken, and the issues seemed unresolved at the end of the session. Tom's final statement about their sunshine commitment did seem to show some insight that improvement would take greater effort.

FEEDBACK CONFERENCE

We began by asking what they had learned from SE. Tom responded that he is now "thinking of it more as a relationship, as a unit together." He said the most beneficial part of the program was the simple tools of "I" statements and restatements. "They're easy vehicles that don't require much thought to use, but are very beneficial."

Debbie said she now views the two of them "as a relationship" rather than as two people "just living here, trying to get along." We asked whether they had found any insights into themselves as individuals. Debbie said, "Sometimes I try to manipulate, by preaching in particular. I also learned that I don't say how I feel, but I project that onto Tom, saying that he's doing something before I say 'I feel this when you do that.'"

Tom said that after listening to the tapes he could "see where I come on real strong as a defense. As a last resort I get real nasty."

Tom and Debbie regretted not having practiced more homework exercises, particularly the shared meaning technique of restatements.

We explained how they can express their commitment to each other by communicating emotions in the following ways: (a) tell your emotions immediately, without implying that the other person has caused the emotion; (b) don't deny feeling angry when your body and face are showing anger; and (c) it's OK to say "I'm confused by what you're saying" when you receive an incongruent message.

Next, we told them how frustrated we had felt when they argued and that we had felt like "shaking them and telling them, 'do this and don't do that.'" We added that we had also felt frustrated with ourselves.

We explained that we want them to feel comfortable about negative emotions, to "give them as much care and respect as the positive emotions," and we asked whether their philosophy opposes negative emotions. When Debbie said she thinks it is wrong to "feel angry without a reason," the female enricher responded, "There's no need. You are angry or you're not angry. You don't say you have to have a reason to feel love." Debbie expressed her ambivalence about this, saying she sometimes feels it's necessary to find a *reason* for the emotion she feels. The enricher explained that emotions are governed by laws different from those of thinking and shouldn't be reduced to the rational elements of the situation. She added that when a reason is sought for a negative emotion, it becomes projected onto the partner in a blaming way.

Debbie did most of the responding, but finally Tom asked for something more specific and concrete. We suggested that a simple statement of feelings, without any blaming connotations, is the essential aspect of open communication; then we reviewed the three points we had made earlier.

We then spoke of our different backgrounds and how we had experienced changes in ourselves as a result of our sessions together. I told them that I had found it easier to identify with Debbie and also that I had been oversensitive to their conflict, particularly during the first session when Debbie had cried and they had decided definitely to separate. "We saw the separation as a sign of strength," Debbie explained. "I was to the place where I was self-sufficient enough to do that."

I commented, "I feel that for the first time we are out of our roles and relating as humans." Tom agreed. Tom had shaved off his beard before this session, and his facial expressions showed much more clearly than before. Tom later said that shaving his beard had made him more vulnerable.

We ended the session by offering further SE if they wish it.

Enrichers' notes.

I felt a real sense of loss or emptiness after the final session. I had somehow felt close to Tom for the first time and wondered why I had *not* felt that earlier. I had been mostly aware of Tom's defensiveness throughout the program. Perhaps the change was partly due to my having replayed the taped sessions, which made me more aware of Tom's hurt feelings. Another factor was the removal of his beard (I identified with this because I recently shaved my beard and have felt quite vulnerable and more open with my emotions).

Supervision.

We discussed the feedback conference and how positive Tom's and Debbie's insights were. This happened in spite of the preceding session in which the couple couldn't get out of their cycle of arguing, and I had poured on the advice. In discussing these events, the coenricher asked why I didn't seem pleased or satisfied with the results. I didn't know why at the time, but I felt a sense of loss.

I explained to our supervisor that when I had listened to the tapes I had felt myself "raising a flag" and being motivated by a sense of resentment, usually because I identified with the weaker partner, assigning her the role of victim. The supervisor asked whether I had ever felt resentment toward him. After thinking about it, I realized that I had and related this to feeling "the victim" of his evaluation. When the supervisor asked me where I wanted to go from here, I explained that I want to be able to continue gaining information from my emotional state and for this to happen more easily.

In discussing my feelings with the supervisor, I realized that my sense of loss came partly from the fact that the program had not gone according to my master plan and that in spite of this the couple had showed great improvement in their attitudes. I saw that my master plan was a function of my life script, which does not tolerate conflict or advice giving. This passive life spirit in part had made me adopt a pride in being facilitative and nondirective, without giving advice. But I had been overwhelmed by the arguments and had been sucked into them myself, with the result that I gave a lot of advice. The fact that the couple had done so well in such conflict-ridden sessions was a threat to my life script, which is why I felt a sense of loss when SE ended.

POSTTEST EVALUATION

The posttest data in general show large increases in marital satisfaction and in satisfaction with one's own interpersonal qualities. On Debbie's

Family Information scale there were large increases in self-disclosure, feelings and emotions, and genuineness. On the other hand, Tom rated himself more satisfied with self-disclosure, feelings and emotions, and confrontation. Tom's ratings dropped in 11 questions on the Primary Communications Inventory and only went up on 1 question, but Debbie's changes were approximately even. Debbie went down in 14 of the questions in the 18-item Family Information scale, and Tom went down in 9 items on the same scale, with very few increases. "Today my spouse loves me." "Today things are peaceful in this family," and "Today I learned something about my spouse" are examples of items marked significantly lower. The other tests show similar decreases in satisfaction and agreement.

It is likely that the testing reflects the situational factor of the arguments preceding and during Session 6 (the posttest forms were given to the couple after that session). Also, the posttests may reflect in part a much more realistic attitude about the quality of their relationship and the effort that goes into a relationship.

In the 10-minute posttest tape, both Tom and Debbie spoke more frequently of their interpersonal needs and abilities as a couple rather than as individuals. They also talked more about the commitment it takes to make a good relationship.

15

Alcohol in the Marriage

James Kochalka

INTERVIEW

Jan and Bob were referred by a friend; they were described as a couple interested in strengthening their relationship.

As I brought the couple into the consulting room, I was struck by their physical presence: Bob is about 6'5", large-boned, and weighs approximately 240 pounds; Jan, also large-framed, is 5'11" and weighs 150 pounds.

Bob's boyish face presents a younger look than his 38 years. His blonde hair is neatly styled in a medium length. His dark slacks and a solid-colored sport shirt hung comfortably on his large frame. Jan, 37 years old, has dark brown hair, which complemented her stylish slacks, tan blazer, and print blouse. Jan and Bob have two children, a 3-year-old girl and an 8-year-old boy. Bob works in sales, and Jan works for a travel agency.

Both have quick smiles, but I noted a somewhat distant look in Jan's eyes. Bob, in contrast, made direct contact and spoke in a deep, almost bellowing, voice punctuated by a resonating laugh. Jan expressed herself more hesitantly, speaking softly but articulately. During the interview, both partners smoked frequently, and Bob quickly lit Jan's cigarettes.

At the outset, Bob pointedly seated himself next to Jan (other chairs were available) and commented, "I don't want him to think we don't like one another."

As I began to explain SE, Bob interrupted, "How stable must one be in order to benefit from enrichment?" Jan echoed a similar concern. Somewhat naively, I responded that the demands would not be great. (In retrospect, further inquiry probably would have provided enough clues to eliminate them from the nonclinical status desired for this case.) After my reassurance, they agreed that they would like to participate.

My only significant observation during the pretests was that Bob is an extremely slow and deliberate reader, in contrast to his rather spontaneous verbal style. He laughed audibly while completing the Sexual Happiness Scale. Jan continued to work quietly.

PRETEST SUMMARY

The following instruments were used as pretests: Marital Happiness Scale, Sexual Happiness Scale, Family Satisfaction Scales (10- and 18-item forms), Semantic Differential, Holmes-Rahe Schedule of Events, and the Marital Questionnaire.

Bob's overall scores on the Marital Happiness Scale are much lower than Jan's, indicating a possibly significant dissatisfaction with their marriage. Also, Bob expressed some dissatisfaction with sexual foreplay, though he saw himself as more satisfied with orgasm.

Jan seemed relatively content but did see Bob as less happy with their relationship. In general, Jan's assessment is more congruent with Bob's assessment of himself than vice versa.

The Family Satisfaction Scales suggest that Bob feels some domestic tension, misunderstanding, lack of love, and some unhappiness with his family. Jan reported being generally more satisfied. Interestingly, each spouse sees Jan as lacking initiative in the relationship.

According to the Marital Questionnaire, Bob engages in a great deal of distracting behavior. Further, he showed significant deficits in the marital tasks of forgiveness and sharing hurt. In contrast, Jan appeared superior on almost all dimensions of the Marital Questionnaire.

According to the Semantic Differential, both spouses have good estimates of self-esteem. Jan selected the highest possible rating on "good" and "useful"; Bob scored himself high on "good," "useful," "superior," "kind," and "pleasant."

The Holmes-Rahe scale shows that Bob perceives a much greater degree of stress in his life than Jan perceives in hers.

Enricher's notes.

I considered three enrichment programs for this couple: Negotiation, Reciprocity, and Assertiveness. Negotiation could address Bob's inability to forgive and share hurt, at least on a content level. Assertiveness might be appropriate for Jan's lack of initiative. Reciprocity could address the issues that Bob is not now confronting equitably with Jan.

SUMMARY OF SESSIONS

Session 1: Marriage Myths

Bob and Jan arrived in a very positive and excited mood. They had just returned from a spiritual meeting and had apparently been much affected by the experience.

After I described the three programs, Bob expressed his disdain for the term *negotiation*. As a salesman, he considers the term taboo. Jan said that lack of assertiveness is a definite problem for her and that she might be interested in that program. Bob countered that the word *assertiveness* makes him uncomfortable. He then related an incident in which he had asserted himself with a used-car salesman. After I helped them get back on the subject, they discussed the programs and chose Negotiation.

Asked to redefine a myth, Jan began by describing it as "a story which has elements of truth in it." Bob agreed with Jan's definition, reiterating the truth he believed inherent in a myth. My suspicion was that each partner had confused *myth* and *parable*. At any rate, I prevailed with a somewhat different definition; that is, a myth is something that people accept as true, but it is not true.

In responding to premarital conceptions of marriage, Jan spoke of her belief that marriage would be a very happy experience, filled with romance and "high" experiences. Bob responded in a TA (transactional analysis) adult fashion (i.e., emphasizing the notion of a working unit, mutual growth, and role flexibility). They agreed that their love had become deeper since they married and that their romantic feelings have been replaced by deeper feelings of concern for each other.

Bob, describing what love was like during courtship, said that premarital love was filled with good feelings, high interest, and his fascination with Jan. Jan said that Bob's premarital love for her boosted her confidence, motivated her, and enhanced her self-esteem.

After they completed and read their lists of words describing male and female characteristics, Bob commented that he and Jan can do identical tasks, with the sole exception of childbearing. Jan said that their lives are characterized by a flexible division of labor; that is, although each partner typically performs certain tasks, each partner helps the other when needed. Bob concluded by saying that he feels especially close to Jan after they have worked together in the yard.

In responding to the myth that arguments equal poor marriages, Bob began by saying that they have no problem negotiating "small" issues but that "big issues present a problem." He said that his strategy during conflict is to retreat from Jan's verbal barrage until he reaches a breaking point, at which time he retaliates by confronting Jan in a deep voice.

Jan said that her inability to negotiate is marked by emotional reactions—screaming and crying. She tends to display these behaviors after small incidents have built up.

Both partners had trouble responding to the question about how each shows respect for the other's viewpoint. Neither could give a concrete example.

Homework.

I asked Bob and Jan to be aware of times during the coming week when the other is met "halfway." Bob responded that he believes there is no fifty-fifty in marriage but that each situation dictates differing amounts of giving. I asked them to think about that, too, during the coming week.

Enricher's notes.

The first session left me with several disparate, though important, impressions. I was first struck by my subjective confirmation of Bob's low score (3) on the distracting scale of the Marital Questionnaire. He indeed had displayed an abundance and variety of distracting verbalizations. I was aware of being "on guard" with Bob, lest he stray too far from the topic.

Though it is early in our relationship, I suspect that each partner has some investment in protecting the other from hurt feelings. Jan expressed a hypersensitivity to criticism from Bob, a statement that Bob said applied to him also. This protective posture may be an inhibiting factor in developing a rational negotiation strategy. A further confirmation of this hypothesis was inferred from Bob's discounting the possibility that negotiation may be relevant in their marriage; Jan, however, said she believes a problem does exist in this area.

Session 2: Focus on the Relationship

Bob and Jan arrived on time and in apparently good spirits. At the beginning of the session, Bob launched into a commentary about the "enlightening" Bible session they had just attended. We chatted briefly on this topic before I asked about the homework assignment (i.e., be aware during the week of times you meet each other halfway).

Jan began, saying she had given "a lot of thought to how we encourage one another" (her understanding of the homework assignment) but had not really come up with anything. Bob responded with an apologetic comment: "I think that the problem is we're still changing gears from the Bible study, but we didn't really do the homework."

At this point, Jan stated in a calm, serious manner that she believes they have a communication problem, citing lack of discussion as a central problem. She related an incident involving an argument that had arisen that evening because Bob and a friend had been drinking at Bob and Jan's home during the dinner hour. Jan said that she had felt "hassled" because they had so little time before their Bible study and our session. I listened quietly and attentively but then suggested that we go on.

Before I began the first exercise, Bob mentioned a discussion he had had with Jan about the pretests. The issue was the great discrepancy between Bob's high stress rating versus Jan's low stress rating on the Holmes-Rahe. In an apparent face-saving comment, Bob stated that Jan's relatively low stress ranking was due to the fact that Bob had attended Bible study class for the first time that evening. His participation in that class makes Jan very happy, so Bob assumed that she would have reported less stress.

In answer to the question "Who are you?" Bob spoke first, describing himself with the following: Bob, me, husband, father, good, resident of Wildwood Road, proud father, confused husband, imaginative person, and a perceptive person.

Jan responded to the question with the following: Jan, your wife, mother of your children, a person, a Christian, your lover, an employee of Worldwide Travel, daughter of my parents, and your friend.

Bob continually asked, "And who is that?" instead of the instructed "Who are you?"

To the question "What can I give you?" Bob listed the following: understanding, love, organization, good to kids, support, fun things, and a fanny pat.

Jan's responses were as follows: love, support, encouragement, a good mother, organized life, pride, a clean house, a fanny pat, and friendship.

To "What can you give me?" Bob listed love, companionship, admiration, respect, good time, lots of money, trip around the world, mother, better organization, and your friend.

When I asked how they felt about doing these exercises, Bob said he thought their comments sounded beautiful but that he was skeptical about the genuineness of their responses because many of their verbal comments were learned.

Jan's response was more pointed: she noted that Bob wants her support but that she doesn't know how to support him since she doesn't know how she hurts him. She alluded to the previously mentioned dinner-time argument. Bob reacted to Jan in a blaming reference to her "trying to make situations more difficult than they were."

After a standard, brief description of family systems, I asked, "Can you name some of the rules of your relationship? Are you aware of your rules about decision making in your marriage?"

Both spouses appeared fatigued and had great difficulty answering. After some time, Jan described their relationship along traditional roles of labor division in the family: the rules are that Bob takes care of the car, lawn, house repairs; Jan's functions include child rearing, cooking, and cleaning. Bob essentially echoed her comments.

Jan responded quizzically to the question about decision making and said that no problem exists in this area. Again, Bob supported her response, citing their mutual participation in child rearing.

Homework.

The homework assignment was to write down all the rules that apply to their relationship and then sit down together to discuss them.

Enricher's notes.

This lesson was significant in that I became aware of SE's diagnostic function and this couple's need for therapy. This awareness was subjectively validated in several ways. First, Jan's unsolicited report of their communication difficulties implied the conflict that exists between them. It was clear to me that even though Jan knows the structure of the program, the underlying marital problems are her primary concern. Second, Jan seems to collude (unconsciously?) with Bob in allowing him to speak for them ("we feel," "she thinks"); yet, on an overtly interactional level, this pattern confounds communication. Third, Bob's abuse of alcohol was intimated in Jan's reference to the dinner-time argument. I inferred that Jan's dinner-time actions had been designed to remove Bob from the drinking situation (e.g., she called for his assistance with light packages and acted "hurried" in the house, which implied a need for help). Fourth, Bob labeled himself a "confused husband." This description, coupled with each spouse's desire for "organization" in the house, may be an allusion to chaotic relational patterns at home. Finally, Jan said that she wants to support Bob but she can't because she hurts him unknowingly. This statement certainly suggests discord and implies deficit of support and a surplus of pain.

It is interesting and somewhat perplexing that Bob commented so illogically about the Holmes-Rahe scale; no items on the scale suggest "an irrelevant" measurement of stress. He is of apparently normal intelligence and displayed no loose associations in thought up to this point.

Bob's distracting tendencies were manifest throughout the lesson: he embellished tangential issues or generalized at length about issues specifically directed toward his behavior.

Though the psychoanalytic concept of transference is not salient to this discussion, at several points during Bob's digressive speaking, I felt an urge to shout, "Shut up! Cut it out! Quit rambling!" In contrast, Jan's communications seemed more genuine and congruent. I resolved to be more direct and explicit in controlling the conversation in subsequent sessions.

Session 3: Communication in Marriage

First, I asked about their homework assignment. Bob said that they had discussed the assignment but had not made a list. Jan reported that she had found the assignment difficult but that she had come up with some rules: (a) If I'm not sure how he's going to receive something, I'll be quiet. (b) I don't usually ask him for help, but then I get mad at him. (c) We try to use positive reinforcement with the children. (d) If Bob asks me to do something, I won't say no even if I don't agree with it. Then I get back at him later. (e) If one of us is mad, we keep the house quiet. (f) We treat everyone in the house with respect. Again, Bob's comments were essentially agreements with Jan's statements.

Jan mentioned that she thought the second lesson had been interesting: she didn't believe she had said that she could give Bob the things that he wanted to have. She asked whether I had a record of their responses. I agreed to mail the information to them; then I began with the first exercise.

Asked to define communication and describe the ways they communicate, Bob began in a textbook style, saying it is "both verbal and nonverbal . . . to adequately convey what you're wanting to and to be receptive to hear what everyone is saying so as not to put words in the other person's mouth." Jan said she had nothing to add to Bob's definition.

Bob added that it is important to consider the "context" of a situation when communicating. He used the example of fatigue at bedtime as an inappropriate time to consider a conflict.

I asked each of them to try to convey a feeling without speaking. Both demonstrated discomfort and anxiety, fidgeting and laughing nervously. Little fruitful discussion resulted from this exercise. Jan said that she saw Bob as nervous; Bob said that he had felt love from Jan's silent message.

In the next exercise, I asked Jan to think of a question she wanted Bob to answer. I instructed Bob to remain silent and distracted, Jan to insist that he answer. Afterward, both were to tell how they felt about doing this exercise.

Jan reported frustration; Bob answered equivocally, saying that he had purposely done some role playing and ignoring but that he had revealed no feeling.

Each was asked to say a sentence or two to the other person and cancel the word message nonverbally. Both appeared relaxed and comfortable; they easily grasped the spirit of the exercise and enjoyed mimicking standard incongruencies in their marital repertoire. For Jan this included a verbal disclaimer of obvious anger and an oblique interest in having sex. For Bob it was a veiled question about dinner location when he obviously wanted to go out. They completed this exercise with a degree of levity that I had not seen in them before.

I used the blackboard to present the manipulative roles—placating, blaming, avoiding, and preaching; then I asked that one play the role of a blamer and the other the role of a placater.

Before beginning, Jan queried Bob as to what role she usually plays. Without hesitation, Bob replied, "Blamer."

During the exercise, Bob acted as placater and Jan as blamer. Each was able to role-play accurately and easily for several minutes. Next, Bob preached and Jan avoided.

When I asked what they had learned about themselves, Bob said that sometimes he does avoid (doing things) but the problem is that Jan doesn't realize the priority system that he has arranged for his activities. Jan said that it had been hard for her to play the avoider. She stated that her avoidance takes the form of looking off somewhere and possibly missing the whole point. She wondered aloud whether she does this deliberately.

For the next exercise, I asked them to talk together for a couple of minutes about an issue of concern to them, but they were to use sentences that begin with "it."

Bob had difficulty staying with the assignment and spoke of irrelevancies (e.g., "Our cat is an it"). Jan's statements began with "it," but she and Bob shared no meaningful dialogue. When asked how they felt, each spouse responded that the exercise had been hard.

In repeating the exercise, Bob often began with "I." Jan's responses were "you" statements, but, again, no discussion took place. Bob remarked that he couldn't do this exercise because "you" sounds "accusatory."

Jan was able to use "we" statements as instructed when Bob repeated sentences beginning "Half of we." Jan said she liked the use of "we" better because it has a "unifying" sound.

Both were able to make "I" statements, and both considered them an appropriate form of communication.

Homework.

Their homework assignment was to make three "I" statements a day during the coming week.

Enricher's notes.

My inferences from this session focused on the couple's manipulative communication patterns. Jan seems to have some investment in being "quiet" in the relationship because this quietness apparently allows her much power (she suggested this in some of her homework rules). Quietness and passivity appear similar to TA's brown-stamp collecting (James & Jongeward, 1971): Jan collects enough "quiets" to trade in on several blames. I think that Jan alluded to this pattern in her comments about avoiding by looking off somewhere. I have seen her lost-in-space posture several times during SE. Apparently she has developed a very economical control mechanism in her quiet behavior, as it does seem to capture Bob's attention quickly (sometimes it also triggers his frustration).

Today's lesson was generally innocuous for Bob and Jan, but I was impressed with their being able to laugh genuinely at each other's incongruent communications. My awareness of the significance of mutual laughter was underscored by an article outlining the clinical use of mutual laughter (Ventis, 1973).

Bob's comments on avoidance were very interesting. Though he acknowledged his avoidance behavior, he *avoided* dealing with it by defining it in a novel way. His response was to Jan's role-played blamer, in which she chastised him for not doing certain tasks around the house.

I am somewhat baffled by Bob's diverse response styles. From a behavioral vantage point, it would be therapeutically instructive to determine the discriminative stimuli that trigger his differential response patterns (e.g., adult definition of communication versus his irrelevant, almost bizarre comments during the exercise on manipulative communication).

My clinical impressions at this time suggest a complementary relationship in which each spouse blames and avoids in polar opposition to the other. Jan responds to blaming by remaining silent and looking away; Bob responds by talking irrelevantly.

Session 4: Communication and Hurt

I began the session by inquiring about their homework assignment—using "I" statements. Bob said that he was becoming aware of three things: (a) they were using each other more often as sounding boards, (b) problems were being related "more discretely" to one another, and (c) they were selecting more opportune times for discussion.

Jan stated that the preceding lesson had "put things together in a new way for her"; that is, she had learned the importance of using "I" statements. She reported that she had definitely used more "I" statements in her conversations with Bob. As a non sequitur to this discussion, Bob made some "We feel" statements, seemingly oblivous to the implications of his message.

The first exercise concerned differences in the message sent and the message received. Bob began by asking Jan, "Didn't we have chicken Tuesday?" Jan responded in machine-gun fashion: "You don't want chicken, you don't like my cooking, and you don't like me!"

Jan then said to Bob, "It's cold in here." Before Bob responded, he qualified his statement by saying he imagined this was said to him in their family room. He then gave a long-winded explanation that essentially covered three areas: (a) "Things aren't to her satisfaction and I couldn't do anything about it." (b) Jan desires physical contact (i.e., to be held). (c) Jan is commenting on the "coldness" of the room decor.

After explaining shared meaning, I asked them to take a few minutes to discuss a real issue. I told them the issue need not be a heavy one— just something both could agree to discuss, using shared meaning.

Before they began, Bob asked for and received clarification of the components of shared meaning. He then made several distracting comments about the number of police cars going by with sirens blaring. Jan cajoled him to "get with the lesson."

They decided to discuss something "close," another dinner-time incident involving Bob's drinking friend. It was clear from the outset that their mutual interest was in rehashing the incident, not in attempting to learn the process of shared meaning. I intervened several times during their mildly intense discussion, asking, for example, "Jan, what do you hear Bob saying?" (or vice versa). These prompts proved only minimally helpful, so I terminated their discussion.

In the next exercise, I asked each to express hurt. Each was to face the partner and take turns saying sentences that begin with the words "I feel hurt by." Jan said she was hurt by (a) "your accusing me of things," (b) "your failure to understand me," (c) (after a pause) "your drinking," and (d) "your accusations." Bob responded very seriously: (a) "having to defend myself in situations," (b) "your ignoring me," (c) "your buying green beans when I put in a tremendous garden," and (d) "your making me feel like all problems are mine."

Asked how each of them wishes the other would express anger, Jan told Bob she wants to be told when he is angry so that she can better understand it. Bob responded similarly but added that he feels there is "no way out" when Jan is angry, because of her aversive expression of anger.

I next asked, "How can you encourage your partner to be more expressive of hurt or angry feelings?" Jan replied that she could talk with Bob in order to understand what she was doing.

Bob responded humorously, saying that the best solution is to take Jan out to dinner and avoid the issue. He then added that he could inquire about her feelings and attempt to discuss them. A brief discussion ensued about the relative merits of their respective strategies during the aforementioned dinner-time situation.

Homework.

Because of my perception of their scarred feelings at the end of this session, I chose not to assign the homework of using the shared meaning process. I did, however, give them a linear (straightforward) letter, which I instructed them to read at home.

Enricher's notes.

This lesson was instructive because it provided an abundance of surplus information. In the first exercise, both partners appeared to demonstrate an "awfulizing" component in their responses, which implied intense feelings (Jan's "don't like me," Bob's sense of responsibility for her dissatisfaction). If these attributions can be viewed as projective identifications of each spouse, they shed much light on how intraorganismic deficits influence the dyad.

Their need for marital therapy was again validated by their quick gravitation to the chronic dinner-time drinking issue instead of focusing on the exercise. The preeminence of this concern is underscored by the fact that the SE format does not provide reinforcement for the discussion of tangential issues. Focusing on the relationship versus content has been validated as a discriminator of clinical and nonclinical couples (Murphy & Mendelson, 1973).

Alcohol is clearly involved in this marriage. My suspicion is that Jan is in the early stages of giving up her protective stance with respect to Bob's drinking. The reticence she demonstrated in saying that Bob's drinking is an area of hurt for her seems to support my suspicion. During their discussion, Jan stated, "It hurts when Mike is around." Since nothing indicates that Mike's behavior is overtly abusive to Jan, I infer that her statement is a euphemism for the hurt of Bob's drinking.

That same discussion also supports my hypothesis of a mutual blaming-distracting (avoiding) dyadic interaction. Jan seems to create performance expectations of Bob (e.g., help with the groceries, kids, dinner); then she chastises him for noncompliance. Bob seems to blame (e.g., "You don't have to get so frustrated," or "You could have done . . .").

Distraction seems to be demonstrated in diverse ways. Bob distracts by initiating interference tasks (e.g., dinner) or by rambling talks on tangential topics; Jan seems to distract by denying her feelings (e.g., on the subject of alcohol).

Session 5: Trust

At the beginning of Session 5, Jan apologized for having "goofed up the lesson" by bringing up personal problems in the preceding session. I thanked her for her concern and assured her that the lesson had not been impaired. Jan continued, saying that she and Bob were aware after leaving that session that they had not used the shared meaning process as directed but that they had really been thinking about it a lot. I rewarded her efforts by saying that there was much value in their continued thoughts and discussion of the process.

In the first exercise, in which each partner was to name three subjects that he or she wished to be more open to discussion, Jan stated that she was unable to bring up any issues that might even hint of criticism because of Bob's inability to accept it. Though she was not specific, she indicated that these could be small things, not just big issues. Jan did, however, list three topics for more open communication: (a) procrastination, (b) business, and (c) (barely audible) drinking. She considers Bob's inability to accept criticism the inhibiting factor in their attempts at open communication.

Bob asked for a clarification of honest communication, wondering how it compared with open communication. After I responded, he listed some general topics for more open communication: (a) the house, (b) buying groceries, (c) where to go for a meal, (d) picking up, (e) short-term finances, and (f) "whether to buy this or that right now." In listing three specific areas, he named (a) disorganization, (b) time, and (c) fault finding. Bob stated that "we're afraid of one another, and Jan is as afraid of criticism as I am."

In the next exercise, I asked them to give examples of inconsistencies between words and actions that diminish trust between them. Jan said that she often verbalizes wanting to help Bob but doesn't follow through, naming as examples sex and lack of organization. Bob said that his problem area is being "verbally optimistic," that is, saying he will carry out various instrumental behaviors but not following through.

In answering when she had last made a mistake and admitted it openly, Jan said that she readily admits little mistakes but that admitting the big ones is more difficult. She then related an episode in which she didn't tell Bob about something that she had forgotten to take with her on a recent weekend trip. Bob described an episode in which he made a mistake in helping his daughter bake a cake and did admit his error.

Next, I asked them to name areas in which they compete and to tell how they feel when they compete. Bob initially said there is no competition in their marriage but that there is a struggle for power. Jan said that she has a hard time admitting she is wrong, so she often fights to have her opinion acknowledged, even if it is not later acted on. Bob agreed that this is typical and again referred to the power struggle that exists between them.

After describing a give-and-take marital relationship, I asked how that idea sounded to them. Bob gave a long-winded description of a problem in implementing the give-and-take, using as an example their current conflict about how to spend a recent commission check. Jan agreed that this is an area of difficulty.

Asked to name the areas for which she is responsible, Jan quickly named the following: dinner fixer, grocery buyer, laundry fixer, menial work around the house (she laughed). She also said that the children are her responsibility, though Bob helps when asked. Bob's responsibilities are major carpentry, plumbing and electrical repairs, cars, long-range planning, financial investments, the yard, and fixing things.

Homework.

For homework they were to note the partner's areas of competence and to divide responsibility for the areas that are not clearly defined.

Enricher's notes.

I noted Jan's opening apology as some kind of approval-seeking behavior.

Jan's barely audible comment that drinking is a difficult area to discuss probably mimics the covertly protective way that the issue has been treated.

In describing inconsistencies that diminish trust, Jan reflected a more genuine attitude than Bob did. She seems to be willing to accept a greater degree of responsibility for improving the relationship.

Each partner seems to try to gain status at the expense of the other in a mutually destructive fashion. There also appears to be a collusion in this relationship in the form of an unspoken rule; that is, "We don't talk about things that upset each other."

Their domestic job descriptions are divided along quite traditional lines, though in general that poses little problem for them. The exception to this satisfaction is the question of handling finances, which apparently is a chronic problem (indicated only by Bob's pretest).

Session 6: Quid Pro Quo

When I asked about their homework, Jan stated two gray areas in their relationship: (a) cleaning up after each other, and (b) who is responsible for preparing dinner when Jan will not be home on time. Bob said that he hadn't been aware that these two areas of conflict existed and added, "I didn't know I was such a mess around the house."

Jan countered, "We have two other people in the house also." At this point, I reviewed the six communication skills that we had discussed before.

I asked each to state as factually as possible the characteristics each would like to see in the other to make marriage more workable. The listening partner was asked to summarize what he or she heard the partner say. Bob said that Jan could use time better, not find problems to the problems, and anticipate the best solution to a problem.

Jan said that she would like Bob to (a) finish things before starting new ones, (b) establish priorities for his tasks, and (c) provide more understanding and acceptance.

Bob prefaced his summary of what he had heard by commenting that Jan's statements were "in a rather narrow vein." I reminded him that his task was to summarize Jan's comments, which he then did, adding that they were all "very valid." Bob tacked on a few destructive comments toward Jan, but I stopped him and went to the next exercise (Jan was visibly disturbed by Bob's caustic remarks).

Each partner was asked to tell the other the ways he or she fails in their relationship and how he or she could change to improve their marriage. Jan reported that she often fails to express her hurt feelings, causing Bob to infer a greater degree of hurt. She also said that she could be less flaky but that she is making improvements in that area. Bob adequately summarized Jan's comments, then said that he could be more assertive with respect to his own wants and needs. He also said that he could be more attentive to Jan.

In describing her principal wishes for their marriage, Jan wished for more affectional behaviors from Bob as well as fewer put-downs. Bob's desires were for more time alone, less judgment from Jan, and more listening.

For the third exercise, I asked each to identify one desire or need that the other partner can fulfill.

After several minutes of guarded, somewhat defensive discussion, they decided to explore Bob's desire to have more time alone. Several points were discussed: (a) Jan's ignorance of Bob's not having enough time alone, (b) the amount of time required, (c) the conditions under which Bob could be alone, (d) how he would communicate this to Jan.

Their interactional styles were marked by a great deal of defensiveness, though they used more "I" statements than they have in the past. Because time was limited, I suggested that one of Jan's issues be negotiated at home during the coming week.

Enricher's notes.

The knot in my stomach at the session's end was congruent with the thought that I was sitting on an emotional powder keg. Both partners were obviously suppressing (not very well) some interpersonal issue of greater importance than the content of SE. I was first aware of this when I asked about the homework assignment and received answers that were trivial as well as discrepant. Their good-front behavior was obvious in light of the more weighty issues that they had brought up in earlier sessions.

Jan's comments about being less flaky were an oblique reference to her low self-concept (as a marital partner). Jan and Bob apparently collude in the decrement of Jan's marital self-esteem (she allows Bob to comment on her performance).

This lesson gave me experiential validation of Gurman and Kniskern's (1978) critique of quid pro quo negotiation strategies. It is clear to me that quid pro quo is predicated on the assumption that each partner can behave in a rational, cognitive mode. I am now skeptical that couples are in fact capable of the amount of rationality required to work in this fashion.

FEEDBACK CONFERENCE

I began by asking to what they considered the benefits of SE. Jan began, stating three things she had learned: (a) new ways of communicating, (b) ways of expressing herself that aren't blaming, and (c) how to better resolve issues between them. Bob said that SE had provided a "vehicle for dialogue" but that he had had difficulty applying it at home. He suggested that a lesson outline given to the couple after each session would help them apply the skills that had been discussed.

He criticized some of the role-playing exercises but was not specific about which ones. Jan's criticism focused on the exercise in which she had had to discuss her failings in their relationship. She said that this exercise does not "build people up" and therefore is inappropriate.

In talking about the linear (straightforward) letter, Jan said that they had read the letter together, and that she believes it was "right, but in a light that I hadn't seen it before." She added that the comments in the letter were quite perceptive. Bob said that he felt I perceived their marriage as so fragile that it needed to be "shored up" with compliments and words of encouragement.

When I asked whether the letter had provided an avenue for discussion, they said that they had read and discussed the letter several times and would continue to do so. (A paradoxical letter would have really mesmerized them!)

Shifting to my feedback to them, I began by congratulating them for having worked so hard to improve their marriage. I noted as strengths their having learned new communication skills as well as being able to see the good in each other. Next, I mentioned the areas they might wish to consider: (a) their difficulty sharing feelings with each other; (b) the lack of clarity in their communication (the incongruence between feelings and words, and their problems in negotiating differences).

I then offered them options for future work, naming three sources for less structured work. Jan immediately said that they would like to receive counseling. Bob was silent, so I suggested that they think about it at home, then call me for a specific referral if they are interested.

PRE- AND POSTTEST EVALUATION

Marital Happiness Scale and Sexual Happiness Scale

Bob's general level of marital satisfaction remains low and relatively unchanged from pretest. The significant change in occupational progress probably reflects his recent $15,000 commission from a sale.

That this marriage is distressed is reflected in Bob's overall decrease in sexual satisfaction, a typical concomitant to troubled marriages. This distress was confirmed when Jan reluctantly admitted that she is not doing her part in their sexual relationship. I suspect that her responses on the Sexual Happiness Scale (all 8s) reflect denial rather than satisfaction.

Jan's mean scores are essentially the same as on pretest. Her report of relatively large changes in the areas of household responsibility (+4) and personal independence (−5) indicate the complementarity in their relationship. Each of these items relates to the couple's ongoing power struggle. As Bob does more around the house, Jan can no longer use his procrastination to gain the upper hand in the relationship, thus lowering her sense of independence.

Family Satisfaction Scale (10-Item)

The mean changes in Bob's and Jan's self-ratings are negligible (−.2 and −.6, respectively), as is Bob's overall rating of Jan (+.1). However, Jan valued Bob negatively (−2.3), that is, became increasingly dissatisfied with him throughout SE. That she rated Bob significantly lower on 7 of 10 items may reflect her digital thinking patterns (i.e., "he's bad") rather than a consideration of particular items. I became aware of Jan's digital thinking pattern during feedback, when she remarked that my letter was "right," implying that letters can be evaluated on a right-wrong scale.

It is interesting that each spouse agreed completely on Jan's "initiative" score (which increased from 3 to 6). I can only speculate that Jan's attempts to gain the upper hand have resulted in some protective dyadic behaviors that are perceived by both spouses. That Bob has received these behaviors negatively may be evidenced by the decrease in his perception of Jan's empathy.

I am surprised at Bob's increase in self-reported self-exploration; it was not clinically apparent to me during SE.

Family Satisfaction Scale (18-Item)

The couple's mean scores showed an increase in family satisfaction for Bob (+1.0) and a decrease for Jan (−1.8). The see-saw quality of their relationship is illustrated by the increases in listening, understanding, and tension for Bob and the decreases in those same areas for Jan. Jan's feelings of less happiness and welcome are artifacts of this complementary phenomenon.

Semantic Differential (SD)

Items on the SD were assigned numerical rankings on a +3 to −3 basis, as suggested by Anastasi (1976). The results indicate that Bob's ranking of self and Jan decreased considerably; Jan's rating of self and Bob show concomitant increases. I attempted to evaluate the SD results according to Osgood's Evaluative, Potency, and Activity factors (Snyder & Osgood, 1969) but found nothing worth reporting.

These results are perplexing. I would have predicted that Bob, who is now gaining more status in the relationship, would have improved his self-concept as well as his rating of Jan. Conversely, I would have expected Jan to rate Bob much lower on posttest as she loses footing in the struggle for power. Can it be that although Jan resents the dyadic interaction, she has somehow differentiated Bob as person from Bob as husband? If so, should not Bob do the same? I can only guess that Bob has somehow internalized his identified-patient status and has attributed that to Jan in some cognitively complex fashion.

Marital Questionnaire (MQ)

The MQ, which consists of 130 items, is expected to be less reactive to situational characteristics than other tests used in SE and may thus produce more enduring and representative results.

Although both spouses improved their total scores (i.e., have become more differentiated), Bob improved to a much greater degree. Their high scores on likeness and priorities indicate that neither defines the self by either sameness or oppositeness to others and that their priorities in the family are structured in a healthy way (L'Abate, 1977, p. 212).

I am fascinated by the MQ's support for the complementarity manifest in the blaming and distracting patterns. It may be hypothesized that at the outset of SE, Jan was in the blaming phase (6) and Bob was responding by distracting (3). However, the spouses have changed roles so that Bob now blames (4) and Jan distracts (4). I predict that these scores will show reversing trends in time.

It is interesting to speculate on SE's effects on Bob's improved marital task scores. Bob would be expected, by virtue of his very low pretest scores, to show more improvement than Jan. Although I was not aware of a great improvement in Bob, I can only guess that SE has had a positive impact on him.

Holmes-Rahe Schedule of Events

This test was checked to see that Bob's perceived stress has been greatly reduced and that Jan has increased her stress ranking.

THEORETICAL SPECULATIONS

In this section, I consider the test results and my clinical impressions in the context of various theoreticians' offerings in the field of marriage and the family. None of my speculations fit perfectly with any particular theoretical model. To me, theoretical models are stepping-stones to be used cautiously across the waters of clinical practice. The theoretician on the bank urging the practitioner to use his or her "stone" can know its soundness only after treading on it personally.

An understanding of Satir's family theory (Satir, 1972) triggered my initial awareness of Bob's distracting behavior. His long-winded, spontaneous, irrelevant talks, coupled with low pretest scores (3) on the Marital Questionnaire, provided enough validation.

Jan's distraction was apparent early in the program. Her distraction took the form of posturing almost catatonically, with a far-away look, denying feelings and withholding verbal responses.

That their dysfunctional communication pattern is more complex than simple blaming and distracting became evident in Bob's blaming behavior (e.g., "If you only did ——, we'd be better off!"). To these verbal transgressions, Jan would predictably respond by distracting.

As the lessons progressed, I became aware of Jan's beginning to blame Bob in various ways. This blaming seemed to be paired with Bob's distracting, and Bob's blaming seemed to tie in with Jan's distracting.

My clinical impressions and the verbal data from the couple suggest that a struggle for power and status exists and is manifest through the blaming and distracting modes. This struggle was humorously, though poignantly, illustrated when Bob stated that Jan would buy frozen green beans in spite of the fact that his garden produces an abundance. Symbolically, Jan is rejecting any dependence on Bob. This relationship apparently does not allow "giving in."

This couple's interactional patterns may be described as complementary, as discussed by Lederer and Jackson (1968). Haley (1963) defined a complementary relationship as "one where the two people exchange different sorts of behavior, such as one giving and one receiving." The complementary, flip-flop quality of their relationship seems evident, though this conceptualization of blaming opposed to distracting is in contrast to L'Abate's (1977) orthogonal structure containing polarities of blaming-placating, and computing-distracting. The Marital Questionnaire results indicate that placating and computing are not involved in the couple's negative feedback.

Bob's relative improvement on the tasks of marriage has in some way precipitated Jan's animosity, as reflected in her satisfaction scores. This may be Jan's attempt to maintain marital equilibrium. Whether or not Jan is aware of her attitudes, the deterioration of one spouse concurrent with the improvement of the other spouse has been demonstrated (Crago, 1972).

16

A Blended Couple

John Lutz

The Reids are a young married couple who have middle-class aspirations. They had been married only 7 months at the beginning of SE. Both are articulate and friendly, though Bonnie is definitely the more verbal of the two; Scott tends to be more jocose. Scott, slightly older than Bonnie, was married once before. He has custody every other weekend of his two young children from his first marriage. His divorce was final around the time he began to date Bonnie. After 2 years of college (where he was a C+ student), he now works full-time as a heating and air-conditioning repairman. Bonnie works part-time as a bank teller while attending college (she is an A student). She is very determined to get her degree but is unsure whether to change her major, which is business.

Scott and Bonnie dated for 5 months before they began to live together; later, they got married. Bonnie said that their relationship improved after they married. Scott, from a working-class background, is the third of five children (four boys and one girl). Bonnie's parents were divorced 4 years ago; her father owns a business, and her mother, who is a bookkeeper, used to do the bookkeeping for the business. Bonnie refers to herself as her mother's best friend. Bonnie has only one sibling, a 12-year-old brother.

My initial clinical impressions were that Bonnie and Scott are an articulate and motivated couple. I was already aware of the differences in their backgrounds and verbal expressions. Both partners spoke about the other to me, though Bonnie appeared to be the spokesperson. Bonnie expressed a desire to work on communication as a way of enhancing their relationship.

An initial pretest battery, consisting of the Holmes-Rahe Schedule of Events, the Dyadic Adjustment Inventory, and the Family Adjustment Inventory, was given to each partner (to be completed before SE began).

PRETEST SUMMARY

Both Scott and Bonnie scored extremely high (over 400) on the Holmes-Rahe Schedule of Events, a measure of life events that require adjustment and an indicator of the amount of change (and stress) one has experienced in the past 18 months. Most of their concurrence for life events and changes were in the areas of getting married, trouble with in-laws, and changes in eating and sleeping habits, residence, living conditions, and number of arguments. Individual changes and occurrences of stress-producing events included Scott's troubles with his boss, the death of a close friend, and separating from his mate (ex-wife) and Bonnie's major personal injury or illness, gaining new family members (Scott's children), and her change to a different line of work.

Their scores on the Dyadic Adjustment Inventory were within 1 standard deviation of the mean given married persons. The areas in which they scored low or expressed disagreement are as follows: Scott—ways of dealing with in-laws, matters of recreation, friends, career decisions, leaving the house after a fight, discussing something calmly, and working together on a project; Bonnie—ways of dealing with in-laws, handling family finances, aims and goals, and household tasks.

On the Family Adjustment Inventory, both partners scored −160 or lower. Scott's areas of dissatisfaction were Bonnie's slowness and lateness, her jealousy of his ex-wife, and his not having time alone or shared interests with her. Bonnie was dissatisfied with Scott's past marriage, in-laws, and his lack of concern for his physical health. She saw their similarity in likes and dislikes as an area of general satisfaction in their marriage.

Enricher's notes.

In choosing possible programs for Bonnie and Scott, I considered the following: Their low-scoring items on the Dyadic Adjustment Inventory were on the consensus subscale; they were experiencing difficulties in negotiating roles, tasks, and boundaries in their relationship (e.g., issues of time together and time apart, increased number of arguments, and Scott's having been married before and having children); they had experienced a large number of life events and changes in the past 18 months; and Bonnie had expressed a desire to work on communication.

The Newlyweds Program seemed a bit too elementary for them, but it does contain a lesson on dealing with in-laws, an acknowledged area of conflict. The Conflict Resolution Program is geared toward specific problems or issues but starts out abruptly with an identified problem of some standing (which hadn't yet been identified or verbalized by this couple). The Negotiation Program, which touches on several pertinent dimensions (marriage myths and moving beyond being "in love" to communication, trust, and negotiation of needs so both partners can "win") seemed better suited to their stage of marital development—posthoneymoon before having children.

SUMMARY OF SESSIONS

Session 1

The lesson on marital myths explores a couple's beliefs concerning three myths: one remains forever in a state of "romantic love" while married; men and women have inherently different attitudes and behaviors, and these differences cause most marital troubles; and if a couple argues, disagrees, or fights, it is a sign that they have a poor marriage.

Both shared their early notions of what marriage would be like. Bonnie, though she has always worked, had thought that she would marry a financially secure man and become a "traditional" wife who would stay at home and raise his children. Scott had thought of marriage as a partnership and as a way to have someone to balance out his life and himself.

After a 5-month courtship, during which Scott traveled (60 miles) twice a week to the town where Bonnie was attending college, they moved in together. The differences between when they were first dating and the present included being less carefree with their money and having more financial considerations, not wanting to be together all the time, and individual differences in styles of handling angry feelings and in times to be together. The last difference included Scott's complaints about Bonnie's slowness in getting ready for bed, Scott's interest in TV in the evenings (when Bonnie wants to spend time with him), and Bonnie's wanting to relax and be alone when she gets home from work (Scott has been home for an hour and a half by that time and wants to talk and spend this time with her).

Scott's list of what men are like included athletic, strong, interested in watching sports on TV, interested in cars, like to clan together, like to watch women, and like to be dominant. Bonnie's notions of what men are like follow: they like to watch TV, they enjoy all sports, they do not like housework, they often need to be pampered, they are *not* afflicted by illnesses, and they enjoy eating, are stubborn, are always right, and make the family decisions. Bonnie sees women as physically weak, ill periodically, always nagging, responsible for *all* housework and paying the bills, gossiping, not doing "real" work, doing the clothes shopping for their husbands and kids, pampering their husbands, and they are supposed to be mentally inferior to men. For Scott, women are sentimental, creative, underpaid, gossips, worried about their appearances; they tend to be late, prefer chivalry, and like expensive jewelry.

When they were asked how they respond to disagreements between them, a major difference in handling angry feelings was brought up. When there is a disagreement, Bonnie gets loud and wants to talk about it and get her feelings out (she said that this was something her mother never did with her father). Scott becames quiet and passive and prefers to talk about it later (after Bonnie settles down). In his family, when his mother got upset with his father, his father would hit his mother. Both partners see their approach to handling disagreements as the only way (and the right way) and want the other to adopt his or her style (i.e., Bonnie wants Scott to express his anger when it occurs; Scott wants Bonnie to settle down before they try to deal with her anger).

When asked in what ways Bonnie is considerate of his viewpoint or his wishes in a given situation, he replied that she sometimes quiets down so that they can discuss a disagreement. Bonnie was unable to name an instance of Scott's showing consideration for her viewpoint.

Enricher's notes.

Bonnie was much more talkative than Scott and frequently told me things about him. If these things seemed critical of him, she quickly added that she can understand why Scott acts the way he does. Scott occasionally played the role of the joker. A number of conflictual issues were brought up, but they quickly moved away from them. The issues included Bonnie's getting to spend only every other weekend with Scott because every other weekend he has his kids from his first marriage; their differences about the handling of angry feelings; and their differences about the times when both want to be together at the same time.

Supervision.

The differences in their styles of handling anger were looked at as differences learned in their families of origin. We discussed their initial patterns of interactions, including the way both partners presented themselves in a new situation concerned with enhancing their relationship (e.g., Bonnie did most of the "explaining" about their relationship and talked a lot to me about Scott; Scott took on a light-hearted, joking role).

My impression is that they, particularly Bonnie, have come for more than simply improving a good relationship. Finally, we explored the interactional pattern of an emotionally eager wife and an overly rational husband. The supervisor suggested I emphasize increasing Bonnie's rational responses (and decreasing her emotionality) and increasing Scott's emotionality (and decreasing his rationality).

Session 2

Asked about their homework—to record and discuss ways in which they meet each other halfway or exhibit give-and-take in their relationship—Bonnie said she had tried to do the assignment but couldn't think of any ways in which Scott meets her halfway. Scott said he simply hadn't done it. Both had completed the daily relationship questionnaires (Marital Happiness Scale).

To the first of three questions, "Who are you?" Scott named five roles in his list of 10 (father, husband, mechanic, son, and brother); three personal characteristics (lazy, shy, and bored with his job); his name; and his trying to be a friend to Bonnie's brother. Bonnie replied with three roles (wife, student, and employee) and five characteristics (hard worker, good friend to have, bad listener, good student, and a person unsure of the future). She also said she is her mother's best friend and a woman. Scott listed *father* third and *husband* fourth; Bonnie listed *wife* first. Several of Scott's answers when Bonnie asked "What can I give you?" were global (security, freedom, and happiness). His other responses were more relationship-focused (love, friendship, yourself, sympathy, and a family). Bonnie's replies when Scott asked this question tended to be more personal in that they included relationship issues and Scott's characteristics (honesty, punctuality, more help with household chores, your self-confidence, yourself, room for personal growth, and money). She also mentioned a secure future and a kitten. When Bonnie asked "What can you give me?" Scott listed laughter, a smile, companionship, freedom, sex, cooking lessons, money, new experiences, me, and a home. Bonnie's answers were a hard time, security, friendship, ways to make and keep friends, lessons on remembering things, a comfortable home, orderliness, financial stability, clean clothes, and myself.

In the second exercise, they named more than a dozen rules and informal agreements in their relationship. A sampling follows: (a) Scott sits on one end of the sofa, and Bonnie gets to put her feet across his lap; (b) Bonnie stays up late to be with Scott, so he wakes her up in the morning; (c) on weekends, Scott lets Bonnie sleep late and makes breakfast for them when she gets up; and (d) Bonnie goes out to get Scott cigarettes, so Scott brings home candy treats for her.

they have not focused on any issues for sustained work. Their manipulative communication styles parallel their styles for handling conflicts and disagreements: Bonnie is louder and more vocal; Scott is quieter and avoids, but he definitely has some control in the relationship.

Supervision.

Distancing and pursuing dynamics were explored. The supervisor pointed out the control Scott achieves with a passive stance; he also commented on the absence of expression of feelings by both partners in their current relational pattern: Bonnie is the more vocal and apparently "emotional" one, and Scott appears the more "rational" and passive; yet, both end up avoiding feelings and intimate sharing. Their avoidance of conflict and their self-presentational levels in SE have implications concerning trust and its place in their relationship.

Session 4

This lesson focuses on communication assumptions and the communication of hurt in couples. It deals with partners' thinking they know what the other partner really means without checking it out and partners' assumption that "If you love me, you'll know what I need, feel, and want, without my having to say it." The first exercise demonstrates that what is said is not what is always received, the second with the process of sharing meaning. Each partner is asked to reflect the message sent and to acknowledge the other's message. In the third exercise, each partner is asked to express feelings of hurt and the ways each can let the other know when he or she is angry.

The exercises generated considerable data on the couple's communication dynamics in general and the sharing of hurt feelings in particular. In the first exercise (comparing the message sent with the one received), it became apparent that Scott and Bonnie have their own communication system worked out for each other: when Scott responded neutrally, Bonnie thought he must really feel negative; when Bonnie said something critical and then laughed, Scott thought she was angry. The problem with their system was that each message sent had at least two meanings, and neither partner was checking out what the other really meant. This became further apparent when, in attempting to practice the shared meaning process, Bonnie was reacting rather than listening and then reflecting Scott's message. Scott's passiveness and avoidance facilitated this pattern. The content selected for this exercise is worth mentioning also: two of the topics were Bonnie's attempts to communicate her need for nurturance (but she hid it in asking for help with housework) and

Bonnie's giving advice to Scott about how to deal with his father and mother.

The exercise in sharing of hurt feelings generated several reactive responses.

Scott: I feel hurt by the way you treat my kids.
Bonnie: Well, I feel hurt that you have kids.
Scott: I feel hurt by the way you feel about my mother.
Bonnie: I feel hurt by the way you wanted to leave my mother's place
the other day as soon as we got there.

Bonnie also expressed feeling hurt when Scott doesn't confide in her or makes decisions without her.

The ways they deal with angry feelings parallel their personal styles. Scott suggested that Bonnie calm down and tell him what is going on (an indication that he misses her message or has trouble dealing with strong affect and that, though she is more emotional, it doesn't result in intimate sharing between them). Bonnie suggested that Scott tell her when he gets angry rather than holding on to it until later. After noting a few other assumptions (e.g., Bonnie: "He knows when I'm angry or hurt"), they decided they could ask more often how the other is feeling and that each could just tell the other when he or she feels hurt or angry.

Enricher's notes.

Particularly during the exercise on sharing hurt feelings, their tones and their affects were different, tenser. The material and the responses were more personal than earlier exercises and revealed some old hurts. Bonnie was noticeably reactive to Scott's messages; she could have asked him what he intended to convey (a more conductive style of communication). Evidently Scott often avoids his feelings (emphasizing rationality over emotion and action) and lets Bonnie make assumptions about what he means or feels. Each complements the other: Bonnie is high on emotionality and action but low on rationality; Scott is low on emotionality and action but high on rationality. Both appear to be low on awareness, as demonstrated by their mind reading and the reactivity in their communication.

Supervision.

The supervisor suggested that I encourage the shared meaning process as a way to increase their communication and the sharing of self. It may particularly help Bonnie, as she has a tendency to react to what Scott says before she hears what he is saying. It will also afford Scott opportunities to share himself and to be more verbal. Additionally, the process requires that Scott be more specific and direct about his feelings, needs, and thoughts.

Session 5

The focus of this lesson is building trust in the marital relationship. The exercises are directed toward self-disclosure in the following areas: subjects that each spouse would like to be more open for discussion between them, examples of each spouse's inconsistent behaviors (words versus actions) that diminish trust in each other, areas of competition, and each spouse's areas of responsibility.

Scott wanted his children, the spending of money, and the planning of separate activities to be more open for discussion. Bonnie mentioned being more open to the needs of the other (when one feels "down," the other should show attention no matter what he or she is doing at the moment), dealing with problems as they arise, and being more flexible and spontaneous in their activities together.

Scott's relationship and interaction with his ex-wife were the example of one way his incongruent words and actions result in diminished trust in his relationship with Bonnie. Although he tells Bonnie he has either negative or no feelings for his ex-wife, he often comes home late after dropping the boys off and treats his ex-wife nicely. Bonnie thus feels confused about Scott's feelings toward her and his ex-wife. Bonnie's example of her incongruent words and actions is saying she doesn't mind doing the housework mostly by herself but slamming cabinet doors and acting angry while doing the work.

The couple's areas of competition include games, where to dine out, and how money will be spent. Scott also mentioned that they argue/disagree over whether any additional education he may get should be vocational or academic. Bonnie wants him to pursue a more academic route; Scott wants it to be more vocational.

Bonnie's responsibilities are cleaning, balancing the checkbook, paying the bills, handling the insurance, and having repairs done on the car (as advised by Scott). Scott is in charge of earning most of the money in the family, maintenance around the apartment, and "being available whenever Bonnie needs me."

Enricher's notes.

Several of the exercises on trust brought out answers that are more phenotypic than self-presentational (L'Abate, 1986b). The answers conveyed a tone of self-disclosure and a personal investment of feeling. Particularly noticeable were responses concerning Scott's relationship with his ex-wife and his children, the negotiation of money, time together and apart, and his and Bonnie's emotional responses to each other. An example of reactive responding (compared with apathetic or conductive) occurred when Scott mentioned (and Bonnie agreed with) his inconsistency in his feelings and behavior toward his ex-wife.

Immediately after bringing this up, Scott mentioned Bonnie's year-long telephone relationship with one of the salesmen at work and how she has talked of going out to lunch with him sometime in the future. Scott said he isn't sure she hasn't gone out to lunch with him already. (Scott and Bonnie's relationship started over the phone when they worked for the same company.)

The issues of Scott's career and education and his responsibility to be available to meet Bonnie's needs have more parental than spousal overtones. In general, the couple appeared more genuine in this session and dealt with more substantive matters than they have before.

Supervision.

We discussed the negotiation of areas in their relationship (money, time together and apart, household responsibilities, and the meeting of emotional needs) according to the dimensions of marital development and phases. The supervisor pointed out the couple's jealousy and reactive styles of responding to conflictual issues.

Session 6

In the final lesson in the Negotiation Program, the couple negotiates, using the rules of communication worked on in earlier lessons: using "I" statements; using shared meaning; matching verbal and nonverbal messages; avoiding manipulative styles; not using past history against the partner. They are to negotiate one need, wish, or desire each could meet for the partner: each partner "wins," or gives something to get something. To get to this final stage, each partner lists characteristics that the other should have to make the marriage more workable. Each then names the ways in which he or she contributes destructively to the relationship. Each then states a specific wish, desire, or need so that the partner will know how to fulfill it.

Ideally, Scott would like Bonnie to be a better listener in fights (not just try to make her opinions prevail), be open and specific about her mother's and her brother's living with them, be more flexible in giving him time for himself, spend more money, and talk about household chores when she's angry about them and about his not helping. Bonnie would like Scott to be neater when working on projects in the house and not leave them lying around unfinished, watch less television in the evening, use his time more constructively, be more direct about his feelings, and do more things to please himself.

The destructive ways in which Scott contributes to the failing of the relationship are watching too much television, spending money too freely, staying up too late at night (not getting enough sleep), procrastinating, and not expressing feelings. Bonnie said she contributes destructively by not being punctual, not trying to change her schedule so it meshes better with Scott's, blaming, bringing up past history when arguing, responding too quickly (not listening to what Scott has to say), and letting Scott spend money when she doesn't want him to. Note the relationship between the ways each acts destructively: spending money too freely (Scott) and letting Scott spend money when she doesn't want him to (Bonnie); not having tried to change her schedule (Bonnie) and staying up too late (Scott).

Scott's principal wishes, needs, and desires for himself in their marriage (he was instructed to be specific enough that both he and Bonnie would know how to fulfill them) were a house, for Bonnie to understand his feelings about his children, for Bonnie to get her degree, for child support to end, to purchase a boat, free time for them to be together, early retirement, and more friends. Bonnie's responses were a home and furnishings for it, more savings, to take more one- or two-day trips, and for Scott to go places with her more (e.g., window shopping for furniture).

The two wishes, needs, or desires chosen for negotiation were Bonnie's getting her degree (from Scott's list) and purchasing a home (from Bonnie's list). Although the two desires seem opposite in terms of complexity and difficulty, Scott and Bonnie negotiated them successfully, showing particularly good skills in negotiating the purchase of a house (something they have been discussing for some time). When they discussed location, Scott asked specifically where Bonnie would not be willing to live. They discussed Bonnie's working full-time and attending school at night and negotiated that as part of buying a house now rather than waiting to save more money. Scott will need to continue to work where he is and forego additional schooling or a job change in the near future.

Enricher's notes.

This lesson continued the trend of increased personal self-disclosure that I had seen in the preceding lesson. They expressed more relationship-specific material than in any other session. Also, they joked less, sincerely expressed their deeper needs and feelings, and acknowledged the relationship-damaging behavior that each has engaged in. Although the desires they negotiated are large, they negotiated fairly well. I'm a little concerned about the emphasis on "having" and the effect that may have on their "being" needs (L'Abate, 1986b). For example, Scott has expressed dissatisfaction with his occupational progress. When asked about this, Bonnie explained (and Scott agreed) that he works so he can enjoy what his earnings can purchase (i.e., his work is more a job than a career).

Supervision.

The supervisor and I discussed preparation for the feedback conference. After soliciting feedback from them about their experiences in SE, I will give them positive feedback, citing their commitment to each other and their relationship as evidenced by their entering and completing SE, along with their flexibility and willingness to grow and learn more about each other. I will tell them that they have made a good start on improving their communication skills and working on their differences. One thing that they need to be concerned about, because it could get out of hand, is their symmetrical posturing about hurt (e.g., in-laws and jealousy). Also, as their marriage is relatively young, they are dealing with negotiating roles and boundaries about which they have often had trouble expressing their feelings and needs. Further SE or covenant contracting will be suggested to help them continue to work on these issues. Marital counseling will also be mentioned as an option that would allow them to continue the work they have begun in SE.

POSTTEST SUMMARY

Scott and Bonnie were again given the Dyadic Adjustment Inventory and the Family Adjustment Inventory. In this section, I include data provided by the couple's weekly averages on the daily relationship questionnaires.

On the Dyadic Adjustment Inventory, both again scored within 1 standard deviation of the mean for married persons. Although Scott's overall score increased 5 points from pretest and Bonnie's overall score decreased 6 points from pretest, her score is still slightly higher than his.

On the Family Adjustment Inventory, posttest scores for both remain below −140. Scott's overall score improved 30 points on posttest, but it is still 20 points lower (i.e., more negative) than Bonnie's score on the posttest (her score improved by 3 points).

In comparing pretest to posttest changes with my clinical impressions, I can mention several relationships. From pretest to posttest, there was a dramatic change in what Scott rated as the area of greatest dissatisfaction—from Bonnie's lateness to her jealousy of his ex-wife. Although Bonnie's making more of an effort to be on time was discussed in several sessions, the issue of Scott's ex-wife and his relationship with her and their children was not explored. It may be argued that this was a more difficult issue for the couple to work through than was the irritation at Bonnie's lateness in getting up or coming to bed. With the improvement of Bonnie's punctuality, another salient issue came to the fore in Scott's rating—his first marriage and his children.

The data supplied through the daily relationship questionnaires, averaged weekly, point out several interesting relationships in the couple's ratings, their behavior and interactions in sessions, and my clinical impressions. Scott's ratings of his happiness with his rearing of his children started out low and continue to decline until Week 4, when he stopped rating it. In at least two sessions, conflict over Scott's children was brought up—once when Bonnie said she doesn't like to share him with his boys every other weekend and again when Scott said he wants Bonnie to understand that he loves his children.

Repeated measures for the dimension of happiness with self and partner communication show a slight trend of improvement for both partners. A functional relationship between SE and happiness with self and partner communication in the marriage and SE cannot be demonstrated empirically because I have no data on the ratings for self and partner happiness with communication for the period before SE.

Scott's ratings on happiness with household responsibilities reflect his being very happy with their arrangement, but Bonnie's ratings average 3 to 4 points lower than his. In several sessions, Bonnie expressed dissatisfaction with their arrangements for household chores but said she expresses her feelings only indirectly to Scott. Scott's ratings of his ability to successfully work out a difference of opinion with Bonnie increased during SE (again, no functional relationship can be demonstrated) and paralleled their increased use of the shared meaning process and Bonnie's use of this process to facilitate a more conductive (rather than reactive) style of interacting with Scott. Bonnie's rating of occupational progress declined slightly and dropped at Week 6, which she said coincided with end-of-the-month billing and closing accounts at her job. Scott's ratings of his happiness with his occupational progress remained in the mid- to low range and was reflected in the couple's differences about whether he should get more academic versus vocational training and in his difficulties with a supervisor, which might mean that Scott will be fired.

A possible lack of communication in their overall happiness with sex was highlighted by their repeated measures: each consistently rated self and partner's happiness with sex as identical, although their ratings differed by as much as 3 points over the course of SE. An alternative hypothesis for this rating discrepancy is that similar rating scales may be calibrated differently (e.g., what is "very happy" for the husband could be a 9; what is "very happy" for the wife could be a 7.5). However, if the alternative hypothesis is correct, one would expect a stable difference between their scores.

Overall, Scott's ratings in several dimensions (personal independence, show of affection, ability to work out differences with his wife, general happiness, communication) for self varied more than Bonnie's ratings for herself in these same dimensions. This finding is revealing in that Bonnie presented herself as the moodier partner, yet she has encouraged Scott to be more expressive of his feelings of anger and hurt as they occur. Scott's self-presentation was that of an understanding, rational, and even-tempered husband. At a deeper level, beyond the self-presentational facade, he may (from Bonnie's reports and his self-ratings) be much more volatile.

SECTION IV
Examples of Specific Programs

17

Affective Programs: Introductory-Experiential and Intermediate-Experiential

Kathy Weeks

Mr. Clifton, who works in an office adjoining mine, heard that I was looking for a family (including at least one child 6 years or older) to participate in SE. After I explained SE to him and he talked it over with his wife and son, the family agreed to participate.

The Cliftons live in an older but pleasant neighborhood in a comfortably furnished brick house. Somewhat cluttered but homey, the living room contains many books, ranging from philosophy to *The Joy of Sex*. They have a stereo system, and I noticed many classical music albums shelved on a bookcase.

Doug, the father, aged 31, is a slim, good-looking man who has brown hair and brown eyes. He is Australian and has a master's degree in sociology. He now works for a social services agency.

Sarah, the mother, aged 34, is small and pretty. She is from the southern United States, and she, too, has a master's degree; Sarah teaches English in a local high school.

Jeff, aged 11, is in the sixth grade. He is small and dark-haired. Gwen, a pretty little girl with curly red hair, is 4 years old. Sarah was married to another man when she and Doug met in the Caribbean, where Doug was teaching and Sarah was a member of the Peace Corps. Jeff, her son from her first marriage, was not yet born. Sarah later divorced her husband but remarried him and divorced him again. She and Doug were married almost immediately after her second divorce. Sarah commented that their background must sound "seamy" to me. Knowing the circumstances under which Sarah was divorced was not important for SE and I sensed a reluctance, especially on Doug's part, to pursue the matter further, so I did not ask for details. I did ask, however, whether Doug had adopted Jeff and he said yes.

During the first years Doug and Sarah were married, the family lived in Spain and in Germany. They traveled a lot, and Doug described it as an "adventure." They have been in the United States for the past 4 years.

As a family they enjoy camping. Sarah likes to sew and garden; Jeff builds models, collects coins, plays sports, and is a Boy Scout; Doug enjoys carpentry work and music (he sings with a local choral group).

They do not see friends or relatives regularly except for Sarah's sister. All of Doug's family are in Australia.

In the past 2 years, this family has experienced stress from the deaths of Sarah's parents. Doug was unemployed for a while, and his looking for a job for several months was very stressful for all of them. I asked about the family's goals. Doug's and Sarah's answers agreed that the goals are to be open and to experience a lot of new things so that the children will develop tolerance and awareness. Doug specified his wish to avoid a "career rut." He described again the first two years of their life together as a family (when they lived in Spain and in Germany). He pointed out that the experience had been a good one for Jeff in that he had been exposed to many things that most children do not experience (e.g., Jeff had attended school in Germany).

The family members then completed the pretests. Doug and Jeff sat together on one love seat, and Sarah sat by herself on the other. I sat between the two love seats in a platform rocker. Overall, their test-taking attitude was cooperative and enthusiastic. The three family members (Gwen was not tested because of her age) talked back and forth, laughed, and teased one another. Most of the interaction, however, was between Doug and Jeff. Gwen went from person to person, playing with the test cards and generally distracting her parents and Jeff. Doug and Sarah shared the chore of entertaining her and keeping her out of mischief. At one point, when she tried to take Jeff's pencil, he hollered at her and shoved her away.

PRETEST RESULTS

On the Bell-Fagan Family Symbols (B-F) the outstanding scores show that the family saw Sarah as most anxious and afraid and Jeff least so.

Jeff's scores on the angry and sad items are also lower than anyone else's scores. The family saw Doug as most angry; in fact, his score on this test item is higher than any other score on any other item. Sarah's score on happy is lower than that of any other family member.

On the Description of Feelings in the Family (DFF) the most noteworthy result is that Jeff saw the family as very smug. In corroboration of this result, the family saw the family members depicted on the test cards as mostly smug. Sarah picked only four cards in this test.

The most eye-catching result of the Family Situations Picture Series (FSPS) is that Jeff saw the family as extremely computing. The family saw the members of the family depicted on this set of cards as computing, also.

The results of the Animal Concepts Picture Series (ACPS) show much similarity among members of the family in terms of the descriptive dimensions of the test. Family members share the same score on various items. For example, the family perceives Sarah and Jeff (in actual terms) as equally harmful and fast. Ideally, the family would like Gwen to be most different from what she actually is; Doug's discrepancy score between "actual" and "ideal" comes next (46).

Enricher's notes and supervision.

This family is markedly cognitive. This conclusion can be justified not only on the basis of the high scores on the computing dimension of the FSPS but also on the basis of the educational level of the parents. In addition, their occupations are cognitive endeavors. The family's goals, as stated by Doug and Sarah, are abstract and intellectual.

Gwen seems to have a lot of power in the family, as demonstrated by the extent to which she demanded the attention of the family members during pretests.

With regard to an appropriate program for this family, the supervisor recommended that I use a feeling-oriented program on the advanced level. The purpose in choosing such a program is to create some balance for this thinking-oriented family.

SUMMARY OF SESSIONS

Session 1

For the first lesson, I chose Working Together, from the Introductory-Experiential Program.

When I arrived, Gwen was still up. Doug and Sarah were getting her ready for bed, which meant that during our first session they were leaving the room to get her out of the bathtub, diaper her, and so forth. After she was ready for bed, she was not put to bed. Instead she behaved much as she had during the interview, creating so much confusion at times that I could not even be heard.

In the first exercise, I asked the family to sit in a circle, join hands, close their eyes, and imagine that they were walking in the country. When I asked, "What are you seeing?" Jeff saw geese, wheat fields, and trees; Sarah saw the same things and added that it was hot and she could smell the grass; Doug saw a lake beside which horses were grazing.

Asked to name a color to tell how each person was feeling, Jeff chose red because to him it meant being handsome and serious. Sarah chose green to correspond to the peacefulness of the countryside image; Doug also named green, for the same reason Sarah did.

When I asked each person to name an animal that best represented how each person was feeling at the moment, Doug named rabbits, saying they remind him of the calm and peace of the countryside. Sarah said she felt like a horse—powerful and graceful. Jeff responded that he felt like a shark, because he was hungry.

The next exercise is a trust exercise in which the members of the family take turns leading a blindfolded family member and being led while blindfolded. Responding to the question of how it had felt to be led around, Sarah said that she had felt unsteady, not in control. Sarah led Doug to an oak table in their dining area; he touched it and commented that he liked the feel of wood because he likes to work with wood. Afterward, he said that he had felt that he might bump into something. Jeff said that he had felt he might trip. When I asked how they had felt leading a blindfolded person, Jeff and Doug answered that leading had given them a feeling of power. Later Doug added that it had brought out the mischief in him. Sarah said that she had felt responsible.

The family members were asked to close their eyes, touch each other's hands and faces, and describe their feelings. Jeff giggled quite a bit during this exercise, but he performed it satisfactorily. He seemed at a loss for descriptive words, but Doug's and Sarah's responses were tender and sensitive. They demonstrated much affection for each other and for Jeff.

In the next exercise, the family gathered their loose change into a pile. Each was asked to pick a coin most like himself or herself, then specify to whom each would like to give the coin and from whom each would like to receive a coin. Later, they were asked how they would divide the money among the family members. Doug picked a quarter, saying that he is one fourth of the family and that it is the biggest coin and worth more than the other coins. Jeff, too, chose a quarter, because George Washington appears on a quarter and Jeff considers himself a great leader, as Washington was. He described himself as a great leader because he leads the boys on raids against the girls at school recess. Sarah picked a dime because it is slim, bright, and attractive. She also remarked that a dime is worth more than a penny, even though it is smaller in size.

Jeff and Doug exchanged coins in the part of the exercise about giving and receiving coins. Sarah said she would give her coin to anybody, and she would receive a coin from anybody. In dividing the coins, at first they divided the total by three, each member receiving an equal share. Then Doug took the coins and handed them out one at a time, as if he were dealing cards. Later he commented that he would not divide the money equally because children should not receive an equal share with parents.

Sarah did not like this exercise. She did not like the idea of having to choose one family member to give a coin to or to receive a coin from. She said that it especially presents a child with a difficult dilemma.

In the next exercise, each family member places himself or herself and the other family members in a living sculpture. Jeff positioned Doug reclining on the floor; Sarah behind Doug, on her knees, holding Gwen; Jeff straddled Doug's legs. Doug placed Sarah on her hands and knees, Jeff rode on top of her, and Doug knelt behind her, his hands on her hips. He said they were supposed to be like a Wells Fargo stagecoach. Sarah sat Doug in a chair, Jeff on his lap, Gwen on Jeff's lap, and then she stood on the edge of the seat, above them. Doug said he knew that her sculpture meant that she had created this family.

When I asked the family how they felt about the lesson, Sarah said that the session would have been less chaotic if Gwen had been in bed. I agreed, and we negotiated a later time for the remaining sessions (after Gwen is asleep). Doug said that the lesson was pointless; that it had no purpose; and that the family already plays games that are unstructured and spontaneous, such as chess and Scrabble. Jeff repeated what his father had said.

Enricher's notes and supervision.

Once again, the very cognitive nature of this family was affirmed, especially in Doug's comments that he could discern no purpose for the lesson and that he considers chess and Scrabble unstructured and spontaneous.

I noted the apparent collusion between Doug and Jeff, especially as demonstrated in the coin exercise, and I sensed a certain pathos in Sarah's response that she would give a coin to anyone and receive a coin from anyone. I think that she sometimes feels left out of the camaraderie between Doug and Jeff.

However, in the touching exercise, she and Doug expressed much tenderness and affection for each other. It was clear to me from their comments and from their nonverbal behavior (glowing eyes, gentle touching) that they love and care for each other.

The supervisor recommended that I continue using feeling- and action-oriented lessons, especially since Doug described the family as more "verbal"—a cognitive mode of behavior.

Session 2

For the second lesson, I chose Expressing Feelings, also from the Introductory-Experiential Program. When I arrived for this session, Gwen was in bed, asleep. The family members' responses follow.

The thing I like least about you——

Sarah to Doug: . . . ignore things, refuse to understand.
Sarah to Jeff: . . . personal habits, not tidy.
Jeff to Sarah: . . . you get mad at me too much.
Jeff to Doug: . . . too busy.
Doug to Jeff: . . . untidiness.
Doug to Sarah: . . . untidiness.

The thing I like most about you——

Sarah to Doug: . . . interests, looks, humor, sensitivity, body.
Sarah to Jeff: . . . sense of humor, interest in everything, especially Gwen and other members of the family.
Jeff to Sarah: . . . you're my mother.
Jeff to Doug: . . . generous, allowance raises.
Doug to Jeff: . . . tolerant of my bad moods, liveliness, curiosity.
Doug to Sarah: . . . resilience, sense of adventure, sensitivity, see right through me.

I have a complaint about something you did.

Jeff to Sarah: You said I'd be back from Scouts by nine o'clock.
Jeff to Doug: You didn't finish chess game.
Doug to Jeff: You pulled Gwen off the swings.
Doug to Sarah: I had to pull your arm around me the other night.
Sarah to Jeff: You should fuss at Doug for having to be back from Scouts by nine.
Sarah to Doug: You didn't put gas in the car.

It hurts me——

Jeff to Sarah: . . . that you said I'm untidy.
Jeff to Doug: . . . that you think I make Gwen cry too much.
Doug to Jeff: . . . don't listen to all my advice, especially about spending money.
Doug to Sarah: . . . that you watch TV after eleven o'clock.
Sarah to Jeff: . . . fuss at me.
Sarah to Doug: . . . try to make me feel that I'm not doing my share.

What I want from you is——

Doug to Jeff: . . . more toughness, perseverance—you give up too easily.
Doug to Sarah: . . . initiative.
Jeff to Sarah: . . . more freedom of movement.
Jeff to Doug: . . . more money.
Sarah to Doug: . . . for you to lead more family-oriented activities.
Sarah to Jeff: . . . for you to stick to a few things—you try to do too many things.

I want to compliment you about——

Jeff to Doug: . . . the advice you give me (sometimes).
Jeff to Sarah: . . . being a good mother.
Doug to Jeff: . . . being pretty smart.
Doug to Sarah: . . . being pretty sharp, holding down a good job.
Sarah to Jeff: . . . being an attractive kid, an asset to the family.
Sarah to Doug: . . . being attractive and desirable.

For the last exercise, I asked each family member to role-play the other two family members. Much of the behavior they mimicked reflected many of the things stated in the earlier exercises. For example, Jeff role-played his father being preoccupied with grading test papers; Doug and Sarah role-played Jeff throwing his clothes around and putting off going to bed; Doug role-played Sarah "glued" to the television; and Sarah role-played Doug being grumpy in the morning. These highlights are just a sample of the behaviors they mimicked in one another. During the role playing, everyone (including me) laughed, and no one was inhibited in role playing. Sarah's imitation of Jeff throwing his clothes around was especially funny. No one used the exercise as an opportunity to blame.

Enricher's notes and supervision.

Doug, Sarah, and Jeff performed the exercises with energy and care. Each family member tried to perform each task with honesty; that is, no one tried to deny negative feelings. I was impressed with their lack of inhibition during the role playing and their ability to laugh at each other and themselves. Although I would still characterize this family's primary mode of functioning as cognitive, I could see in this session that their cognitive nature is balanced to a larger extent than I had realized by an ability to get in touch with their feelings—both good and bad—and to have fun.

In supervision I was told to rely on my own judgment in choosing the lessons. My tentative strategy will be to use the advanced affective lessons (which require mostly verbal interaction) but to include an action-oriented exercise as an introductory exercise for each lesson.

Session 3

When I arrived for the third session, I learned that the family had had company for the past several days (in fact, their company had just departed that morning).

I could tell that the family members were tired. They tried to participate with as much care as in the previous session, but they lacked their usual energy.

I began with an action-oriented exercise. I asked Doug and Sarah to encircle Jeff with their arms and catch him as he, eyes closed, swayed freely between. Jeff was stiff in performing the exercise, and despite encouragement to relax, he had difficulty doing so. The family's responses to the next exercise follow.

Which feelings does this family like?

Jeff: Happiness, joy.
Sarah: Trust, fidelity.
Doug: Excitement, interest, curiosity.

What feelings does this family dislike?

Jeff: Anger, depression, despair.
Doug: Boredom, being misunderstood, frustration.
Sarah: Unhappiness, being pressed for time.

Tell your family something you are proud of.

Doug: My wife, myself, my family.
Sarah: My family.
Jeff: My family, the television (gets us out of boredom), my house.

Asked to "compliment everybody else in the family for what they are proud of," the family agreed that it is difficult to compliment someone. Doug qualified this feeling by saying that sometimes it is not as difficult to compliment someone as it is to think to do so. Jeff said that he felt "embarrassed" when complimenting someone. I asked him whether he could tell me why he felt embarrassed, but he could not.

In the last exercise, the family was to talk together about a mutually agreed topic. Doug, Sarah, and Jeff agreed to talk about where they will go to live next. When I asked each family member to make a single statement about their topic, they answered as follows:

Jeff: I think we should move to San Francisco.
Doug: I think we should move to Europe or Africa.
Sarah: I think we should do a great deal of investigation before we decide
where we're going to live.

Enricher's notes and supervision.

The most striking responses were made in the first exercise, in which each family member told something he or she is proud of. No one, except Doug, mentioned taking pride in self; even Doug did not specify anything in particular about himself that he is proud of. Each family member, however, expressed pride in the family. This sameness, together with the fact that no one expressed pride in anything personal, makes me question the degree of differentiation in the members of this family.

Session 4

In the first exercise (from Knowing Your Family), the family members pretended they were robots and weaved around the room. Once again they demonstrated their ability to play, and they seemed to enjoy the exercise.

I then began the lesson called Direct Feelings (from Intermediate-Experiential Program). The exercises and their responses follow.

Tell things that the rest of the family could do to make you feel good about yourself.

Jeff: More money, nurse shark in the aquarium.
Sarah: Compliment me.
Doug: I already feel good about myself.

It would hurt me a great deal if you were to——

Jeff to Sarah: . . . yell at me.

Jeff to Doug: . . . spank me.
Doug to Sarah: . . . dismiss my feelings as invalid.
Doug to Jeff: . . . roam with buddies and break the law.
Sarah to Doug: . . . discount my feelings (example: stare at your shoe while I'm talking to you).
Sarah to Jeff: . . . make me the villain when I'm trying to correct you.

Share a secret within the family.

Sarah: Secrets are kept for healthy reasons.
Jeff: If I tell my secret, Daddy might spank me.
Doug: I'm not Jeff's natural father.

The family had difficulty stating what does or would hurt them. Through this exercise I learned that Jeff had told his parents (or they had found out) that recently he and his friends had been up to mischief of some sort and that Jeff, fearing punishment, would not say what they had done. Although the family used this exercise and the one that followed to talk about this incident, the mischief was never explained.

Also, Doug used the last exercise as an opportunity to say that he is not Jeff's natural father. As he spoke, he had his hand over his mouth and appeared somewhat nervous. Doug said that the fact he is not Jeff's natural father had never been mentioned in front of Jeff. I was reminded of the pretest, when I had asked Doug whether he had adopted Jeff.

Jeff's behavior during this session was distracting: he squirmed and giggled a lot, and most of his answers were silly. Sarah frequently coached him in his responses; that is, she interpreted the questions for him when his answers were silly or did not seem to relate to the exercise.

I think Jeff's not telling Doug what he and his friends had done is causing a strain between them. At the time the incident was mentioned, Doug was sitting in a chair across the room from Sarah and Jeff. When they did talk about the incident, they spoke in intellectualized terms, especially when Jeff said that what he had done was exciting and Doug described the situation as the result of urban living in which children do not have harmless ways to "act-out" and experience the kind of excitement Jeff was describing. Doug's example of harmless mischief was building a tree house or chasing chickens.

Enricher's notes and supervision.

Because of this session, I decided that this family has difficulty dealing with hurt and being open. However, I am aware that I have been a little uncomfortable in working with this family because I see Doug at work. In supervision we explored the possibility that this family's reticence to elaborate and to discuss negative feelings is partly due to my knowing the father; the family members, too, may be feeling uncomfortable. I do not wish to exaggerate the situation, and the family members have been quite open with me about positive feelings, so I am inclined to believe that the lack of depth in their responses may be a "little bit of me and a little bit of you," as the song goes. I believe that they probably do deny negative feelings, as evidenced in both Doug's and Sarah's comments that they discount each other's feelings when they argue.

My supervisor recommended that I avoid confronting the family with exercises that require them to deal with more negative and possibly threatening feelings. He suggested that I use lessons that allow the family to have fun.

I learned a valuable lesson from this experience: It is not good to try to do SE with acquaintances. Doug and I see each other only fleetingly at work; however, our contact is frequent enough that my effectiveness as an enricher has been impaired and their capacity to derive maximum benefit from SE has been limited.

Session 5

In this lesson, the family fantasized about what they would do in a number of situations, for example if they were marooned on a desert island, inherited $1 million, won the vehicle of their choice. They fantasized in detail about the cruise they would take to Tahiti on the yacht purchased with the $1 million. Interestingly, if they could win any vehicle, they would choose a Jaguar over a fully equipped van, even though the van would be more practical.

The family sat together on the sofa across from me, Sarah in the middle. They interacted with warmth and humor, and they allowed each person to contribute to each response, without interrupting. They did not take turns answering; without becoming chaotic, they talked back and forth about what they could do in each situation.

Enricher's notes and supervision.

The most outstanding aspect of this session was the way the family communicated. The family enjoyed themselves, but their enjoyment did not allow them to shout one another down or one person to try to dominate the discussion. Their behavior bespoke a certain courtesy toward each other (it also might have signified that they were tired after the day's activities and did not have the energy they might have had otherwise). Frequently, they have apologized for interrupting each other, or Sarah has asked Jeff to be quiet when he has digressed too much.

Session 6

Once again the family was asked to fantasize, this time about where the family would be in 5 years and then 10 years. The family discussed the possibility of living in Australia or Germany. Sarah fantasized that she would be teaching in a university. Doug fantasized that he would complete a PhD degree in sociology and would be teaching full-time. Jeff commented that he would be in the 11th grade. Most of the conversation about where the family would be in 10 years centered on Jeff's college plans. He expressed a desire to go to law school, and he, Sarah, and Doug discussed how he would have to make good grades in high school and win a scholarship.

Enricher's notes and supervision.

This session was a quiet, serious one. The family joked a little, but mostly they talked thoughtfully about the future. Once again, each person spoke without being interrupted. The family seems to feel positively about the future. They have set realistic goals and are aware of what they must do in the present to secure the kind of future they want.

Posttest Session

During the posttest, the family was quiet. Doug and Sarah sat together on a love seat. Jeff sat on the floor to their left. They did not talk as much among themselves as they did the first time, perhaps because the test had lost its novelty. As in the pretest, Jeff and Doug tried to "psyche out" the tests. For example, on the Description of Feelings in the Family (DFF) answer sheet, above the card numbers, are the words *sad, distracted, smug,* and *mad,* and *intensities;* they tried to figure out what the test measures. Doug could not understand the distracting stance depicted on some of the DFF cards; apparently because he did not understand what the stance meant, he refused to consider those cards as possibly depicting feelings in his family.

PRE- AND POSTTEST EVALUATION

The most noteworthy result of the Bell-Fagan Family Symbols (B-F) is that Doug was seen as less angry and Sarah as less anxious and afraid than on the pretest.

On the Description of Feelings in the Family (DFF), Doug saw the family as more smug than mad; Jeff did not see the family to be nearly as smug as he did at the time of the pretest, although he still saw the family as mad. Sarah saw the family as more mad. The family saw the young son and the young daughter depicted on the cards as more distracting than they did on the pretest.

Jeff still saw the family as very blaming and computing on the Family Situations Picture Series (FSPS) but more blaming than computing on the posttest. Doug and Sarah saw the family as much more computing than they did on pretest.

Pre- and posttest results on the Animal Concepts Picture Series (ACPS) show very few differences. The most noteworthy result is that on the "actual" part of the posttest, Gwen was seen to be very different from the other members of the family: smaller, more good, more harmless, and more passive. My early speculation that Gwen was the family pet may have been more accurate than I realized at the time.

FEEDBACK CONFERENCE

First, I asked the family what they thought of SE. They said that they thought they had benefited from it and expressed appreciation for the opportunity it had provided them to say things to each other they would not normally say—especially compliments. SE had also, they said, enabled them to talk concretely about the future. They said that there were parts that they did not like, because they were negative and divisive, such as the coin exercise. They noted that I had seemed somewhat "ill at ease" in the beginning and that my lack of ease had made them feel ill at ease. I confessed that I had felt a little uncomfortable because I knew Doug from work and asked them whether this fact had affected their attitude. They said that it had not, but Doug said that he had not invested as much as he might have because he felt that they were "doing me a favor," as it were, because I needed a family to work with for my enrichment course.

In my feedback, I told the family that I saw them as a family whose members care for each other. I told them that I liked their humor and the way they shared happy times but I wondered about the sad times in their family life and how they deal with hurt. They responded that they did share negative feelings, and they thought they were improving all the time in telling each other when they feel anger and other emotions.

SUMMARY

This family did appear to be very caring. The relationship between Doug and Sarah appeared to be a very loving one: They looked lovingly at each other; they said loving things about each other. Some of their exchanges had sexual overtones, which conveyed the impression that they share sexual attraction and satisfaction. I saw no evidence of a struggle to dominate either each other or the family; they seemed to share their roles as parents without much conflict.

At first I suspected some sort of collusion between Doug and Jeff. They seemed very chummy, and I wondered whether Sarah felt left out. Later, I decided that the generational lines are firmly drawn, as Doug and Sarah seem so close and unified in their roles as parents.

I was struck by the power Gwen has in the family. In the three times I saw her, Doug and Sarah (especially Sarah) seemed almost permissive with her. This impression is tenuous because I did not see her and the family interact that much. During the times I did see her, though, she seemed demanding, mostly of attention, and in general her demands were met.

Sibling rivalry certainly exists between Gwen and Jeff, and I wonder whether Jeff resents the attention Gwen receives, not to mention the fact that their parents seem so solicitous of her demands. I also wonder whether Jeff sometimes feels lonely. Doug and Sarah seem very affectionate toward each other, but despite the fact that they said positive things about Jeff, I do not remember Sarah's hugging him or touching him much, and I do not think Doug touched him at all.

Jeff saw the family as blaming and computing on the FSPS, and I suspect that his perception was not distorted very much. Jeff seemed to act-out frequently, and I think Doug and Sarah have been having to exercise discipline more and more with him (not only when I was present). Perhaps Jeff has been trying to get some of the attention Gwen receives. At one time, Jeff was talking baby talk, and Sarah said, "Jeff, you're not Gwen."

The family may be improving in expressing negative feelings, but I suspect that their expressions of anger and hurt take the form of "you" statements instead of "I" statements, which would account for the blaming and anger seen in this family. Insofar as the family's smugness and computing are concerned, I am reminded of Doug's and Sarah's comments to each other that they discount each other's feelings.

This family's computing nature has been consistently borne out. They would benefit, I think, from more SE, in which they could learn to express their negative feelings constructively and without hurt. If I worked with them again, I think I would assign homework in which Doug and Sarah would give Jeff one big hug a day.

18

Advanced Affective Programs: Introductory-Experiential and Various Modified Lessons

Deborah Huntley

The family consists of six members: Kenneth, aged 44; Marie, aged 40; Walt, aged 24; Ben, aged 23; Melissa, aged 18; and Cindy, aged 14. Kenneth is salesman and part-owner of the company. He attends junior college at night and plans to transfer to a local university in the fall. Marie is a senior at the university. Walt is married and attends a university in another city. He served 3 years in the military after graduating from high school. He has been married almost 2 years. Ben went to college for 2 years but became bored and quit to join the military. Melissa, who graduated early from high school, has been away at college for 2 years. She is coming home to attend a local university that has a particularly good program in her major field. Cindy is in the ninth grade at a local public high school.

Kenneth and Marie grew up in the same neighborhood in Chicago, Kenneth from a poor family and Marie from a rich one. He is the oldest of four siblings. She has a younger sister. They got married when she was 15 and he was 18, but they did not tell her parents or his father. Marie continued to live at home; Kenneth was a freshman in college and working. She got pregnant, so they made plans to leave town. When

Marie became ill (related to her pregnancy), her mother took her to a physician. Her parents then found out about the marriage and pregnancy, but they did not accept the marriage and had it annulled. Kenneth and Marie moved to the Southwest, where they were married again. They have been married for 25 years.

Three years ago, they decided to do something together because the children were growing up. Marie passed her high school equivalency test, at Kenneth's urging, and they decided to attend college together. Although Kenneth has worked for the same company for 25 years, they have moved a number of times. They now live in a nice apartment and plan to stay in the large southern city to which they moved 6 years ago.

Kenneth and Marie have been very active in the community; now most of their energy is invested in school. Cindy is a member of the high school vocal ensemble, is a class officer, a member of Young Democrats, and she enjoys swimming. The family shares a common interest in theater and music and have been in many productions together. They like to socialize and have many friends. Kenneth and Marie have set aside Friday nights for time together.

The family seems to be very close. They telephone the family members who live away from home every week. They seem creative; for example, they post rules and let the children set their punishments. The children are allowed to try anything at home. They communicate openly about sex and finances.

When I asked them what they would like to work on, they mentioned that Melissa's coming home to live will mean readjustment. Marie has grown very close to Melissa in the years she has been away and does not want Melissa's coming home to push them apart. They asked that Melissa be allowed to join our sessions. With the supervisor's approval, she was allowed to join, but she did not participate in the pre- or the posttests.

PRETEST RESULTS

The family's scores on the Bell-Fagan Family Symbols (B-F) are close together on the anxious-afraid end of the graph, falling in the intermediate range. The scores differentiated on the other end of the graph are loving, quiet, and happy. Marie has the highest score for loving, the lowest for quiet, and a fairly high score on happiness. Kenneth has the highest score on quiet and the lowest on afraid-anxious, but none of his scores are very low. Cindy has the lowest score for happiness; the rest of her scores fall in the midrange.

In the Description of Feelings in the Family (DFF), Kenneth saw the family as slightly mad. Marie saw the family as slightly mad and distracting. Cindy saw the family as mad and a little bit smug. All the scores are very low and near the axes. In the family-sees-member section, Kenneth was seen as a little bit mad and distracting, Marie as neutral. Both teenaged-daughter and young-daughter cards were picked for Cindy: On the teenaged-daughter cards, Cindy was seen as slightly mad and distracting; on the young-daughter cards, she was seen as slightly mad and smug. Again, the scores are low and near the axes.

In the Family Situations Picture Series (FSPS), Kenneth saw the family as a little placating; Marie saw the family as slightly placating and computing. Cindy saw the family as computing. All the scores are very low and near the axes. In the family-sees-member section, Kenneth was seen as placating and computing, Marie as computing. Older-daughter and younger-daughter cards were chosen to represent Cindy. On the older-daughter cards, she was seen as slightly placating; on the younger-daughter cards, she was seen as slightly blaming and computing. All the scores are very low and close to the axes.

On the Animal Concepts Picture Series (ACPS), the real and the ideal are very similar. The only person who really changes from real to ideal is Cindy, and the change is not great. The change is moving closer on the continuum toward good, fast, harmless, pleasant, and passive. As the family took this test, they commented that they like themselves as they are, and this seems evident in the results.

The overall pretest results support my impression that the family is creative and open.

SUMMARY OF SESSIONS

Session 1

Melissa was home from college and joined our session. After I described the affective programs, they were still a bit unsure about which one to choose; Marie and Melissa liked the Introductory-Experiential Program, so I began with the first lesson, Working Together.

In the first exercise (the family sits in a circle, holding hands, and imagines themselves taking a walk in the country), the imagery was very detailed, including all the senses. The family members interjected loving and appropriate humor. They chose colors to describe the way they felt; Kenneth, green; Cindy, yellow; Marie, blue; and Melissa, red. All said the colors denoted peace, happiness, tranquillity, and aliveness. They also chose animals to represent themselves: Kenneth, a soaring eagle; Marie, a rabbit; Melissa, a turtle; and Cindy, a cat.

Kenneth started making up the story using all the animals, and the other family members joined in. The rabbit and the turtle were in a race, the cat was watching, and the eagle was soaring overhead. There was some disagreement over who would win the race. Cindy suggested that the cat would join the race and win. Kenneth said the eagle would get hungry and swoop down and eat the rabbit. Melissa and Marie teased each other about who would win, then decided it would be a tie.

In the exercise involving touching, Cindy was disruptive and giggled a lot: she did not want to touch anyone, nor did she want anyone to touch her. Melissa took the exercises more seriously and seemed to enjoy them. Cindy, at 14, is at a stage in which she is conscious of touching, particularly in public. She said she felt silly and embarrassed. Her parents commented that when the family members sit together on the parents' king-sized bed at night, talking, she holds both her parents' hands.

The next exercise, the trust walk, the family had done before in a drama group. Melissa led her father around and vice versa. Cindy led her mother around and vice versa.

In the money exercise, the family had more than $5 in change. In choosing the coin most like oneself, Kenneth chose a quarter, Marie a penny, Melissa a nickel, and Cindy a shiny new penny. When asked to exchange coins, every member swapped with every other member. In dividing the money, Kenneth said that he and Marie would keep the money in a pool and give out money as needed (Marie agreed with his answer). Melissa said she would give all the money to her daddy (except 30 cents for herself) because he could manage it better. Cindy said she would give Melissa and her a dime each and give the rest to their daddy.

In the family sculpting, each member sculpted typical family scenes. Kenneth posed the family for a family snapshot, with Marie holding two fingers over Cindy's head. Melissa had Kenneth reading the paper; Cindy sitting at his feet, watching TV; and Marie on the sofa studying, drinking coffee, and smoking. Cindy arranged the family similarly except that she was lying on the sofa, feet in air; Melissa was sitting beside her; and the parents were sitting together on the opposite sofa. Marie said that since the family had been together in the other sculptures she would do them as individuals: Kenneth was washing the car, Cindy practicing routines for drill team tryout, Melissa practicing a part in a play, and Marie on the bed, studying.

When I asked the family what they thought of the session as a whole, Kenneth said he hadn't learned anything. Cindy said it was fun but agreed she hadn't learned anything about the family because they have done many things like this. Melissa said she had enjoyed it. Marie said she felt the lesson was three levels too low for them. After this feedback, we looked more closely at the affective programs. Marie finally said a cognitive-experiential program might be better (Kenneth and the children wanted Marie to decide because they felt she knew more about these things). I told them I would think about the change and discuss it with my supervisor. None of the family seemed happy with the fact that they had had fun and enjoyed themselves; they wanted to learn something concrete.

Enricher's notes and supervision.

Before the session began, Melissa and Marie were talking about Melissa's wanting to be different yet feeling that she is like her mother. She seemed torn between the two, actually wanting both at times. I think the story they made up reflects this. At the beginning of the session, the family assumed that a visitor of Melissa's could sit in on the session. Since this was the first session with the family and I did not know how an observer would affect them, I requested that she not observe. She said this was agreeable to her because she had some studying to do. Kenneth did not seem too pleased but said nothing. During the session, Kenneth got up to go check on the visitor. I could see he was bothered by her being left out, so I invited her to observe. There was no change in how the family acted: they were very verbal and open, and took no notice of the observer. My supervisor suggested that in the future I allow observers and have them give their impressions to the family at the end of the session. The supervisor agreed to the change in programs but warned me against getting hooked by letting the family put the responsibility for SE on me.

Session 2

Ben, who was home on leave, joined the session.

In responding to the first exercise, What is important to you today? Cindy said going swimming and that it was her dad's birthday. Ben said waiting for his brother and sister-in-law to arrive. He said all seven are seldom together and that it makes his mom happy when everyone can come home at one time. Melissa said getting an A in her English class. Kenneth said, "My birthday, having the family together, and I'd like to be alone for an hour." Marie mentioned that Kenneth had said he would like to lock the bedroom door (with her and Kenneth inside) and put Vaseline on the doorknob.

In the next exercise, I asked about the life experiences they consider important. Cindy said participating in the All-State Chorus concert and getting kissed. Ben said graduating from boot camp, when he got an award and his mom was there to receive it with him. Kenneth had a hard time with this exercise. He said that every experience had been important—meeting his wife, getting married, the birth of each child, the opportunity to own his own business, a trip to Europe. He said that nothing mundane had ever happened to him. Marie said she found everything exciting and that she had gone through many phases: she mentioned the 25 years with Kenneth, the kids, theater shows, politics, their son's wedding. She added that all experiences are important—one experience leads to another. Melissa said going to college early, acting in plays, and participating in a dance-athon.

When I asked them to share the saddest moment of life, Cindy said not making drill team, but she took it back. Ben mentioned one bad fight his parents had had years before: His mother had planned to leave for a while. He got so upset that he went into his bedroom and started jumping up and down and screaming on his bed. The tantrum was so bad that he worked himself into a fever. His mom had to stay home because he was sick, and his parents worked out their differences. Neither parent remembered the incident. Kenneth did say that he remembered Ben's tantrums as well as some of Marie's (his tone was sarcastic, and in a sense he put down his son).

Kenneth said that his saddest moment had been when his mother died, when he was 18. He added that this is the only personal tragedy he has experienced. Cindy's saddest time was when her two cats died (she said she cried for a year). Then she added that she had also been sad when her great-grandmother died.

Melissa said people don't remember a sad thing unless it's a tragedy. She said the most recent sad moment she could remember was when she wrote a letter to her deceased great-grandmother and then cried because she knew her great-grandmother wouldn't get it. Several family members teased Melissa about the letter, but Marie came to her defense, saying it had not been silly. She had sent her Uncle Milt a telegram when he died because she couldn't be there for the funeral and she had wanted her thoughts said. She had asked the rabbi to read it to her uncle after the funeral service.

Marie said her saddest moment was the first time she saw her father cry—at his mother's funeral. The children said they had never seen their dad cry and requested in unison "Cry for us, Daddy." Kenneth laughed and said, "Wait until the bills come on the fifteenth."

Next, I asked the family to express their feelings to each member nonverbally. (I chose this exercise because Cindy had had so much trouble with the touching exercise.) Playful and teasing, they took turns kissing and hugging each other. Kenneth teased Cindy about having given them so much trouble during the past week.

All were asked to name something good they could do for themselves as individuals. Ben said he was going to see the credit union counselor and work out a budget (money is his biggest problem). Kenneth said he will pass his chemistry test and lose 5 pounds. Melissa said she will jog a mile a day and lose weight. Cindy said she would pass her algebra test, do yoga, and lose 2 pounds. Marie said she wanted to break her weight barrier this week.

The family members were asked to say why love is important to them. Melissa said that love is a human necessity. Cindy said it helps her get going—"My parents love me and encourage me." Ben said he knows the family loves him, even when he does something wrong or things go bad: "When I'm feeling down, Mom can always tell. The love from my family always picks me up when I'm feeling down." (At this point, Marie cried.) Kenneth said that love motivates him, as does the fact that people depend on him. He considers love a necessity and said that he is a product of it. Melissa said she had been raised with it and had learned to give it. She added that love makes her not be lazy. Marie said love is what keeps her going and that she needs to give as well as take love.

Asked to name the ways love is expressed in the family, they answered that love is expressed verbally, by hitting, and by kissing. Ben recalled that the last words they heard as children before they went to bed were "I love you." Kenneth said that love is the glue that holds their family together. Ben interjected that they are a sarcastic family; Kenneth countered with a minisermon on how theirs is a very expressive family, very open with feelings and thoughts. He concluded that no one in the family purposefully hurts another.

In sharing their fantasies about themselves, the family teased each other about sex and fantasy. Cindy said her fantasies are to become president of the United States, outsing Kelly Brewer, have lots of musical talent, and have a boyfriend (she proceeded to describe her ideal boyfriend). Melissa's fantasies are to be a famous actress, conquer the world, and find a cure for muscular dystrophy. Ben said his fantasy is to be a singer and a musical director. Marie said her fantasies are her first grandchild, getting a doctorate, growing old with her old man, and going to an island alone with Kenneth. Kenneth's fantasies are to hit a home run for the Braves (at the bottom of the ninth with the Braves down by two runs), being able to make love just one more time in a night, live in a white house on top of a hill and look down on a domain that is his, and fly a plane.

Ben commented that he had been taught to set goals that he can reach, so he never thinks of a goal he can't reach. He considered all the fantasies mentioned within the bounds of possibility.

In the last exercise, the family was to imagine living alone on an island and describe what they would do to survive. Ben said they could move to the other side of the island. Marie said that Ben and Melissa would come up with all the right answers. Kenneth suggested that the island be Manhattan Island, with no people but with a stocked refrigerator and a full wine cellar in every house. The family really liked that idea. Marie suggested that they could take over a theater and put on a show. Ben said that all the grown-up children would have to live apart on the island because they have different views and would fight all the time.

Enricher's notes.

The family's creativity is evident in their answers. They are extremely verbal, very achievement-oriented, and they emphasize the positives.

At the end of the session, Kenneth asked whether I was getting what I wanted. When I replied that SE is for the family, he said he was concerned that I might think the family was trying to present a good image by not discussing many negative things. I told him I had not felt they were covering up or presenting a false image.

Several times Kenneth asserted his power in subtle ways. I think it is important for him to feel that he is in control of the situation. The family generally considers the exercises ambiguous and would prefer more structure so that they could feel that they are learning something. I think Kenneth sees me in a judging role and is afraid of what I might think. He has a lot invested in keeping his family together.

Supervision.

When we discussed my impressions, my supervisor suggested that a transactional analysis (TA) program might be appropriate. He said that in achievement-oriented families, the positives tend to be emphasized and the negatives forgotten.

Session 3

For Session 3, I modified a transactional program designed for the families of alcoholics.

In the first exercise, I asked the family members to describe early childhood memories. Kenneth said he grew up in a loving household. Children were to be seen but not heard around adult company. As a child he was not allowed to socialize with company. His earliest childhood memory is that at age 3 he fell out of a second-story window (he was not badly hurt). His mother wanted him to be a dentist, and his dad wanted him to be a baseball player. The oldest of four children, he had a lot of responsibility as a child. He was close to both his parents, particularly his mother. Marie said she had no relationship with her parents: Her father was very authoritarian, and her mother was his puppet. Her childhood memory was being made to eat all the food on her plate because of starving kids in Europe.

Cindy and Melissa described their relationship with their parents as warm and loving. Both have been taught to try things at which they are good and can excel. They have been taught to set goals that are within reach.

All family members except Marie described their births (she was never told about hers). At this point, the family comforted her, and Cindy suggested they make up a story for Mommy's birth. Their story was full of humor and centered on their grandmother's having found Marie under a cabbage leaf. Grandmother, needless to say, was described as very Victorian.

The family's favorite fairy tales or Bible stories follow: Cindy—stories in which she was a part (her mother always put her in the story); Melissa—Noah's ark; Kenneth—a story about a good king (Marie couldn't think of a favorite story).

Enricher's notes.

The family liked this program better and the session went well, but little new information was revealed.

At the beginning of the session, I mentioned my impression that the family has some trouble with ambiguity (I had to define ambiguity for the girls). The family agreed and confirmed that they are more comfortable with structure (understandable, considering their achievement orientation).

Session 4

Again I modified the transactional program for this family. After I explained ego states, the family did ego-grams for each member (including self) and gave them to each other.

Some important issues arose from these ego-grams. Cindy sees Melissa as 40% Critical Parent; Melissa could not understand that and denied it. Kenneth was seen mostly as a Critical Parent and a Nurturing Parent; he saw himself mainly as an Adult. As they traded ego-grams, they made comments such as "I'm not like that," but when each member was asked about the ego-grams, they were for the most part pleased and felt they reflect the way they are. Although I emphasized *now* and the fact that the situation would change in a few weeks when school ends and tension is not so high, no one wanted to change anything.

The family had a little trouble identifying ego states in some of the written transactions, but Cindy caught on fast and helped the others.

Kenneth had labeled his statements Adult when actually they were Critical Parent statements. When I pointed that out, he got angry, wadded up his piece of paper, and threw it at me. Cindy said, "Daddy is acting like a Rebellious Child.'"

Enricher's notes.

The family really got involved in doing the exercises, and they enjoyed learning something new. Kenneth, to protect himself, becomes distracting when the exercises get into an area that may bring out some issues for him. He seems insecure about his position and wants to be sure things stay the same. He is the most resistant to change and is not very good at looking at his weak points.

Supervision.

My supervisor suggested I use the triangles concept for the last two sessions.

Session 5

About 10 minutes of this session was spent discussing the homework from the preceding week (ask a family member to respond to you in a certain ego state; that person in turn may request the same of you).

Marie had asked Cindy to respond as an Adult, and Cindy asked her mother to be a Nurturing Parent. They had handled their responses well. Cindy mentioned that she had not said anything to Melissa about being a Critical Parent. The sisters immediately got into an argument about using each other's clothes, each blaming the other. I asked that they deal with that problem later. In the meantime, Kenneth got up and started watering the plants. When I asked him whether he had done the homework, he said he would like to do it with Melissa next week. He wants her to be more Adult, and she wants him to be more Adult, less Critical Parent.

In responding to how the mother-father-child triangle applies to each person, Kenneth saw the longest side of the triangle as his father; he saw his mother's side and his side as equal. In his own family, he considers his side and Marie's side equal, the children's side the shortest. Marie saw the longest side of the triangle as her father, the next longest as hers, and the shortest as her mother's. Cindy and Melissa agreed that their parents' sides are equal and their sides shorter. Cindy said her side would be shorter than Melissa's, since she is the baby of the family. Cindy sees Melissa as having more power. In this exercise, the family repeated information they had learned from the TA exercise, but they did use some creative analogies.

The family had some trouble with the I-you-we triangle. They said they use "I" to mean all of them and that they call this the "editorial I."

Enricher's notes.

Again, the family's creativity emerged. The aspect of blaming came out for the first time between the daughters. The family is asking for some changes in themselves through the use of the homework exercise, which they want to continue. Kenneth was again distracting and reverted at times to digital thinking. I suspect he has learned his creativity from his wife and the other family members.

Session 6

In the first part of the session we dealt with the rescuer-persecutor-victim (R-P-V) triangle. Cindy and Melissa really felt this triangle applies to their family: They said their mother is the persecutor most of the time, their dad is the rescuer, and they are the victims. They admitted that their mother is occasionally the rescuer. Neither Cindy nor Melissa could see themselves in any role except victim.

Neither girl felt very well: They were tired from having stayed up late the night before, and Melissa had a stomachache. The lesson moved slower, and the parents talked less.

During all the role-play exercises, the girls took every opportunity to point out bad things about their mother. Kenneth commented that this must be "dump-on-Marie day." Marie rarely responded to the girls' blaming. Cindy and Melissa did not want to break up the R-P-V triangle. Kenneth played psychologist and said Cindy does not do her work around the house just to get her mother's attention. He said he usually walks in on the middle of fights between Marie and one of the girls and ends up trying to appease both sides.

Rather than end the last session on a negative note, I ended with an exercise on behaving like grown-ups. They discussed assuming responsibility for oneself, speaking only for oneself, and talking in the present. Each member of the family expressed the desire to be more of an adult.

Enricher's notes.

This lesson really hit home. Apparently the girls had stored up resentment toward their mother. Melissa and Cindy prefer not to take responsibility for themselves; at times, they seem to want to be children rather than adults. Since Kenneth has been in school, Marie has been the parent most of the time, but Kenneth is the peacemaker when he is at home. I think Kenneth likes to be thought of as protective and loving rather than a Critical Parent. Both girls seem a little immature, but Marie has commented that Melissa has grown up a lot since she went away to college. Cindy, I think, is really fighting growing up.

POSTTEST RESULTS

On the Bell-Fagan Family Symbols (B-F) test, all three family members' scores are varied and spread apart, except that Marie and Kenneth have very close scores on afraid-anxious. Marie has the lowest scores on anger and quiet, and the highest scores on loving and happy. Kenneth has the lowest scores on loving and happy, and the highest scores on afraid-anxious and sad.

On the Description of Feelings in the Family (DFF), Kenneth saw the family as slightly mad and smug; Marie saw the family as slightly mad and distracting. Cindy saw the family as slightly mad and distracting. The scores are very low (no score over 2). In the family-sees-member section, the father was seen as a little sad and smug, the mother as a little sad and distracting, and the younger daughter as a little mad. Again, all scores are very low (no score over 4).

On the Family Situations Picture Series (FSPS), Kenneth saw the family as slightly placating and distracting; Marie saw the family as computing; Cindy saw the family as blaming and computing. The scores are low (highest score is 10). In the family-sees-member section, Kenneth was seen as slightly placating and computing, Marie as slightly blaming and computing, Cindy as a little blaming, and Melissa as slightly blaming and computing. Again, the scores are low (no score over 6).

In the Animal Concepts Picture Series (ACPS), Kenneth's scores are identical for actual and ideal. Marie's scores change a tiny bit from actual to ideal but follow the same pattern. Cindy's scores change the most from actual to ideal, but the change, which is on the continuum toward powerless, small, good, quiet, harmless, pleasant, is not great. The posttest results reflect the family as I experienced them; in other words, the testing and my experience with them are in agreement.

In comparing the pre- and posttest results, I see some changes in the family, which can be explained by several factors. The pretests were done before Melissa returned home. Her presence adds a new dimension to the family and raises new issues. This family, unable to rely on families of origin, has formed its own survival support system, and the members have a lot invested in seeing the good about themselves and are achievement-oriented. I hypothesize that SE has helped the family become more aware of itself as it really is. Through the lessons, they were able to take a closer look at their interactions. The TA program and the work on triangles allowed them to examine their negative aspects and weak points.

FEEDBACK CONFERENCE

First, feedback was obtained from the family. Melissa said she had really liked SE and that she had learned more about her mom's and dad's lives. She believed that her parents had learned more about their daughters. She had become aware of the good things about herself and learned that she can be an adult. Marie said it was important to her that the family had sat down together as a group 1 hour a week. She said she had learned more about each family member and liked the fact that the family had been able to talk on an adult level. Cindy, in a bad mood, at first said SE had been a waste of time. She then said no, it hadn't: she had learned about ego states and triangles. She mentioned the R-P-V triangle as important. Kenneth said SE had been interesting and that he had learned to look at things differently. He had liked having the family discuss things as a group but said he hadn't learned anything new about his family (Cindy agreed). Melissa challenged her father on that, but to no avail. In reaction to Kenneth's statement, Marie shrugged her shoulders and seemed a little disgusted.

In stating their assets and strengths, I mentioned their humor, their verbal skills, and their ability to express positive and negative feelings openly. Kenneth asserted his control and jumped the gun by asking me whether I considered their humor a cover-up. I responded that I would like to continue with what I had to say. I told them these assets could be used very productively. Then I posed the negative aspects in the form of three questions: "Is your humor sometimes used to avoid pain and hurt feelings? Do your verbal skills sometimes get in the way of expressing hurt? When you express negative feelings, are you sometimes expressing blame instead of seeking constructive change?"

The family discussed these questions openly and in detail, and concluded that all three happen at times. I was particularly pleased that Kenneth could consider these questions without becoming defensive.

The family chose not to participate in more SE, commenting that they are happy with themselves as they are.

SUMMARY

I consider the enrichment of this family successful. I had difficulty finding an appropriate program for them, but TA and the triangles exercises were very useful. I think that if the family had been able to complete all the triangles work, they might have been better able to resolve some of the issues raised. It concerned me that a lot of new issues were brought out in Session 6 and had to be left hanging, but I am confident the family can handle the issues effectively when they are ready.

The family balances being, doing, and having. They are what Kantor and Lehr (1975) would define as an open-type family. Lewis, Beavers, Gossett, and Phillips (1976) would define this family as healthy. They seem to be coping very well, and they are creative. Neither of the parent's family of origin was creative, so this family has developed its own creativity. The fact that the parents left their families of origin at such a young age and have been physically separated from them has aided the parents' differentiation. I think more conflict will arise in this family as the children differentiate themselves further, but the family will find a way to cope with it.

19

Working-Through and Cohabitation Programs

Edgar Jessee and Rosemary Bleyer

Steve and Pamela have been living together for the past 6 months. Steve, aged 28, is a public attorney who frequently acts as counsel for poor people. He is the younger of two children; his father is retired, and his mother is deceased. Steve has been married once but is now divorced, and he has no children from the marriage. Steve has lived in four cities in the past 8 years.

Pamela, aged 30, is currently a secretary but for several years was a schoolteacher. She, too, has been married once and is now divorced. She is the older of two children; her father works in manufacturing, and her mother is a school principal. Pamela has lived most of her life in a small midwestern town and moved to a large southern city only in the past year.

INTERVIEW

During the first few moments of the interview, Steve and Pamela appeared somewhat anxious, talking about trivia and laughing nervously. When we asked why they sought SE, they began to argue in a rather blaming manner. Pamela started and appeared to be the pursuer. Steve reacted in a very intellectual, rational, and nonfeeling way, as opposed to Pamela's outbursts of feeling and angry affect. Steve used computing to gain distance from his feelings and basically implied that it is Pamela who has most of the problems. Pamela presented herself as the one pushing for SE, but Steve also seems willing and, at some level, committed (he even agreed to pay for SE if necessary). Pamela sees their problem as sexual dissatisfaction; Steve mentioned "communication" as the area he would like to work on.

After intervening in the argument and attempting to gain control of the situation, we tried briefly to help clarify each person's feelings. We administered the pretests at the end of the interview.

Enrichers' notes.

We have reached three conclusions. (a) The primary question is whether therapy or SE is indicated. (b) The couple's relationship is unstable, and they might terminate SE at any time. (c) We need to establish the fact that we are in control of the sessions and not allow any more of the blaming and fighting we observed in the interview.

Supervision.

Our supervisor suggested that we should have low expectations for this couple: on the pretests, Steve rated himself as far superior to Pamela, and Pamela fed into this viewpoint. He suggested that we confront Steve and Pamela with this fact, as well as the other test results. According to their pretest scores, the couple has sufficient difficulty to warrant therapy. It was decided that we would offer SE only as at least a three-program undertaking.

SUMMARY OF SESSIONS

Session 1

At the beginning of the session, we told Steve and Pamela the results of their pretests. Basically, their scores are low, particularly in areas of warmth, respect, sex, and level of hostility. They generally agreed that the scores seem accurate, although Steve disagreed somewhat with the scores on "respect" and "hostility." We also confronted them with the superiority-inferiority relationship indicated by their pretests. Pamela agreed she plays into this relationship; Steve said that he doesn't think he is superior but that perhaps he *feels* as if he is.

We noted that our expectations for one SE program are low and told them that it would take at least three programs for SE to be effective. We discussed therapy and SE; then the couple asked to talk alone to decide which they wanted. After 10 minutes, we returned to the room, and Steve said that they would like to do the series of SE programs. Pamela said tearfully that she would prefer to go into therapy but that Steve would not agree. At this point she said that Steve was saying that she was the one with the problem and that it was up to her to do something about it. Pamela agreed to participate in SE but clearly blamed Steve for their not entering therapy (Pamela did not mention the possibility of individual therapy for herself). Each seemed to say that the other person is the one with a problem.

Before ending our meeting, we finally agreed on the Working-Through Program.

Enrichers' notes.

We believe we did establish that we will be in control of the sessions from now on, although this might be challenged from time to time. We also believe that we now have a deeper understanding and appreciation of Steve and Pamela as individuals.

Supervision.

Two relationship triangles were applied to our couple. Our supervisor suggested that Steve and Pamela are very involved with "doing" and "having" but that they are avoiding "being." Also, both seem to see themselves as the rescuer in a rescuer-victim-persecutor triad (Steve works with poor people, and Pamela sees herself as the savior of their relationship).

Session 2

The first lesson in the Working-Through Program is focused on making "I" statements rather than "you" statements. Steve and Pamela seem to avoid themselves by blaming each other. In fact, an argument occurred that beautifully illustrates their incongruent styles of communicating. We stopped the argument after a few minutes and played it back on the tape recorder. Both were "amazed" to hear what had happened. Pamela acknowledged that she had been blaming, and Steve acknowledged that he was using computing to avoid dealing with his feelings. This interaction seemed to depress Pamela somewhat—I think she began to get in touch with some old depression—and although she talked about being upset, she focused on a rather superficial issue. At this point, Steve attempted to "rescue" her and actually showed much warmth in doing so. We reinforced their sharing of feelings and their ability to be warm with each other.

The homework assignment was to practice making "I" statements. Both seemed genuinely interested in learning this new skill.

Enrichers' notes.

We were glad to see the couple's ability to be intimate, but we wondered whether this pattern—a fight leading to intimacy—is a common one for them. We were also encouraged by their willingness to practice the new skill we offered and hope that this indicates a high degree of motivation. Perhaps Steve and Pamela now realize that some help is available and that they can be a part of the process. It will be interesting to see who resists the change now that it appears possible.

Supervision.

We again discussed the victim-rescuer-persecutor triangle and the ways in which both are victims and rescuers. Our supervisor advised us to incorporate this idea into the paradoxical letter to be given to them later. He confirmed that the Working-Through Program seems especially applicable because of its emphasis on the self and its role-reversal exercises.

Session 3

In this session, we used Multiple Viewpoints, the second lesson in the Working-Through Program. The lesson deals primarily with needs and feelings, and with economic and situational pressures. (I was not at the session because of illness but did listen to the tape later.)

First, Steve and Pamela were asked how their practice of "I" statements was going. Both, particularly Pamela, replied they had been trying very hard but that it was still difficult. They were encouraged to keep practicing.

Nothing really surprising occurred in the session. Both gave businesslike answers to the questions about pressures, and they did not seem to have an in-depth awareness of their feelings. However, Steve tuned in to the question about individual needs—"I think I need love." This was one of the first times Steve has expressed some real feeling. While he spoke, his head was lowered, and he spoke in an unusual tone of voice for him.

Enrichers' notes.

We are pleased with Steve's ability to open up and get in touch with some of his feelings. Perhaps he will be more open to growth than we first believed.

Supervision.

The focus of supervision was the paradoxical letter and the inappropriateness of one enricher's meeting with a couple. Our supervisor explained that our contract with these people calls for both of us to get together with them and that if one can't make it we should cancel the session.

We discussed specific patterns for the paradoxical letter—the couple's feelings-computing relating and their inferiority-superiority characteristics.

Session 4

In this session, we worked with a role reversal. Steve seemed to switch roles very easily and played Pamela's part with real feeling. Pamela, however, had a very difficult time with the whole exercise. She complained that she could not "get into Steve" and that Steve was playing her wrong. It was very hard to carry out the exercise, but we went ahead anyway. I had not expected this resistance and felt confused through most of the session. Pamela seemed very anxious and engaged in several maneuvers that were apparently designed to bring Steve or one of the enrichers to her rescue. The rescue did not take place, so basically Pamela seemed stuck with herself.

Enrichers' notes.

We believe that Pamela is beginning to feel the threat of change and is doing her best to resist it. Although she is trying to resist change, she is also getting in touch with some of her hurt. She is still very confused in her feelings and seems unable to clarify them. Pamela seems to be a particularly good distracter, so she may need some nonverbal role playing to avoid her verbal distracting. Steve, on the other hand, appears to be growing, shows insight, and displays a lot of motivation for learning more.

Session 5

We again dealt with role reversal, but this time we tried a nonverbal role reversal in order to avoid Pamela's distracting. We used the pursuer-distancer theme that we had observed earlier; that is, Pamela pursues Steve about his emotions in an attempt to avoid herself, and Steve distances from this by computing and eventually not communicating at all. Initially, Pamela refused to do the exercise but agreed after we pressed her. Once they began, they did extremely well and we complimented them on their portrayals of each other. Both were able to get a feeling for the other's situation and exhibited some genuine understanding of their incongruent patterns of communication. At the end of the session, we gave them copies of the following letter.

Dear Pamela and Steve,

We are impressed by the way you complement each other in your relationship. With one of you working from the intellectual realm and the other from the emotional realm, together you create a total, blended person, able to experience and analyze all aspects of life. We hope that both of you work to preserve and protect this complementarity.

We're pleased with the way you focus on your work and your relationship rather than being preoccupied with yourselves. Since you've settled into this pattern, you can maintain the balance of power that now exists. We wonder whether this delicate balance would be disrupted if a change occurred.

Enrichers' notes.

Pamela may be close to getting in touch with her depression. Steve seems very amenable to learning much more about the relationship and seems to be undergoing first-order change. Pamela, however, because of her resistance to changing the relationship, seems more accessible through second-order change.

Supervision.

Today we talked about the digital quality of thinking exhibited by both partners—there appears to be very little variation of intensity. We also talked about Pamela's distracting and decided that the nonverbal role playing worked well. Our supervisor suggested that we deal with Pamela's depression in the feedback conference.

Session 6

Before we began the lesson (intimacy), some interesting interactions occurred. Pamela began talking about job interviews and asked to speak with the female enricher for some helpful hints. The interesting thing was that I (the male enricher) was directly and obviously excluded. The female enricher avoided Pamela's ploy, and we began the lesson.

One of the interesting things that came up was the ways in which each avoids being intimate with the other. Steve said that when Pamela wants to be intimate and he doesn't, he talks in an intellectual manner; Pamela said she keeps herself very busy, which precludes much chance for intimacy. A particularly interesting pattern emerged when we asked how they avoid being intimate in bed. Pamela said she goes to bed early and wakes up early; Steve said he comes to bed late, usually after Pamela is asleep.

Pamela commented on the paradoxical letter, saying it was a "nice" letter and thanking us for writing it. We told her we would talk more about the letter during the feedback conference if they wished, and we asked them to read it again during the next week.

Enrichers' notes.

Pamela seemed to be trying to create a new triangle (excluding me) in the hope of creating a new alliance and taking some of the pressure off herself. Such a maneuver may also be another distracting attempt at resisting change. From her comments about the letter, it also seems obvious that Pamela is very much resisting change.

Supervision.

Pamela's manipulative attempts were discussed, and our supervisor suggested that they are designed to help Pamela avoid intimacy with herself. We also discussed the couple's emphasis on doing rather than being. We learned that many times the one who agrees with the letter is the most resistant to change.

Steve and Pamela are in a hooked system in which they cannot live with each other or without each other. Thus, any attempt to change that system will be met with opposition. Selfhood seems to be sacrificed for selfishness.

Session 7

For our last session, we used the lesson Fears, Hopes, and Expectations from the Cohabitation Program. We did this because we felt the contracting session from Working Through was inappropriate at this point— this couple has much work to do on their relationship. For the first time, the couple began to seriously investigate their fears and hopes for the future. Steve mentioned that he was afraid they would begin taking their relationship for granted, as had been happening in the last few weeks. He said he did not see the relationship as a permanent one but neither did he see it as ending in the near future. He also expressed a fear of not being able to do all the work involved in making a relationship work, although he admitted he had surprised himself by doing the amount of work he has done thus far in SE.

Pamela displayed much confusion, as she apparently usually does when anxious and fearful. She talked about "voices" in her head that had told her the relationship would not work even before it began. In general, she exhibited a fatalistic attitude; she apparently set herself up to lose in this relationship as she has done with other things in the past. Basically, Steve and Pamela seemed in touch with their depression for the first time, and the atmosphere of the session was heavy and painful. We congratulated both of them for being able to get in touch with their hurt.

Enrichers' notes.

Pamela does seem to be somewhat in touch with her depression and may be face-to-face with herself, a very uncomfortable and unusual situation for her. Our hope is that Steve will not be hooked into rescuing her and thus inhibit any chance for real change to occur. The feedback conference should give us a good chance to deal with their depression.

Supervision.

We discussed the depression we have been seeing in the relationship. Our supervisor suggested that we use *hurt* instead of *depression* if the couple has difficulty admitting that they are depressed. He also suggested that they had gotten themselves into the relationship to avoid their depression. We are to deal with the depression in the feedback conference by following specific steps: (a) positive reframing, (b) asking whether their liabilities control their assets, and (c) asking "Who controls your depression?"

We decided that a verbal contract would suffice for engaging in another series of SE programs.

FEEDBACK CONFERENCES

First Conference

Steve and Pamela arrived in very good spirits. Pamela very quickly asked for our assistance with an upcoming interview. This was the first of a series of instances in which Pamela sought our attention in a way that directly excluded Steve. After we had consistently avoided these ploys, Pamela finally said she felt that she was not being understood and expressed much helplessness. Again, we focused on the relationship and how this pattern of interaction is expressed in the relationship. Finally, Pamela said she guessed she was trying to get Steve and herself into therapy, even though she knew Steve did not want therapy (actually she had not checked this with Steve).

Later Pamela attempted another alliance, this one with the female enricher, who again frustrated Pamela's attempts. At this point Pamela contradicted her earlier statements about feeling "very good" and "feeling comfortable enough to say anything." She seemed again in touch with her depression.

Steve remained quiet most of the time and seemed still in touch with the hurt that had been opened up during the preceding session. Steve seemed reluctant to give up his depression and had not responded to Pamela's initial statements about feeling "so good." Steve resisted the term *depression* but very much identified with *hurt*. He said, "Things are still unresolved, but I'm feeling better about this process." He made many statements that indicated he wanted to stay with his hurt, such as "I'm a slow learner" and "Things change slowly for me."

First, Steve and Pamela took the posttests. Then we asked for feedback on the program. Both were very positive about their experience and said that the role playing had been most meaningful to them. Both partners, particularly Pamela, seemed in very good spirits (in direct contrast to the depression evidenced in the preceding session). We commented on this and complimented them on having been able to get in touch with their hurt.

We were able to move on and have Steve and Pamela consider how the liabilities in their relationship control the assets. They were able to say that their avoidance of their depression actually cancels out many of the assets of their relationship. We told them that we wanted to meet with them in a few weeks to hear how things are going and the decisions they make. We did express our concern about the depression we've seen. Both were agreeable to meeting with us in 2 weeks.

Supervision.

Our supervisor cautioned us to be very aware of this couple's depression. Pamela's statements about feeling really good seem incongruent with her recent expression of depression. Apparently much of their depression is related to "old stuff," hurt that has been brought to the surface by their interactional patterns in this relationship. He also suggested that we contact the couple if they do not get in touch with us.

Second Conference

Asked how they had gotten along during the past 2 weeks, both said that they were very pleased with the way things were going. They said they were happier, were having fewer fights, and were enjoying each other more. Next, we asked whether they had made any decisions about their future. They replied that they had not discussed future plans and had felt no real need to do so.

Pamela said she had been thinking about a contract and wondered whether we could help with that. Steve agreed to a contract, and we helped them do this, using Lesson 6, The Contract, in the Cohabitation Program. The length of the contract was agreed to be 2 months. Neither partner would commit to marriage, but both agreed to consider it. Steve was not willing to give up sexual partners (although he said he has had none since their relationship began), but Pamela was willing to do so. Each agreed to give up 2 nights a month purely for the partner's enjoyment. They said they had had no difficulties with their arrangements for financial and household responsibilities and thus wished to leave those out of the contract. Both signed the contract and agreed to go out to dinner in 2 weeks to assess how it is working out. Both partners expressed a desire to participate in more SE programs and agreed to call us in a week to let us know what they want to work on.

Enrichers' notes.

We are pleased that the couple was able to ask for a concrete set of rules in the form of a contract. They seem to be viewing their relationship somewhat more realistically now and seem more satisfied with their relationship. We are also encouraged that they are interested in more SE.

Supervision.

We reported on our second feedback conference and went over the contract. Our supervisor advised us not to make important decisions on the phone (the only decision made by phone is a change of time): "Decisions you want to make about your life are too important to make on the phone."

We also were told that contracts help a couple focus on specific areas and clarify issues. Our supervisor observed that contracts are especially useful in therapy.

Third Feedback Conference

We arranged the third feedback conference after a 2-week period in which the couple did not call us. Both Steve and Pamela reported that things had not been going well—in fact, they said they had been ready to move out at one point. The past week had gone well, however, so well that both expressed a hesitancy to get back into SE because they feel "more pressure" on the relationship when they are working on SE.

Pamela reported that sex was not good for her now and that she was interested in the program called Sexual Fulfillment for Couples. Steve said he was having no problem in this area but would agree to that program to help Pamela out; his preference was the Assertiveness Program. We tried to point out the inconsistencies that they were expressing—wanting help but not wanting it now, and a sexual problem affecting only one person. The issue was resolved when they learned of the fee and decided not to continue with SE. They said they had the money but did not want to continue for that sum. We assured them they could call us at any time if they decided to seek help (they are to call us when their contract is up).

Enrichers' notes.

The future of Steve and Pamela's relationship does not look very bright: they seem immobile (both need help in focusing on their relationship, as evidenced by the 2 weeks during which they discussed nothing about their relationship) and their current priorities, which do not include paying a modest fee for sessions. The areas that the couple expressed a desire to work on—sexuality and assertiveness—do seem appropriate for this couple.

Supervision.

We reported that we had had our last meeting with the couple because of their reluctance to pay the fee for more sessions. Our supervisor outlined several useful approaches in future situations that involve sexual frigidity. He suggested clarifying questions: "Who is responsible for your sexuality?" "What does sexuality mean to you?" "What do you want to do about it?" "How much of your sexuality is related to your depression?" He pointed out that this information is essential for dealing with the frigidity and with the depression (the two are probably closely related—"I'm not worthy of enjoying myself"). He further observed that when there is no orgasm in the woman, there is usually premature ejaculation in the man; wherever there is a frigid woman, there is an inept man. Finally, he advised that if they do not call back with a progress report, we should call them.

EVALUATION

Self-Differentiation

The first area to be examined is self-differentiation within the relationship and the family of origin. Relevant historical data reveal that Pamela grew up, married, and lived in her hometown until her divorce a few years ago. During her first marriage, she was a schoolteacher, like her brother and similar to her mother, who is a school principal. This indicates a lack of differentiation from her family of origin. However, Pamela left home and changed occupations after her divorce, which indicates a greater degree of self-differentiation than previously exhibited. Pamela's scores of 7 (pretest) and 6 (posttest) on the Likeness Grid indicate difficulty with differentiation within the relationship.

Steve's historical information reveals an earlier separation from parents due to the death of his mother and his having gone away. Perhaps a clue to possible lack of self-differentiation can be found in the fact that Steve's mother was a secretary, as is Pamela, and his parents were married when they were about the same age as Steve is now. On the Likeness Grid, Steve scored 10 on the pretest and 7 on the posttest. The decrease in scores can perhaps be explained by his increasing involvement in and commitment to the relationship, and the resultant difficulty of differentiating feelings, role, and task.

Priorities

Steve's and Pamela's priorities in the relationship appear to have been and continue to be structured in a healthy way. On the Priorities Inventory, both scored 10s on the pretest and 9s on the posttest, indicating that the priority structure is self first and relationship second. However, the lower scores on the posttest may indicate that the relationship is becoming more important to each of them. Even so, the posttest scores are still in the high range.

Communication Patterns

Before SE, Steve and Pamela were using very incongruent patterns of communication. Steve seemed very rational and digital in his approach and used his rationality to intellectualize his feelings. The low scores of 6 for computing and for distracting lend credence to this observation. Steve attempted several times to avoid a question by intellectualizing out of context. Pamela was using blaming, placating, and distracting; her placating style of communication occurred in our sessions whenever she seemed close to being in touch with her own hurt. Her pretest score of 5 for placating substantiates this observation. Pamela used the distracting style (she scored 7 on distracting on pretest) whenever Steve used a computing style. This interactional style was exhibited numerous times during the early sessions, particularly when change in the relationship was threatened. She also used the blaming style (she scored 7 on blaming on pretest) extensively during the early sessions, as demonstrated by her frequent remarks about Steve's "making her" feel or behave in a certain way. There was a distinct absence of "I" statements.

After SE, we could see a distinct change in each partner's style of communicating. Steve is now doing much less distracting (posttest score of 8) and dealing much more with his emotions. Because of his emphasis on the "rational" and his digital thinking, this transition has not been easy for him. Steve's posttest score on blaming dropped from 10 to 5. When SE began, Steve seemed to view the difficulty in the relationship as exclusively due to his own shortcoming, his inability to operate on a feeling level. Now Steve seems to be blaming Pamela for some of their difficulties. Steve's drop in the placating scores from 9 to 5 at first seems inconsistent with his increase in blaming Pamela, but it may reflect that Steve is now much more involved and concerned with the relationship and perhaps is attempting to smooth over some of the hurt both partners have recently become aware of. During the sessions, Steve seemed to have difficulty dealing with his own hurt and frequently tried to avoid the hurt by denying it.

Pamela's posttest scores of 7 on placating and 8 on blaming represent marked improvements, and our clinical observations support these findings. Pamela is not using blaming or placating as often as she did; however, she continues to use distracting, especially when dealing with her hurt. Her scores on distracting did not change from pre- to posttest.

In general, the partners are using more congruent patterns of communication. This has been observed in our sessions and is reinforced by the couple's very accurate perceptions of each other on the posttests.

Conflict Patterns

During our initial sessions, it became clear that Steve and Pamela were manifesting their communication difficulties in an approach-avoidance pattern characterized by emotional pursuing and distancing. Pamela pursued Steve with much talk about how he made her feel. This style of emotional blaming was difficult for Steve, the computer. Thus, when Pamela pursued, Steve distanced by intellectualizing or staying silent, which in turn caused Pamela to push harder. Pamela thus effectively avoided the hurt in herself by focusing attention on Steve. Steve seems to have been able to avoid "being" by intellectualizing and concentrating on "doing"—much of which is illustrated by his spending long hours at work.

Evidence of Pamela's need to avoid confronting her hurt can be found in several areas. First, the historical information indicates a rather severe emotional cutoff from her family: Pamela left home, divorced, and began a new occupation almost simultaneously. On Family Information (18-item) Pamela's score of 3 indicates she has a poor relationship with close relatives. Other pretest scores suggest a poor self-concept. On the Semantic Differential, Pamela saw herself as not very pleasant, good, or useful; she also generally rated herself as inferior to Steve.

Posttest and clinical observation indicate a change in the pursuing-distancing interaction. Pamela scored higher on blaming and placating; Steve scored higher on distracting. We have seen less emotional pursuing by Pamela and fewer attempts at emotional distancing by Steve.

Relationship Satisfaction

Posttest results indicate much more satisfaction with the relationship for both partners. The ratings on Family Information indicate general improvement in the relationship, especially in listening, understanding, conflict, and tension. The 10-item Family Information scores indicate improvement in a number of ways: Both Pamela and Steve indicated a significant increase in warmth and respect in their relationship.

Results from the Sexual Happiness Scale also indicate much improvement (no scores decreased markedly from pretest to posttest). Pamela's scores illustrate dramatic self-improvement, some spouse improvement, and mutual levels of satisfaction on most items. Steve's scores indicate minor self-improvement and significant spouse improvement. In general, the scores indicate they have much more accurate perceptions of each other in addition to more self and spouse satisfaction. This change in satisfaction with sex seems particularly significant because sexual dissatisfaction was a major presenting problem and seemed to be a primary manifestation of the couple's relationship difficulties.

Further evidence of relationship improvement can be seen in the posttest results on the Semantic Differential. Both partners' ratings of self and spouse show a strong sense of equality, which was not shown on the pretests.

Self-Satisfaction

The partners' personal satisfaction has changed somewhat since the pretests. Steve's posttest scores on the self part of the Sexual Happiness Scale and the self-satisfaction items of Family Information indicate slight to moderate improvement in personal self-satisfaction. Improvement is particularly clear in communication, warmth, and forgiveness; dissatisfaction remains in self-disclosure, feelings and emotions, confrontation, self-exploration, and physical health. The only area that shows significant decline is concreteness. On the posttest of the Semantic Differential, Steve rated himself as softer, less powerful, and less independent.

Clinical observations support these findings. Steve does seem more satisfied with himself and has described himself as more satisfied. Also, he has described work as more enjoyable and has recently received a raise. Steve's low score on concreteness might be explained by his recent attempts at communicating in a more feeling way, with less intellectualizing. He has described these attempts as extremely rewarding but also very difficult. The emotional confusion quite possibly makes it more difficult for Steve to separate and distinguish elements in a computing, intellectualizing manner.

Pamela's posttest scores on the Sexual Happiness Scale and on Family Information also indicate much improvement in self-satisfaction. On the Sexual Happiness Scale, Pamela showed dramatic improvement in almost all areas; her scores did not decrease from pre- to posttest. On Family Information, Pamela showed substantial improvement in relationship with close relatives, listening, understanding, and acceptance. On the 10-item Family Information, Pamela showed an increase in warmth and empathy but a decrease in self-exploration.

Pamela's ratings on the posttest Semantic Differential exhibit a more positive self-concept. She now sees herself as Steve's equal and shows significant change in seeing herself as useful and important.

Clinical observation again seems to support most of these findings. Pamela does seem to listen more effectively—a fact supported by the increase in congruent communication in the relationship. According to Pamela's self-report, she is aware of more understanding, warmth, and acceptance for her. The depression observed in the last few sessions may explain the decreased scores. Pamela recently said that she used to think she knew herself pretty well but that she now realizes she is just beginning to be aware of some parts of herself. Therefore, the low scores on self-disclosure, feelings and emotions, and self-exploration may well be explained by Pamela's depression at the time. Also, the observed withdrawal associated with Pamela's depression may account for her decreased score on confrontation. One item that remains unclear is her increased score in her relationship with close relatives. We did not pursue this topic, nor has Pamela brought it up. We hope this indicates a trend toward increased differentiation from her family of origin, but further SE and testing are needed to explore this finding.

CONCLUSIONS

In conclusion, SE seems to have helped this couple in several areas. Both partners are much happier with their relationship. They are communicating feelings, wants, needs, and expectations more congruently. Conflict in their relationship has decreased markedly. Steve has exhibited an improvement in his ability to communicate and express his feelings and therefore seems somewhat happier with himself. Pamela seems more in touch with herself in being able to experience hurt and value herself.

Despite these improvements, several areas deserve further attention. Pamela needs further examination of her depression and her lack of differentiation from her family. Steve needs practice in dealing in a more emotional realm and needs to examine his new patterns of blaming and placating.

20

Eclectic SE: Conflict Resolution, Negotiation, and Exercises on Triangles

Susan P. Gantt

INTERVIEW

Jon and Amy, both in their 20s, are a very attractive couple. When we asked them to tell us something about themselves, Jon very clearly took the lead and Amy briefly added information. Jon had recently enrolled in school full-time; he had banked the money from selling his retail business in order to go to school for the next several years. Amy had been very influential in his beginning school (education has always been very important to her and to her family, although not to Jon's). Amy is working full-time as a secretary and part-time (at night) as a salesclerk. Both described Jon's beginning school as a very significant step in their lives. Amy also plans to return to school eventually (she completed 3 years of college). Exactly when she can go back to school depends on Jon's career plans (for example, whether or not he goes to graduate school). Amy's main plan at this point is to help Jon get through school.

We described SE and answered the couple's questions. Both indicated some concern about the contract: Jon wanted to know explicitly what the feedback conference would involve, as it was mentioned in the contract; Amy was concerned about being videotaped, which was also delineated in the contract. We told her that we have no plans to do videotaping and that she could alter that part of the contract. After we explained the feedback conference, both agreed to participate and signed the contract.

Amy and Jon met in Jon's father's store, when Amy was a junior in high school. Jon had finished high school and was working for his father. They dated for almost 2 years before deciding to get married and have now been married for 2 years. Amy described Jon as having been "wild and woolly" when they first started dating (he was living in his own apartment; she was still living at home with her parents). Both were dating other people, but Amy said she had been "after" Jon early and had decided that she would simply have to wait until he settled down. Roughly 8 months to a year after they began dating, Jon did become serious about Amy. They were married when Amy was 19, Jon 22. Jon said he felt a need to explain that they had gotten married so early "to get Amy out of a family situation that was very rough."

Amy, the second of four children, described her father as having a serious drinking problem. She made very little mention of her mother. Amy was very quick to say that things with her family are now good, though they had not been at the time she married Jon. Part of her reason for wanting to marry Jon was to get "love, affection and a chance to be loved" and to get out of her family situation.

Jon sees himself as having a very strong relationship with his family. His only sibling was born when Jon was 13 years old. He especially feels that he has a good relationship with his mother, though he said that Amy resents that relationship; Jon went on to say that Amy has a bad relationship with his mother. Although his main purpose in getting married was to get Amy out of her family situation, he said he did have positive expectations about marriage (he was not able to define those expectations very clearly).

When we asked about the areas of their marriage that they wished to improve or strengthen, both mentioned that Amy's conflict with her mother-in-law is a particular source of anguish for them. Jon talked about wanting to mesh qualities and learning to appreciate differences in each other. He described Amy as making snap decisions, snap judgments; he sees himself as very slow in making decisions because he likes to think. They agreed that Amy is quick to get angry, and Jon said he is learning to be quiet when she is angry.

Their manner of fighting was mentioned as another concern. Jon described Amy as the mean one; both described Jon as quieter and less reactive during fights. Both mentioned cleaning the house as a major source of disagreement, although they seemed to feel that this is somewhat better now because Jon has assumed more responsibility for the house since Amy has added a part-time job and he is going to school.

We ended the interview by administering the pretests. Amy completed all the tests very quickly; Jon was much slower and more deliberate.

Enrichers' notes and supervision.

There were some gaps in the family history (mostly in Amy's family), and we did sense her reluctance to talk very much about her family. Since "getting away from her family" had been part of her motivation for getting married, the topic is evidently painful.

The persecutor-victim-rescuer triangle seems prominent in this couple. Both are clear that Jon rescued Amy (victim) from her father (persecutor) by marrying her. Some triangular interaction also seems to be involved in the relationship of Jon's mother, Amy, and Jon.

Considering our observations and the areas they had mentioned as areas they would like to make stronger—meshing and appreciation of differences and the ways they fight—we decided that either Conflict Resolution or Negotiation would be appropriate.

SUMMARY OF SESSIONS

Session 1

We presented and described briefly the two programs that we saw as most relevant—Negotiation and Conflict Resolution. After a brief discussion, they decided on Conflict Resolution, and we began the first lesson.

In the first exercise, they role-played a conflict situation. They resolved this easily because Amy gave in; she showed little interest in arguing her position in the role-play. Both said that the situation in the role-play was not very realistic for them.

After we talked about *avoidance* and *distancing* as behaviors in fighting, Jon described himself as an avoider and said that he considers avoiding the best behavior he can use. He continued, saying he frequently leaves when he and Amy fight. Amy interjected that this is good because she then simmers down. Jon described himself as a reserved optimist and Amy as a pessimist. They described several recent fights: typically, Jon would leave the room, Amy would throw something or hit him, and then they would act silly and make up. Both agreed that they can work out some fights or conflicts but others they can't work out. Amy also mentioned that she is distracting when she accuses Jon (during a fight) of being like his mother.

In the last part of this session, we focused on destructive and constructive fighting. Jon described Amy as very "sharp" and "nasty" in her fighting. Amy said she sees herself as destructive when she accuses Jon of being like his mother, whom she considers interfering and aggressive. Both agreed that when Jon's family is brought into an argument, the fighting becomes destructive. Jon considers Amy jealous of his "good family"; he also described her as having a low tolerance and basically not liking people. Amy believes that Jon is dominated by his mother. (Both seemed fairly comfortable discussing their arguments and opinions of each other.) Constructive fighting, for them, is a fight in which Jon is rational and logical, and Amy controls her anger.

The homework assignment was to complete conflict resolution forms on their arguments during the coming week.

Enrichers' notes and supervision.

Amy participated more in today's session, and both seemed at ease in describing their styles of fighting (they even laughed when describing them). Jon strongly felt that his avoidance style is functional in fights with Amy.

A pattern of pursuer and distancer in their fighting styles has become evident. Typically, it is easier for a pursuer to stop pursuing than for a distancer to stop distancing, but Amy is particularly sensitive to judgments (or perceived judgments) about her. Our supervisor reminded us to be especially nonjudgmental in our interactions with Amy (she seems particularly sensitive to a perceived judgment made by the female enricher).

We also discussed our curiosity about how enmeshed Jon is with his family and to what extent Amy becomes odd person out.

Because Jon places a premium on being rational and logical, we will attempt to explore with Jon the instances in which logic does not work.

Session 2

As usual, the couple bounded in with enthusiasm; they began almost immediately to talk about the record they had kept of their conflicts during the week. They had decided to record only their major conflicts, although both were aware of several minor conflicts that had occurred. As Amy said laughingly, minor conflicts were kept minor because "I knew somebody would report them."

The major conflict of the week, which both had written up, involved an argument over Jon's mother. Jon's mother had called, and he had talked with her for 25 to 35 minutes, during which Amy indicated three times, nonverbally, that she would like him off the phone. Then Amy screamed it once from another room and repeated it in front of the phone. He eventually got off the phone, and although he was angry, he chose to just ignore Amy in order to "get her." It worked, according to Amy, because she got madder and madder, and threatened to break Jon's wooden turtle. As she said later in the session, he was not understanding how she felt, and she was doing everything she could do to get his attention. Jon said that he then did something that he had never done before—he used *her* tactics. He said he grabbed their wedding pictures and threatened to rip them in half if she broke his turtle. Evidently, this broke her escalation of the fight. A short time later Jon tried to be affectionate, but Amy was evidently not in the mood for affection and soon went to bed.

Both described the conflict as unresolved, and neither was satisfied with it. The whole conflict had arisen after a brief period of intimacy that had been interrupted by Amy's coughing. Amy's added perspective on this story was that everything Jon had said was correct, except that she had just gotten home from work and she believed his mother had intentionally called at that time, knowing that Jon and Amy have very little time together. Amy felt that Jon's mother needs to realize that he is not her son anymore, and she wants Jon to agree with her instead of treating her like a "paranoid or something, although I may be." Jon said that he can't agree with her, because to agree with her would be to give up his position.

They also described a minor conflict: Jon had rolled down the window to listen to the sound of the car, and Amy had wanted it rolled up. Jon said he had eventually rolled the window up so that they would not have a major disagreement but that his annoyance had stayed with him for about a day. Amy confirmed his statement, saying that he had been distant for about a day. Later in the session, they described this behavior as pulling back, keeping bits and pieces back in order not to get hurt. We tried to draw a distinction between understanding and accepting Amy's feelings (i.e., Amy's hurt) and agreeing with her, but the distinction did not seem at all clear to Jon.

In the next exercise, they were able to resolve a role-played conflict over a television program. Amy said she felt good about how they did this, but she did recognize her small stab at Jon in the process, telling him he was acting like someone neither of them liked. Jon said that he didn't like the "stab," and he revealed after the role-play that though he had agreed to watch his program only during the commercials of "her program," he had had other plans in mind that he had not mentioned. During this discussion, Jon's pattern of fighting became even clearer to him. Though the conflict wasn't major, he followed his typical pattern: he basically agreed with Amy but did not tell her everything he was planning to do. He kept part of it to himself—that he was going to switch channels more often than he said he was. Amy said that this did not bother her; she felt that he had listened to her and that she had influenced him and that his holding back was one way for him to keep his self-respect. She added that one of the things she likes about him is that he does listen to her and is willing to be influenced by her.

The final exercise in the lesson was to work on a list of constructive steps for arguing. They started very slowly. Initially they started with broad, general rules about what they *shouldn't* do. Gradually they proceeded, Jon very much taking the lead, to list positive things to do. We provided a lot of clarification, and they finally concluded that the sharing of feelings is important. This seemed to be a real turning point for Jon in that he said he thought it would be more constructive if he didn't hold back what was going on with him. Both were still struggling with the difference between thinking and feeling. Although Amy said she wanted her feelings to be understood, Jon also said that, many times, he thinks Amy does not understand the facts of his position. We talked very specifically about how his willingness to share depends upon her willingness not to attack.

The following are Jon and Amy's steps for constructive arguing:

Ground Rules

1. Discipline own anger.
2. Avoid attacking each other (stay on the issue).

Steps

1. Try to bring facts (and feelings) out openly for understanding.
2. Understand and communicate an understanding of the other person's feelings.
3. Think of all possible solutions.
4. Make a joint decision (negotiation or compromise).

We ended the session with the homework assignment, which included using their steps for constructive arguing in their fights. Jon seemed very concerned about not being able to do it.

Enrichers' notes and supervision.

Several areas have become clearer to us. Jon attaches great importance to rationality and logic, and he uses them to defend his position. A main part of his struggle with Amy is that she isn't rational. In keeping with this, Jon has great difficulty distinguishing *feelings* and *thoughts*, and in distinguishing his acceptance of Amy's feelings from agreement with her position (and giving in to her). Amy fights to get close; Jon moves away to keep from being smothered. Amy's pattern of distracting and blaming and Jon's pattern of computing and placating also became clearer in this session.

We decided to alter the next homework assignment to include some practice with feeling statements (e.g., "I feel hurt because . . ."; "I feel angry when. . . ."). They do not share hurt and anger; their arguments are not resolved. We also decided to be especially attuned to reinforcing any "feeling" statements that Jon makes.

Session 3

We began by asking about their homework. Amy and Jon had concluded that there had been no conflicts, so neither one had written up anything. When we pressed them, they mentioned a conflict that had occurred the day before, but both seemed very reluctant to describe it (eventually, Jon described it). Neither had seen it as significant enough to write up (as homework). Their resolution of the conflict had been that Amy went to work and Jon stayed at home and studied; when they were back together again, they were ready to make up, and so they forgot about the conflict. Both said they were satisfied with that outcome, but at several points either or both looked as if they could get actively involved in fighting about it again.

The conflict had occurred at a picnic they had attended with Jon's family (to celebrate a relative's birthday). After eating, Jon had remarked that he was full and that he didn't want to move. Amy's response was that he was just trying to get out of studying, or something to that effect, which he interpreted as her wanting to leave to get away from his family. Amy was also irritated because Jon had responded "in public," and they had been observed by the preacher's daughter. Amy did say that the one step for constructive fighting that she had used was that she had not attacked Jon, although she had thought about doing it at one point. Jon said he had been unable to remember any of the steps at the time.

We reviewed the steps and discussed how they might have used them. As usual they got stuck at the accepting of feelings (Step 2 in their list). As they put it, "saying to each other, 'you're hurt,' leaves us nowhere." We drew the distinction between accusing the other person of being hurt and recognizing, accepting, and acknowledging how the other is feeling. Jon seemed to struggle especially with this distinction, though both seemed to find it meaningless.

The next exercise in the lesson was a role-play in which Jon acted distant; to our surprise, it fell flat. Amy had a very hard time playing the role and never quite carried it out. Still, their pattern of dealing with conflict reemerged. We again pointed out the pattern, and both seemed to "re-see" the pattern; in this case, Amy's pushing for reconciliation and asking for anything she can do to make the situation better while Jon holds her at a distance for a while, then accepts her advances and apologies. We discussed some of the ways their role-play could have been more constructive, but both seemed content with it as it was.

In the final exercise of this session, a discussion of feelings and conflict, they returned to their difficulty in identifying each other's feelings. Amy at this point suggested that part of their problem is lack of communication. She made her suggestion when I was repeating something Jon had said to me; she had not understood what he had said—she had, in fact, misunderstood. She pointed out that she has always thought no one understands Jon but that she was beginning to wonder whether it is simply she who does not understand Jon. We noted that both have felt frequently that neither was understanding the other and that their communications often pass each other by, neither understanding what the other is saying.

We again asked them what they could do to deal with conflict more constructively. The first thing, Amy said, is for Jon to believe her. Jon responded, "If you wouldn't lie, I would." All this was said jokingly, but basically Jon said that if Amy would agree to tell the truth (she says she always does), he would agree to believe her. The second thing Amy mentioned was that each should agree to stay, not leave, until a conflict is resolved. Jon said he would stay for a reasonable period of time. At this point, we asked them if they were willing to contract with each other on these points.

They agreed, and we prodded them to make their agreement more explicit. They decided that for the second item, a reasonable time would mean that the partner who wanted to leave must at least listen to the other's reasons for considering the conflict unresolved. Jon's criterion was that he would stay as long as they were progressing, or as long as he could be convinced that they were progressing. In discussing this, Jon said, "I don't have the ability to argue, so I pull back into my shell." Amy responded that she is tough to argue with. Amy then suggested a third item—both would agree to try to follow their steps for constructive conflict resolution. Jon seemed somewhat hesitant, but they agreed that their struggle would come with Step 2 (feelings). The contract was written, and both agreed to abide by it for 1 week (when it would be renegotiated or renewed).

Toward the end of the session, Amy asked me (the female enricher), "Are we really in trouble or are we really normal?" My coenricher responded with an answer that seemed clear to her. Jon seemed to try to keep us from answering by saying, "They haven't done enrichment before."

Enrichers' notes and supervision.

This session seemed much slower than the preceding one. We were struck by their lack of listening and communication skills and their inability to distinguish acceptance of feelings from agreement with feelings. We were also surprised at their lack of involvement in the role-play, which we considered directly relevant to their situation.

Most of this session was spent zeroing in on the typical patterns that have been emerging: distancing, pursuing, being right, maintaining one's self. Our supervisor suggested that it might be useful to find out more about Amy's relationship and involvement with her family. Who is it in her family that is part of her triangle?

Amy pursues because she wants Jon to make her happy. Jon distances, though he often orchestrates reciprocity. Amy refuses to reciprocate; instead, she placates. Jon wins and is on top when she placates. Amy's anger seems closely related to her hurt, but instead of bringing Jon closer, it moves him further away, so she placates to get him back.

Because the Conflict Resolution Program has only four lessons, we discussed which program to use in the remaining sessions. Communication and sharing of feelings seem to be the central issues, though the triangle of Jon, his mother, and Amy is also prominent. We decided to integrate an exercise on triangles into the next lesson and to use lessons from Reciprocity or Negotiation for the last two sessions.

Session 4

We began by asking how they had used the homework assignment. According to Jon, they had had only one minor conflict ("it was easy and the kind we can handle") until the day before the session. Both felt they had used the steps in resolving the conflict (buying a new car), but neither had kept a written record. Jon and Amy had "forgotten" about the contract they had made, although they said they had pretty much stuck to it in spirit. The difference that they had observed in their fighting was that each seemed able to bring the other back when one got off the track.

In discussing the conflict of the day before (over some land Jon owns), it became evident that for Amy, it remained unresolved. Jon said that Amy wanted to make a snap decision without having all the facts. She said she had been struggling not to attack his family on the issue, since Jon owns the land with his father. Later in the session, Jon suggested that he and Amy switch roles on this conflict. They did, and we asked them to exchange chairs when they reversed roles. Jon played Amy's role beautifully; he even commented at the end that it had been great fun because he had had no responsibility and he had not had so many things to think about. Amy found Jon's role difficult and complained that she had had to think about "this, this, this, and this." She obviously struggled while playing his role, although she was able to play this role better than any of those she has attempted in other sessions.

Both seemed to find the role reversal helpful, and Amy commented that she was feeling more like the decision was theirs together, not just Jon's.

The third exercise was a role-play (the reverse of the preceding week's) in which Amy was distant and removed from Jon. She found it very hard to stay distant. Jon recognized and acknowledged Amy's hurt in the role-play. (It was at the conclusion of this exercise that they took each other's roles and continued their discussion of the land issue.)

During this session, we explored the role that Amy's family plays. Jon said they see Amy's family pretty often; Amy said they see them only every 2 or 3 weeks but that they see or are in contact with Jon's parents weekly. Amy described herself as not being as tied in with her parents as Jon is with his. Then she rephrased, saying that it is they who are so dependent on Jon.

Amy asked me (the female enricher) what she should do about the problem with her mother-in-law ("Should I talk to her or what?"). This was the second session in a row that Amy had directly asked me a question about what she should do. I replied that I really wasn't close enough to the situation to know what she should do and couldn't tell her what to do anyway, but that I felt she was doing something by dealing with the problem with Jon.

For homework, Jon and Amy were asked to make a list of things each can do to facilitate conflict resolution. We suggested that they include the occasional switching of roles.

In discussing plans for the next two sessions, we suggested that we focus on communication and dealing with hurt in communication. Both seemed very receptive to the idea of communication, but neither responded to the dealing with hurt.

As we concluded the session, we gave each of them a copy of the following paradoxical letter. Amy commented, "I was wondering when we were going to get this."

Dear Amy and Jon,

   The purpose of this letter is to deal with the aspects of your relationship that we have observed above and beyond the enrichment process. We want to put these observations in writing because what we have seen is far too important for us to consider verbally. By putting our observations in writing, we will all have a better opportunity to reflect on them.

We are impressed by the way in which you use conflict to achieve intimacy and closeness and that you each maintain your own individuality through your fighting. We're glad that you care enough to fight instead of being indifferent to each other.

We have a suggestion to help you become more intimate through your fighting. The next time one of you feels unloved and wants attention, don't tell the other, but start a major fight. The next time the other one of you feels you are getting too intimate through your fighting, get out of the fight by retreating into your shell or by being rational and logical or by leaving the room.

We wonder whether it is possible for both of you to be united at the same time. As long as you emphasize being right, you force the other person to be wrong and you cannot be united. Only by giving up being right or wrong can you be together. Are you strong enough to unite?

We enjoy working with you both and appreciate your efforts in entering into the sessions so actively.

Enrichers' notes and supervision.

We discussed the possibility of integrating an exercise on the persecutor-victim-rescuer triangle into one of the remaining sessions. We also talked about how we would deal with the letter if they bring it up during the next session: we will listen but refrain from a lot of discussion; if we are pushed, we will tell them that we will discuss the letter further in the feedback conference.

We also discussed Amy's "What should I do?" questions and decided that if she asks again, we will ask her what it is she wants us to say.

Session 5

This session was based on the third lesson in the Negotiation Program, with a short section on the persecutor-victim-rescuer triangle.

Asked about the homework, they reported that they had not had any fights and had forgotten about making a list of constructive things to do in fighting.

In the first exercise, on defining communication, both seemed bored. In the second exercise, on nonverbal messages, Amy struggled with being silent and Jon struggled when he was asked to keep pushing Amy for a response.

The third exercise concerned manipulative communication roles: blaming, placating, preaching, and avoiding. Amy chose to act the role of blamer and Jon chose placater. After several minutes (without being asked), they switched roles. Next, Jon played the preaching role and Amy the avoiding role. Both were able to relate to the roles. Jon said, "I like to smooth things over," and Amy said, "I don't ever placate."

At this point, we introduced the triangle. Amy described herself as victim, Jon's mother as persecutor, and Jon as rescuer. Jon agreed but said he also sometimes sees himself as victim and Amy as persecutor. Amy disagreed and reiterated her view that Jon is too close to his mother.

In the final exercise, we asked them to talk together for several minutes, first using only "it" statements, then "you" statements, then "I" statements. Jon said that he found the "you" statements most comfortable; Amy pointed out that using "you" is *blaming*. With some prodding, they discussed the usefulness of "I" statements.

For homework, each was asked to make three "I" statements a day.

Enrichers' notes and supervision.

We were surprised that neither Jon nor Amy referred to the paradoxical letter that each had received the preceding week. They did report *not* fighting, and we noticed that they seemed more intimate and nonverbally involved with each other at the beginning of the session and less involved with us.

We felt uncomfortable with the triangles exercise. We were left with the impression that Jon was seeing *only* the usefulness of being a rescuer, not the liabilities. We decided, if time permits, to go further with the triangles during the last session, trying to get them to explore the pros and cons of being locked into these three roles.

We also discussed their lack of cooperation in doing the homework and decided that if the next assignment is not carried out, we will confront them (mildly) about it.

Session 6

This session was taken from Communication and Hurt, the fourth lesson in the Negotiation Program.

Jon opened the session by reporting how valuable the homework had been. He added that they had been feeling guilty that they hadn't been doing their share when they had neglected to do the homework. Jon had found that the "I" statements forced him to clarify what he was saying. Amy was less excited about using them, and both remarked that making "I" statements had been difficult.

When we explained crystal-ball communication and asked them to comment on it, both responded as if they were beyond this idea. In the first exercise, we asked each to read a statement to the partner, who was then to state the message received. Jon read a statement, and Amy immediately assumed that the message was that he was criticizing her. This was a very powerful interchange; Jon realized immediately that she was misreading him. Amy had to work very hard to see the message he had intended, even after he stated it explicitly several times.

The second exercise focused on the shared meaning process (repeating what the partner has just said). We explained it, demonstrated, and then asked them to try it, first on single statements and then in a dialogue. Jon initiated a topic, which we soon realized was new information for Amy: He informed her that he had gotten a job that morning. Evidently, they had discussed this in the past, but Amy had been assuming that he would wait until the quarter ended. She was angry and concerned that a job would interfere with school. They discussed the issue for about 7 minutes, using the shared meaning process. Jon did it very well and spent most of the time repeating what Amy had said. Finally, Jon asked when he would be heard. We asked Amy to listen and reflect Jon's statements. She found it harder to use shared meaning without distorting it and putting Jon down. Both described the interchange as productive. Amy commented that it was the best thing yet and that she liked it. Jon responded to her: "What you're saying is you think I need it." "No, that's not it," Amy said. "It was also tough for me, but it seemed productive." Jon had shifted, unannounced, into shared meaning and discovered that he was not, in fact, hearing what Amy was saying.

The final exercise was focused on the sharing of hurt: They took turns completing sentences beginning with the words "I feel hurt by." Jon included in his list of hurts "when my family gets put down," "when you feel that you have hurt me." Amy's list included "when I look back on how I act," "when you [Jon] get mad at Molly [dog] and I feel blamed," "when I don't keep house," "when we're not getting along well," "when my family doesn't call me or they aren't concerned," "when I hurt you." After this exercise, Jon said he felt solemn. Amy commented that she doesn't like to talk about hurts, since she already knows they're there.

The final question we asked was how each wants the other to express anger. Jon said he wants Amy to express anger in a "calm, sensible way." Amy said she wants Jon to express anger "with a smile on your face" and "without reprimanding me."

Enrichers' notes and supervision.

Amy seems more resistant to change than Jon is. We discussed what it is that she is getting out of keeping the situation the same. Amy originally "got" Jon by being hurt and needing rescuing; perhaps she believes she needs to stay hurt to keep him. The issue of power and control in keeping him away from his mother is also part of this. Her perceptual framework and cognitive set also seem particularly resistant to reorganization.

We (and our supervisor) were puzzled as to why Jon chose to inform Amy of his new job in a role-play (perhaps he feels safer and stronger in the session). Neither of them expressed many feelings in the shared meaning exercise. If there were another session, we might find it useful to address cognitive and affective levels.

We also discussed their use of hurt and anger and the pattern they seemed to follow in the "expression of hurt" exercise—getting intimate, then pulling back.

FEEDBACK CONFERENCE

We started by asking what changes they had seen as a result of SE. Jon remarked that it did work *if* they tried but that it depended on their seriousness and sincerity in carrying it out. When the model for dealing with conflict has broken down, he said, it is "not because we didn't know, but we just didn't use it." Amy mentioned that Jon stays around and talks more than he used to, that she is controlling her temper more, and that remembering the pattern has helped keep her closer to the issue, though "not perfect." Jon said they are having fewer arguments and staying more on the issue; when they get off the issue, a reminder brings them back.

Amy remarked that a surprise has taken place; she doesn't understand it and finds it "strange": She is not having in-law problems anymore, and she doesn't argue with Jon's mother so much. She even commented that she "felt hurt for the way I felt about them." Amy also said she had "for some reason, cleaned up the house at midnight, wanting to please him," and felt "more organized in her mind."

Jon said he considers the programs good and that he particularly likes the "I" messages. Amy said that all the sessions were good, though some of the exercises were irrelevant, and that she had not liked the tests. She said that in general she had been pleasantly surprised because "I came in with a negative attitude that this won't work." Amy remarked that "it was not easy. . . . I'm not orderly and I had to concentrate and think of rules . . . and think before talking, which I usually don't." Jon said that he "had wanted someone to tell me *how* to do it [but] I wasn't spoonfed. . . . That's good and bad. We had to learn to feed ourselves." Amy responded, "We now know how to feed ourselves if we want to."

A passing reference to the letter evoked several responses. Amy said that she liked it up to a point but after that it didn't make any sense and seemed "phony." She felt she "couldn't afford to give up the good times." The beginning part "made me feel better that you didn't think we were some heathens." Jon reported that "the letter didn't really offer me anything overall," and he "questioned the reasoning behind it." As he put it, "I read it and re-read it, and we read it together out loud, and it still didn't make any sense."

Next, we shared with them the strengths we see in them as a couple—openness, caring, willingness to change, honesty, their trust in each other.

This feedback seemed to evoke lots of thoughts. Jon talked about his inability to hold his ground with Amy in fighting. Amy began to talk about how good it made her feel to hear positive things, since a secret fear of hers is divorce. She explained that her older sister, after 5 years of a seemingly happy marriage, had gotten a divorce. She also began to talk of her fear of being like her father, who had always put her down. She mentioned that students in one of her sociology classes had discussed how people tend to be the same kind of parents to their children as their parents were to them. Even though she had found SE awkward, she felt it was worthwhile if "I don't end up hating myself."

Amy also expressed some fear about no longer having any guidelines. She went on to say that Jon is so wonderful and she isn't and that he provides her with love "not just like a husband and wife but almost like a child." Jon was very quiet during all this. We told Amy that we also saw strengths in her and had been describing those as well. Amy said that she had only heard us describing strengths they have together, which are mostly Jon's. At this point, we commented on several of her strengths; her response was to find reasons that these "strengths" are really negative. When we pointed out that she was preventing herself from hearing strengths, she really seemed to understand.

At the end of the session, we explained the options for SE and for therapy. Both seemed interested but expressed concern about time. We left the decision with them but gave them clear information about what to do if they decide to pursue further SE or therapy.

We have been impressed by the changes that this couple has reported. What seems most important is that they seem to have a sense of their own ability, hence their responsibility, to affect what happens in their relationship. Amy's "surprise" change—no longer fighting with her mother-in-law—seems related to the closeness in their relationship. Amy's fighting with her mother-in-law was an attempt to get Jon closer to her and away from his mother; this left Amy in a victim position, waiting for Jon to rescue her (which was how Amy had "gotten" Jon close to her originally). During SE, Amy found other ways in which to be close to

Jon, and her feelings toward her mother-in-law "magically" disappeared. When Jon was not attacked, he was able to distance himself less. The paradoxical letter seemed to unite them more and also left Amy freer not to attack her mother-in-law.

We also discussed the way Jon stays in a one-up/one-down position with Amy: he is strong and good and wonderful in relation to Amy, who is bad. We wonder how much of his feeling good about himself depends on her feeling bad about herself.

PRE- AND POSTTEST EVALUATION

The test battery consisted of the following: The Family Satisfaction Scales (10- and 18-item), the Marital Questionnaire, the Sexual Happiness Scale, and the Semantic Differential.

Both Amy and Jon have overall high ratings on the pretest battery. Amy's ratings are consistently higher than Jon's (Amy gave ratings of 10 to many items).

Overall, their scores moved closer together on the posttest battery. Jon's scores increased slightly, and Amy's decreased slightly. For example, on the Sexual Happiness Scale, Amy moved from a mean of 8.53 to a mean of 7.0, Jon from 5.88 to 7.90. This general direction is consistent with our observation that they have moved closer together.

THEORETICAL THEMES

Differentiation

Amy and Jon entered marriage from two very different kinds of families: a very close, tight, and secure family (Jon's) and one that was highly diffuse and conflict-laden (Amy's). In terms of L'Abate's levels of differentiation, Jon's family of origin and his relationship with them was symbiotic; Amy's was very close to an autistic position. Amy described herself as separated from her family; she sees Jon as being "too close" to his. Amy's degree of differentiation from her family seems clearly grounded in oppositeness—she wants the closeness she never had there, is fearful that she, too, will be like her father (toward her own children), and is overly uncomfortable and jealous of Jon's closeness with his family. What I struggled with initially in conceptualizing their levels of differentiation in their marriage was Amy's evidently very powerful desire for symbiosis and how this fit in with her "oppositeness." Only in the dialectic of symbiosis and autism does it begin to make sense. What she looks for in Jon is closeness she could not have in her family of origin;

yet her oppositeness gets in her way of "quite getting there." Jon, in his own process of individuation, feels uncomfortable with "being too close" ("I can't hold my own with her, you know"), but he feels good about himself (as her rescuer).

Pursuing and Distancing

Amy pursues; Jon distances, as he says, because "I can't hold my own with her." Their pursuit/distance pattern seems to be related to a rescuer triangle. Amy pursues, then stops, gets silly, and becomes the victim, who is "bad." At this point, Jon stops distancing and "rescues" Amy. Out of their pursuit and distancing interaction arise a victim and a rescuer.

Amy's way of bringing Jon close is to become the victim, the undeserving; then Jon moves in to take care of her.

Space and Time

Jon clearly fits the computing and placating roles. His tempo is slow and deliberate in contrast to Amy's snap decisions and her blaming and distracting. Simultaneously, their dialectical opposites are evident. Amy placates after she blames, by acting silly and helpless. Their self-presentation includes Amy as the introvert ("she doesn't like people") and Jon as the extrovert ("he likes to be with people"), but on a phenotypical level, these polarities reverse.

CONCLUSIONS

For this couple, SE's preventive and paratherapeutic functions are clear. Changes occurred for them and for their relationship, the most significant, perhaps, that they gained a sense of their ability to make their marriage better. In this vein, the diagnostic function seems evident in two ways: (a) SE gave the couple a view of the areas in their marriage that need strengthening; and (b) it provided us with a fairly extensive picture of their relationship, its functioning, and their areas of dysfunction.

21

Mentally Handicapped Children

Victor Wagner and Jerry Stein

INTERVIEW

The Tyler family, a middle-class family, lives in a comfortably furnished older house that they purchased 1 year ago.

Clint Tyler, aged 34, has a PhD in chemistry. He taught for several years at a local college but now teaches and coaches in a private school. Clint seems to be in good health—he is well built and seems physically fit.

Lucy Tyler, aged 37, has a BA and credits toward an MA in English. She gave up a job with a public relations firm before Corey, the youngest daughter, was born. Lucy is now a full-time housewife and mother, but she is active in the community and involved with women's liberation activities. She plays tennis a lot and seems quite healthy, although she is slightly hefty.

Caroline, the oldest daughter, is 8 years old and a third grader. She is quite intelligent and reads books far in advance of her age. She is friendly, talkative, quick in responding and quite energetic. She is fond of animals, interested in nature shows on TV, and enjoys sports, especially swimming.

Candace, aged 7, is a retarded child, classified as moderately-severely retarded. Her physical and mental ages correspond to those of a 2- to 3-year-old child in most respects. In some behavior, she is less mature, in others slightly more advanced. She is unable to walk or talk, but she is partially toilet trained (she often "makes mistakes"). During the past year, Candace has learned to feed herself. She is very affectionate, showing her emotion through kissing, smiling, and clapping her hands. Candace suffers from seizures (petit mal), but grand mal seizures are prevented by daily medication with phenobarbital. She has a scholarship to a school for special children, which she attends daily.

Corey, 11 months old, seems to be normal and in good health.

Clint and Lucy are Unitarians, but Lucy is more active and attends services more frequently than Clint. It was through the church that they had signed up for SE.

Enrichers' notes.

Our initial impression was that the difficulty of having a retarded family member was affecting all family members. Lucy told us she felt the birth of Candace had forced Caroline to grow up more quickly, that she was being pushed out of her childhood. Lucy feels guilty about this and very sad and burdened by having a retarded child. Clint's outlook is more positive: he enjoys Candace for herself and admires her ability to give love with no hooks or strings. Lucy feels that Clint does not share equally in the responsibility of caring for Candace; Clint does not agree.

Supervision.

We decided, with our supervisor, E. E. Dunne, to use the program called Mentally Handicapped Children. (The work with this family illustrates how lessons can be combined to complete a program more quickly. The Tylers had planned a trip that left us only 6 weeks to complete all sessions.) When we next saw the family, we suggested the program, and they agreed.

PRETEST RESULTS

On the Bell-Fagan Family Symbols (B-F), the total cards chosen were Clint, 43; Lucy, 62; Caroline, 51. On the loving subscale, Lucy came out extremely high, perhaps reflecting not only love but her position as commander-in-chief. Although Caroline and Lucy gave Lucy many cards on this subscale, Clint did not. Caroline came out extremely high on the happiness subscale, in contrast to both parents, who were quite low. All family members gave her many cards on this subscale.

On the Description of Feelings in the Family (DFF), Lucy saw the family as distracting and sad; Caroline saw the family as sad and slightly smug; Clint saw the family as mad. The results match our initial picture of the family. Lucy can be seen through Clint's eyes as being quite mad;

Caroline sees the family generally as being sad and perhaps as not considering her very important, hence smug. Lucy's view of the family as distracting and sad most likely reflects her feelings about her own situation—sad and always jumping from one thing to another.

Both Lucy and Clint were seen as slightly smug on the family-sees-members section; Clint was viewed as slightly mad, Lucy as slightly sad. Clint's indifference (passive aggression) can be related to his being viewed as mad and smug. Lucy's sadness and smugness may reflect her being the boss but always complaining about not being happy in that role.

On the Animal Concepts Picture Series (ACPS), all scores are clustered in the central range, and no actual-ideal score is over 30. The closest is Caroline's discrepancy of 29 between her actual and ideal cards.

SUMMARY OF SESSIONS

Session 1

The session took place in the family's living room, a comfortable room with several easy chairs, a fireplace, and a TV. It wasn't until late in the session that Lucy moved from one end of the room to sit on the floor in close proximity to everyone else.

Exercise 1: How does it feel to be you in this family?

Clint said he felt comfortable in the family, kind of flowing along and relaxed.

Caroline said, "When Mom yells at me, I feel small like an ant, but then I yell back and feel like a volcano." She reported feeling happy when her dad makes her feel good, for example, when she's hurt herself. Caroline likes to comfort Candace after their father yells at her, but she also gets mad at Candace for urinating on her toys.

Lucy said, "I feel burdened. I do most of the work around here." She feels that Caroline is being shoved out of her childhood and that she (Lucy) must make things up to her because she did Caroline in. She feels frustrated in her relationship with Candace because she can't discipline Candace (because of her handicap), so she gives Caroline a double dose. Lucy doesn't feel Clint is carrying his weight or assuming the father role.

Asked whether anything said by any family members was surprising, Lucy replied that she was surprised by Clint's feeling that he carries at least half the burden. Lucy sees a triangle: she disciplines Caroline, who goes to Daddy, who comforts her. Lucy said later in the session that she thinks Clint spends too much time with the children or reading the newspaper and not enough time with her.

Exercise 2: How did each of you feel when you were told of Candace's handicap?

Lucy felt very sad and didn't want to admit that Candace was both physically and mentally retarded. She felt bad for herself, sorry for herself, angry at herself, and bad for having brought Candace into the world. She felt responsible, sure that she had failed.

Clint, too, felt sadness, but his sadness was for Candace—sadness that she would miss her childhood. Clint had commented earlier that at one time he and Lucy had thought they couldn't have children and had considered adopting. The only restriction they had placed on the agency was that they did not want to adopt a retarded child. Despite that, he said that when Candace was born he felt no sadness for himself or for the load he would have to carry.

Caroline felt sad, just sad.

Exercise 3: Do you think what you were told about Candace's condition is accurate?

Both parents feel that Candace has progressed well and is now capable of doing things the doctors said she would never be able to do.

Exercise 4: What positive things have resulted from Candace's handicap?

Clint feels better about handicapped children. He also believes that he is more comfortable with mentally retarded children and adults. He feels lucky to have Candace because of what she can give.

Caroline feels closer to the family because of Candace. Lucy at first could not think of anything positive, but she went on to say that it has been educational and an experience in intellectual growth. She feels that she has become more sensitive to everyone, especially to handicapped people, because of Candace.

Exercise 5: Role-play another family member.

Caroline's first choice was to play Corey, saying she has always wanted to be a baby and that she really likes Corey. Caroline refused in this round to play her mother (and said she did not want to be a "yelly" person but a nice, quiet person). Clint played Lucy but found it difficult to play Lucy to the hilt. He felt more comfortable playing Caroline. Lucy played Clint but found it difficult. She felt the role was very foreign to her.

The second time around, Lucy played Clint, and Caroline played Lucy. In this role-play, Lucy felt she came to a new insight, seeing the child Caroline between Clint the protector and Lucy the prosecutor.

Enrichers' notes.

Our initial reaction was that the session had gone well. Caroline was occasionally distracting (not paying attention, making noise), but her behavior was not too bad and she did get very involved in the role playing. Lucy was also sometimes distracting, throwing out irrelevant comments or talking out of turn or leaving the room briefly. Clint, apparently motivated, paid attention and answered the questions. He did not distract or get up to leave the room during the session.

Our impression is that Lucy, frustrated and angry, is isolated from the rest of the family and feels overburdened. She doesn't get the attention and help she wants from Clint, and she sees Caroline as more allied with Clint because of his placating nature. Clint feels comfortable, but he is perhaps too aloof and intellectual, not really feeling what Lucy is going through. Caroline, very active, bright, and attention-demanding, knows how to manipulate both parents.

Session 2

The family seemed eager to do the lesson (Specific Feelings), and everyone had worked on the homework assignment (think about being another person in the family; choose the best time and the worst time to be that person). Interestingly, Lucy said that she would not want to be Clint when he is getting up in the morning to take care of Candace. Lucy constantly says that Clint doesn't share the responsibilities for the children; yet, she considers this time, when Clint has a specific role to fill, the worst time to be Clint.

Exercise 1: Have you ever pretended to anyone that your family is different from what it really is?

Clint said he has pretended that his family is happier than it really is. Lucy has tried to put up a good front; she has recently permitted herself to be more honest with other people (about the children), but she still presents a facade about her relationship with Clint. Caroline also has pretended that her home is happier than it really is; she portrays her mother as super nice, even though her mother yells at her sometimes.

Lucy said that in general she believes she can empathize more with Clint's needs than he can with hers. She feels frustrated because of insufficient money to do things for herself and for the children. She would like to go back to work so that she would have her own spending money and feel more independent.

Exercise 2: Tell us something you've done to make the family happy.

All three had difficulty thinking of something an individual has done to make the family happy. Caroline, for example, couldn't think of anything she does to make her mother or father happy, but eventually she realized that she does do things such as setting the table and baby-sitting.

Clint said he couldn't think of anything he does to make the family happy but that one-to-one he makes Caroline or Lucy happy. He finally said that ice cream at the park makes the whole family happy. Lucy believes that everything she does makes the family happy—all the chores and responsibilities, the washing, cleaning, cooking, taking care of the kids.

Exercise 3: Tell us something you've done to make the family mad.

Clint said he makes Lucy mad by being less sociable than she would like. Caroline thought in terms of her mother, for example, when she made her mother mad by spilling a glass of milk. Lucy then prompted her to say, "Mom gets mad when I interrupt her conversation with 'big people.'" Lucy complained that Caroline does this constantly and that she (Lucy) has been unable to control this particular behavior. Caroline could not think of anything she had done to make her father mad.

Asked how each of them makes the family sad, Clint said he makes the family sad when he has a fight with Lucy. Caroline said that their fights make her scared.

Lucy said that she does not do anything to make the family sad but that she does do things that make the family angry, such as dictating and setting the pace. She said that she is used to a faster pace and everybody hates her for it but that if she doesn't play the role of moderator and controller nothing will get done. She went on to say that maybe she is mad at herself for having to play such a role but that her father raised everyone to be like robots and march along. She said finally that nobody would function if she didn't play this role, although she hates it.

Exercise 4: How do you show your pride when one of you does something to be proud of?

Clint spoke of showing pride in the children; he didn't mention Lucy at all. Lucy said she feels proud when she gets Clint to go to church with her. Lucy seemed to be putting Clint down, implying "Well, Clint never goes to church, so when he does, I can display him to the community." She went on to say that she sometimes feels that Candace is an object of pride.

Exercise 5: Tell us about your assets.

Caroline said that her assets include riding a bike well, reading, climbing trees, writing well, and making the family happy. Clint said he does math well, is an excellent teacher, is easy-going, doesn't get upset easily, is nonaggressive, and has an ability to shut off the world. Lucy said she is a good conversationalist, a good ping-pong player, supportive of people, excellent with kids, lives in the now, and has a take-charge nature.

A big point of contention is that certain things that Clint considers assets Lucy considers liabilities; for example, Clint feels that being non-aggressive and easy-going and being able to turn off the outside world are assets. Lucy considers Clint's lack of assertiveness and his distracting techniques liabilities. The reverse also holds true: Clint does not consider Lucy's take-charge nature an asset. Clint believes that he can be assertive with the children but that Lucy pushes him around.

Lucy said she is used to judging herself harshly because Clint judges her harshly, especially her strengths in being assertive and taking charge. She also feels that it is difficult for her to get affection and warmth from Clint and that her assertiveness leaves a distance between them. She believes that females in general intimidate and bully Clint. Clint agreed that Lucy's assertiveness keeps him away but said he does feel close to Lucy, although he does not show his affection overtly. He said that in general he has a hard time making people believe that he feels close to them, but he doesn't worry much about whether people realize that he feels close. Lucy said laughingly that it was revealing to her that "Clint feels close at a distance." Clint said he shows affection and warmth much better with kids than with adults.

Session 3

There was tension in the air as the session began. Lucy seemed upset and nervous and couldn't sit still. She got up four or five times during the session to fiddle with something in the room. Caroline had trouble sitting still, too. The family had thought about and worked on the homework (to quit doing two things that make the family mad or sad and to begin to do two things to help the family). Clint felt he had begun to work on being more assertive; however, his assertiveness had caused friction with Lucy. Visitors had been expected, and Lucy had asked Clint to clean up a room. Clint had said he would do it after he finished dinner, which Lucy did not like. Lucy intervened to say that when guests come, Clint treats himself like a guest, too; he doesn't share the responsibility of preparation, so she never gets to enjoy the company. She admitted that she had invited these guests without consulting Clint and that when he found out he was less than enthusiastic. Lucy protested that she had invited them because she had thought Clint would be pleased.

Lucy went on to complain that during the 12 years they have been married, Clint has never volunteered or offered his help in anything. She called his attitude very immature.

Exercise 1: What opportunity would you like that would help you or the family?

Lucy said she would like the opportunity to work but followed that by saying she's going to be forced to go to work sooner than she would like. Several times Lucy made a positive statement, then attached a negative phrase. Money is a problem, so she believes that life would be easier if she were working. However, she feels that the most important thing is that her working would increase Clint's respect for her. Lucy feels torn because she "has been programmed to be a mother." She thinks that the children would do all right without her, but she wants to be totally involved in their childhoods, not missing any of the experiences.

Lucy said that Clint takes his cues from other people. If she worked and other people respected her opinions and thought she was great, Clint, too, would think so. Clint disagreed with Lucy's analysis and said that Lucy would feel better about herself if she were working, which would in turn make other things better (e.g., she would not take things out on him so much). Caroline said that if her mother went to work, the house would be quieter.

Exercise 2: Name one strength in each of the other family members.

Lucy said Caroline's strengths lie in her persistence and her curiosity but confessed she finds Caroline's persistence hard to handle at times. Lucy had difficulty in naming Clint's strength but eventually said his strength is with his children and his compassion for them. Her voice sounded a little sad, as if he had compassion for the children but not for her. Clint was surprised that Lucy considers his patience a virtue. He had assumed she would look at patience as passivity. Lucy interjected, "With the children I feel it is patience; toward me it is passivity."

Enrichers' notes.

There seems to be a great deal of frustration in Lucy. She feels unable to communicate effectively with Clint, and his attitude and general lifestyle seem to amplify the issue. He is easy-going and passive; Lucy is a bit hyper and depressive. It does seem though, that in his own passive way, Clint gets what he wants and quietly controls a great deal of what happens; Lucy, on the other hand, seems to be playing the martyr role. Clint and Lucy look at things through very different eyes, but we hope these sessions are helping them to understand each other better. Lucy has said in every session, "That's very interesting"; "I never knew that"; "That's an important insight." Clint is more of an enigma; he answers all the questions quite thoroughly and to the best of his ability, but he responds more like a computer.

Session 4

The family, especially Lucy, seemed much more relaxed and in a better frame of mind today. There was more laughter, kidding around, and an easing of the tension that had dominated the preceding session.

Exercise 1: What do you do to have fun when you go out as a family?

Both Lucy and Clint had difficulty thinking of things the family does for fun. Lucy said that the family has trouble functioning as a unit and they don't often try. She said that she has fun with the family as much as she can—when she is not actually taking care of duties. She went on to say that she doesn't have much unity with Clint and isn't really sure whether they have fun together when they go out.

Clint rarely goes anywhere or does anything on his own initiative. He said he goes to a movie with Lucy when she wants to, but he doesn't call a friend to go to a movie that he is particularly eager to see. For example, Lucy mentioned that Clint had wanted to see *The Eiger Sanction;* she wasn't interested and had urged him to call one of his friends, but he never did it. Clint rarely goes anywhere with friends and very rarely telephones anyone. His friends are his colleagues at work. Of the movie situation, Lucy commented further, "If Clint and I can agree on a movie, we go, but we very rarely agree" (Clint likes action-adventure-police movies and books; Lucy prefers more emotional subjects).

Lucy enjoys going to parties and would like to give some parties. She feels that she "owes" it to many people who have invited her to parties. Clint said he feels uncomfortable at parties and would rather do something better, such as watch TV. When asked what she could do to make going to parties more enjoyable for Clint, Lucy said, "Not go." Clint (and the enrichers) interpreted this to mean that if Lucy didn't go and didn't pester him to go, he would feel better. Lucy, however, thought that Clint had interpreted her statement to mean that he would have a good time at a party if he went alone and she didn't go.

Exercise 2: How isolated or how involved are you in the community?

Both Clint and Lucy feel that they are community-oriented and are fairly active in their community. Lucy believes that she could be doing more work in the community; Clint said he doesn't have the time to be more involved than he is.

Exercise 3: How do you feel about the term mentally retarded?

Caroline said her friends know that Candace is handicapped and that she can't walk or talk or say her ABCs, but her friends don't make her feel bad or sad because she has a retarded sister.

Clint considers the term a good descriptive term. Lucy said she prefers *handicapped* to *mental retardation* because it gives her a chance to explain what Candace's condition really is. She feels that the term *mental retardation* conjures up too many fantasies.

Session 5

Exercise 1: How has this family changed in the past year?

Clint mentioned his change of job, Corey's birth, and the move into a new home. His new job brought a substantial cut in salary and raised his tension level. He feels that getting adjusted to the new job has taken away some of his energy: He comes home later and doesn't get to see the children as much.

Lucy said that the past year had been very difficult and had brought too many changes at one time.

Caroline said that the past year had brought a lot more noise and a lot more work to do. She said her father used to do more work than he does now. Now he just sits around like a bump on a log and reads the newspaper. Lucy interrupted Caroline at this point to say that both she and Caroline feel that Clint gives too much at school so that when he comes home he is too tired to give to the family.

The family had difficulty coming up with positive changes in the past year. Clint mentioned Caroline's learning new things, Corey's growth, Candace's learning to feed herself. Lucy was hard put for an answer but finally said Candace's improvement and the purchase of a home—the first they have ever owned. She added, however, that it is ironic that she finally has a home but at a time when her family life seems so unstable.

Exercise 2: What will this family be like in 1 year? In 5 years?

Caroline answered that it will be even noisier: "Mom will be yelling at something; and Dad will be yelling at Mom." She said that in the grown-ups there will be grumpier noise and among the children, happier noise.

Lucy said she had no idea: "Things could get better or worse. Things have got to get better—they can't get much worse. If they don't get better, there probably won't be a family."

Clint said a lot depends on his job situation. In general, he feels that the family itself will probably be happier. He said he worries sometimes about the family staying together, but he's not sure what he could do to prevent the family's falling apart. Then he said, "being more relaxed, not getting uptight, just getting along better." He shifted his position when he concluded, "I don't worry that much about the family falling apart. I am more worried and concerned about financial problems."

Exercise 3: What do you look forward to or wish would happen in your future and your family's future?

Clint hopes to go back to teaching college but added that although there are no jobs right now, he hopes that will change soon. He hopes Candace will learn to walk and that her seizures will dissipate. He hopes for Caroline's continued success in school. He hopes that Lucy will be happier, but he doesn't know what he can do to help Lucy feel happier.

Lucy responded at this point that Clint could help by noticing her when she does positive things with the children. Also, "he could be home more, and if and when he gets free time I want him to give me the option of approving his extra hours. I want him to clear his free time with me because there is so little of it."

Caroline looks forward to traveling and wishes for wings so that she could go all over—to Hawaii, Chicago, New York (and she would like to take her mother and father along). She worries about dropping through a hole, being on a mountain and falling off (her mother has nightmares similar to these fears), and about her parents leaving her alone.

Lucy looks forward to reconciling her differences with Clint. She fears that Candace may die; she is afraid when Caroline leaves the house alone. She doesn't fantasize about bad things happening to Corey because she keeps Corey so close. Lucy said that not all the things that she is interested in center on family but that all her worries center on the family. She added that Clint does not get paid enough for what he does but that he never has and probably never will because he doesn't assert himself.

Lucy feels that what is important to her at this moment is getting to the feelings of the family and working on them so that "we know where each of us is at. Clint comes in and doesn't give us any verbal signals as to where he is at." Lucy said that although she is more explosive and volatile and can be hard to deal with, she is more honest than Clint. "What's No. 1 important is better communication with Clint. I don't even think he's listening now."

Exercise 4: Describe the happiest moment and the saddest moment in your life.

Both Lucy and Clint consider their happiest moments the births of the three children; their saddest moment was the realization that Candace is severely retarded.

Lucy added that she still can't accept Candace's retardation and the idea that it will never significantly change. She hopes for a miracle. She thinks God is getting her for absolutely no reason: She is a pure person, was a virgin when she got married, and has done everything right. She said that she can't help seeing Candace as a terrible burden, whereas Clint considers Candace a gift—that he is honored among men because Candace is so pure that she gives her love without strings or hooks.

Supervision.

We discussed with our supervisor the topics we should talk about in the feedback conference. It was difficult for us to come up with three statements about things that work in the family. Things that don't work were quite easy to find, but stating them in a nonthreatening manner took work from all three of us.

FEEDBACK CONFERENCE

We began by asking each member of the family to tell us what he or she had got out of SE.

Clint told us that he had enjoyed the sessions but that most of all he had looked forward to our coming. He had found the role-playing exercise in the first session the most interesting part of the program. He felt the most useful thing was beginning to think about personal strengths and weaknesses, assets and liabilities.

Caroline said she had enjoyed the role playing and doing the Animals test (Animal Concepts Picture Series) but that in general she felt that it had been a waste of time. Her response matched her attitude and behavior throughout the sessions—pestering us to do more role playing, to give her the cards, and generally being very difficult to control.

Lucy said she had enjoyed the sessions but felt that everything had been too quick; she felt that she hadn't had time to do everything as well as she could have. She mentioned that thinking of the family as a unit is something she has not been used to but something that is good for her. She feels the sessions have provoked her into thinking and that this will be beneficial in the long run.

We then gave the family our positive feedback. They have positive relations with their children and take good care of all of them. We told Lucy and Clint that we feel they are working on more effective communication with each other. We commented that the family is very friendly and comfortable to be with; we had felt relaxed and at ease and had enjoyed their company. We told them that we consider their friendliness positive and that it is reflected in their community activities.

Next, we proposed three areas for the family to work on.

1. The family would benefit if they could start to approach and deal with their disagreements and feelings toward each other more directly.
2. It would be good for the family to discuss and decide democratically who should be responsible for what in the family so that everybody can reach agreement and the parents can share equal amounts of responsibility for the children.
3. Issues of responsibility in general seem to be a problem area in this family. It seems that each family member has not adequately dealt with the issue of how much responsibility to assume for other people versus how much responsibility to assume for one's own needs, feelings, goals, and life plans.

Lucy was very much interested in (and took notes on) our feedback. Our last statement, which was the closest we came to dropping a hand grenade, affected Lucy. She looked at Clint and asked what he thought of it. In his usual monotone, he replied, "Fine."

POSTTEST RESULTS

On the Bell-Fagan Family Symbols (B-F), the numbers of cards chosen were Clint, 51; Lucy, 68; and Caroline, 37. As on the pretest, Lucy received a majority of the cards and again came out high on the loving subscale. (Again, this can be interpreted as partly a function of her dominant role in the family.) Caroline again was on opposite ends from both parents on the happiness subscale. Perhaps both Clint and Lucy look at Caroline as the one bright spot in their lives and this is reflected in their giving Caroline many happiness cards. Lucy's anger is more clearly differentiated on the posttest: her score has increased quite a lot—both Clint and Caroline gave her more cards that relate to that subscale.

On the Description of Feelings in the Family (DFF), all three members viewed the family as more distracting than they did on the pretest. Both Clint and Caroline viewed the family as mad; Lucy was right in the middle. The family viewed its members as mad and distracting. Lucy was seen as mad and smug. Clint was viewed as highly distracting, a significant change in his score, as he had been viewed as mildly smug on the pretest.

On the Family Situations Picture Series (FSPS), everyone was seen as blaming and computing. The blaming corresponds with everyone's being viewed on the DFF as mad. A possible interpretation of the computing in the FSPS and the distracting in the DFF relates to the general state of affairs in the family. Lucy had said she is the general, so FSPS may reflect her taking charge—having people do this, do that, no questions asked. The distracting may indicate people who are being forced into roles or into doing things about which they feel ambivalent, for example Lucy's giving orders but not liking the role. When Lucy's order is not obeyed, she gets distracted and a fight results; when her order is obeyed, she questions herself and Clint and Caroline question her authority (although usually not verbally). Thus arise confusion and distraction. It is easy in this family to give and take orders (at least on some levels), but the giving and taking on clear feelings (since most feelings in this family seem to be ambivalent) is difficult.

On the Animal Concepts Picture Series (ACPS), some significant discrepancies occurred in the actual-ideal (A-I) scores. Clint has an A-I differential of 39 for Lucy, which can be seen as a reflection of her dissatisfaction with the way things are going in their relationship. Lucy has an A-I differential of 33 in reference to herself. She is not happy with herself or her situation, but she seems to be trying to change (one probable reason for the A-I differential). Lucy's A-I discrepancy for Caroline may be a situational function (Caroline was not very cooperative in the sessions). It is also possible that Lucy is investing more hopes and aspirations in Caroline so that she can be the great person that Lucy feels she herself isn't. Caroline's A-I score for herself is significant but not very much changed from the pretest.

SUMMARY

Initially, Lucy seemed the dominant force in the household. We saw her in this role and in speaking of her role. Lucy sees herself as the person responsible for running the family—the take-charge person, the commander-in-chief. She believes that if she weren't running things, nothing would get accomplished. Lucy's position in the family represents many contradictions within her. She is the aggressive-assertive member, but she complains that Clint doesn't assume enough responsibility, doesn't take the father role, isn't assertive enough. Yet, she constantly tells him what to do. In one session, she even said Clint should clear all his free time through her. She doesn't really seem to like the dominant position, but she is not sure whether to consider assertiveness-aggressiveness an asset or a liability. She feels burdened with too much responsibility but believes that nothing will get done if she doesn't do it or see to it. Lucy looks to Clint for support and reinforcement, but the nature of their marriage and their personalities make the giving and receiving of support difficult for both of them.

Lucy told us in one session that her father ran his house like the army—he was the commander-in-chief and her mother was a martyr. Lucy seems to have incorporated both traits into her personality: She is the commander, but she is also sad and mad and guilty. Several times, she mentioned questioning why God has given her a retarded child. She said she is pure and good and does not deserve the burden. In relation to Caroline, Lucy feels guilty and responsible for making Caroline grow up quickly. The first session gave Lucy some insight into the dynamics of the Clint-Lucy-Caroline relationship. In a role-playing exercise, Lucy saw how she yells at Caroline, tells her what to do, punishes her; when things get too hot and heavy for Caroline, she goes to Daddy for comfort and protection against mean Mommy.

Lucy is dominant and at least outwardly in control of running the family, yet she needs and wants support. The family is not doing well financially, and Lucy is thinking of going back to work. She feels, though, that the most important benefit that she could reap from working is increased respect from Clint. She mentioned once that Clint can so intimidate her at parties that just a look from him can make her clam up.

Lucy is clearly dissatisfied with herself and her relationship with Clint. The themes of burdens, responsibilities, and frustration were heard from her in all the sessions. Despite that, Lucy seems to be working as best she can to strengthen herself and improve her relationship with Clint. Lucy is in individual therapy, and she persuaded Clint to attend a couple of group sessions with her. She was very attentive and said at least once in every SE session, "That's really interesting. I never looked at things that way." She had the most affect in her voice and several times seemed on the verge of tears. At the end of each session, she faithfully took out a pencil and paper and wrote down the homework.

Clint is the passive member of the duo, but his passivity reaps its rewards and he can be seen as passive-aggressive. Clint is most comfortable when he withdraws from the world. He told us he has always been able to sit down, pick up a book, and be oblivious to his surroundings. He is most comfortable reading scientific journals, participating in seminars, or reading police adventure stories. He seems quite immature emotionally, especially in relation to Lucy. Lucy once mentioned that the two significant women in Clint's life (aside from her) are his mother and his sister, both of whom (she said) are very dominant ladies. Clint became quite agitated at this remark and nonverbally showed more emotion than he showed in any other session.

We got the impression that Clint looked at SE as an interesting and enjoyable diversion. He answered all questions in the exercises adequately and always worked on the homework, but he didn't seem personally involved. He seemed to hear Lucy's words but not Lucy. He gave answers to the questions but seemed not to relate the questions and answers to himself and to his family.

Clint's laissez-faire attitude is characteristic of his relationships at home, work, and play. He has very few friends (he could remember only one time in the past year that he had telephoned a friend), does not enjoy going out socially, and goes places only when Lucy pushes him. His attitude causes conflict with Lucy, who is more energetic and would like to do more things with Clint. Caroline characterized her father more than once as sitting like a bump on a log, reading a newspaper. Apparently, though, being a bump on a log is pretty much what Clint is and what he wants to be. He doesn't see the relationships between his attitude and Lucy's feelings of dissatisfaction and unhappiness. Clint considers his passivity and even-temperedness assets; Lucy sees them as liabilities. However, after a session that focused on assets and liabilities, trouble and fighting arose on the homefront: Clint had tried to assert himself when Lucy told him to clean up a room (she had said "Now!"), and both had become angry and upset. Both have a lot invested in their particular roles, and although Clint doesn't like getting pushed around, he gets his benefits from it. He doesn't have to think too much and can, without too much difficulty, remain a bump on a log, withdrawn from the world.

Clint seems to have a good relationship with the children. Lucy said Clint generally can show his feelings and emotions better to children because it is less threatening, and Clint concurred. Even in his relationship with the children, though, Clint seems a bit outside, looking in. He told us he enjoys sitting around and watching Corey grow. He seems to have a nice relationship with Caroline, taking her places, enjoying her company, feeling proud of her accomplishments. His attitude toward Candace seems quite good: Although he feels very sad for her, he loves her ability to give her love freely. However, many problems exist between Clint and

Lucy vis-à-vis the children and their respective roles and responsibilities toward them. Clint believes he carries 50% of the weight; Lucy believes that almost the entire burden rests on her.

Caroline, for the most part, did not enjoy our sessions very much and was inattentive and often distracting. She did the role-playing exercises well and gave very insightful portrayals of her mother and her father. One theme Caroline repeated during the sessions is that her house is very "yelly" and noisy. Caroline seems very bright, precocious, and spoiled (she whined when she did not get her way).

Both parents seem very proud of Caroline and have a lot invested in her—perhaps too much. On the pre- and posttests of the Bell-Fagan Family Symbols, Caroline was viewed as extremely happy, especially in relation to the parents, who are both quite low on this scale. It seems that Caroline is carrying a heavy burden and has a lot of pressure on her to "be happy." This may be detrimental as she grows up, but some of this burden may shift to Corey as she gets older.

The family has difficulty functioning as a unit. Lucy remarked in the feedback conference that one thing that she had learned was to begin to look at the family as a unit. Many problems exist in the family. Communication is impaired because all members take a blaming stance. Negative confrontation and not listening to others are common. The family seems entrenched in the sameness of roles that bring some things to each of them but prevent them from differentiating and truly enriching their family lives. Change is difficult—in this family, particularly so. Each day, Lucy puts on the general's sword, gives orders, makes sure everything gets done; in the evening, she nails herself to the cross and laments the burdens and responsibilities she must carry.

Clint agreeably and passively "puts up" with Lucy's bitchiness, bossiness, and domineering. He shakes his head, does what he's told, then reads the newspapers, muttering under his breath. (Once when Lucy was out of the room, he advised one enricher not to get married.)

Clint and Lucy feed off each other's weaknesses, but Lucy seems to be growing impatient and wants to change. Clint is still too comfortable on his log. As the parents go, so go the children. Caroline has a lot of intelligence and a lot of creative energy; her emotional well-being and growth will reflect how her parents come to grips with their difficulties.

We cannot say that this family was truly enriched. Certainly there was some communication, information exchange, and examining of issues and problems from different (new) perspectives. Although we did not see any significant change, we believe that their work in SE can be a foundation for change if they can incorporate what they learned into their lives.

SECTION V
Special Cases

22

A Resistant Couple

Bari Zwirn and Edgar Jessee

Matt and Emily, who have been married 10 years, live in an attractive two-bedroom brick house in a middle-class neighborhood. Emily is in her early 30s, has brown hair and eyes, and is attractive but slightly overweight. At the interview, she wore minimal makeup and a homemade dress over a print blouse. Her voice was soft and childlike; at times, she expressed some hesitancy. Generally, Emily was very cordial, but she often laughed nervously. Matt is also in his early 30s (1 year younger than Emily); he is 5'10" and slightly overweight. His hair and eyes are brown, and he wore a sports shirt and slacks. Matt is a manager in a software company; Emily is a student and housewife (she did take a part-time job during SE). Matt was very verbal most of the evening and frequently monopolized the conversation. Tony, aged 6, the only child in the family, was not included in SE.

INTERVIEW

As we discussed SE, both expressed some nervousness and concern about the threatening aspects of the process. After we had explained fully, they agreed to participate. They mentioned the improvement of communication as a goal for both of them; further, it will satisfy a job requirement for Matt.

Matt is the oldest of eight children in a very chaotic, low-income family. His parents were divorced when he was very small. His mother remarried, but Matt ran away when he was 14 because of the mutual dislike between his stepfather and himself. He described his relationship with his mother as a warm and caring one. Matt reported that he had never again gone home except for one short visit when he was 17 (during that visit, he and his stepfather got into a fight). Matt stayed with friends while growing up and claims that it was his high IQ that enabled him to escape his family. He also reported having done very well in academics and sports during high school.

The patterns in Matt's family include physical separation, in the form of divorce or elopement, whenever severe emotional problems arose. Two of the children have been divorced; all the children ran away from home before they reached age 18. The sibling Matt feels closest to is a younger brother who has recently entered the army and married. Matt said that he is the only child who has begun to make something of himself. The siblings do seem to exhibit much dysfunction—from failing marriages to institutionalization in a mental health facility.

Emily, the younger of two children, described her childhood and adolescence as sheltered and protected. She also described a close relationship with her parents and an unwillingness to leave home. Emily's brother was the black sheep because he defied his parent's wishes and was "wild." He is now head of a physical therapy department at a local hospital. Emily talked about her parents with a mixture of affection and resentment; she commented that she had always understood how much she had been sheltered and protected. Emily identified her dependence as the main problem in their marital relationship, a view Matt heartily concurred with.

They talked about their marriage in terms of growth and development—from a very naive and unequal state at the beginning of marriage to the current "satisfactory" condition. The couple met in high school and were married after Matt's 2-year military service. Their courtship was turbulent because Emily's family did not accept Matt. The first few years of marriage were spent in another state, where Matt was studying to become a minister. Emily said she idolized Matt during that time and was very content to play the role of traditional housewife. Matt, however, became upset at her dependence and the infringement on his freedom that the marriage caused. They separated and began divorce proceedings; at the last possible moment, they decided to stay together and soon afterward moved to a large southern city. They described no other separation or crisis situations except for a brief separation last year because of Matt's job. Emily said, however, that one of her major fears is that Matt will leave her (Matt laughed but did not deny the possibility).

Enrichers' notes.

Matt and Emily come from distinctly different, almost opposite, backgrounds. Matt's chaotic family background exhibits a pattern of separation as a means of dealing with conflict. Emily's sheltered background evidences extreme togetherness, which explains her separation anxiety. Matt occupies the father role and seems to treat Emily as a father would treat a child. Emily colludes through her subservient but mildly rebellious behavior, her dress, and her voice inflection. Both appear fairly comfortable in this parent-child marriage.

Interestingly enough, though, Emily's dependence on Matt is a concern of theirs. Both said they would like Emily to be more independent; yet Matt reinforces Emily's dependence, and Emily apparently makes few attempts to be independent. This incongruence between words and action appears to be one of the paradoxical aspects of their relationship.

Supervision.

Our supervisor, Gerald Weeks, suggested that because of the couple's apparent acceptance of their relationship system, they may be very resistant to any change within that system. Obviously, no crisis exists at this time. We discussed which program might be most appropriate. Because of the inequality in this parent-child system (Matt replaces Emily's father; Emily replaces Matt's siblings), we decided on the Equality Program.

PRETEST SUMMARY

The pretest battery consisted of the Marital Happiness Scale, the Marital Questionnaire, the Semantic Differential, and Family Information. On the Marital Happiness Scale, the couple rated areas of their relationship (e.g., sex, communication, money, social activities) on a 10-point scale, *very satisfied* to *very dissatisfied*. The Marital Questionnaire consists of 13 subscales on various dimensions of the relationship (e.g., computing, distracting, sharing the good, sharing the hurt). The Semantic Differential consists of 20 polar adjectives (e.g., good vs. bad, smart vs. stupid) that are used to describe oneself and one's partner on a 7-point scale.

The overall scores on the Marital Happiness Scale are in the moderately high range. Emily's average score is approximately 9 on a 10-point scale, Matt's approximately 8, which indicates general satisfaction with their relationship or extreme denial. Both partners noted specific areas of dissatisfaction: Matt was unhappy with money, sex frequency, foreplay, kissing, and intercourse; Emily was unhappy with household responsibilities, social activities, communication, and sex (overall).

Some noteworthy discrepancies appear in their scores. Matt believed he was more satisfied than Emily in communication and personal independence but much less satisfied in sex (overall), intercourse, and orgasm. Emily believed she was less satisfied in personal independence but more satisfied in general happiness. These areas—communication, personal independence, and sex—suggest areas in which conflict may exist.

The Semantic Differential shows that both partners have favorable self-concepts. Interestingly, both rated Matt in a more favorable light on almost all dimensions (the same superiority-inferiority picture they presented in the interview).

The scores on Family Information are also in the moderately high range. Matt's scores average 8.6 on the 10-item scale, 7.4 on the 18-item scale. Emily's scores average 7.2 on the 10-item scale, 8.6 on the 18-item scale. Emily omitted two items: "Today my spouse loves me" and "Today I learned something about my spouse." Emily gave low ratings to relationship with close relatives, "Today my spouse understands me," concreteness, and initiative. Matt indicated dissatisfaction with feelings and emotions, self-exploration, and "Today I feel this marriage has potential." Again, these results confirm what we saw in the interview. Inequality and emotional satisfaction are two basic issues with this couple.

According to the Marital Questionnaire, both partners engage in a great deal of computing and distracting (our clinical impression of them was that they tend to compute and that they often distract through their computing; apparently their computing manifests itself as a form of distraction). Emily also has a low score (4) on placating; apparently she deals with conflict by attempting to smooth things over (perhaps she does this to keep Matt from walking out on her). Matt also has a significantly low score on priorities—perhaps indicative of his giving his work top priority. Overall, the scores for both partners exhibit wide range and variation. The totals (Matt 94, Emily 86) are in the moderately high range.

The test results generally substantiate our initial observations. The couple's areas of dissatisfaction are selfhood, communication, and emotional satisfaction.

SUMMARY OF SESSIONS

Session 1

We discussed the test results and our impressions with Matt and Emily and offered three program choices: Negotiation, Conflict Resolution, and Equality. After discussion, they chose the Equality Program.

In the first lesson (Old Roles), we asked each spouse to consider the advantages and disadvantages of their old roles. An interesting dichotomy emerged from their answers: both talked about the freedom to pursue their individual interests, but Matt was using this freedom frequently while Emily was doing so only rarely. Emily also had great difficulty assuming Matt's role in the role-reversal exercise. We interpreted this as Emily's difficulty or resistance to assuming a more assertive role. By not asserting herself, Emily is maintaining the status quo in the relationship and keeping her child position.

Enrichers' notes.

We noted especially the inequality of their roles and their lack of emotional exploration. Matt mentioned control many times as extremely important to him; Emily listed Tony, Matt, and her education, in that order. She seems to defer to Matt constantly. We found ourselves less frustrated by Matt than we had been initially; he systematically answered questions but did not tell anecdotes.

Supervision.

Our supervisor suggested that this is a "traditional American marriage," that they are a classic couple with a parent-child polarization, which usually takes the form of denial. Both have power but deny it—Matt in his computing and Emily in her helplessness. We noted that Emily's responsibilities include all the menial work (yard work, shopping, cooking).

Session 2

During the second lesson (Femininity-Masculinity), the overall theme of the session was set by the couple's insistence that they already understood these concepts completely. They went through the motions but did not seem involved and gave intellectualized answers to all the questions. To get past intellectualizing, we asked them to name their favorite movie stars. Matt responded with James Coburn and Jaclyn Smith; Emily named Burt Reynolds and Barbra Streisand. Matt mentioned movies in which James Coburn has played the strong, emotionless macho male and Jaclyn Smith has played the sex-object who wears a facade of independence. Emily spoke of Burt Reynolds as someone who is "wild, rebellious, and often on the wrong side of the law." She said that all Barbra Streisand's movies involve her initial dependence on her husband but that she gradually surpasses him in fame and fortune.

Enrichers' notes.

We were more supportive of them, and we met with less resistance and distracting and more cooperation. They do not deal directly with conflict or emotion; rather, they let them subside. They obviously spend a lot of energy on keeping peace. Matt seems to relate through distance, as he did with his primary family. Emily colludes by keeping peace (as her parents did—she never saw them fight or kiss) through her fear of separation.

Supervision.

We discussed their parent-child, see-saw relationship and how to communicate that in a letter. We recognized the effect of *not* confronting them and intend to use support carefully. We decided to deal with manipulative roles in an addition to the next lesson (role-playing Satir's four styles). We discussed the letter and chose power (denying it) and dealing with feelings through thinking as our main points. We thought also of discussing their lack of differentiation from their families and the lack of separation in their marriage but decided that the first two issues are more important.

Session 3

The couple did follow through with the contract but attributed little meaning to it. In this session, we used exercises designed to increase sharing feelings. As might have been predicted, they had an extremely difficult time with the sharing of feelings—both positive and negative. Emily complained that Matt does not express his love often enough; Matt said that Emily does not show anger.

When we reached the exercise about communicating in conflict, both refused to role-play, saying they would not fight because it might result in serious problems after we left. They further stated that they never fight because they have such good communication. We complimented them on their ability to communicate so perfectly. As we left, we gave them the paradoxical letter.

Dear Emily and Matt,

The purpose of this letter is to deal with our observations of your relationship. We want to put these observations in writing because they are too important for us to deliver orally, and all of us will have a better opportunity to reflect on them.

We want to congratulate you for being such an extraordinary couple by never misunderstanding each other. You seem to have an in-depth understanding of each other's feelings. It is obvious that you have devoted much thought to this pursuit. Consequently, we feel your thoughtful understanding will enable you to continue your present degree of sharing feelings.

We are impressed by the amount of influence you have in your marriage. We want you to continue to use the enormous power you have. But in order to protect the roles you have set up in the relationship, one of you should continue to deny your power but use it to control the relationship while the other pretends to be helpless. At all costs, you should continue to cooperate with each other by maintaining the roles we've described.

We find you warm, intelligent, and caring people. We look forward to continuing our work together.

Enrichers' notes.

We were amazed at the energy spent in not fighting and not feeling anger. Emily seems to be the good mother (her way), and she maintains sameness through good behavior. Matt lives in the same emotional distance he did as a child. Emily mentioned that anger was not allowed in her family and that she has no model for anger. We noted that they relate to us as the persecutors in the triangle, from whom they must protect and distance themselves. Any confrontation to their system creates collusion and a strengthening of their front.

Supervision.

We discussed the aspects of emotional rather than physical distancing and how this couple deals with fighting by separating. This pattern is especially true of Matt (divorces in the family, leaving home). We agreed to have them do nonthreatening role-plays ("We know this is not a problem with you") and to listen for metaphors and distraction in the exercises that deal with sex.

Session 4

The subject of this lesson is achieving equality. Matt again sought to control the session, using computing to distract from the issue. After I complimented him several times on his intellectualizations, he stopped and was more compliant during the rest of the session. With the approval of our supervisor, we used an exercise from Lesson 3 in the Negotiation Program for our final exercise. Each person was asked to role-play Satir's (1972) four communication styles. Both did this well and again exhibited their primary styles of communicating by expressing their preference for computing and distracting.

At the end of the session, Matt told a story about taking control of a computer away from the operator and giving it back to him only "when he agreed to be a good little boy." This metaphor seemed to say that Matt perceives SE as a threat to change and that he will not give us the power to invoke change.

Enrichers' notes.

The letter was not mentioned. We discussed Matt's story of several situations in which he had expressed anger and the person involved died. To Matt, anger leads to death. Emily married someone like her mother—unaffectionate. We were encouraged to see them get into the role playing, especially since they had discounted manipulative techniques ("We've both worked in sales and can spot them"). Perhaps role playing couched in a paradoxical presentation would be effective with them.

Supervision.

Matt controls sessions as he does lovemaking. Lessons on anger and hurt might be helpful. Matt frequently discusses work and perhaps uses stress at work as a metaphor for the relationship. At one point, he had told us about jamming up the computer system of a person who had tried to tell him what to do. That story was certainly directed at us. We also talked about the changes we see in them and considered what we might want to say at the feedback conference.

Session 5

Before we began, Matt launched into another metaphorical statement about his work: basically, he would be working long hours for many months to come and everything else would have to be put aside. We interpreted this to mean that work is still first priority and that nothing we can do at this time is going to change this couple's relationship system. Not surprisingly, the couple refused to write a contract for achieving equality in their marriage.

Enrichers' notes.

We discussed their resistance to change and how Matt speaks of it metaphorically through work ("too much pressure"). Emily is enjoying her job; he seems to want to keep stress and continue to overcome obstacles. It interests us that board games (e.g., backgammon), which are structured and computing, are their typical family interaction. We believe that Matt is sharing more with Emily, but his priorities seem to be work, family-child, marriage, self.

Supervision.

We discussed their resistance to contracting for change and related it to their familial patterns. We then looked at their test results and discussed the feedback conference. We decided that it will be best not to give any negative feedback or feedback that they might find confronting.

FEEDBACK CONFERENCE

Matt and Emily expressed different views of what they had gotten from SE. Both said it had been fun. Emily said she had gained a great deal—that she knows Matt better, she sees new things, and perhaps Matt sees her a little differently too, especially as less dependent (no comment from Matt to that). Emily also said they've had more conversations with each other. Matt had found the sessions "entertaining" and admitted he had sometimes tried to give us a hard time.

Neither remembered the letter very well and claimed to have misplaced it. They considered the letter vague and commented that it said nothing, at least nothing new. Matt went into a long diatribe on the importance of formalized, clear language. The letter, he said, was "not useful to us at all." Matt claimed to see "a few new things" because of SE.

Emily related that they had had a spat and the world hadn't caved in and that she had come home highly inebriated (unusual for her) and their roles had been reversed. She also expressed interest in more SE (for her and friends), which Matt did not respond to.

Enrichers' notes.

Matt commented on how glad he is that the quarter is over (he's not in school), and we think he was alluding to SE. We think they will look over the letter again but will not continue SE because it's too threatening to Matt. We wonder whether Emily's negative feelings about Matt's bowling have more to do with his drinking those nights. We realize they have used us as "therapists" (by telling us many details of their lives) and the sessions as a social hour. Emily's "changes" seem still to be changes only with permission.

Supervision.

Initially our supervisor had suggested that this couple exhibited little desire to change and thus probably would not do so as a result of SE. We have discovered that both partners collude to keep the relationship the same. Emily has continued to exert her power through helplessness and dependency; Matt has exerted his influence yet denied his power.

We learned early in our sessions that confrontation would not be effective with this couple, and our supervisor suggested that we compliment and accentuate the couple's proclamations about their wonderful marriage. This strategy proved to be very effective as a means of controlling the session but seems to have elicited little change. Even the paradoxical letter appears to have had little immediate effect.

The final conclusion in supervision is that this couple has evidenced very little change. We hypothesize that they are colluding to keep the relationship the same. However, some aspects of the relationship do appear different. Emily has gotten a part-time job and is now proclaiming herself to be less dependent on Matt. Also, during Weeks 5 and 6, the couple said they were enjoying their time together much more.

PRE- AND POSTTEST EVALUATION

The overall difference in scores between the pre- and the posttests is not significant. However, the posttest scores tend to be slightly higher, especially for Emily.

On the Marital Questionnaire, Emily's average score increased 1 point. Her particular areas of improvement are enjoyment, seeing the good, sharing hurt, and placating. Forgiveness, computing, and distracting remain problem issues. In fact, the only decrease in her scores is on distracting (from 6 to 4). Matt's posttest scores are also somewhat higher but reflect little change. He does show a 3-point upward shift on priorities, but he also exhibits an increase (downward shift) in computing and distracting. This couple seems to be using the same incongruent communication patterns; perhaps, though, Emily is deriving more satisfaction from the relationship.

The Marital Happiness Scale reveals very few new developments. Matt's scores reflect no significant change, except for a change to equal ranking for spouse and self on a few items. The only significant change on Emily's posttest is a 3-point increase in communication.

The results of the Family Satisfaction Scales substantiate the findings from the other tests. Matt's scores show no change in satisfaction; Emily's scores reveal slightly more self-satisfaction. Emily's scores do show significant positive changes on concreteness, initiative, and understanding of spouse.

The results of the Semantic Differential show a tendency to grade spouse and self more in the middle, with fewer extremes. Matt's scores, again, reveal no difference or trends; Emily's show slight improvement in her self-concept (smart, superior, soft, unselfish, aggressive) but no real change in how she views Matt.

Generally, the test results support our clinical impressions. Few significant changes have occurred in the couple's relationship system. Emily's results do indicate more self-satisfaction, which may eventually bring about some degree of relationship change. Perhaps our paradoxical letter and frequent paradoxical supportive statements reinforced the system, as evidenced by more dysfunctional scores on distracting and continued low scores on computing and emotional expression.

A THEORETICAL INTERPRETATION

This couple can be viewed in terms of L'Abate's (1976) theory of personality development within the marriage and family. Matt and Emily exemplify a very undifferentiated couple (self-differentiation implies the setting of clear boundaries of one's feelings, role allocations, responsibilities, and marital and work functions). They were unable to differentiate themselves on feeling, responsibilities, and marital and work function boundaries. On the continuum of likeness, this couple can be described as same-opposite. Their oppositeness is demonstrated by their having chosen each other as mates—coming from completely opposite family backgrounds. Their sameness is demonstrated by their refusal to change themselves. Their oppositeness is also demonstrated in Matt's pattern of dealing with conflict through separation and Emily's pattern of attempting to smooth over and deemphasize the differences—attempting to keep them more the same. Thus, they use their oppositeness to keep themselves the same as a couple.

The couple's inability to deal with hurt is also a comment on their level of differentiation. More differentiated couples would be able to share hurt feelings; less differentiated couples would focus on anger. Matt and Emily do not deal with hurt and rarely confront anger. Their unwillingness to express anger toward each other seems to be due to unrealistic fears (separation anxiety). Matt's family members have always left when anger resulted, as evidenced by the number of runaways and divorces in his family. Also, Matt had two experiences in his life in which someone died shortly after he became angry at them. Emily's fear seems related to the dependency and helplessness she exhibits while playing the child role in this parent-child marriage. Emily's family avoided conflict and stressed sameness and symbiosis. Thus, Emily has invested so much of her self in Matt that his leaving would threaten her existence.

The priorities in this family are clearly work first and marriage second; the self is rarely considered. Matt and now Emily, too, with her new job, define self by occupation. In fact, Matt has used occupational metaphors to talk about the relationship. As expected, Emily colluded and offered little opposition. There is evidence, however, that Emily is gaining some sense of self. Matt clearly has a poor self-concept and avoids looking at himself.

Because this couple values work so highly as a self-description, they can be assumed to place an inordinate emphasis on doing, as opposed to being and having. The emphasis on doing is reflected in Matt's working long hours and Emily's going to school and working part-time. The couple's future goals—continuing advancements in education and in job hierarchy—also reflect an emphasis on doing. Having occupies a minor role and is occasionally exhibited by Matt's boasting statements about having done better than anyone else in his family. The couple is not, however, preoccupied with money or goods. The third side of the triangle—being—appears very small indeed. Neither seems to have an in-depth awareness of self, much less a desire to change and to focus on the self.

The couple's style of communicating can be examined in terms of computing, distracting, and placating. Matt is excellent at intellectualizing in a digital manner in order to avoid looking at himself. Emily also engages in computing at times but mostly avoids examining herself and the relationship by placating. However, at the end of SE, Emily was exhibiting somewhat more self-assertion in response to Matt's computing (she inevitably gave in to him when she felt stress). Both display a computer nature in their use of digital thinking. A prime example of this was their inability to see "interdependence" as an option to "independence" or "dependence." Also, this digital thinking was involved in their inability to see how two separate, strong individuals could form a stronger relationship foundation than could two complementary individuals. In short, they keep themselves in a centripetal bind through their digital thinking and their insistence on being the same or opposite. Unfortunately, their defenses were so strong that even the paradoxical letter did not seem to work.

This relationship also can be viewed in terms of the rescuer-victim-persecutor triangle. Matt was the rescuer when he married Emily (the victim) and brought her away from her stern parents (the persecutors). Evidence of Matt's rescuer role can also be seen in his earlier decision to become a minister. Matt has attempted to protect Emily from the world, much as her parents did. As a result, Matt became the persecutor and Emily began to express ambivalent feelings toward him, just as she had with her parents. They attempted a similar pattern with us. Matt sought to be the rescuer and protector by making us the persecutors and interpreting SE as threatening. Emily was the one threatened, the victim, because she was the one identified with the problem. We avoided participating in this triangle by supporting their claims to be a perfect couple.

23

A Failure to Enrich

Edgar Jessee and Kathy Weeks

INTERVIEW

Rick, a law student, and Donna, a schoolteacher, have been married only a few months. They met when they were 14, dated for 5 years, separated for 2 years, lived together for 1 year, then married a few months ago. Rick is Jewish, and Donna is Catholic.

Both come from large families of four or more children. The males in Rick's family have a long history of being attorneys; the females in Donna's family have a history of being teachers. Rick's family immigrated to America after World War II (Rick's father spent 2 years in a concentration camp during the war). Family reunions are very infrequent, and members of the extended family do not seem to be close to one another.

Rick seemed reluctant, but willing, to participate in SE. He said he wanted to avoid therapy and mentioned that his time is limited. We agreed that we would try to cover two lessons per session.

Rick and Donna described their marriage as a "happy" one with "no real problems." At the beginning of the interview, their anxiety level seemed high, but as the session progressed, they relaxed. Rick's anxiety increased at the end of the session but was somewhat eased when we answered several questions about the first session. Donna appeared eager and interested in the program. Rick leaned back in his favorite chair, far away from the rest of us.

Enrichers' notes.

We were relieved and pleased that our couple seemed normal and functional. We discussed several factors, such as the history of attorneys and teachers in Rick's and Donna's families. Generally, we felt the session went very well. Our main concern at this point is Rick's apparent resistance, as evidenced by his statements concerning the lack of time for SE.

Supervision.

The results of the pretests confirmed our impression that we were working with a fairly "normal" and healthy couple. Significant findings include lower scores on the priorities, placating, and distancing scales of the Marital Questionnaire. One implication of these scores is that this couple perhaps places their marriage first, themselves as individuals second. Because both are engaged in family professions, they may not be well differentiated from their families of origin.

Our supervisor suggested that we compliment the couple on having scored so high on the tests and tell them that it will be very hard to improve on such a good thing. At this point, Equality, Reciprocity, or Negotiation seem good program possibilities.

SUMMARY OF SESSIONS

Session 1

In this session, we covered the first and second lessons of the Negotiation Program. The first lesson deals primarily with myths, romantic love, role stereotypes, and conflict. We observed several interesting patterns in Rick's and Donna's responses. They do not openly engage in conflict; they always avoid disagreeing and seem to have some investment in presenting a united, "peaceful" front. They said that they had had to compromise on only one occasion since they married. Both tended to avoid answering some of the more open-ended projective-type questions; for example, "What are some of your myths about men and women?"

The second lesson is focused on defining perceptions of each other and the relationship. Donna seems to define herself in her marital relationship; Rick is in charge of creating most of the relationship rules, and Donna is in charge of the practical side of the relationship (balancing the checkbook, paying the bills). Both continually cited Rick's lack of time as an excuse for many of their relationship patterns and rules.

Enrichers' notes.

We discussed the couple's reluctance to answer several of the questions. Rick's dominance and Donna's acceptance of his superiority seem to be a predominant theme in their relationship.

Supervision.

We began with a brief review of the couple's test results and a rundown of our first session. Our supervisor suggested that the couple may be concerned primarily with "doing" and "having" while avoiding "being" and are expressing this avoidance in their inability or resistance to the questions. We also brainstormed some ideas for the paradoxical letter to be given to the couple after the next session.

Session 2

In this session, we covered Lessons 3 and 4 of the Negotiation Program. The exercises primarily deal with communication within the blamer-placater and computer-distracter frameworks, the nonverbal cancelling of messages, and shared meaning.

The tenor of the session was bored resistance. Rick and Donna responded superficially and made numerous references to time. We succeeded in completing both lessons in a little more than an hour. Rick and Donna said repeatedly that they were not learning anything, and they seemed determined to imply that they were not going to learn or change no matter what we did.

We gave them the following paradoxical letter at the end of the session.

Dear Donna and Rick,

We are impressed with the way you have ordered your marriage and the definition of yourselves along clear-cut traditional guidelines. Since you have already decided what you will become, we wonder what decisions you've made about who you are now as human beings. We appreciate how neatly you have separated responsibilities and roles between you. This is a distinct asset now, but could this asset become a liability later in your marriage? Given the effectiveness with which you act out your roles, have you given any thought to what might happen if you were to reverse roles? We understand the importance you place on having and doing, but we are asking ourselves what importance you place on being, for yourselves and for each other.

Enrichers' notes.

We took particular note of the boredom and resistance in tonight's session. We speculated that the couple is very invested in the status quo and determined not to change at this time. We also noted a definite absence of any discussion of feelings.

Supervision.

Donna met with our supervisor before our supervision session and voiced, rather heatedly, her discontent with the letter. Her chief complaints seemed to be that the letter was not only obscure but largely inaccurate. She said that the letter was a "therapeutic device" that had been forced on them and that they were not in therapy.

In our supervision session, it was suggested that we let Donna and Rick ventilate their feelings about the letter but that we advise them that content discussion would be delayed until the feedback conference. We were also instructed to confront Rick and Donna with an examination of their motivation for participating in SE. If they are participating solely for Donna's fulfillment of a class requirement (as we suspect), we are to advise them that they may terminate SE and Donna will receive course credit.

Session 3

Rick and Donna postponed the scheduled session, giving time problems as the reason. The paradoxical letter was not mentioned.

At the beginning of the rescheduled session, Rick and Donna asked many questions and made several statements about the letter. Their questions included the following: "What did the letter mean?" "What right did you have to make such an assessment?" Their statements were very angrily expressed and centered on the obscurity of the letter and its intended content. We allowed them to ventilate their feelings and then told them we appreciated their having shared these feelings with us. When they pressed for an explanation of the letter, we explained that the letter was purposely vague and that we would be glad to discuss its content during the feedback conference. Rick continued to press for an explanation of the letter's content and said that he wouldn't go on until he was given an explanation. We focused on their motivation for SE, tying it into Rick's question by explaining that the last lessons would not be radically different from the first, mentioning their earlier comments about their discontent with SE so far. Rick said the only reason he had agreed to participate was to help Donna; Donna said she was participating only to satisfy a course requirement.

They further stated that they had learned virtually nothing and were very disappointed. We offered them the option of terminating and assured them Donna would obtain full course credit. Rick was reluctant to terminate at first and said he would do whatever we wished. We returned the responsibility to him but said that if they do not wish to participate actively, the usefulness of the sessions for us is also affected. Donna then spoke up and advocated termination; Rick quickly agreed.

After making their decision, both began to speak honestly of their feelings about SE. They said they had never become involved in it or taken it seriously. They said that they had found many of the questions very hard to answer. We told them that we would miss our sessions with them but agreed that they were not making use of the program and that termination was perhaps indicated. We complimented them for having expressed their feelings about the program. By this time, the atmosphere was warm and friendly, and all angry feelings were far removed. Rick and Donna then scapegoated the program and assured us that termination was "nothing personal" toward us. We told them that we had not interpreted their termination as a personal act and that if in the future they wished to participate in SE, the opportunity would be available.

24

A Case of Double SE

Margaret S. Baggett, Edgar Jessee,

and Flo P. Dawson

FIRST SE
by Margaret S. Baggett and Edgar Jessee

Brian Logan, aged 24, and Sherry Logan, aged 23, learned of SE through a graduate student and wished to participate to enhance their marriage. Their motivation was exemplified in many ways, for example, their patience in remaining on the waiting list for two quarters.

The Logans are recently married. They are from the same town but did not know each other well in high school. They rediscovered each other in college and lived together for short periods before they married.

Sherry is the youngest of four sisters. Her parents are happily married. Like her mother, Sherry married a man a year older than she, and like her mother, Sherry feels rejected by her mother-in-law.

Evelyn, Sherry's mother, is her parents' only surviving child (her older sister, described as a genius, died of leukemia at an early age). Evelyn's parents divorced when she was young; her father remarried and lives in Los Angeles. Evelyn learned to "pinch pennies," and, like her mother, Sherry does this now. Evelyn worked her way through college and became a schoolteacher.

Sherry's father, the oldest of four siblings, worked in a retail business. His mother was a controlling woman who wanted him to become a lawyer, like his father, for whom he was named. He rebelled, however, and moved south.

Two of Sherry's sisters are married, one unhappily. She describes them as close, for the most part. Lindy, the unmarried sister, lives in the same

344

city as Brian and Sherry. In describing her sisters' jobs, Sherry was careful to include the authority and importance of their positions (manager, director). There seems to be a lot of same-oppositeness in this family. The family tells the offspring to be like it, but some of them rebel.

Brian is older than his one sister. His mother tried to control him, but he rebelled. His parents do not get along well at all. His father is an engineer and his mother seems to be of the country-club set, although she has returned to school for a master's degree. Brian learned the role of older brother, and Sherry learned the role of youngest sister. They married appropriate role partners.

Brian's father was an only child and named after his own father. His paternal grandparents were happily married but Victorian. Brian's mother is the older of two girls and comes from a family of ministers. Brian's mother and maternal grandmother have hearing problems; Brian describes Sherry as "tuning him out," not hearing him when he talks to her. Brian's paternal grandparents are very close and claim that parts of one reside in the other (symbiotic disposition?).

In summary, there seems to be more sameness than opposition in Brian's family. The controlling women are present here, too, however. Brian and Sherry see the problems in Brian's parents' marriage and in Sally's (Sherry's sister) marriage and are striving to avoid them in their own.

INTERVIEW

Brian and Sherry are dissatisfied with their status and feel they have not yet started on their future, on which they focus. Brian, a graduate student, deplores the fact that Sherry is the breadwinner. Sherry looks forward to Brian's earning the living because she will then be able to return to school for graduate study. They are experiencing pressures from role reversals but seem to be adjusting to them quite adequately.

The couple's apartment is in a middle-income, relatively close-in city neighborhood. It is neat and clean, though sparsely furnished, as would ə expected of newlyweds. Plants and a fish tank suggest an interest in living things.

Brian and Sherry are very attractive people; both have clean, shiny black hair and slender builds. Sherry is of average height; Brian is tall. Both wear glasses at times.

Sherry is soft-spoken and appears shy but clearly sets the tone of the marriage because she earns and handles the money and uses the rules her family followed (e.g., never leaving each other angry—they sit down and talk through feelings at the time of the disagreement). Brian allows her to wield this power, yet he seems uneasy about it. He appears restless, angry, dissatisfied, but he does not seem to know why. He also has temper outbursts followed by guilt. Throughout the interview, he was quick to blame and criticize himself, spreading his "shoulds" about liberally (which Sherry allowed). Despite Sherry's aloof control, she lounged on the couch in an open, seductive position, her feet on Brian throughout the entire series of sessions. Whereas her verbal behavior appeared closed, her nonverbal behavior suggested ample openness.

Sherry and Brian voiced concern over their many trivial arguments, which seem to stem from their basic differences in approach. Sherry is neat, methodical, compulsive—a computer. Brian is freer, messier, more gregarious, and he appears to occasionally have difficulty following the rules Sherry attempts to enforce. We wondered how open to change Sherry would be: she has a great investment in the regimented areas of their marriage, and Brian seems to have done the most changing in their relationship.

In summary, Sherry seems to control the relationship, and Brian allows her to do so. Yet, they are aware of an undefinable feeling of uneasiness in their relationship. They seem very bright and motivated, and though they are quite functional, they exhibit patterns that could lead to dys-functionality if not checked.

PRETEST RESULTS

Brian and Sherry cooperated willingly in the test session. Sherry became ensnared by her compulsive reading of the test (e.g., poor or vague wording). Brian exhibited uncertainty in his marking, frequently changing his answers.

On the Marital Questionnaire, Sherry scored 6 on likeness, which was expected because of her adherence to the rules she learned in her family. As was also expected, she scored 6 on computing, followed by 7 on placating and on distracting. Some of this behavior may be reflected in her control through helplessness. She also scored 6 on caring, on pro-tectiveness, and on responsibility. Sherry seems to care a great deal, but she does tend to take responsibility for the marriage and, in this way, overprotects Brian (if she is responsible for them, he doesn't have to be). She scored highest on blaming (9) and seeing the good (8). Brian blames himself enough for both of them, and she allows him to do this. Sherry's grand total is 90.

Brian's overall score on the Marital Questionnaire is 104, a little higher than Sherry's. His likeness score is 7, indicating that he has some problems in differentiating from his family of origin, just as Sherry does. His lowest score is on priorities, indicating that he places the marriage before himself. This is confirmed by checking individual answers on the questionnaire. Computing and distracting are the lowest (7); blaming is a 10. The blaming score is unexpected, since he appears to blame (himself, particularly) a great deal. Most of his tasks are 9s, except protectiveness, which is a 6 (this score was expected—when Sherry appears helpless, Brian protects her).

On the Semantic Differential, their scores are similar, reinforcing the hypothesis about their lack of differentiation. Each seems to see the other as a little smarter and more useful than the other. Both agree that Brian is noisier, Sherry quieter.

On the Marital Happiness Scale, Sherry scored mostly 9s and 10s; Brian scored 8s and 9s. Sherry tends to deny more than Brian does. Their overall scores are 241 (Brian) and 269 (Sherry). Sherry was least happy about household responsibilities; Brian was least happy about money.

Sherry scored a total of 162 on Family Information, and Brian scored a total of 153. Brian was least happy about his relationship with close relatives, and Sherry agreed with that rating.

On the Primary Communications Inventory, Sherry's total score is 86; Brian's is 92. Brian was least happy about self-disclosure; Sherry was most satisfied with self-exploration.

In summary, this couple seems basically undifferentiated from their families of origin, therefore, from each other. Sherry computes and controls; Brian protects and blames (though the blaming is not reflected in the test results). Neither is satisfied with their occupational status, and both seem concerned about problems with close relatives.

SUMMARY OF SESSIONS

It was agreed at supervisory sessions that this couple might benefit from the Negotiation Program, with appropriate lessons from Working Through or Conflict Resolution.

Session 1

Brian and Sherry had rearranged the furniture since the pretest session so that we were a little closer together, though not much. Both times, Sherry has been seated on the couch when we arrived and reached for the door from there, not getting up.

The couple's love and caring for each other are apparent, but they worked almost too hard (Brian especially) to answer the questions. Sherry is quieter and seems more reserved than Brian, who seems to be the more anxious one. Sherry controls through her omnipresent stability.

The unhappiness with close relatives seems to pertain to Brian's mother, but they did not elaborate. When they were asked to discuss marriage myths, they denied having any, saying that marriage is, for the most part, what they expected. Sherry exhibited a little resistance; Brian made an incredibly earnest effort to answer each question fully and thoughtfully (he typically takes a long time to answer, though he presents a barrage of words). Brian said he had expected to have fewer trivial arguments, and Sherry said she had hoped not to have to handle financial affairs.

Brian said that friendship and support had replaced romantic love, and Sherry said that a fondness had developed and that she now trusts Brian more. They appeared undifferentiated when they answered (they agreed with each other a great deal).

In their definitions of male and female qualities, much stereotyping was apparent. (This may be part of the reason they are uneasy about role reversals—Sherry supports the family while Brian goes to school.)

They said they "yell and scream" in disagreements and that they could show respect for each other by listening.

Enrichers' notes.

Sherry seems to externalize when she focuses so often on money. Brian seems to place the marriage before himself ("she is my right arm"). Brian needs to please; Sherry needs to learn to express feelings.

Sherry is quite helpless (another form of control) in some areas, for example, her timidity in social situations and her fear of driving.

Both believe they are realistic about their marriage expectations, but they are unaware of their unrealistic expectations (such as discussing each argument when it happens).

Sherry first sat on the floor at Brian's feet; then he joined her on the floor. Later, Sherry returned to the couch and sprawled out (she usually lounged on the couch during our sessions).

Session 2

Again, Sherry lounged on the couch, even more seductively than before. (As they begin to explore their relationship, does she become more seductive in order to distract Brian from looking closer?) She seemed more resistive than Brian, saying that she had learned nothing new, but she admitted that she has viewed areas of their relationship a little more closely. If Brian is resisting, he is doing so indirectly, as illustrated by the time he requires to answer a question and by the incomplete sentences with which he bombards the questions. Sometimes he avoids answering questions altogether.

Homework.

For homework, Sherry and Brian had been asked to think about the times they met each other halfway during the week. They said they had cleaned the entire apartment when Brian got home from school one day.

Brian: She's feeling guilty about that. She has to do it otherwise.
Sherry: We both hate housework. It's not fair that he has to do that alone.
Brian: It has to be done, but she's tired when she gets home on Friday and doesn't like to do it when she gets up on Saturday.
Sherry: Weekends are the only time we have together.
Brian: We're both antiroutine.
Sherry: I made the bed this morning and picked up and didn't say a word.
Brian: I know what she did—she cleaned up my study room.
Sherry: It's hard to think of things where we meet each other halfway.
Brian: I know something else she did. My brother-in-law came through town, and she fixed breakfast (pancakes) for us all.

Brian tried hard to think of examples, but Sherry had difficulty. Finally Sherry said, "It was helpful. We talked about it, and it makes you think about what you're doing." Brian agreed.

Enrichers' notes.

Brian continues to try hard to please and to protect Sherry. Sherry appears to be the wise one, the one who "knows what's best," the rule-maker, the mother. Brian is at once the protector and the recalcitrant little boy who is his own worst critic. (Is Brian running parent tapes?) Brian does motherly things for Sherry (tells her to eat breakfast, eat her vegetables, do the laundry). Would he do this if he were the main breadwinner? Is Brian's enjoyment in watching wrestling on TV a release, a vicarious experience? Does Brian like other violent sports?

They intellectualize, avoid talking about self, and have difficulty answering "Who am I?"

The following issues are pertinent:

1. Brian is protective and puts himself down.
2. Brian is dissatisfied with his occupational status.
3. The partners lack differentiation.
4. Brian fears the marriage is not working.
5. Brian has a real investment in the marriage. What is it? He's very involved with Sherry's family. Is there something in his family he's missing and is fulfilling through Sherry and her family?

6. Brian's mother also sounds like the dominant figure in the marriage. Brian says things are resolved with his mother. If his mother and his wife are alike, will he admit problems with his wife?
7. What about Sherry's timid little voice, her helplessness, her seductiveness?
8. Is the double message in Sherry's family that one is to be independent verbally but dependent nonverbally? Is Sherry doing this to Brian?
9. Is being different threatening?
10. Sherry sends incongruent messages: her body language is open; her verbal messages are closed.

Supervision.

We discussed the paradoxical letter to be given to the couple after the next session. The main issue is control: Who's controlling whom? Who is in charge here? Sherry, Brian, or both? Is there polarization in who's in charge? Who is the most responsible for the marriage? Sherry cares so much for the marriage that she takes charge, and Brian lets her. They divide nicely: Sherry takes responsibility inside, Brian outside. If he takes responsibility and doesn't do it right, she takes it back. He's protective; she's helpless.

Session 3

Sherry is showing a great deal of resistance by distracting (getting up, checking fan). Brian has shown more interest and seems to relate issues in past sessions to current ones. Tonight's discussion about using shared meaning seemed helpful to them.

They had done their homework (practicing "I" statements). Despite Sherry's resistance, both remain highly motivated. Brian's speech is becoming clearer, and Sherry is beginning to express herself more.

Sherry told Brian she feels hurt when he compares her with his mother. She also said she feels hurt when he doesn't tell her when she has done something to offend him (this violates their main rule—discussing disagreements when they occur). Brian feels hurt by things she says about his family. Sherry, too, violates her rule about discussing disagreements when they occur. She said she often picks at Brian for little things when she is really angry about something else but won't acknowledge it.

We gave them a paradoxical letter at the end of the session.

Session 4

Both seemed a little uncomfortable about the paradoxical letter. We told them we would discuss the letter in the feedback conference, and they were agreeable to that.

Sherry presented a great amount of resistance tonight. She couldn't seem to get into the lesson and responded only briefly or agreed with Brian's answers. Because of this, the lesson was not as effective as it might have been. The letter seemed to have made Sherry, in particular, a little more cautious in her behavior. Because this couple is so involved with control (control by Sherry and by Brian's mother), dealing with open-ended questions (with no rules to help them answer) forced them to depend on the I-ness within each of them.

Both had enjoyed the homework and had found shared meaning very helpful because they had been forced to listen more closely to each other.

Sherry and Brian denied that there are any areas in which they fail to be honest with each other. As the lesson continued, they responded more fully and openly. Their greatest competition seems to be in the instrumental areas, when Brian tries to deal with the outside world on behalf of the couple. Sherry "lets" him do this because "he needs to learn how." She, having worked in sales, has had adequate experience in this area and takes over for Brian when his inadequacies (temper and impatience) defeat him. Again, Sherry is the controlling mother, taking full responsibility for them in their marital relationship.

They still seem to be struggling with the issues we identified at the beginning of the sessions, but with more awareness. They are bringing more and more specific issues out into the open.

Session 5

Brian and Sherry told us that they discuss the lesson after we leave and that they've learned things they had not known about each other.

In discussing the homework, it seems they agreed that Sherry is more competent in planning and structuring (balancing checkbook) and that Brian is better at socializing (Sherry the computer, the rule-maker; Brian the more emotional partner). Several times Sherry "corrected" Brian. These are examples of her mothering, structuring, and judging when rules are broken. Brian readily admits his guilt, incompetence, and short-comings, like a recalcitrant but repentant boy.

Sherry: Brian made $5.34 in errors by entering checks wrong.
Brian: I got into it again. I'm totally incompetent in this.

In one exercise, Sherry asked Brian what he meant by "dogmatic." Then she said, "I must think about a better way to say it." Does Sherry have difficulty facing her control?

Brian is quite concerned about not being as considerate of Sherry as he could be.

Sherry said they could "always be willing to let each other do some things" in responding to how they could spend more time together and not grow apart. At one point, Sherry said to Brian, "You can discuss it, too. Is there anything else you want to add?" Is Sherry modeling the expert role?

In an exercise about where they would be in the future, Sherry finished a sentence for Brian, but she finished it wrong.

Brian: The only unknown—
Sherry: —is financial.
Brian: No, an area that offers a university.

Does Sherry play into Brian's guilt about her supporting him while he's in school? This was mentioned several times.

Sherry said at various times, "I wish I could go back to school one day"; "I wish I had more energy when I get home after work to do more things. I feel really bad when Brian has to do the dishes because I'm so tired." She also wished "to be more on our path for the future."

For Sherry, the only unknown about her going back to school is financial (does she lack faith in Brian's ability?); for Brian, the only unknown is their future location near a university.

Another exchange about their future went like this:

Brian: Something we need to work for [Sherry's going back to school] because you want to and you sorta gave it up for me.
Sherry: We haven't talked that much about my going back to school.

In Exercise 1, Brian wanted Sherry to be more patient, less dogmatic (inflexible). He took some of the edge off by saying he, too, was guilty. Sherry resisted the "dogmatic" aspect and put some of her blamed impatience on Brian because he misunderstood what she meant.

Sherry wanted Brian to be more patient and control his temper better. Brian agreed, saying his temper hurts Sherry, and chastised himself for not being fair to her by losing his temper before he listens to her.

In Exercise 2, Sherry said she could be more patient, could avoid picking at Brian for small things, and could be less "arbitrary" (which she substituted for "dogmatic").

Brian heard Sherry say, among the other things, that she could say things so that he could understand.

In naming the ways in which he could change, Brian said he is impatient, loses his temper, is dogmatic (he couldn't say this about her without putting it on himself also?), inconsiderate, and gruff. He also said he needs to listen more.

In expressing wishes and desires, Brian had difficulty separating his wishes and desires from those for the marriage.

Sherry wished (a) to get along better with in-laws; (b) to be on the path for their future; (c) that Brian will be with her (said they'll be happy); (d) not to be so impatient; (e) to go back to school; (f) that Brian wouldn't get so upset with Tammy (Sherry's sister); and (g) that she had more energy when she gets home from work.

Brian wished (a) for a good job, happiness, and security; (b) to have two kids, adopt a third; (c) to do things together as a couple; (d) to resolve problems with his parents; (e) to go to Europe for their 20th anniversary; and (f) to not grow apart, but to spend time together.

For discussion, Brian chose Sherry's No. 5 (go back to school); Sherry chose Brian's No. 6 (not to grow apart). They chose areas in which they agree but noted they could use their new skills to discuss areas in which they do not agree.

Sherry seems to be offering resistance; Brian seems to be trying to tie what he is learning into a meaningful whole.

Supervision.

We discussed the issues of control and likeness, or lack of differentiation.

PRE- AND POSTTEST EVALUATION

Sherry's overall scores on the pre- and posttest of the Marital Questionnaire rose from 90 to 98 points. Her likeness score improved 1 point (from 6 to 7), which indicates that she is becoming more differentiated from her family of origin and therefore (we hope) from her husband. Her priorities score jumped from 8 to 10, an indication of her increased awareness of issues and self. The dysfunction scores (including her 6 on computing on the pretest) increased 1 point, except for distracting (much of Sherry's resistance is enacted through avoiding by distracting). All scores on the tasks improved, except responsibility, which dropped from 6 to 5, and seeing the good, which dropped from 8 to 6. Forgiveness stayed the same. These seem to be the areas in which Sherry exhibits control. Her initial reaction to awareness of her control may have been to try to strengthen it. When her control is threatened (responsibility), she sees less good. The mother in her is losing control, which she tries to strengthen, and the little boy in Brian is now seen as engaging in more misbehavior (not following orders as well). Forgiveness may pertain to the problems with Brian's mother, as well as to issues in Sherry's relationship with Brian.

Brian's score on the Marital Questionnaire has also improved, from 104 on the pretest to 112 on the posttest. His likeness score is the same as on pretest (the issues with his parents are still unresolved), but his priorities score has doubled, from 5 to 10. Perhaps he is increasingly aware of himself but still lacks the ability to differentiate himself from his family of origin and his wife. Computing and distracting improved by 1 point (from 7 to 8); blaming and placating scores remained the same. On the tasks, protectiveness jumped from 6 to 9, perhaps because Sherry's assertiveness is beginning to take more honest and congruent channels and he can deal with it more openly. Her incongruent messages (nonverbal canceling) and her helplessness are disappearing, taking with them Brian's need to protect her. Sharing hurt dropped from 9 to 7, perhaps because of Brian's awareness and beginning recognition of the hurt he experiences in his poor relationship with his mother. As he becomes more aware, his initial reaction is to share less. His forgiveness score, like Sherry's, remained unchanged.

In summary, it appears some positive changes have been effected in this couple's relationship. They are becoming more aware and more honest with each other.

On the Semantic Differential, Sherry saw herself as less good, more square and selfish, and more important (reflects her giving up the guise of helplessness), more dangerous, and less aggressive. She saw Brian as much less good, useful, smart, superior, noisy, fast, kind, friendly, and selfish. This may reflect the changes in him as he becomes more autonomous and releases some of his defense mechanisms of noise and confusion. (Brian marked answers only once on the posttest, not crossing out and re-marking as he had done on the pretest.)

Brian's scores for himself on the Semantic Differential are similar to the pretest scores, except that he rated himself more unselfish, dangerous, powerful, strong, and independent (perhaps reflecting his newly aroused feelings of selfhood). He rated Sherry essentially the same as on pretest except that he saw her as softer, less aggressive and dangerous, more powerful and more independent. These ratings could reflect her beginning to differentiate from him, relinquishing some control over him, but gaining some control over herself as she gives up her helplessness.

On the Marital Happiness Scale, Sherry's score rose from 269 on the pretest to 279 on the posttest. She is still least satisfied with household responsibilities but seems to see the couple's general happiness as better. Her slightly lower scores on sex may indicate less denial and resistance on her part. Brian's score increased from 241 to 273 on this scale, reflecting his general improved happiness in every aspect of his marriage. He appears less tense and more sure of himself as well.

On Family Information, Sherry's score fell from 162 to 159. She seems to have been having some difficulty with work lately; otherwise, her scores have not changed much. Brian's scores fell from 153 to 141 from pre- to posttest. He is less satisfied with his occupational progress and with his marriage (reflecting his increased awareness in general).

On the Primary Communications Inventory, Sherry's scores increased from 86 on the pretest to 90 on the posttest. She appeared more uniformly satisfied with the expressive aspects on the posttest. Brian's scores decreased from 92 to 83. He seemed a little less satisfied in general with the expressive aspects of his marriage. Perhaps this reflects his new understanding and awareness of self.

The posttest scores indicate a general positive change over the pretest scores. Brian and Sherry seem more aware of themselves and of aspects of their relationship, such as control, interdependence, differentiation, and incongruencies. As they have become more satisfied with some, they have become more dissatisfied with others. The positive changes are Sherry's control and Brian's priorities.

FEEDBACK CONFERENCE

Brian and Sherry believe they have received many benefits from SE (perhaps their high level of motivation was further heightened by the fact they paid $5 per session!). Sherry, surprisingly, was the more vocal of the pair when it came to extolling the virtues of their experience. She said she has learned to argue constructively, to listen more to what Brian says, and to be more congruent. The congruency is illustrated by her recognition of the difference between her verbal message and what she really means (she is thus more aware of herself and of her husband). She said she understands Brian better and can see their differences more clearly, which indicates the beginning of differentiation. She said that their arguments about housekeeping had diminished, which she insightfully contributed to lessened misdirected anger. Further, she said she understands their responsibilities better. Sherry admitted that in the beginning she had felt "hesitant" about SE, threatened by the possibility that we might consider them "crazy" and by Brian's disapproval of some of her actions. Later, she discovered she really wanted to know more about what Brian thinks and feels. It was interesting that she could identify her resistance and work through some of it.

Brian, too, believes that gains have been made. He said they are listening more and arguing less. He noted that Sherry is more congruent and that she "comes to the point more." He described himself as more patient and objective, able to stand back and not talk for Sherry. This description reflects his beginning to find a definition of self apart from the marriage. He reinforced this idea by declaring that he is more aware of his feelings.

The issue of the letter arose, and both expressed uncertainty about the meaning and intention of our use of *interdependence*. We asked for their ideas on the topic, admitting that their accusation of vagueness was indeed legitimate, since we had hoped they would find meaning in it for themselves. (We were applying interdependence to them and to their relationship with their families.) The issue of Brian's family arose again. Sherry is very close to her family and said their relationship had changed very little since her marriage. Both admitted more distance from Brian's family, and Brian voiced his concern that Sherry overreacts to his family, particularly his mother. We acknowledged their concern and noted later that this area needs further exploration.

We complimented Brian and Sherry on their strength and motivation. They are a caring, intelligent, personable, responsible couple, and we told them so. We further complimented them on their heightened awareness and their ability to change, as evidenced by their having learned new skills and practiced more effective methods of communicating.

We added, however, that they sometimes fail to be interdependent. They polarize their responsibility by forcing one to be in charge within the marriage and the other to be in charge outside the marriage. They need to share responsibilities and to resolve some of their feelings about their conflict with Brian's parents, since it is a major concern and causes disagreements between them.

Last, we asked them where they wanted to go from here. They chose to continue SE and were distressed (particularly Sherry) that the female enricher would be unable to continue to work with them. They suggested continuing SE later if both enrichers would be available. We explained the circumstances and reassured them about continuing SE with a new enricher on the team.

CONCLUSIONS FROM FIRST SE

Brian and Sherry are a highly motivated couple who seem capable of becoming aware of and dealing with the issues in their relationship that may force them to change. They are genuinely interested in improving their marriage and very willing to work toward that end.

On the self-presentational level, they seem to have only minor areas of discord—household responsibilities and other relatively trivial areas. Brian is the gregarious one; Sherry is timid, controlling through her helplessness and her need for Brian's protectiveness. On the phenotypical level, Sherry sets the rules, and Brian allows her to do so. Her family of origin is the originator of the rules she follows so inflexibly and compulsively. She is the controlling mother, and he is the recalcitrant son. On the genotypical level, neither has differentiated from the family of origin and therefore from the marriage. Sherry defines herself by commission, by the rules and standards she lives by, and by Brian's approval of her. Brian defines himself by omission, losing sight of himself in the marriage. Without the marriage and his failure to live up to the rules (thereby becoming the bad little boy), his self-definition is vague.

Brian's mother is a controlling figure from whom he has rebelled. But he married another controlling woman. Sherry married a man like her father—warm, friendly, humorous. He, too, had rebelled against a controlling mother and married a controlling wife. Brian and Sherry are unconsciously perpetuating the roles they learned in their families of origin.

Before SE, their level of awareness was very low, but they have shown amazing ability for insight, with a minimum of guidance. The issues of control and of interdependence between themselves and their families have surfaced and are being dealt with expressively. They require further work in these areas and in personal definitions of the self. They were somehow aware that their inability to get along well with Brian's family was hindering their successful marital adjustment. They need to further clarify this problem and the feelings accompanying it.

In conclusion, Brian and Sherry are highly motivated and desirous of positive change in their relationship. Problems of differentiation from families of origin, self-definitions, control and interdependence, family of origin relationships, and the clarification of goals in their careers (a more future issue, perhaps) still exist. They have made gains in insight and awareness: Sherry admits her initial resistance and the incongruencies in her verbal and nonverbal communication; Brian is beginning to realize his separateness from Sherry. This realization is exemplified by his attempts to avoid speaking for her and by his emerging understanding of his responsibility to the relationship and of the control Sherry must exert when he allows her to be responsible for him.

This is a delightful couple who are functioning adequately but who could become less functional if their relationship continues in the present direction. The prognosis seems excellent.

SECOND SE
by Edgar Jessee and Flo P. Dawson

The Logans' motivation is apparent in their willingness to continue SE and to review openly with the new enricher their earlier sessions.

Brian seemed more open to change than was Sherry, who stood to lose her control in the relationship. She saw Brian as the problem and retreated when the focus turned her way, bringing Brian to her rescue. She frequently mothered him, scolding and shaking her finger. Brian occasionally exhibited an explosive temper. They said that in problem solving, Brian tends to overkill and Sherry to deal too soft a blow. Sherry frequently distracted with her persistent laughter and "playing dumb." They continued to exhibit a lack of differentiation by checking with each other before answering questions and in speaking for each other; Brian said that they are still working on negotiation skills and many of the same problems as before but that he has greater awareness now and that learning to share feelings has been the most helpful to him.

PRETESTS

Brian and Sherry were tested at the beginning and at the end of the first enrichment and were not tested again until the end of the second enrichment. The posttest scores of the first enrichment were used as the pretest scores for the second enrichment.

SUMMARY OF SESSIONS

Session 1

The first session was an opportunity for the couple and the new enricher to get to know each other. Brian and Sherry were very warm and responsive, although a degree of anxiety was evident in their movements and voice inflections. Asked to summarize the first enrichment, Brian and Sherry said that it had been very helpful, but they were vague in describing how it had been helpful: "It made us face issues we probably wouldn't have talked about." The most specific change they had observed was a decrease in the number of arguments they have—particularly arguments over trivial things (the presenting problem). They have shifted the focus from their relationship and said that Brian's mother is one of their main problems. We did not react to this red herring but let them present what they wanted to, knowing that we could deal with it later if it came up again.

Enrichers' notes.

Many of the patterns observed in the first enrichment were readily apparent. Sherry continues to exert control, both through her helplessness and through her mothering. Brian continues to go along, although he is using more "I" statements than before and thus does show some signs of separating himself from the relationship. Both still show evidence of avoiding a focus on their relationship (e.g., bringing up Brian's mother).

Supervision.

Our supervisor suggested that we avoid external issues that the couple attempts to bring up when the focus is on their relationship (for example, blaming their difficulties on their families). When they throw out red herrings, we are to refocus on their relationship.

We also talked about working together. It is very important for one enricher to have the other's permission before moving into unexplored territory with the couple. The analogy of doubles partners in tennis was suggested as a helpful model.

Session 2

Tonight we began our work together, using the role-playing exercises from the Working-Through Program. We were able to apply the role playing to a recent conflict Brian and Sherry had experienced. They were dealing with a salesclerk who was pictured as incompetent. Brian initially handled the interaction but soon became very angry and exploded at the clerk. Sherry stepped in, assumed control, and handled the situation. The couple admitted that this is a frequent pattern with social encounters and that in their own conflicts Sherry controls the resolution. Sherry described Brian as incompetent in this area. Brian said that he dislikes this kind of experience and finds it frustrating. Brian was able to see how he played into Sherry's controlling mother role by playing the explosive, rebellious child. Sherry, however, was reluctant to give Brian the opportunity to display his competence and generally seemed uncomfortable with giving him control.

Enrichers' notes.

We have isolated the following dynamics: (a) Sherry is still presenting Brian as the problem, and he continues to collude in this. (b) Brian plays the child role, and Sherry plays the mother during conflict. (c) Sherry says she wants Brian to share more feelings, but when he does she discourages him through her controlling and mothering behavior. (d) Brian is expressing some awareness of his role in this process. (e) More role playing with role reversal might be appropriate for this couple.

Supervision.

Our supervision centered on the couple's lack of self-differentiation within the relationship. Both partners lack a clear self-boundary and seem so loyal to each other that they are unable to separate. Each seems to communicate, "You are responsible for me." Our supervisor suggested that their likeness interferes with the learning of communication skills. Because we have seen marked improvement for short periods, then gradual regression to the old problems, our supervisor suggested that we use a paradoxical technique to induce change in this couple. We are to state that we've reached a point at which we are very pessimistic about them and their progress, so we must have failed. Having said that, we are to leave.

Session 3

We began by asking about the homework. They had done the homework but had misinterpreted what we considered obvious instructions. Instead of working on what prevents each of them from sharing feelings, they had thought about what prevents each of them from bringing up their own thoughts and ideas. We worked with the couple's definition of the homework, which eventually boiled down to an absence of sharing feelings and a fear of sharing. They had great difficulty elaborating why they were unable to share their feelings and looked to us to help them with this problem. We tried to use the lesson on role reversal to work on some real conflict situations. Basically we discovered that they fear that expressing their feelings will ultimately drive them apart.

At the end of our session, the couple began to exclaim (as usual) about how much they had learned tonight. We used the paradoxical maneuver suggested in supervision, saying that they were dealing with old issues repeatedly and that they seemed unable to institute any real change.

Enrichers' notes.

The focus in tonight's session was the sharing of feelings. We also noted that the couple again sabotaged the homework. They seemed very surprised when we said that no real change was occurring. Although they did not respond verbally, it is our hunch that we will hear about it next time.

Supervision.

Our supervisor suggested that the couple's confusion is being highlighted and noted that facing their confusion is not easy. If they get

upset, what are they going to look at? If we disagree with them, they
have to look at themselves more closely; if we agree, we enter into
collusion with them.

Their relationship system isn't changing. For them, change is talking,
not doing. We are to remind them not to say "you" but to say "we"
("you" is judgmental and divisive—distancing). They need to get away
from verbal communication and use more nonverbal communication.

We might tell them that we appreciate what they have done in terms
of performance but ask them, "What about underlying issues?" We might
also ask about the end of the preceding session: "What did you hear?
What were you feeling?"

Session 4

First, Brian and Sherry asked about the end of the preceding session.
They said they were angry because we had told them that we saw no
real change, yet they feel change is taking place, albeit slowly. Sherry
appeared most upset and frequently said that Brian was trying to change
but that it would take time. At this point, Brian disagreed and said that
he knew what we were talking about and that maybe the changes hadn't
been as deep as they thought. Both indicated that they had given extensive
thought to their relationship (and the issue of change in it) since our
last session. We congratulated them on this and generally attempted to
reframe the situation positively without "softening" our statement about
the lack of deep change.

Brian and Sherry then pushed for our evaluation of their difficulties
and what they could do about them. We briefly outlined the key
problems—likeness, control, awareness—and offered them an exercise
"if you *really* want to change." They readily agreed to proceed, and we
used one of their recent conflicts to illustrate our points. Sherry seemed
to hear what we were saying about her control, but she attempted to
deny it later.

Their homework assignment was to use the experiential role-playing
lesson as a contract for new conflict behavior.

Enrichers' notes.

We seem to have put the couple in an untenable position: we have
said they aren't changing; they insist they want to change. Now we
have given them a behavioral contract that will necessitate change. They
must either comply or acknowledge the fact that they don't want to
change. Their only other alternative is to discount our observations (which
they have already acknowledged are fairly accurate) or discount the

contract, which they helped write. We expect them to follow through with the change dictated by their contract.

Supervision.

We began by reporting our observations on our paradoxical intervention. It did produce an explosion, which should lead to change. Our supervisor pointed out the importance of congratulating the couple on their ability to get angry and thus share their feelings. This in itself is a big change for Brian and Sherry, one that we hope to explore in future sessions.

Session 5

In this session, we covered the lesson called Sharing Feelings. Sherry had great difficulty with the lesson. She began by being unable to do the role-playing exercises. She also expressed the fact that she always has control over her emotions; however, when we complimented her on this ability a few minutes later, she denied it. Everyone, including Brian, became annoyed at Sherry and confronted her with her inconsistencies and lack of commitment to the lesson. Sherry only became more defensive. Finally, we quit confronting and agreed with her. At this point, she seemed to be able to see some of the things she was doing and slowly backed away from her confrontive and defensive stance.

Enrichers' notes.

We have concluded that confronting Sherry does not work. Perhaps the best strategy to use with her is paradoxical interventions. She gets very uncomfortable when she has little control over the sharing of feelings. She seems to need to be in control to feel comfortable. Brian, however, reacted enthusiastically to tonight's session and shows the potential to want to change the current balance of power in their relationship.

Supervision.

Several helpful suggestions were offered in supervision today. (a) Since confrontation is not working with this couple, we should agree with them and highlight the good points that they present. Confrontation strengthens this couple's system. (b) Sherry's need to be in control probably carries over into their sexual relationship.

Session 6

Tonight Sherry was much more cooperative, and we complied by not confronting her. Yet, both were rather cool and uninvolved in the lesson (Achieving Equality). They went through the motions of answering all the questions but exhibited little affective involvement. They commented that this lesson was not particularly helpful for them and that they had thus remained essentially uninvolved. We did not challenge their reasons but said that perhaps the content would be more meaningful in the future.

Enrichers' notes.

Brian exhibited some protectiveness of Sherry by distracting whenever issues arose that could evoke conflict. Sherry colluded in his distraction by trying to bring up the red herring of Brian's mother again.

Supervision.

It was suggested that perhaps Brian and Sherry were distancing from the intensity of Session 6 (by their rather cool behavior), signaling that they did not want to get into any problem issues.

Our supervisor suggested that perhaps this couple has gone as far as they can with SE. We discussed giving them more homework assignments and fewer sessions with us.

Session 7

We briefly discussed the events of the past week, administered the posttests, and gave Brian and Sherry a homework assignment for the coming week.

The couple reported few problems or conflicts within the past week. They were quick to point out that difficulties still arise but that they are handling them better now, primarily through sharing feelings. The major disagreement that had arisen was the question of whether Brian should play intramural football. Brian wants to play, but Sherry objects because she fears for his physical safety. The issue seems to involve Sherry's motherly protectiveness and the question of individual desire versus relationship pressures. Therefore, their homework assignment was to distinguish the difference between actions of selfishness and actions of selfhood.

Enrichers' notes.

We are encouraged that Brian and Sherry believe they are handling their conflicts better. Sherry's need to control and Brian's "childishness" arose again in the issue of whether he should play football. They became hooked in a mother-child interaction, which temporarily precluded the sharing of feelings. However, they finally shifted into a primarily adult-adult interaction and shared their feelings effectively enough to satisfy both of them.

Supervision.

It was suggested that we congratulate the couple on their improvement—"The way you have improved is tremendous!" Also, we should praise their persistence, work, and general relationship.

POSTTEST EVALUATION

On the Marital Questionnaire, Sherry's scores range from 6 to 9, for a total of 98 points. She still scored lower on likeness (7), responsibility (5), and seeing the good (6). She identified strongly with her family of origin and Quaker background, seeing them as unchallengeable. She admitted that she does not want to share feelings or negotiate all issues, only the big ones, and that she depends on her conscience in making her own decisions, after which she tells Brian what she has decided. The scores on seeing the good (6), forgiveness (7), and blaming (1) reflect the fact that Sherry sees Brian and his mother's relationship as their problem; she is reluctant to accept a share of the blame and responsibility for the problems in the relationship. Sherry also scored 7 on protectiveness, distracting, and computing. She demonstrated in the sessions her ability to distract from uncomfortable personal issues and to compensate with more "rational, logical" approaches. Placating, enjoyment, and caring received scores of 8; priorities received 10. SE has further clarified the couple's priorities (i.e., issues are becoming clearer), but they are not yet satisfied with their success in dealing with the issues.

Brian's scores total 112; his scores range from 7 to 10. Scores of 7 were given to likeness and sharing hurt. Brian is aware of withholding feelings and, to some degree, his and Sherry's lack of differentiation. He has not resolved his problems with his family and sees himself as somewhat of a problem in the marriage. Scores of 8 were given computing, distracting, and forgiveness, 9 to placating, caring, enjoyment, protectiveness, responsibility, and seeing the good. Brian's habitual apologizing and blaming himself is diminishing some. He seems to sense Sherry's refusal to be wrong and protects her in it, a role he has played with his mother and his sister. A score of 10 on priorities seems to reflect his ability to take care of himself, a characteristic we did not observe early in this second program. Possibly, for him, priorities are his interest in working on their marrige relationship. We did not expect a 10 on blaming because Brian tends to blame himself.

On the Sexual Happiness Scale, Sherry's scores total 279 (self 123, spouse 124, individual 132, ranging from 7 to 9). Household reponsibilities was scored 7; money, occupational progress, frequency of sex (spouse), foreplay (self), kissing (spouse), fondling (self), and orgasm (self) were scored 8. Each remaining item was scored 9. Sherry rated herself as slightly less satisfied in foreplay, fondling, and orgasm. Brian's total score on the Sexual Happiness Scale was 273 (self 124, spouse 124, individual 25, ranging from 8 to 9). He rated Sherry as slightly more satisfied in frequency of sex and social activities; he rated himself as slightly more satisfied in kissing and in orgasm.

On Family Information (18-item), Sherry's scores total 159, with scores ranging from 5 to 10. She had previously expressed some dissatisfaction with her occupation and scored that item 5 and occupational progress 7. Except for present relationship with close relatives, which was scored 8, Sherry scored every other item 9 or 10.

Brian's scores total 141, ranging from 5 to 10. He scored present occupation 5 and occupational progress 7. Another 7 was given to present relationship with close relatives, indicating the confusion in his sorting out loyalties between family of origin and new marriage. The remaining items were scored 8 and 10, all scores of 10 going to his relationship with Sherry. He omitted two items, religious participation and parenthood, which falsely lowered his total score.

On Family Information (10-item), Sherry's total score is 90 (she scored each of the 10 items as 9). These scores indicate a high degree of satisfaction in her present relationship with Brian.

Brian's satisfaction is apparently high in this area also; his total score is 83, with scores of 8 and 9.

On the Semantic Differential, Sherry rated herself as slightly good, superior, smart, friendly, kind, important, pleasant, quiet, strong, and slightly soft, helpful, powerful and independent. She gave herself a higher rating on useful and neutral ratings on small, slow, aggressive and dangerous. She rated Brian slightly favorably on most items. She rated herself slightly more useful and selfish but somewhat smaller and less aggressive than Brian.

Brian rated himself highest on noisy and useful. He rated Sherry as slightly more quiet, harmless, big, soft, unselfish, and good; he rated himself as slightly more helpful and friendly. The remainder of his scores are in the neutral range.

PRE- AND POSTTEST COMPARISON

In comparing the posttest scores from the first enrichment (using them as pretest scores) with the posttest scores from the second enrichment, we found that most scores show slight improvement or remain the same.

Both partners exhibited fairly high scores with somewhat narrow ranges and only slight variations. Using this general pattern as a guide for the pre- and posttest comparison, we wish to mention the exceptions to this trend.

On the Marital Happiness Scale, Sherry's total score on marital happiness is 99, ranging from 4 to 9, which is similar to her 98 on the tests used as pretest. She decreased her ratings on priorities, blaming, and protectiveness (2 to 3 points), and increased responsibility (4 points). Sherry may have felt less protective and blaming toward Brian by the end of this program as her unwillingness to change became more apparent. In her resistance to change, she possibly saw herself as being even more responsible than before. Brian's total score on the Marital Questionnaire is 104, with a range of 5 to 10. He showed a decrease of 2 points on blaming, 4 points on protectiveness, and 2 points on seeing the good. These scores reflect his awareness of the importance of differentiation in the marriage and his diminishing habit of blaming himself. By the end of the second enrichment, he felt less protective of Sherry and was more able to speak up for himself.

On the Sexual Happiness Scale, Sherry's ratings remain essentially the same—a total of 276 compared with 279 points on the pretest. She showed a slight increase in happiness and household responsibilities and a slight decrease in money and occupational progress. During SE, she became more aware of Brian's willingness to help her at home when she speaks up for her needs.

Brian's scores, too, remain essentially the same—a total of 272 compared with 273 on the pretest. He gave each item a rating of 8 or 9.

On Family Information (18-item), Sherry's scores remain the same except for a slight decrease in satisfaction with occupational progress.

Brian's posttest score is 160, compared with 141 on the pretest. He eliminated religious participation as well as parenthood on the pretest; he eliminated only parenthood on the posttest, falsely lowering the pretest score. His scores remain in the range of 7 to 10. One exception is a 3-point increase in satisfaction with present occupation, which may mean that his increased self-esteem in his marriage is carrying over into other areas.

On Family Information (10-item), Sherry's total score is 82, compared with 90 on the pretest. The difference is accounted for by a drop of 1 point in most of her ratings.

Brian's total score is 90, compared with 83 on the pretest. The difference is accounted for by an increase of 1 point in most of his ratings. This slight trend reflects our clinical observation that exploring their relationship has led to greater satisfaction for Brian and to less satisfaction for Sherry because her position is being challenged.

On the Semantic Differential, Sherry did not change any of her ratings about herself. All the ratings are in the middle range except that she moved 1 point toward useful; none of the ratings moved more than 1 point. This is in keeping with Sherry's perception that she is not part of their problem. Neither did Sherry change her spouse ratings more than 1 point except for aggressive-helpful, which she moved 2 points toward aggressive, and quiet-noisy, which she moved 3 points toward noisy. These ratings probably reflect Brian's new ability to stick up for himself, to be somewhat more confrontive, and to stop blaming himself.

Brian's change in his position in the marriage is apparent to both of them because Brian also did not change any of his ratings except selfish-unselfish and tough-soft, both of which he moved 2 points toward selfish and tough. Brian rated Sherry within 1 point of the pretest ratings on this scale except for tough-soft, which he moved 4 points toward tough, and strong-weak, which he moved 2 points toward weak. These contradictory ratings may be explained by the fact that a person needs to be strong to admit being part of a problem and tough to persist in being right. Sherry meets both requirements. (These ratings may also be incidental.)

The ratings on the Semantic Differential confirm our clinical observations that Brian is more willing than Sherry to change personally for their marriage but that he has continued to protect her position.

FEEDBACK CONFERENCE

Brian and Sherry reported that they have an increased awareness of how they interact in their relationship. They also reported fewer conflicts and an ability to work out those conflicts by sharing feelings. Brian is more assertive, and Sherry is relinquishing some of her power.

We congratulated them for having worked so hard and told them we had benefited from working with a normal couple. We told them that there still seem to be a few problems they should be aware of. Briefly, they have not yet separated and explored their selfhood completely. They have come a long way in sharing feelings, but they need to continue working on this area. We mentioned also the issue of control and Sherry's assuming the mother role while Brian plays the rebellious child. We presented possible options, but they chose to do nothing right now.

CONCLUSIONS AND RECOMMENDATIONS

From their families of origin, Brian and Sherry brought many behaviors that have contributed to entrenching each of them in those positions in their new marriage. Sherry's behavior and her description of her sisters indicate that control is an important issue in her family. Both partners indicated that Brian's position in his family had been one of mediator, placater, peacemaker, caught between his coercive mother and his way-ward sister. Two SE programs have allowed them to discover their own contribution to the cycle of their conflicts, especially to the mother–bad boy relationship. They have found considerable success in resolving these conflicts, through practicing the sharing of feelings with each other. This one communication skill has given them better communication and real acquaintance with each other. They have become aware of their need to move away from dependency in the relationship toward individual development and separateness. Brian's change in this area is more ap-parent than Sherry's; he has moved from placater to a more assertive role and is experiencing much success with this. Sherry seems not to have yet decided to yield some of her control to Brian, but she is aware of the need to do so. As they adjust to their new positions in the marriage, we have recommended that they determine their goals and continue either in SE or in therapy, as a couple or as individuals.

25

A "Straight" Family

Cinda Caiella

This case study illustrates how SE can work with a variety of families, in this case, a drug-dependent family. The objective results and the satisfaction expressed by this family have given us sufficient confidence to continue this approach with other drug-dependent families.

INTERVIEW

At the interview, I met the Adams family, a blended family chosen by Straight, a program for chemically dependent families, and Jessica Hall, a junior staff member of Straight, who sat in on all sessions to provide liaison with Straight.

After explaining SE in general, I noted that the Adams family had been chosen as a "good" family that could give good feedback and thus help us evaluate the program.

Dan and Beth Adams have been married for 3 years; he works in electronics, and Beth does part-time clerical work. Dan, aged 41, has been married twice before; he has two children (one of whom is autistic) from his first marriage. Julie, aged 16, is, for the third time, in Phase II in the Straight program; she has been in Straight for 11 months but has had trouble going through the phases smoothly. Jason, aged 10, was described by the Straight observer as the forgotten child, one who seeks attention but who has not yet worked out a relationship with his stepfather.

The observer also confided that Beth, aged 39, was married to an alcoholic for 15 years, that it had been hard for her to divorce, and that she still suffers from a lack of self-confidence. Beth has an older son

369

(aged 20) who lives south of the city, is married, and is expecting his first child soon. The family had lived in that area, near Dan's job, but moved to another county, near the Straight offices, because of the amount of time they are required to be at Straight. Unable to see her son as often as before the move, Beth misses him very much.

Carrie, Dan and Beth's child, is 18 months old. Living with the Adams family are three other teenaged girls, Straight members who board with the family as part of the program.

So that I would know about Straight, its terminology, and its rules for families, the observer provided materials that are given to families as part of their orientation to Straight. Many times during the first session, I asked questions about terminology (e.g., "insecurity raps") that the family was using, primarily to see whether the family could explain the terms to an outsider. The family has adopted not only the Straight jargon but the practices, and they have incorporated into their family the ideas behind the jargon and the practices. The Straight program seems to be working well for them, providing them with the tools they need to grow and develop as a family. In the discussion about which program might be useful for them, the communication and problem-solving programs seem similar to the approach used at Straight, differing primarily in terminology. Because the family is new (blended) and already trying to change through Straight, we discussed choosing a program that deals with life goals—what the family is aiming for.

To see whether the Clarification of Values Program would reach the family as currently structured, I tried some questions. First, I asked, "What are some of the important rules in the family?"

Jason answered first: not to joke when the girls are at home; not to scream at Carrie; have his mother oversee and schedule his homework because he can stay up and watch TV if he gets his homework done (Beth added that Jason has some trouble at school).

Julie responded that she has to do her "moral inventory," eat, be responsible for others, be in bed by midnight. She also noted that the family has to read the Bible and say the Lord's Prayer every evening (her mother interjected that the family is religious and that reading the Bible is a Straight suggestion that they have readily adopted). Julie continued, saying that she must not leave a fight: "I must stay to work it out, without profanity; I must not go to bed without resolving it."

Beth answered that she can no longer expect the children to "do as I say, not as I do" (especially about smoking). Another rule is to respect her authority; that is, her husband is her authority. She has to do mountains of laundry and cook, but she consults with Dan about any rules that are needed.

Dan began by going through a long list, the rules on the Straight handout. When questioned, he explained that the family has adopted all the rules of Straight and that the rules are working fine. He and the rest of the family (except, perhaps, Jason) found it strange that I asked them about adopting these rules; the Straight observer kept adding that certain rules are required of the Straight program participants. It was somewhat difficult to get a sense of the family apart from Straight; the uncertainty became more apparent when I asked whether the rules keep the family from doing things that they value. All answered no and could think of no rules that they wish to change.

To get them to consider their values more directly, I asked: "What would you like to be when you're 'grown up,' in the future?"

Julie answered that she would like to be on the staff at Straight, to be active in church, and to travel and share what she has learned. Jason wants to be a mechanic or a missionary. He explained that an uncle, Beth's brother, is a missionary and that he is currently home for a visit.

Dan said that he wants to retire (he enjoys carpentry and also likes camping). Dan helps with computer work, and when pressed about which job he would like to advance to before retirement, he mentioned research analyst. Beth responded that she wants to be "myself, wife, and mother. I clean house well. I would like to buy an old house and renovate it and have a lot of land. I'd like to be a 'country grandmother,' watching my grandchildren play on the land."

Supervision.

In supervision we discussed including the Straight observer as a coenricher.

PRETEST RESULTS

Jason did not complete the pretests.

Homes-Rahe Schedule of Events

Although there have been many changes in the family in the past 18 months, there was much agreement among the responses made by Beth, Dan, and Julie.

Beth noted stresses related to sleep, eating, recreation, social concerns, church, family get-togethers, arguments, residence, health, traffic tickets, personal achievement, working hours, a small loan, and vacation.

Dan indicated stresses from business readjustment, a son's leaving home, work responsibilities, living conditions, Beth's going to work, a different line of work, marital reconciliation. These were in addition to the stresses that Beth noted. Julie added to her mother's list traffic tickets and line of work.

Family Life Questionnaire (Rochester Scales)

Both husband and wife consider themselves happier than before (their scores were only two places apart on this item). Beth noted disagreements more often; Dan said less often. Beth and Dan agreed that the main problem of the past year has been Julie's drug problem. On spouse's love and affection, Beth was a little more disappointed than was Dan.

The family has undergone much stress and many changes. Only 3 years earlier, they had Julie's problem to work through plus marriage plus Jason (who was not even mentioned in the tests). Their marital arrangement is fairly traditional; both are fairly satisfied, from a middle-class background, and religious.

SUMMARY OF SESSIONS

Session 1

Jason, who was away at camp, missed this session.

I was somewhat concerned about getting the same kind of "required" answers that the earlier questions had elicited, but I began with cognitive-experiential exercises on family strengths.

Before the session began, Beth mentioned that she had had a reaction to the preceding session, specifically to my statement that the family had been chosen as a "good" family. Beth said that she had felt very down because they are not good enough and have so far to go. Dan concurred, saying that he has felt "despair" because they are not good enough and mentioned that he had had a minor fight at work.

In Exercise 1, I asked everyone to name his or her strengths. After some trouble deciding who would go first, Beth began. "I am stronger with the kids and the family, not backing down, standing up, and feeling competent." Dan said that his strengths are awareness (a Straight term, which I asked him to define) of people (Dan noted that he is better at this with kids than with adults) and confidence in himself, noting that he has become more outgoing, even at his work, where he used to feel isolated.

Julie answered that her strength is tough love (another Straight term), which she explained with an example: "Mother sets herself apart and I won't let her." Dan added that tough love is a caring love; the Straight observer also explained the term and added that Straight had used it before the Tough Love Program adopted it. Beth acknowledged that Julie gives her a hard time but that it is for her (Beth's) own good. Dan summarized by saying that the family has become more caring and is improving in strength and respect (another Straight term) for others.

When I asked them to name the strengths in one another, Julie began: "Mom has changed a lot; she sticks up for herself but has time for all of us, including Dan." Dan added that Beth has awareness and identifies problems, and noted that he and Beth work together to grow and help each other.

Beth said that there has been a big change in Dan, that he has gotten tougher. Julie listed Dan's awareness, his listening, and his relationship with Jason. Beth added that Dan shares, is easy to talk with, and shows feelings and love.

Beth said that Julie's strength is her love. "She gives hugs; she's getting stronger with me and is proud of me." Dan said that Julie's strengths are her ego, awareness, strength, tough love, and caring; he added that she still has responsibilities around the house.

There was some general talk about Jason, Carrie, and Beth's older son, thus including them in the family. Beth contrasted the family with "friends" at work and those outside Straight, who cannot understand what the family is going through and who do not share their values, such as not swearing or drinking. She made a point that she and Dan would repeat many times: I was the first outsider with whom they have been able to share what has happened to them. Julie mentioned other families who share at open meetings.

Because the family was clinging to the Straight jargon and seemed to have little confidence in themselves (even though they said they had changed), I went on to fantasy exercises to see how the family would function in wildly unstructured situations. These exercises are less personal than the preceding ones, which the family found difficult.

First, I asked, "How would you spend $10,000?" Dan answered that he would go camping, buy a recreation vehicle, go to the mountains in the fall when it's cool, just get away and relax. Beth would go to the Bahamas (where they had spent their honeymoon), where there's peace and tranquillity and where she'd like to shop and eat. Julie said that she would go to Hawaii when she reached the seventh step, the ultimate phase of the Straight program.

The goals they mentioned are individual goals. To get at problem solving, I chose another exercise. "There is danger—you are in a boat that is drifting. What would you do?" Julie responded that she would pray and catch birds so that they could use the heads as fishing bait. Beth said that it would be "every man for himself" but that she would pray and look to Dan. Dan answered that he would try to get a means of locomotion, such as a female whale. Beth contended that Dan, with his camping experience, should be able to save them.

Next I asked them how they would survive is they were marooned on an island. Beth said that they could invent games and communicate (she commented that it didn't sound bad). She mentioned that they would need food and would miss Cokes.

Dan expressed a Crusoe fantasy: his health would be better and he would be able to do things such as open coconuts. Julie said that, with Dan, she would learn and would meet the challenge. She commented that she would miss TV and radio but that if they had a Bible, it might be OK.

Supervision.

The family's self-image has come through all the programs. I noted that doing the exercises has been slow because the family wants to process everything, as they have been doing at Straight. The supervisor suggested that I concentrate on gamelike exercises that are light and fun. Can they have fun as a family (i.e., not duplicate Straight business)?

Session 2

For this session, I drew on earlier, successful work with a single parent and a 9-year-old for whom I had researched family drawings and art exercises.

The first instruction was to scribble on a piece of paper (this kept baby Carrie happy). The Straight observer and I also drew, leaving the family to work on their own.

When the scribbles were finished, the instructions were to look at the scribbles and find or make a picture in them. Beth made PacMan, a pig, of her random scribbles. Dan had made boxes; on the reverse, he demonstrated (to Julie's delight) a doodle that he had done in school— a box that contains every number and every letter of the alphabet. Julie had drawn various shapes, which she made into a heart, *hello*, a man's face, a starfish in the sea, curled fingers, a sprinkler seen from above, a flower. Last was Jason's drawing, which he had a hard time calling anything; he finally decided that it was a mountain with a man's face in it. He also wrote the alphabet on his page, sitting to the side of the family group while Dan explained his box doodle.

The next instruction was for the family to draw one picture. There was much discussion among the family members as they decided how to do this, asking twice whether each member was to draw some or they were to choose one idea that would then be drawn by one person. I deliberately kept the instructions vague. The family powwowed while the Straight observer and I talked about her life in Straight, as a member and a staffer, her college courses, and her career plans. The family took a long time to complete their drawing. I overheard, "Add Carrie." Dan drew first, then Beth, then Julie, then Jason (in age order). They shifted positions at each person's turn, leaving the paper in place on the table. They seemed somewhat hesitant to stop and show the drawing.

The picture, drawn on the reverse of Jason's scribble-drawing, showed a house, a tree, the sun, Dan in his camper, and the dog, Brutus, near some swings in the yard. Inside the house was a stove, a Bible, a book, a motorcycle, a Christmas tree, a hamster, a computer, and a pet snake—all clearly labeled. Julie had labeled the drawing and had drawn many of the objects inside the house. Jason had added the snake and the dog, Beth the stove and the house outline, Dan the motorcycle he wished for and the picture of himself in the camper. The family considered the picture a good representation except that they have no pet snake.

The next exercise is from Using Your Imagination, in the program called Knowing Your Family. I instructed the family to work together to make a machine with sound and movement; the family members were to have physical contact with one another but not to talk as they made the machine. This exercise proved difficult. With some talking and a little physical contact, Dan lined them up and tried to make them work as pistons in a car, every other one bending at the knees, then the other members bending at the knees. Beth never understood and tried to bend along with both groups. Jason remained off to the side. Julie said that it had to make noise, which she did hesitantly; the others did not follow her lead. Dan explained that the machine was supposed to have been pistons, adding, to everyone's laughter, that it had become a broken motor. This exercise took the family a long time to begin and to complete.

Supervision.

The supervisor observed that the fun exercises had been good and suggested that I make a list of all of them.

Session 3

This session began with Introspecting, from the Experiential-Cognitive Program. I asked the family to relax (eyes closed) and be aware of their breathing. After a few moments, I asked them to listen and describe what they heard. They responded as follows: the Straight observer—a Straight meeting down the hall; Dan—the sound of his breathing; Julie—the air-conditioning, the meeting, the sounds of others' breathing.

Exercise 3, a breathing exercise, was difficult for everyone because they had become aware of their breathing during Exercise 2. Beth mentioned how hard it was for her to breathe while thinking about it.

I then returned to Using Your Imagination, from Knowing Your Family, and gave the following instructions: "Keeping your eyes closed, imagine yourself in a movie theater; look around and see an animal on the screen. See yourself as the animal; look at it closely. What kind of animal is it? What movements does it make? Noises? Be that animal."

Jason said that he would be a leopard, eating another leopard, growling and making sounds like a cat. Julie said that she would be a donkey, stuck on a cactus, crying. The Straight observer said that she would be her cat, pouncing on a lizard, purring in the back of the throat. Dan said that he would be a giraffe, its head moving back and forth, silent. Beth would be a gorilla, little, lying around in the trees, making a high-pitched squeal.

In Exercise 4, I asked them to imagine the animal in a cage and describe how it feels. Then they were to describe the animal when it's free and tell where the animal is when it's free.

Beth said that the gorilla would be lonely without others but would be free in the jungle, killing. Julie said that the donkey would be lonely in a cage. The donkey, when free, would be in the mountains, drinking from a creek and playing. The Straight observer said that the cat would be scared in a cage; when free, it would be in the backyard and the woods, climbing trees. Dan said that the giraffe would be cramped in a cage. Free, the giraffe would be taking long strides across the prairie. Jason first said that the leopard would not be as happy in the cage. The leopard would be free in the trees but would like the swinging tree, bananas, peanuts, and the attention he would get in the cage. Jason then changed his first statement and said the leopard would like it better in a cage.

Next, I used Sculpting, from Working Together. This exercise was chosen as a good nonverbal exercise to explore the feelings and the structure of the family. The family had had so much trouble doing the machine exercise that I was unsure of their ability to do the sculpting.

First, the family members, in turn, were to position the family in a living sculpture, demonstrating the current family structure. Julie volunteered to sculpt first and placed chairs in a line, facing out. She put Beth and Dan next to each other, Dan's arm around Beth, both turned a little toward Carrie on the left. Jason was placed to their right in a "speak no evil" pose. Julie left herself out. (Jason laughed to himself throughout Julie's sculpting.)

Jason started to do the family next, as it had been 2 years earlier. When he got stuck, Beth took over. She placed Jason, hands to his eyes, to the left of a triangle made up of Dan, herself, and Julie. Beth's finger was pointing at Julie; Julie's stance, hands on hips, was defiant. Julie almost began to cry, saying later that she had felt hurt. Beth agreed that it was hard to relive that time (2 years earlier), which had been just before Julie joined Straight. The family had been in turmoil; she and Julie had been fighting all the time.

Jason then sculpted the family, placing four chairs in a square, Beth and Dan facing each other, Carrie and Jason facing each other, Julie seated in a chair against the wall. The family was doing the budget, and Dan was pointing and gesturing at Beth, who was trying to attend to Carrie. Jason explained that Julie was away at Straight (relief filled Julie's face as she learned why she had been banned from the table). The family laughed at the enactment of doing the budget, breaking the tension from the earlier sculpting. Time ran out while Dan was trying to think of a sculpting situation (he had been a fairly reluctant participant).

Supervision.

We discussed the power of sculpting, and the supervisor reminded me to tell the family in the feedback conference how far they seem to have come in the past 2 years.

Session 4

Jason missed this session; he was visiting relatives in another city.

I wanted to return to goals and self-esteem but keep the exercises in the realm of fantasy, so I used exercises from various lessons and programs.

First, I asked them to imagine themselves as famous historic persons. Julie could not at first think of one but finally said, "Anita Bryant, because she stood up and didn't worry about what people thought of her" (she later apologized twice for this answer, saying she just couldn't think of an historic person). Beth said that she would be Joan of Arc, full of courage and strength, willing to die for her beliefs. Dan said that Abraham Lincoln popped into his mind because of his character, strength, and determination. Dan added that Lincoln had changed the way people thought and that he was a self-made man.

Next I asked them to choose living persons they admired (not scientists, as specified in the instructions, because I wanted to make the exercise easy for the family and also wanted to ease Julie's feelings). Beth chose Mother Teresa of Calcutta, about whom she had read. Dan chose Jerry Lewis, a "humanitarian actor." Julie said that movie stars came to her mind—Sandy Duncan, for example, who is comfortable with herself, even though she has only one eye.

Asked to describe the ideal car, Julie said that it would be bigger than the one they have. Beth, observing that they have five girls, asked, "How about a Cadillac station wagon?" Dan's response was "a hearse." Julie said, "a Lincoln Continental, with velour, automatic seats." She said that Dan could get a hat like a chauffeur's. Beth added, "a Lincoln Continental—not red, but black." Dan suggested a gray Mercedes. Dan and Beth talked about color, but Beth conceded immediately to the idea of a Mercedes. Julie added that it should have a hitch for Dan's camper.

For the next exercise, I asked, "Where will each of you be in 5 years?" Julie said that she might be married or might be at home, that she would be 21 years old, might have a maid, might be pregnant, living on the land in a simple house with a pond and swings. She would cook, grow flowers, visit her mom, help with kids, volunteer at church, and do baby-sitting.

Beth said that she would have a country house and a garden. She would be a grade mother for Carrie's school. She would have children and grandchildren, would quit work and stay home. Dan said that he would have a home away from the city, a more solid career, would watch more football and would watch Jason play football.

When I asked, "Where will each of you be in 10 years?" Beth said, "I'll be 49, Carrie only 11; I'll be the same as in 5 years." Julie said that she would be 26 years old, have two kids, would be adopting more (over the age of 9), redoing furniture, and would have hobbies and a house. Asked what she would need, Julie said that she would need money—a bank loan—and that she would need to learn to cook and get a husband.

Continuing in the same vein, I asked them to describe the family future, the family goals. Beth mentioned family vacations, Sundays together (all would live in the same town), and a toy room for the children. Julie said that they would have home movies and that they would be protective of what they have. Dan listed patience, being realistic, finding meaning in life, closeness.

Next the family members were asked to share a dream or a fantasy. Julie described a dream. Jesus would come to Stone Mountain and the good would go to heaven. "I'm scared that I'll be left on earth and judged. I've had this dream since we lived in Greenville and our bikes were stolen." Dan said that he dreams infrequently. When asked for a fantasy instead, he said that it is nonsensical—a house with doorways only, a stairwell to nothing. He said that he does dream this fantasy occasionally and can see it clearly.

When Beth said that she couldn't think of anything, Julie interjected that Beth had told her of a dream in which a man was chasing her and she was unable to scream. Beth answered that she had been mad at Dan when she dreamed that.

FEEDBACK CONFERENCE

The family members repeated how much they had enjoyed telling an outsider about Straight and their experience in it. I told them that they are very much a family, especially so, considering that they are a blended family who have been together only 3 years and that they have had to deal with problems and change from the beginning. I commented how nice it is that they have incorporated the Straight program into their lives (e.g., reading the Bible at night) and how nice that each of them has goals that are reachable and desirable, both for self and for family togetherness.

Dan commented that he couldn't understand why some of the exercises had been chosen. I tried to explain that the choices were partly a result of my being new at working with Straight and not wanting to duplicate the good work of the Straight program. Dan said that he would be willing to help coordinate or recruit other Straight families for SE.

Julie mentioned that she had not liked choosing the famous person but that she had liked the fun things. The family began talking about fun things they have done, such as having once thrown a pie on the floor and of Dan's "little boy" imitation (a little boy whose teacher won't let him go to the bathroom), which I persuaded Dan and Julie to do right then. I suggested that occasionally, when everyone feels like it, the family might have a crazy meeting instead of their usual serious family meeting.

I fed back many other positives about how the family members are changing to become what they want to be; this time, they seemed to accept the positives.

POSTTEST RESULTS

I allowed the family plenty of time to complete the posttests during the session (Beth was somewhat distracted because Carrie was sick).

On the Holmes-Rahe Schedule of Events, Jason had some trouble reading the items but checked personal injury (had cut his hand), personal achievement, and most of the items checked by the other family members. Dan's, Beth's, and Julie's responses remained the same as on the pretest.

On the Family Life Questionnaire (Rochester Scales), Dan's answers became somewhat more positive, noting fewer disagreements. Beth's answers stayed closer to those on the pretest. The answers connote a fairly traditional marriage in decision making. One interesting point in the pre- and posttests is that Dan picked the wife's affection and support as the two most important aspects of a marriage; Beth picked the husband's affection and support as the two most important aspects. Each is waiting for the other to make things right.

SUMMARY

The drawings and the sculpting and problem-solving exercises indicate the family's style, which is not very expressive and not one in which they use much physical touching. Although the family has been very separated, they seem to have welcomed Straight's idea of sharing thoughts and feelings, the ideal of closeness. The interactions of Beth and Julie are quite enmeshed; they had been most at odds before Julie joined Straight. Dan is a source of amusement to Beth and Julie but is viewed as a tower of strength. The family is quite passive, looking outside for help and direction. They expressed little self-esteem and seem fairly rigid in interaction and thinking. Fairly conventional and somewhat isolated from others whom they see as different (threats), they are attracted to Fundamentalism and the Straight philosophy. It took some time for the family to share their interactions with me.

I liked using the fun exercises with this family, which had been so Straight- and process-oriented at the beginning of SE. Sessions became looser, although some exercises remained difficult (e.g., problem solving together, touching). They were somewhat in touch with their emotions but seemed to fear expressing them, akin to the "walking on eggshells" phenomenon that is seen in the family of a recovered alcoholic—the family is afraid of rocking the boat of what is working and afraid of being able to succeed without the treatment program.

Because Jason is further out of the family (evidenced by his missing two sessions and by his comments and behavior), he is freer in some ways. Julie shows traces of fantasy and immaturity but is holding up well (school had started before the last session, and a dropout from Straight had pointed her out to all the other students; Beth commented on Julie's ability to handle the situation).

There is a pattern of stress and change in the Adams family. Straight seems to be helping the family not only with Julie's problem but with their problems as a "chemically dependent family" who are coming to grips with change and with being a blended family. There is a lot of passivity and waiting for someone else to do something, but Julie's problem and Straight have forced them to meet problems without backing away. They have individually taken on the philosophy of tough love (a responsibility toward each other that borders on enmeshment).

The family became more open as sessions went on, and they were always willing to do the exercises. Fantasy was hardest for Dan; seeing and accepting positives was hard for Beth. Julie was very much in touch with problems in the family and was willing to take much of the blame upon herself. She shows some immaturity but does perhaps appear closer to her age than she probably did when she was a "druggie." Jason does seem very much an outsider, the forgotten child, especially when compared with the darling baby, Carrie, who receives much attention from the family and from others who come into contact with them. Jason's contributions were insightful, and the family sometimes recognized his insight.

Although one difficulty was Straight's constant supervision, the experience was useful and is worth continuing.

REFERENCES

Anastasi, A. (1976). *Psychological testing.* New York: Macmillan.

Azrin, N. H., Naster, B. J., & Jones, R. (1973). Reciprocity counseling: A rapid learning-based procedure for marital counseling. *Behavior Research and Therapy, 11,* 365–382.

Crago, M. A. (1972). Psychopathology in married couples. *Psychological Bulletin, 77,* 114–128.

Crosby, J. F. (1973). *Illusion and disillusion: The self in love and marriage.* Belmont, CA: Wadsworth.

Egan, G. (1973). *Face to face.* Belmont, CA: Brooks/Cole.

Gottlieb, H., & L'Abate, L. (1974). Sexual Happiness Scale [additional items for Azrin's Marital Happiness Scale]. Atlanta: Georgia State University.

Gurman, A. S., & Kniskern, R. M. (1978). Behavioral marriage therapy: A psychodynamic-systems analysis and critique. *Family Process, 17,* 121–132.

Haley, J. (1963). Marriage therapy. *Archives of General Psychiatry, 8,* 213–234.

Holmes, T., & Rahe, R. (1967). The social readjustment rating scale. *Journal of Psychosomatic Research, 2,* 213–218.

James, M., & Jongeward, D. (1971). *Born to win.* Reading, MA: Addison-Wesley.

Kantor, D., & Lehr, W. (1975). *Inside the family: Toward a theory of family process.* San Francisco: Jossey-Bass.

Knox, D. (1975). *Marriage: Who? when? why?* Englewood Cliffs, NJ: Prentice-Hall.

Kochalka, J., Buzas, H., McHenry, S., L'Abate, L., & Gibson, E. (1982, October). *Structured enrichment: Training implementation with paraprofessionals (a pilot project).* Paper read at the annual meeting of the National Council on Family Relations, Washington, DC.

L'Abate, L. (1973). The laboratory method in clinical child psychology. *Journal of Clinical Child Psychology, 2,* 8–10.

L'Abate, L. (1976). *Understanding and helping the individual in the family.* New York: Grune & Stratton.

L'Abate, L. (1977). *Enrichment: Structured interventions with couples, families, and groups.* Washington, DC: University Press of America.

L'Abate, L. (1986a). Prevention of marital and family conflicts. In B. Edelstein & C. Michaelson (Eds.), *Handbook of prevention.* New York: Plenum.

L'Abate, L. (1986b). *Systematic family therapy.* New York: Brunner/Mazel.

L'Abate, L., Ganahl, G., & Hansen, J. C. (1986). *Methods in family therapy* (pp. 46–48). Englewood Cliffs, NJ: Prentice-Hall.

L'Abate, L., & McHenry, S. (1983). *Handbook of marital interventions.* New York: Grune & Stratton.

L'Abate, L., & Rupp, G. (1981). *Enrichment: Skill training for family life.* Washington, DC: University Press of America.

L'Abate, L., & Wagner, V. (1985). Theory-derived, family-oriented test batteries. In L. L'Abate (Ed.), *The handbook of family psychology and therapy* (Vol. 2, pp. 1006–1031). Homewood, IL: Dorsey.

L'Abate, L., & Weinstein, S. E. (1987). *Structured enrichment programs for couples and families.* New York: Brunner/Mazel.

Lederer, W. J., & Jackson, D. D. (1968). *The mirages of marriage.* New York: Norton.

Lewis, J. M., Beavers, W. R., Gossett, J. T., & Phillips, V. A. (1976). *No single thread: Psychological health in family systems.* New York: Brunner/Mazel.

Minuchin, S. (1974). *Families and family therapy.* Cambridge, MA: Harvard University Press.

Moos, R. H. (1976). *The human context: Environmental determinants of behavior.* New York: Wiley.

Murphy, D. C., & Mendelson, L. A. (1973). Communication and adjustment in marriage: Investigating the relationship. *Family Process, 12,* 317–326.

Navran, L. (1967). Communication and adjustment in marriage. *Family Process, 7,* 173–184.

Olson, D. H., Sprenkle, D., & Russell, C. S. (1979). Circumplex model of family systems. I: Cohesion adaptability dimension, family types, and clinical application. *Family Process, 14,* 1–35.

Satir, V. (1972). *People making.* Palo Alto, CA: Science and Behavior Books.

Schulz, D. A., & Rodgers, S. F. (1975). *Marriage, the family, and personal fulfillment.* Englewood Cliffs, NJ: Prentice-Hall.

Snyder, J. G., & Osgood, C. E. (Eds.). (1969). *Semantic differential technique: A sourcebook.* Chicago: Alein.

Spanier, G. B. (1976). Measuring dyadic adjustment: New scales for assessing the quality of marriage and similar dyads. *Journal of Marriage and the Family, 38,* 15–28.

Ventis, W. L. (1973). The use of laughter as an alternative response in systematic desensitization. *Behavior Therapy, 4,* 120–122.

Wildman, R. W., & Wildman, R. W., II. (1974). *Wildman Comprehensive Sex Survey.* Unpublished survey, Milledgevill State Hospital, Milledgeville, GA.

AUTHOR INDEX

PROGRAMS INDEX

TESTS INDEX